ONEIDA

ONEIDA

From Free Love Utopia to the Well-Set Table

E L L E N   W A Y L A N D - S M I T H

PICADOR

New York

www.picadorusa.com
www.twitter.com/picadorusa • www.facebook.com/picadorusa
picadorbookroom.tumblr.com

Picador® is a U.S. registered trademark and is used by St. Martin's Press under license from Pan Books Limited.

For book club information, please visit www.facebook.com/picadorbookclub or e-mail marketing@picadorusa.com.

All insert photographs are courtesy of Oneida Community Mansion House.

Designed by Greg Collins

The Library of Congress Cataloging-in-Publication Data
is available upon request.

ISBN 978-1-250-04308-5 (hardcover)
ISBN 978-1-250-04310-8 (e-book)

Our books may be purchased in bulk for promotional, educational, or business use. Please contact your local bookseller or the Macmillan Corporate and Premium Sales Department at 1-800-221-7945, extension 5442, or by e-mail at MacmillanSpecialMarkets@macmillan.com.

First Edition: May 2016

10 9 8 7 6 5 4 3 2 1

For my father

CONTENTS

INTRODUCTION

IN 1948, LOUIS WAYLAND-SMITH, MY GREAT-GRANDFATHER, WAS VICE
president and treasurer of Oneida Limited, one of America's top three
manufacturers of silverware. And, for the first time in a long time, he had
unusually good financial news to report. When the United States entered
World War II in 1942, Oneida had halted silverware production and converted its factories to manufacturing hardware for the war effort, pumping
out everything from surgical instruments to Curtiss propellers for the
Helldiver bombers leading the charge in the battle for Japan. After the war's
end, things were touch-and-go as the company undertook the difficult process of converting back to silver production. During the initial months of
1946, Oneida battled absenteeism, high worker turnover, and a general
drop in productivity. But in his annual report to the stockholders on January 31, 1948, Oneida Limited's president, Pierrepont B. Noyes, was able to
state that 1947 had been "the most satisfactory year, from the standpoint of
volume of business and earnings, in the history of the Company," with net
earnings topping three and a half million dollars.[1]

While Oneida might not have been producing its usual product line of gleaming silver teaspoons during the war, it had not ceased brand building, and the company was now reaping the benefits of an enormously popular advertising campaign that had kept the Oneida name front and center in consumer consciousness. The luminously colored ads, splashed across the pages of *Life* magazine and *The Saturday Evening Post*, depicted a handsome, uniformed soldier embracing his sweetheart, with the banner "Back Home for Keeps" printed confidently across the top of the page. Spawning a "pinup craze" among stateside wives and girlfriends pining for their servicemen, such sentimental images of home and hearth pushed Oneida ahead of its silverware competitors to earn the status of number one in consumer brand recognition. Once the soldiers were, in fact, home for keeps, Oneida's advertisers seamlessly shifted to rosy pictures of couples exchanging engagement rings, with the altered slogan "This Is for Keeps" urging future brides to choose Oneida silverware for their timeless trousseaux.

With the wind of 1947's financial success in their sails, Oneida's management began to plan a centennial celebration to take place the following summer, commemorating the company's improbable origins in a utopian Christian commune founded by Pierrepont Noyes's father, John Humphrey Noyes, in 1848: the Oneida Community. The company even commissioned an official history to memorialize the event, *The First Hundred Years*, by the patrician New York historian and novelist Walter Edmonds. Edmonds's paean to Oneida was tinged with the same nostalgic romanticism that, in 1936, had earned the author a popular success at the top of the *Publishers Weekly* bestseller list for his historical novel, *Drums Along the Mohawk* (a mere four notches down from Margaret Mitchell's blockbuster of the same year, *Gone with the Wind*).

John Humphrey Noyes and his followers, Edmonds wrote, had been Christian Perfectionists, religious dissenters and reformers in the best American tradition. Intent on forming a community resembling the early church as described in the Acts of the Apostles and calling themselves Bible Communists, Noyes and his followers pooled all their possessions and lived and worked together as an extended family, striving to become one body in Christ through total selflessness. But if they sought to restore the communal harmony of the age of the apostles, Noyes and his band of Bible Communists were no starry-eyed romantics. As the twin dynamos of the market revolution and the Industrial Revolution were transfiguring the American landscape in the 1840s, John Humphrey Noyes and his followers energetically embraced capitalism and the technological wizardry of the modern era, from the steam engine to the telegraph, as the wings that would bring to fruition the New Jerusalem. Pried loose from the selfish interests of the property-owning few and transformed into "the servant of Communism and the spirit of heaven," modern capitalism would usher in a reign of peace and plenty unknown since Adam's expulsion from the Garden of Eden.[2]

Edmonds went on to explain in *The First Hundred Years* that, while the Oneida Community had dissolved as a social and religious entity in 1880, the bold "experiment in human relations" initiated by Noyes Sr. was carried forth in the economic sphere by Noyes's son Pierrepont and his fellow Community descendants, who took the "old principles of sharing and equality" inherited from his father and applied them to the industrial production of silverware. Oneida Limited prided itself on the equity and dignity that it accorded all its members, from the lowest factory hand to the president of the company himself. It was an institution that, true to its founder's principles, held that "every man and woman whose work contributes to the success of the company is entitled to an equitable share in the company's profits," prizing the common good over private individual interests. Edmonds's commemorative history closed with a selection of glossy black-and-white photographs of the company and its homey, small-town environs, from the village block hardware store ("Merchandise is displayed on the sidewalks in a neighborly way") to the stately trees surrounding the old communal homestead, "proud of their ancient lineage" and "living reminders of the thought and vision of those who planted [them] generations ago."[3]

Oneida Limited's centennial celebration opened on a sunny Saturday in July 1948 and was a grand affair. It was held in bucolic Noyes Park, equidistant from the cozy, clustered bungalows of the worker village and the tree-lined hamlet, across the bridge, where management lived in larger houses surrounding the ancestral Mansion House, a 93,000-square-foot Victorian brick mansion built by the original Community. On the gaily festooned grandstand a pretty soprano belted out an organ-accompanied rendition of "The Star-Spangled Banner," and a beaming Pierrepont Noyes crowned the "Silver Queen," chosen from among the loveliest girls on the company's secretarial staff. The wide-eyed audience was treated to five-cent hot dogs and ice cream, not to mention a dizzying slate of spectacles, from the Gaudsmith Brothers and their French Poodles Pantomime Comedy Knockabout Act to Sensational Rob Cimse on the seventy-five-foot High Whirling Motorcycle Trapeze. The celebration closed with dancing under the stars to the strains of Jimmy Dorsey's orchestra. The Oneida Limited centennial was, in short, a taste of postwar America in all of its glory: patriotic, prosperous, and unfailingly cheerful.

ONLY A YEAR BEFORE, IN 1947, A MORE COMPLICATED RETROSPECTIVE ceremony of sorts had taken place: a group of Oneida Limited officers emptied a vault full of documents, diaries, letters, and papers dating from the Community days and loaded them into the back of a truck, which they proceeded to drive to the town dump. There, they burned everything. The event came to be known in following generations as "the Burning"; like most family secrets, everyone knew about it, but no one talked about it. The identity of the family members who spearheaded and carried out the mission remains, even today, every bit as mysterious as the contents of the documents they reduced to ash. Unlike Edmonds's carefully constructed narrative of the family company in *The First Hundred Years*, the story in the vault was, decidedly, not a story anyone wished to pass on.

The family knew, without having to be told, the nature of the threat that lurked in the archival vault. For if the original Oneida Community had been an association devoted to re-creating the spirit of universal fellowship uniting the Apostolic Church, their definition of communism had gone well beyond anything imagined by Peter or Paul. Relinquishing selfish ownership of property meant nothing, John Humphrey Noyes insisted, unless Christians also relinquished selfish ownership, including sexual ownership, of persons in the form of marriage.

"I call a certain woman my wife," Noyes penned in an 1837 letter to a friend outlining his sexual theology. "She is yours, she is Christ's, and in him she is the bride of all saints." Only "Complex Marriage," the open and equal sexual union of all Community women with all Community men, could approach the holy unity enjoyed by the saints in heaven. Far from being "one of the most iniquitous systems ever devised and propagated under the name and garb of Christianity," as one apoplectic clergyman fumed against the group in 1849, the ideal of nonprocreative sex among multiple partners was touted by the Bible Communists as a religious sacrament of the highest order.[4]

Such an unorthodox sexual arrangement, which the Oneidans practiced as an integral part of their peculiar brand of Christianity for a full thirty years, from 1848 until 1879, was understandably a thorn in the side of later generations of descendants like my great-grandfather Lou, who, having been born during the turbulent period of the Community's breakup in 1880, narrowly missed being born out of wedlock. In the wake of the Community's final dissolution, this younger generation—"apologetic or grieved at the radical beliefs of their forefathers," according to one outside observer at the time—embraced monogamy with puritanical zeal, desperate to shed the stigma of being a band of bastards and fornicators in the eyes of the world.[5]

Rejecting the more unorthodox sexual theories of their elders, these post-1880 descendants took the fledgling joint-stock company that had been entrusted to them and devoted themselves, single-mindedly, to building Oneida Community Limited into a shiny national symbol not only of America's industrial strength but also of the country's dedication to social equality and the golden rule. If John Humphrey Noyes and his original followers had imagined themselves a "city on a hill" leading America toward the promise of Christian salvation, Pierrepont B. Noyes and his fellow descendants refashioned for Oneida a more secular goal: it would light the way toward a more equitable and brotherly vision of the American social contract.

And so, even as one version of the Oneida story was being given the imprimatur of the family in an official commemorative book, another version was reduced to ash. One story told the tale of the Oneida family's entrepreneurial spirit and capitalist vigor, mixed with a dose of fair-minded Yankee egalitarianism and Christian brotherly love: a hopeful way forward in a time when the ideological split between communist and capitalist, the collective and the individual, was poised to divide the world in two. The other told the tale of a people who, refusing to accept agape or caritas as the pinnacle of Christian love, vigorously reclaimed eros as a legitimate means of expressing Christian fellowship between men and women. That story told the tale of a social experiment in which three hundred people had, for the space of thirty years, blasted traditional gender roles, rejected the age-old truism that a woman's primary function was to bear children, and reimagined traditional family structures, breaking open the "selfish" circle of father, mother, and child to build a more inclusive and—in their view—more authentically Christian community of interconnecting relationships, radiating out infinitely from Jesus at the center, like the light from a star. (According to the literary critic Edmund Wilson, who visited the Oneida family compound in the 1920s, Pierrepont Noyes's young daughter Constance, when asked to identify the baby in a picture of the Sistine Madonna, replied artlessly, "Why, that's little Cousin Jesus"—a testament to the curiously expansive definition of "family" that persisted at Oneida decades beyond the breakup.)[6]

Looking back, it seems perfectly obvious that these two narratives were incompatible, and it is understandable that one had to be rooted up and destroyed in order to give the other room to flower. But what a strange, dreamlike place must America have been if, for a brief space of time in the 1840s and 1850s, free love and industrial prosperity, communism and capitalism, women's lib and millennial Christianity appeared to share a sunny future together.

This book tells the story of the rise and fall of the Oneida Community in nineteenth-century America and of how the twentieth-century descendants who ran Oneida Community Limited alternately assumed and evaded the uniquely American legacy bequeathed to them before finally watching it vanish altogether when Oneida filed for bankruptcy in 2006. To follow the story of this commune-cum-capitalist powerhouse is to revisit a very American story: that of the tension between radical social critique and unapologetic accommodation, between a commitment to equality and an unshakable faith in the reality of divine election, between Promethean madness and hardscrabble realism, between communal harmony and individual striving. It is, finally, to shine a light on the most perplexing contradictions of the American character and—perhaps—of the human heart.

1

A Minister Is Born

WHEN JOHN HUMPHREY NOYES'S MOTHER, POLLY HAYES NOYES, TOOK a deep breath after the travail of childbirth to see that her firstborn son was a "proper child"—that is, one apparently hearty enough to buck the odds of making it through the bitter New England winter to see his first birthday—she prayed on the spot that he might become a "minister of the everlasting gospel." Polly's prayer would be granted twenty-two years later, in 1833, when John Humphrey received his minister's license from the Yale Theological Seminary. But on the day of his birth, as she fell back upon her pillows in sweet exhaustion, this prim and conventional Congregationalist could hardly have anticipated the theological edifice her infant son would one day construct. For John Humphrey Noyes would not become just any minister; his brainchild, the Oneida Community, would blend a utopian ethic of total selflessness, communism of property, and divinely sanctioned free love into one of the most baroque interpretations of Jesus' "everlasting gospel" ever attempted.[1]

Born into a prosperous New England family in Brattleboro, Vermont, on September 3, 1811, John Humphrey was the fourth of nine children. Polly

Hayes Noyes was a strong-minded, deeply religious woman who demanded that matters of spirituality be kept foremost in the raising of her children. John Humphrey's father, John Noyes Sr., was of a more secular character; a 1795 graduate of Dartmouth College, John was first a teacher and then a successful Brattleboro businessman, spending a two-year stint as a representative in Congress from 1815 to 1817. Letters that John Noyes wrote home to his wife from Washington in 1815 hint at his enjoyment of the city's cosmopolitan privileges, foreign to the native Vermonter: "The style and manner of proceeding, the dignity which every member seems to feel, and the living at our quarters, all are very, very different from what we have in Vermont. A man cannot but feel animated, and as it were elevated." "We live full well enough for our health," he continued later in the same letter. "Our meat and poultry are of the first quality. . . . Brandy and wine very good and very dear. Plenty of oysters, apples, chestnuts." While he was gallant (or cagey) enough to write to his wife that the "pie, apples, and the wine lost their charms" when he thought of the comforts of home, one senses the sensual enjoyment he took in "the bustle, the show and parade of great folks." Later in life, he would become a rather pronounced alcoholic; only when he received a formal written letter from his wife and children begging him to cease "indulging [his] degrading appetite" was he jarred from his pleasures.[2]

"In the highways and byways of business he was a born Solomon," John Humphrey would later recall of his father, one who "in social and commercial life . . . found his natural sphere." The competing claims of religion and a worldly life were twin currents traversing the Noyes household. "Lay not up for yourselves treasures upon earth," warns the apostle Matthew, "where moth and rust doth corrupt, and thieves break through and steal," but, rather, "Lay up for yourselves treasures in heaven" (Matthew 6: 19–21). Flying in the face of the good evangelist, John Humphrey Noyes would devote his life to brokering a fragile truce between treasures on earth and those in heaven. Perhaps only the collision of two such vigorously opposed natures as the saintly Polly Hayes and the carnal John Noyes Sr. could have spawned a compromise as brilliantly bizarre as John Humphrey Noyes, who would close this parental gap between spirit and flesh by claiming, among other things, that the sexual organs were the "first and best channel of the life and love of God" and that getting salvation was "a business—like getting a living"—in other words, that spiritual and earthly pursuits were, in fact, one and the same thing.[3]

Young John was a thoughtful boy—as a child, he was fond of going to bed early because "he wanted to think"—and from the first a natural leader. As his mother recalled in later years, "I can see him now marching off up the hill at the head of a company of his playmates, all armed with mullein stalks." Sent away to school in Amherst, Massachusetts, when he was nine years old, John Humphrey sent letters home that reveal a boy seized by homesickness but anxious not to upset his mother on his account: "Mamma, I must say that when I am not reading, or writing, or studying, I am home-sick. Yes, I am homesick. . . . But away with all this! I fear I have distressed you already. . . . Tell Papa that I am studying Cicero, and that I have got to the fourth book of Virgil." When he was ten years old, his family relocated to the village of Putney, Vermont, within easy communication of his new school, Brattleboro Academy, where John would complete his preparation for college. Endowed with a ruddy, freckled complexion and a bright red shock of hair, John Humphrey early gave signs of a passionate nature to match; a friend from his Brattleboro days referred to him as "inclined to give way a little too much to the *libido corporis*."[4]

Just which "lusts" of the body the young boy had a particular weakness for is not divulged in the friend's letter; it is clear from his diaries that, by the time John Humphrey had entered Dartmouth College as a freshman in 1826, a partiality for the ladies was chief among them. This journal, begun at the age of eighteen in 1829, provides glimpses of a teenager struggling with para-lyzing shyness in his relations with the opposite sex. He was further ham-pered by the conviction that his red hair and freckles rendered him physically repulsive. John Humphrey compared himself to the "Black Dwarf" in the Walter Scott romance of the same name, a tortured, loveless figure whose deformed body and "long matted red hair" forced him to sequester himself in the forest as a hermit. The young collegian's interactions with women were, accordingly, nothing short of torture. In one diary entry, he berates himself: "Oh! For a brazen front and nerves of steel! I swear by Jove, I will be impudent! So unreasonable and excessive is my bashfulness that I fully believe I could face a battery of cannon with less trepidation than I could a room full of ladies with whom I was unacquainted."[5]

Despite his best resolutions, John Humphrey continued to experience acute anxiety and embarrassment in social situations. Once, at a wedding party, he mistook the name of a lady he was introducing to a company of gentlemen; he recorded afterward that he could "feel [his] cheek burn with shame" upon recollecting the "scornful smile [that passed] over the countenance of a certain lady" who, sitting near, overheard his blunder. A sense of intense social shame and self-loathing, especially when he felt himself caught in the gaze of the opposite sex, was one of the strongest currents in young Noyes's emotional life. At one point, he had even resigned himself to remaining unmarried and becoming a philosopher, renouncing the physical world for the life of the mind.[6]

Yet John Humphrey's social fortunes took a turn for the better upon graduation from Dartmouth. In 1830, when he entered into training as a lawyer at his brother-in-law Larkin Mead's practice in Chesterfield, New Hampshire, John Humphrey unexpectedly found himself at the center of a robust social scene. He and his classmate "Put," also an intern in Mead's practice, were catapulted into the enviable position of being the only two college graduates of a crew of eighty or ninety young men and women attending a nearby school. "Bewitched" by his female companions, John Humphrey nonetheless complained that the continual round of balls and parties raised his emotions to a painful pitch of overexcitement: "impatience of absence from those seraphs, jealousy of my competitors in gallantry, and the dolorous reflection that the school would close in thirteen weeks were constantly dragging me down from the pinnacle of felicity which seemed to be almost within reach. . . ." Drawn as he was to the *libido corporis*, John Humphrey was acutely affected by desire's painful obverse: the ache of pleasure denied or delayed.[7]

Somehow John Humphrey was able to overcome his shyness long enough to tentatively court a young woman who is recorded in his diary only as Caroline M—. The dances where he met her might have been held in one of the academy's buildings or in a hall hired in town: one can almost hear the squeak of the freshly polished floor, the clink of teacups at the refreshment table, the sweep and rustle of ladies' skirts. The gauzy, high-waisted, ankle-length frocks of the Empire period were no longer in vogue, but dresses had not quite yet evolved into what was to become the standard armor of the

Victorian woman, thickly petticoated, wooden-hooped, and tightly corseted into the shape of a dinner bell. Caroline would have worn a dress that dropped all the way to the floor, with sleeves swollen like cream puffs and a pinched wasp waist—possibly corseted, but in either case symbolic, in its tightness, of the strict emotional control women were increasingly expected to exercise as moral heads of the Victorian household. The popular ladies' hairstyle at the time was closely plaited and center-parted with bunches of ringlets at the ears. With the flickering candlelight bouncing off Caroline's curls, perhaps making her dark eyes snap, one imagines John Humphrey's heart tightening as the orchestra gave the signal for another quadrille and the dancers took their places.

Noyes even penned a rather sweet, if sophomoric, poem to Caroline that he copied in his diary, a country idyll in fashionable hymn meter:

> Mark, Caroline, yon western sky.
> Deep-tinged in crimson light.
> The sun's red glories haste to die.
> And swift comes on the night.
>
> . . .
>
> Then hasten, ere the twilight ends.
> Far down the vale we'll roam,
> Nor pause till o'er us night descends,
> Then Love shall light us home!

Alas, John Humphrey's dream of an enveloping night illumined by the star of love was to remain unfulfilled. (Indeed, if we are to believe Noyes's own later account, he would remain a virgin until the night of his marriage.) When the academy's school year finally drew to a close, John Humphrey abruptly ran home to Putney, forgoing even a parting interview with his beloved Caroline, upon whom he never laid eyes again. This precipitous disappearance in the face of a situation he felt at a loss to master was just the first of what would become a series of such retreats over the course of Noyes's life. In any case, in his relationship with Caroline, the young Noyes proved himself unable to heed the advice he had once given to a lovesick Dartmouth chum to "never read Byron, . . . and above all to repeat every five minutes: 'Faint heart never won fair lady.'"[8]

Yet just as John Humphrey had steeled himself, like Macbeth, to "jump the life to come" in favor of worldly pursuits, religion came knocking. In the fall of 1831, at his mother's prompting, Noyes attended a religious revival in Putney and, against all expectations, experienced conversion. The year was the watermark for religious revivals that had been sweeping across the Northeast for over a decade. "The Second Great Awakening," as it came to be called, resulted in the conversion of hundreds of thousands of middle-class souls to Jesus and, perhaps more important, to a strikingly new way of thinking about their relationship to God and the world. The dour Calvinism of the Puritans depicted humans as sinners in the hands of an angry God, waiting passively to be eternally damned or lifted up to join God's elect—resigned, in any case, to their status as "loathsome insects," in the words of Jonathan Edwards, dangled over the pit of hell. In contrast, the new revival religion emphasized humans as active moral agents capable of steering their souls—and the fallen world around them—toward the perfection promised by the advent of God's kingdom on earth. Instead of waiting passively for the millennium to come, humans had a duty to reform their world and thereby hasten the King's arrival.[9]

The effect of the revivals was to ignite within the American national consciousness the spark of millenarianism: the belief that the Second Coming of Christ and the advent of his one-thousand-year reign were nigh. Some converts took this message quite literally. William Miller, a Baptist preacher and farmer in northern New York, performed a complicated calculus based on the prophecies of Daniel to predict that Christ would return very soon, indeed: on October 22, 1844, to be exact. Other converts stuck to a looser timeline. Christ was coming, and, in anticipation, good Christians were duty-bound to set their house in order by reforming such ugly social blights as alcoholism, the poor state of America's prisons, slavery, and women's mistreatment at the hands of men. Abolitionists Frederick Douglass and William Lloyd Garrison, as well as the feminist Elizabeth Cady Stanton, were carried to prominence in the 1840s on this wave of intense social activism and compellingly framed their ideas in the messianic language of the revivals. Humans, it was believed, had an obligation to at least meet God halfway in ushering in paradise on earth.

Later in his spiritual journey, Noyes would fully embrace the reformist spirit stirred up by the revivals, concocting his own millennial timeline no less bizarre than that of the Millerites and building his own miniature version of the coming City of God. Initially, however, one senses that Noyes's conversion simply provided the exhausted teenager with a welcome exit from the dark labyrinth of sexual desire, disappointment, and shame that had marked his adolescence. Tempted by the pleasures of the flesh yet wracked with ambivalence about his right to a place at the sexual table, Noyes had spent the last five years of his life agonizing over whether society or solitude, sex or cold philosophy was to be his ultimate fate. Now, suddenly, he had an answer: the "meridian splendor" of God's light had pierced his heart, out-shining the romantic love-lit nights he had imagined in the presence of Caroline. Referring scornfully to the love poem he had so recently penned to his sweetheart, Noyes scribbled in his diary: "These three verses cost me an hour of labor. How much better would that hour have been spent in framing a hymn to the praise of God." Pledging himself to the "happiness of heaven," Noyes could now safely disparage the "groveling world" of earthly desires. "Hitherto the world, henceforth God!" he penned hopefully, turning the page, he trusted, on the melancholy pleasures of the flesh.[10]

But the flesh was to give him trouble yet. Indeed, considering the thin margin separating the religious ecstasy so prevalent at nineteenth-century revivals from the sexual sort, what Noyes may initially have sought as a steady spiritual substitute for the painful ups and downs of carnal love would, in fact, lead him into no less complicated territory. These revivals encouraged extravagant outpourings of emotion from people who normally sat through buttoned-up church services with bland and silent piety. At a typical New England "protracted meeting," a charismatic preacher would alternately pray with and sermonize to a gathered audience over the course of three or four days of meetings, exhorting them to repent and accept Christ. Those with the temerity to admit themselves sinners in need of salvation would crowd to the front of the hall and occupy what came to be called "the anxious seat," in full view of the expectant congregation, who scrutinized them for signs of conversion. Cries, tears, groans, and fainting were taken as external tokens that the Holy Spirit was doing its appointed work.

The most famous of these revivalist preachers, Charles Grandison Finney, narrates his own conversion in the autumn of 1821 as an ecstatic flood of love coursing throughout his body: "[T]he Holy Spirit descended upon me in a manner that seemed to go through me, body and soul. I could feel the impression, like a wave of electricity, going through and through me. Indeed it seemed to come in waves of liquid love, for I could not express it any other way. It seemed like the very breath of God." These "waves" reached a peak of almost unbearable intensity, until Finney cried out, "'I shall die if these waves continue to pass over me. . . . Lord, I cannot bear any more.'"[11]

In his autobiography, Finney goes on to detail an impromptu revival staged by an unlikely Congregational deacon, who, normally spare of words and possessed of a thin, reedy voice, this time "soon began to wax warm and to raise his voice, which became tremulous with emotion." He rocked back and forth on his heels, then on his chair, bringing it down against the floor again and again "so that they could feel the jar in the room." The audience melted. "The brothers and sisters that were on their knees began to groan, and sigh, and weep, and agonize in prayer. . . . [N]o one in the room could get off his knees. They could only weep and confess and melt down before the Lord."[12]

If these depictions of divine rapture sound sexual, it is because they were. Indeed, one of the well-noted aftereffects of the spiritual ecstasy circulating at these revivals was a surge in sexual activity between attendees. In an 1820 pamphlet entitled *Methodist Error; or, Friendly Christian Advice to Those Methodists, Who Indulge in Extravagant Emotions and Bodily Exercises*, John Fanning Watson warned against the popular revival indulgence in "the practice of shouting, leaping and jumping, and other outward signs of the most heedless emotions."[13] Noting that most of those affected with the "leaping" mania were not only women but "women who while single are conspicuous in these things, [yet] desist altogether after marriage," Watson insinuated that indulging in "heedless emotions" was a particular danger for young women whose sexual drives had not yet been properly channeled and controlled by marriage. The possible spillover from religious to sexual excitement was, he suggested, a constant danger.[14]

A sympathetic reviewer of Watson's "friendly Christian advice" seconded his views, urging that those prone to leaping "inquire, whether their emotions are the result of the operation of the divine Spirit, or whether they are not merely the excitement of animal feeling; and the effects of an over-heated imagination, or what is equally to be deplored, the delusions of Satan." In the popular imagination, a distinct association existed between re-vival behavior and relaxed sexual mores, such that one critic estimated, in 1843, that "there are probably more wrangles by day and debauches by night within one mile of a camp [meeting] of the usual size, than occurred in the whole nation of Israel at seven feasts of tabernacles."[15]

That Noyes, tortured by sexual frustration in his adolescent dealings with the opposite sex, should find something congenial in the pent-up sexual energy of a revival meeting is not surprising. Noyes would later offer an ex-planation for this common confusion of religious and sexual feeling, or the fact that "the most decided manifestations of intercourse with the spiritual world, in whatever sects, are always complicated with social novelties." Such an overlap was perfectly sensible, given that passionate, receptive natures, open both to influxes of divine love and divine inspiration, are the Holy Spirit's paths of least resistance in manifesting itself on earth. Just as, "if a gun is over-loaded and bursts in firing, we shall find . . . that the force of the powder found the weakest spot in the barrel, where there was least resis-tance," so it is among "babes in understanding," those who have not hard-ened themselves against passion, that "the spiritual world might be expected to break out first." The revival's sexual shenanigans were not pure nonsense, Noyes later theorized, but signs—crude and untutored, to be sure, but signs nonetheless—of the coming fulfillment of Christ's gospel of Love on earth.[16]

But Noyes had not yet reached the point of fusing sexual and religious inspiration. For the moment, the two remained opposed impulses: his mother's ascetic piety in pitched battle with his father's full embrace of worldly pleasures. For the moment, the "meridian splendor" of God's love had fully eclipsed the seraphic glow of his Chesterfield dancing partners.

IN NOVEMBER 1831, DETERMINED NOW TO DEVOTE HIMSELF TO GOD, JOHN Humphrey Noyes entered Andover Theological Seminary. Freshly plucked from the profane world as he was, he fully expected to find himself immersed in an atmosphere "little less heavenly than a habitation of angels." Noyes learned to his surprise that his Andover fellows were, instead, an earthly lot, and that "there was, at least, as much levity, bickering, jealousy, intrigue, and sensuality there, as in any equal gathering of young men with which I had ever been connected." Discouraged by his Andover colleagues' lack of spiritual seriousness, Noyes decided to pick up stakes and continue his training the following fall at Yale Theological Seminary.[17]

In New Haven, he threw himself into the cause of antislavery, working among the African American community there and, in the winter of 1832, helping to found the New Haven Anti-Slavery Society. Noyes also joined forces with the New Haven Free Church, one of a number of splinter groups inspired by Finneyite revivals that arose in opposition to the Calvinist orthodoxy of the mainstream churches. Despite his rather conventional bourgeois upbringing, Noyes now sought his natural companions among the unchurched and the disenfranchised. He found they offered a palliative to the professional religious "scholars" he frequented in the cosseted world of the seminary, who, he felt, stifled true religiosity. For such professional churchmen, Noyes argued, "religion becomes . . . an external business, a prospective means of subsistence" rather than an affair of the heart. Noyes felt strongly that spirituality was not a ratiocinative project but, rather, lodged in the solar plexus, that region of the heart that he would, in later writings, identify as the corporal dwelling place of the soul and the organ through which humans could communicate with the divine.[18]

But once ensconced at Yale, Noyes found that, while the spirit might be willing, the flesh remained weak. "I cannot send abroad my thoughts in any direction without crossing the track of some polluted image," he lamented in a diary he began while at Andover, "and a thousand needless suggestions of impurity occur daily to blast my endeavors after holiness." Noyes wrote of his desire to be cured of sin, comparing it to a cancer for which he desperately wished a magical antidote: "I have been wishing today I could devise some new way of sanctification—some patent—some specific for sin, whereby the curse should be exterminated once for all." Noyes's Puritan ancestors had been quite at home with the idea of the natural depravity of man. For them, the curse of Adam, the unregenerate flesh, was the prison house of the spirit, and the constant battle between "The Flesh and Spirit," in the words of Puritan poetess Anne Bradstreet, was the very stuff of life, not a calamity that might somehow be averted. "Sisters we are, yea twins we be / Yet deadly feud 'twixt thee and me," Bradstreet's allegorical "Spirit" warns her sister "Flesh." While Charles Finney and his revival religion, with its emphasis on loving grace and the possibility of redemption, had worked to soften this Calvinist strain in the American soul, it still did not go far enough for Noyes. To have a soul touched by sin, tarnished by "polluted images," spotted with imperfection, was, quite literally, unbearable to him.[19]

From his early days, Noyes was haunted by the story in the third chapter of Genesis of the expulsion from the Garden of Eden. That humans should be exiled from Paradise, barred by a cherubim with "a flaming sword that turned every way to guard the way to the tree of life" (Genesis 3: 24), appeared to the young seminarian not as a righteous punishment for the transgression of a law, but as an intolerable loss, a source of inconsolable sadness. Was there not some magic potion, he wondered miserably in his diary, some spell that could remove the curse, like the magic kiss in fairy tales? Noyes was peculiarly susceptible to magical thinking. Unable to confront his social fears and insecurities head-on, he often responded to perplexing or painful situations by simply absconding, as he had when he abandoned his first love, Caroline. The same logic was at work in his wrestle with sin: rather than accepting sin as a sorrowful fact of life to be reckoned with, he fantasized that it might, like a bubble, simply vanish into thin air.

As an adolescent, Noyes had endured humiliation in social interactions with his peers, his burning face and ears becoming as red as the carrot-colored hair about which he was so self-conscious. Acutely sensitive to the sting of social shame, Noyes accordingly felt deeply for Adam and Eve's shame upon finding themselves naked, as recorded in the enigmatic verse from Genesis: "And they heard the voice of the Lord God walking in the garden in the cool of the day: and Adam and his wife hid themselves from the presence of the Lord amongst the trees of the garden" (Genesis 3: 8). To magically reverse the baleful consequences of original sin, to render the "tree of life" once again accessible to humans: this was to become Noyes's holy grail.

Noyes was to find his antidote to sin soon enough, in the doctrine known as Perfectionism that was percolating within the New Haven Free Church. Perfectionism saw the reformist ethos of the American Protestant revival culture and raised it one: the sinner could not only reform himself by making the right moral choices but also be made "perfect"—free from sin—simply by accepting God's grace. What mattered was not the letter of the law but the spirit, not outward acts but the inward disposition of the heart.

The Perfectionist claim to be sinless was nothing new; for centuries, the heresy of antinomianism, or the belief that Christians are freed by grace from any obligation to the earthly law, had been a thorn in the side of institutional Christianity. The thirteenth-century Brethren of the Free Spirit, for instance, was a mystical sect that believed that their members constituted an elite cadre of immortal, perfected supermen, the incarnation of the Holy Spirit, who represented the culminating stage of Christian history. Beyond law, and thus incapable of sin, these heretics engaged in promiscuous sex as a token of their oneness with the divine essence and as an affirmation that, to them, all was permitted.

Though the Brethren were dutifully hunted down and burned at the stake by the church, their spirit continued to crop up, here and there, throughout early modern Europe. In seventeenth-century England, amidst the tumult of the Glorious Revolution, the "Ranters" (so-called for their boisterous bouts of drinking, whoring, and cursing) emerged as yet another sect seduced by the allure of sinlessness. Proclaiming the mystical oneness of God, the Ranters argued that the very concept of sin was theologically inconsistent: if God was one and indivisible, then to label anything within His creation "sinful" was blasphemy. In his 1650 tract *A Single Eye All Light, No Darkness; or, Light and Darkness One*, Lawrence Clarkson explained his theological reasoning: "This to me by Reason is confirmed, and by Scripture declared, *That to the pure all things are pure*: So that for my part I know nothing unclean to me, no more than it is of it self, and therefore what Act soever I do, is acted by the Majesty in me." Swearing and praying, whoring and fasting were, in the Ranters' theological version of the proverbial night in which all cows are black, one and the same thing.[20]

The claim to be beyond law took on slightly tamer forms in the New World. In 1638 the prophetess Anne Hutchinson, criticizing what she perceived to be the legalistic, bean-counting approach to sin in the Puritan theology of the Massachusetts Bay Colony, declared herself free from law and, instead, bound only by the covenant of grace. Convicted of heresy, she was promptly banished from the colony, ordered by the Reverend John

Wilson "in the name of Christ, Jesus and of this Church as a leper to with-draw [her] selfe out of the Congregation." (Hutchinson found refuge in neighboring Rhode Island, only to meet an unfortunate end some years later when she and all but one of her fifteen children were massacred by Indians at a settlement in eastern New York—a fate that her Puritan perse-cutors would, no doubt, have interpreted as just deserts.)[21]

Given his desperate need to feel himself justified in the eyes of others (and since his conversion, in the eyes of the Supreme Other, God), Noyes found in this latest branch of the Christian Perfectionist tree precisely what he was looking for. Immersing himself in a feverish study of the New Testa-ment, Noyes now began to formulate a radical reading of the Gospels that offered scriptural sanction for his newly adopted Perfectionist creed. Noyes insisted that the Second Coming of Christ and His thousand-year reign was not, as the orthodox believed, an event in the future but had in fact already transpired at the time of the destruction of the Temple of Jerusalem in AD 70, when the members of the primitive church—Christ's apostles and followers—had been resurrected and raised to glory in an invisible spiritual kingdom in the heavens. Christians had misread the Book of Revelations to interpret the millennium as coming to pass on earth, when in fact it was a heavenly event, restricted to a select circle of Christ's followers, and was but a prelude to the larger extension of Christ's kingdom to all humanity. According to Noyes's calculations, then, the millennial era predicted by the Book of Revelations had ended in AD 1070, and for the past 760 years or so the saints of what Noyes referred to as the invisible world had been twid-dling their thumbs, waiting for mankind to be ready for what Noyes imag-ined as an "annexation" of the visible world to heaven. Now that Noyes had arrived to apprehend God's secret plan and to explain to his blinded breth-ren that sinlessness could be achieved in the here and now, that time was at hand.

According to Noyes's revised biblical timeline, Christians were no lon-ger living in the age of prophecy but in the era of fulfillment. On the day of the Pentecost, Jesus said, "If any man thirst, let him come unto me and drink. He that believeth on me, as the Scripture has said, out of his belly shall flow rivers of living water. This spake he of the Spirit, which they that believe on him should receive" (John 7: 37–39). Noyes's gloss on this verse, however, interpreted it as Jesus' promise of redemption not at some future time but in the heart of the living present. As Noyes penned in one of his many meditations upon grace, "A great river is flowing in humanity; and whosoever will may drink of it as he pleases. It is not something that is yet to be sent—that we are to wait for and expect in the future—it is a river of life that is now running within easy reach of every one of us." One had only to partake of this water of the Holy Spirit to become justified—sinless—before God.[22]

Noyes drank deeply of this river. On February 20, 1834, he preached a sermon at the Free Church on the text "He that committeth sin is of the devil," taking the verse quite literally: only he who had fully accepted Christ's river of grace into his heart, thereby cleansing himself of all sin, could lay claim to the title of Christian. Upon lying in bed that night, Noyes received a new baptism of the spirit: "Three times in quick succession a stream of eternal love gushed through my heart and rolled back again to its source. 'Joy unspeakable and full of glory' filled my soul. All fear and doubt and condemnation passed away. I knew that my heart was clean, and that the Father and the Son had come and made it their abode." Washed clean once and for all were the "polluted images" that had formerly "blast[ed] his endeavors after holiness."[23]

If in nineteenth-century New Haven Noyes's claims to be sinless were not enough to earn him death at the stake or banishment, as had been the case with the Brethren of the Free Spirit and Anne Hutchinson, they were sufficient, all the same, to land him in hot water with the heads of the Divinity School. News of Noyes's heretical sermon soon reached his teachers, and, several days later, the illustrious theologian Dr. Nathaniel Taylor consequently paid a visit to Noyes in his rooms. Named Professor at Yale's newly created Theological Department in 1822, Dr. Taylor had been critical in forging Yale's reputation as a haven for progressive-minded Christians seeking a compromise between old-school Calvinist teachings and the gentler theology of revival religion. Countering the Calvinist belief in predestination, Taylor preached the power of Christians to shape their own moral destinies through free will and emphasized sin as the consequence of freely chosen sinful acts rather than the inevitable result of natural human depravity. On the face of it, Nathaniel Taylor was sympathetic to an interpretation of the Gospel that prized grace above the law. Still, Noyes's claim to have cast off his sinful nature altogether and to have achieved perfect holiness on earth went one step too far.

Ushering his former mentor into his rooms, Noyes proceeded to accuse him, through a series of annoyingly passive-aggressive syllogisms, of being "of the devil": "Thereupon I asked him if he did not commit sin," Noyes recounted of his confrontation with Dr. Taylor. "He admitted that he did. I then repeated the text—'He that committeth sin is of the devil.' 'You say then (said he) that I am of the devil, do you?' 'No, (said I;) you said you committed sin, and I only quoted the words from the Bible, 'He that committeth sin is of the devil.' 'Well (said he) you are a sinner now, if you was not when I came in, for you have not treated me courteously.'" But Dr. Taylor's bruised feelings did not deter Noyes from the path he was blazing toward perfect holiness.[24]

Despite Noyes's offer to relinquish his minister's license, Dr. Taylor and the Yale Department of Theology not only formally stripped him of his right to preach but demanded as well that he evacuate the seminary premises immediately. Sympathetic friends gathered round Noyes, asking whether he intended to continue preaching now that his license had been revoked. To which Noyes replied haughtily: "I have taken away their license to sin, and they keep on sinning. So, though they have taken away my license to preach, I shall keep on preaching."[25]

Noyes had now lost his position and his reputation, and his friends were "fast falling away," he would recall in later years. But he was not completely friendless, claiming at least one supporter: a young woman named Abigail Merwin, who, having heard of Noyes's reputation through the Free Church, requested an interview with him. "She appeared to be in perplexity, and eager for the truth," Noyes wrote of his first meeting with Abigail. Noyes proceeded to a full conversion: "I put to her the question, 'Will you receive Christ as a WHOLE SAVIOR, and confess him before the world?' She answered promptly, 'I will.' Immediately a manifest change came over her spirit. Her countenance began to beam with joy. She said afterward that she received at this time baptism of the glory of God, which so overwhelmed her that she seemed on the point of passing to the other world." Abigail Merwin's ecstatic near-death experience mirrored the "waves of liquid love" testified to by Finney, and the "stream of eternal love" rolling three times through the heart of John Humphrey Noyes. The next day at the Free Church meeting, Abigail publicly professed holiness with Noyes by standing up and singing aloud from the hymn "Welcome, welcome, dear Redeemer, / Welcome to this heart of mine."[26]

In his *Confession of Religious Experience*, Noyes would romanticize Abigail as his partner in the battle for Perfectionism, bravely standing in the front lines of their adversaries' fire in the early days of the movement: "Her power of argument and her position as my first convert placed her with me in the front of the battle and in the full glare of the public gaze, and she nobly sustained the trial." Noyes's image of himself and Abigail, arm in arm in a halo of Perfectionist glory, nobly sustaining each other in the "full glare" of their enemies' contempt, reveals the prized place Abigail filled in Noyes's later heroic recasting of his life. More important, Noyes's decision to fully embrace the persecuting gaze of the unholy provided him with a means to evade the ever-threatening eye of judgment. Unable to stand the scorching social gaze that shamed him in public, he simply reversed it so that the persecuting "gaze" of contempt served instead as a measure of his own elevation. In other words, Noyes took the unbearable image of himself as the target of a social mockery and turned it on its head: others' disdain served only to measure his divine election and the "eminence" toward which "God [was] calling and leading [him]." Persecution, whether social or religious, would only serve to magnify the glory of Noyes's eventual triumph.[27]

It was soon after Abigail's conversion that Noyes had another important spiritual conquest: this time, over Charles Weld, a fellow Perfectionist to whom he had been recently introduced and whose tendency to strike a paternal pose toward Noyes irked the young preacher. For if Noyes had been exiled from the respectable circle of orthodoxy, it now became of the utmost importance for him to jockey for a position of prominence among the ragtag band of preachers who had clustered around the New Haven Free Church and were starting to give shape to the fledgling Perfectionist movement. Here, as in the case of the persecuting gaze he suffered heroically alongside Abigail, power would work itself out in Noyes's mythical imagination as an epic battle of glances between him and his enemies.

Noyes narrates, with some relish, his ocular domination of Weld during the course of a Free Church meeting. As he was preaching his recently discovered doctrine of perfect holiness, Weld was apparently cast into a sudden paroxysm: "In the midst of my discourse I was interrupted by a strange sound. I looked around and saw Weld sitting with his eyes closed, his countenance black with horror, his hands waving up and down, and his lungs laboring with long and rattling breaths." The shocked congregation ran to the man's aid until, at last, the fit passed. When Weld met Noyes's eyes, the latter "looked at him steadily . . . [until Weld's] countenance softened into a smile, and he dropped his eye."[28]

Having "dropped his eye" in this battle of gazes with Noyes, the stunned Weld was later able to explain the onset of the seizure: "From the beginning of [Noyes's] discourse, the words of [his] mouth, he said, were like fire to his spirit. They scorched him more and more, till he could endure no longer, and he thought of rising and smiting [Noyes] in the pulpit. Instantly upon this, the word came to him—'Touch not mine anointed, and do my prophet no harm.' " In his Dartmouth and Chesterfield days, on the chivalrous field of courtly love, Noyes's "competitors in gallantry" might have blocked him from the "pinnacle of felicity" he seemed continually on the edge of achieving. But here, in his conquest of Weld, Noyes had lighted upon an antidote to help him cope with the pesky problem of gallant competitors, both sexual and religious: he invented for himself a supereye that could literally stun and paralyze his enemies, knocking them clean out of the ring and clearing the field for his total domination.[29]

In Abigail Merwin, Noyes had a muse to guide him along his journey toward the eminence God had marked out for him. But if every Christian odyssey requires its Beatrice, it demands as well a ritual passage into the underworld. And so, stripped of his preaching license, cut off from Yale, and slipping into the role of an outcast, by the spring of 1834 Noyes began his descent.

2

Noyes in the Underworld

L EAVING NEW HAVEN AT THE END OF MAY 1834, NOYES SET HIMSELF UP in New York City in a boardinghouse on Leonard Street, intending to devote himself to writing. Leonard Street was adjacent to the infamous Five Points neighborhood, an area of lower Manhattan situated at the confluence of Anthony, Orange, and Cross Streets. Once lush and bucolic, with a five-acre lake called the Collect as its geographic center, slaughterhouses and chemical tanning factories took over the area in the late eighteenth century, turning the once-verdant lake into a putrid swamp. In 1802, the area was razed and filled in an attempt to rehabilitate the neighborhood.

The Collect had become a residential and commercial district that, for the space of a decade or two, housed a moderately successful community of artisans, merchants, and shopkeepers. But with the decline of its artisan culture at the turn of the nineteenth century, the neighborhood took an economic dive; soon, crowds of impoverished Irish Catholic immigrants and African American freemen swept in to occupy its rows of rickety, two-story, brick-and-wood houses, which had cheap rents. This mix did little to raise the area's social cachet, while its low-lying situation made it a hotbed for cholera outbreaks. The epidemic of 1832 spread like wildfire through its tenements, where outhouses and drinking wells were located cheek by jowl. As though unable to cut ties with its reeking, sinking foundations, by 1830 the Collect—now named Five Points—had become the prostitution center of Manhattan, sensationalized across the media as the proverbial den of iniquity, rife with drunkenness, gambling, and whoring. The very year that Noyes would move into his boardinghouse, the frontiersman Davy Crockett wrote a travel memoir recording his experience in Five Points, commenting, "I would rather risque myself in an Indian fight than venture among these creatures after night. . . . [T]hese are worse than savages; they are too mean to swab hell's kitchen."[1]

Why Noyes directed his steps to Leonard Street that day in May 1834, we will never know. Some combination of economy and missionary zeal no doubt factored among his motives. But whatever the case, his choice of rooms overlooking the moral cesspit of Manhattan—the ground zero of sexual temptation—would greatly influence what Noyes later characterized in his *Confessions* as his "strange experience in New York." Sitting alone in his hired room on one of his first evenings on Leonard Street, Noyes experienced a religious vision he would afterward describe to a friend as a "marriage feast" with Christ. Noyes's blow-by-blow description of his wedding night with the Son of God abounded in sexual metaphor; after it was over, the vision left Noyes pining like the ravished bride of the Song of Songs for the lover whose "fruit was sweet to [his] taste" (2:3).[2]

Noyes was, of course, no innovator when it came to describing his religious vision in unabashedly sexual terms. Christian mystics had always figured the face-to-face meeting of the believer and his God as a spiritual marriage, a blending of bride and bridegroom in ecstatic oneness. The sixteenth-century Carmelite nun Teresa of Avila, perhaps the most notorious in this line, depicted her encounter with God as an act of divine penetration, at once painful and sweet: "I saw in his hand a long spear of gold, and at the iron's point there seemed to be a little fire. He appeared to me to be thrusting it at times into my heart, and to pierce my very entrails; when he drew it out, he seemed to draw them out also, and to leave me all on fire with a great love of God. The pain was so great, that it made me moan; and yet so surpassing was the sweetness of this excessive pain, that I could not wish to be rid of it." Teresa's vision was immortalized a century later by the baroque sculptor Gian Lorenzo Bernini; his stunning white marble statue of the ecstatic saint, collapsed in the throes of spiritual union with Christ, has rightly been characterized by Simon Schama as "hover[ing] on the borderline between sacred mystery and indecency."[3]

But Noyes's Leonard Street vision would have given even Saint Teresa's erotic fireworks a run for their money. There, in his shabby garret, Noyes recounted how Christ "entered the secret chamber of my soul," and Noyes was at a loss for words to describe the "glories of the feast" that ensued: "At one time the love of the Lamb seemed like celestial fire rushing through every fibre of my body, and every susceptibility of my soul. At another, it seemed like a bubbling stream of living water. At another, it was like a quiet mighty but peaceful river, rolling its pure waves through my bosom. At another, it was like an ocean in which I sunk, and sunk, and found no bottom, and even my spirit mingled with the very essence of the God-Head." Noyes quotes from the Song of Songs, describing himself as literally having a sex hangover the morning after the love debauchery: "This morning I am sick of love. . . . Now indeed I am married, and will henceforth wait only on my husband. I know he will give me all the desire of my heart."[4]

Noyes interpreted his marriage-feast vision as confirming his growing faith that there did, indeed, exist a path back to paradise, back to a place where loss and absence, shame and sadness could be magically wiped away: "We may now over come by the blood of the Lamb, and enter the holiest of all. The cherubim and flaming sword are withdrawn at the gate of Paradise. Adam may return, and eating of the tree of life, become immortal." Through this ingenious fantasy of sex with the godhead, Noyes was able to reverse the traumatic expulsion from Eden, the source of human shame and sorrow, while indulging in the sublimated satisfaction of his strongest sexual urges.[5]

But no spiritual pilgrimage is complete without a journey through the valley of temptation, by which the Christian hero justifies his status as God's chosen one. As the ecstasy of his marriage-feast vision gradually dissipated, Noyes felt Satan's minions gathering their forces against him. "A murky spiritual atmosphere began to gather around me," Noyes narrated in his *Confessions*. "Strange thoughts coursed through my brain unsuggested by my own reflections and uncontrolled by my will. I felt with shuddering that the Evil One was near." Like Christ in the desert, Noyes was about to endure a three-week standoff with the devil.[6]

In his manic state, Noyes stopped eating and sleeping and instead wandered the streets of Five Points and lower Manhattan. He proselytized to prostitutes and sailors, slept on the benches of the Battery, devised a theological argument rebutting Copernicus, dabbled in theories of metempsychosis, became convinced he was Lucifer incarnate, and in general did battle with "every thing within and around me [which] seemed to be full-charged, and, as it were, crawling with the dark, nauseous spirit of Satan." At one point Abigail Merwin appeared to him in a vision as Satan's emissary, disguised as an angel: "I saw her, standing, as it were, on the pinnacle of the universe, in the glory of an angel; but a voice from which I could not turn away, pronounced her title: *Satan transformed into an angel of light.* I gave her up, and cast her from me as one accursed."[7]

Convinced that Christ's final judgment was imminent, Noyes hurried out of his rooms one day and anxiously watched the sky for the appearance of the Son of Man. One imagines his rapt face turned heavenward as he stood alone in the chill gray mist of the Battery at dawn, in a coat by now well wrinkled and dusty in every seam, a hollow-cheeked John the Baptist for this latter century: "It was a terrible moment, when the red canopy above seemed just bursting for the descent of Christ with his mighty angels, in flaming fire, to take vengeance on the world." Finally, after three weeks, Noyes's fearsome visions began to abate. He sought relief for his blistered and swollen feet in the healing salt water off the wharves. With his mind cleared and his feet soothed, Noyes interpreted this immersion as a baptism of sorts, a ritual cleansing of the poisonous temptations that Satan had sent to corrupt the young saint. Like Christ, who had thrice resisted the devil's snares in the wilderness and remained faithful to his God, so Noyes emerged victorious from his confrontation with the evil one.[8]

Later, Noyes would adamantly deny that he had passed through a "crazy" period in New York, insisting instead that it was God's way of testing him in the fire of faith, of training him to navigate the rough-and-tumble world of spirits, both heavenly and diabolical. His New York experience had given him "an acquaintance with the principalities of the invisible world . . . [,] practical skill in discriminating between divine and diabolical manifestations

and impressions, and a boldness . . . in facing and exposing spiritual impos-
tors." In short, Noyes insisted that his wandering in the spiritual wilderness
of New York had given him the requisite skills to become God's prophet on
earth, able to discriminate between messages that were hell-sent and those
that, on the contrary, were stamped with a divine origin. Noyes would compare himself years later to a telegraph station, linked by a wire to the spiritual
world whose "vibrating" signals he was continually fielding and triaging.
"Our most valuable business as Christians," he would write, "will be to perfect ourselves in this kind of telegraphing and keeping signals constantly
going back and forth between us and heaven." Signals from Hades—the
term Noyes adopted to refer to the realm of the unresurrected dead—were to
be exposed for what they were: deceptive messages sent by Satan to ensnare
and tempt humans into the path of error.[9]

But among many members of his entourage, friends and enemies alike,
Noyes's apprenticeship in spiritual telegraphy was quite simply chalked up
to insanity. And so, while this three-week stint as a hallucinating vagabond
prophet in the bowels of New York City may have given Noyes confidence
in his spiritual credentials, it did little to ingratiate him with his family and
former friends, who found his antics not only worrisome but deeply embar-
rassing. "[H]ad I trusted to stories, [I] should have believed him a downright
madman," wrote Noyes's brother Horatio, a classics student at Yale, soon after
the wanderer's return to New Haven. Noyes's parents were, for their part, in
despair over their son's precipitous fall from grace at the seminary and rumors of his faltering reason, and insisted that he return home to Putney to
recuperate. "I guess John . . . is pretty well broken down," wrote Polly to
Horatio on June 18, 1834. "I hope he will come home to Mother as soon as
possible . . . I shall not give up my confidence in his ardent piety and filial
gratitude till I see him."[10]

Noyes found an ambivalent welcome on his return home to Putney, his
father having "given up all hope" for him after rumors of his "fantastic per-
formances in New York," and the neighbors striving to avoid "mentioning
[his] name in [the family's] presence for fear of hurting their feelings." Noyes
did a creditable job of appearing sane in front of his friends and kin, but by
the end of the summer his colleague from the Free Church, James Boyle,
was calling him back to New Haven to begin work on a Perfectionist news-

paper aimed at disseminating the doctrine of perfect holiness. And at the end of July, despite the misgivings of his family, Noyes returned to New Haven.[11]

Boyle and Noyes's newspaper was titled, quite simply, *The Perfectionist*. The name had originated among the movement's critics as a term of derision, but Noyes insisted on adopting it anyway, "anticipating the time of its redemption from infamy." In the introduction to the first issue, which appeared in August 1834, Noyes was at pains to disabuse his readers of the many misconceptions buzzing around about the movement and "the varying and incongruous images of Perfection, conjured up by the word in the various fancies of men, from a picture of a monk in sackcloth and ashes, to that of a seraph with six wings." In a series of dry, rather tedious articles arguing arcane theological points, Noyes would use the paper to publicize what he meant by perfection: humans' ability, through Christ's grace, to attain perfect holiness of intent, or perfection of the spirit, that rendered perfect obedience to the outward letter of the law a matter of secondary importance.[12]

But as the official spokesperson for New Haven Perfectionism, Noyes had bigger bogeys to fight than images of six-winged seraphs and monks in sackcloth. Throughout Christianity's checkered history, splinter cults and sects who claimed to be beyond sin as taught by the church had invariably engaged in sexual experimentation (or, at the very least, had been accused of it by their enemies) to prove that they were not bound by earthly law. This latest branch of the sinless tree was no exception. The Perfectionist preacher Erasmus Stone, based in central New York, in the town of Salina, had a religious vision in 1834 in which he saw a mighty host of distraught men and women rushing about, each frantically searching for a lost soul mate. The minister's religious gloss on the dream was that humans, while in earthly form, are nearly always paired in marriage with an incompatible mate; on the day of judgment, when the graves are opened, each soul will at last find its true spiritual bride or husband and be reunited for eternity. In heaven, earthly marriage with its legalistic, soul-deadening binding of unlike souls would have no place. Stone's doctrine of "spiritual wives" spread like wildfire among Perfectionist camps in Massachusetts and New York, where it became common practice for believers to enter into quasi-clandestine "spiritual marriages" with partners outside their legal marriages. While these unions were reputedly chaste, meant to be marriages of spirit only, rumors inevitably spread that some pairs were dabbling in more carnal forms of fellowship.[13]

What ensued was a turf war between New Haven Perfectionism, headed by the prim and intellectual Noyes, and the more raucous, amorous branch of New York Perfectionists. Simon Lovett, who oversaw a congregation of mostly women saints (as they called themselves) in Brimfield, Massachusetts, set out on a pilgrimage to Noyes with the aim of converting him. The silver-tongued Noyes, however, turned the situation on its head, converting Lovett instead, and in February 1835 the two of them headed back to Brimfield on a proselytizing mission. At Brimfield, Noyes was immediately struck by the disconcertingly "free" manners of Lovett's female congregants, who exchanged kisses and terms of endearment with their male coreligionists. Sitting next to a Perfectionist beauty named Hannah one evening, Noyes received an unexpected kiss from the admiring girl as they parted for bed. Noyes—who, despite his fantasies of sex with God, remained physically chaste—panicked at this carnal invitation and, without communicating his intentions to anyone, left the next morning, making "a bee-line on foot through snow and cold—below zero—to Putney, sixty miles distant."[14]

Noyes's instincts had been sound. A few nights later, the revivalist fervor in Brimfield assumed a "social and fanatical form" when Mary Lincoln and Maria Brown crept into Simon Lovett's bedroom at midnight and crawled into bed with him to prove their chastity in the face of temptation. Becoming hysterical at the ensuing scandal, Mary Lincoln had a vision that God was about to destroy Brimfield with fire from heaven and that all who would be saved must flee to the mountains. "They set forth at nightfall, and tramped through mud and rain to the top of a neighboring mountain, throwing off their clothing as they ran. There they prayed that the avenging bolts might be stayed; and as a result of their intercession, they afterward said, the city was saved."[15]

Noyes scrupulously took his distance from the "Brimfield Bundling," as the scandal came to be called in the press, and its juicy tabloid blend of kissing, streaking women, rainstorms, and hellfire. But if Noyes vehemently disapproved of the sexual experimentation rampant among New York Perfectionists, the question of sex in heaven—or angel sex, as he chose to think of it—was another matter altogether. At the time of the Brimfield Bundling, Noyes was actively mulling over in his own mind the relationship between men and women among the saints of the invisible world and came to the conclusion that sexual intercourse between spiritual soul mates was an integral part of resurrection life.

Noyes's obsession with proving the existence of sex in the afterlife may have been spurred by the sense that he had already lost his chance for earthly sex. During the summer of 1834, as he was convalescing from his "New York experience" in Putney, Noyes had received disheartening news from New Haven: Abigail Merwin, his first convert, had defected from Perfectionism. Noyes was devastated at the news, but it was not until he got wind of Abigail's engagement to a Mr. Merit Platt, in the fall of 1835, that he was moved to write to her. Noyes opened his letter by denying any intention to interfere with her "earthly engagement" to Mr. Platt, as he had passed beyond such trivial matters: "I dwell where 'the fashion of this world has passed away,' and as I cannot go back to those whom I have left asleep, so I have no desire to disturb their dreams until they shall hear that voice of the Son of God, which will effectively break their slumbers and sever every earthly tie." Noyes's pompous distinction between himself and the sleepers who had not yet been enlightened with his God's-eye perspective allowed him to acknowledge Abigail's engagement and, at the same time, to wave it away as nothing but an earthly dream that would melt with the coming of God's kingdom. Having been instructed by God as to "the place which the marriage relation will hold in the coming dispensation"—in other words, that resurrected bodies would have sex—Noyes assured Abigail "by the word of the Lord you were given to me" and that God had joined them "in an immortal marriage, and . . . what God hath joined together man cannot put asunder." Throwing off his squeamishness, Noyes was happy to reverse himself now that it suited his purpose and adopt Lovett and Stone's theory of spiritual marriage. Noyes's belief in angel sex was key to his fantasy of holding on to Abigail, whom he considered his own legitimate spiritual wife.[16]

Abigail's nuptials to Mr. Platt were delayed until the winter of 1836. But Noyes, after declaring in his letter to Abigail that he had shuffled off the mortal coil of earthly cares and would be content to possess her in heaven, spun around and made the decidedly earthly decision to pack up his belongings and move to Ithaca, in central New York, where the newlywed Mr. and Mrs. Platt now made their home. In a letter to his mother, Noyes was unambiguous about his reasons for the move: "I went for the purpose on the one hand of starting the paper and the kingdom of God in the center of New York State, and on the other of pursuing and confronting Abigail Merwin, who had deserted her post as my helper." One can only imagine Abigail's surprise on finding that the wild red-haired preacher, of whose New York hijinks the Merwin household was well aware, had set up shop in the same hamlet where she lived with her new husband. Noyes's plan was to begin publishing a second Perfectionist newspaper, this one titled *The Witness*, and to lay the foundations for the coming kingdom of God in the comforting—if begrudging—presence of his spiritual wife.[17]

In Ithaca, Abigail refused to acknowledge him, revealing herself quite patently unwilling to resume her place as his spiritual "helper." In the face of this rebuff, Noyes's thoughts on how the marriage relation would play out in heaven began evolving toward a more communal model. On January 15, 1837, Noyes confided in a letter to his friend David Harrison his new vision of the "marriage supper of the Lamb": "When the will of God is done on earth as it is in heaven there will be no marriage," he wrote. "Exclusiveness, jealousy, quarreling have no place at the marriage supper of the Lamb. I call a certain woman my wife. She is yours, she is Christ's, and in him she is the bride of all saints. She is now in the hands of a stranger, and according to my promise to her I rejoice. My claim upon her cuts directly across the marriage covenant of this world, and God knows the end." Frustrated by jealousy over having to share Abigail with an earthly husband, Noyes had to invent a system in which exclusiveness was banned and all were wed to all. Unable to eliminate his rival, Merit Platt, Noyes would do the next best thing: eliminate the very notion of sexual rivalry altogether.[18]

Noyes's letter was not destined to remain private. Harrison gave it to Simon Lovett, Noyes's old Brimfield Bundling buddy, and from there it fell into the hands of Theophilus Ransom Gates, an itinerant preacher and editor of *The Battle-Axe; or, Weapons of War*, a Philadelphia news sheet dedicated to the ideal of Christian free love. Gates—who would be immortalized locally when, in 1843, he and a cohort of free lovers streaked naked down the aisle of the Shenkel Church in North Coventry Township in Chester County during Sunday services—believed marriage a curse and an apostasy. He advocated instead a more open arrangement whereby "one Battle-Axe would go to the home of another, state his or her call to a saintly marriage union, and the pair might live together for a day or a lifetime before a new inspiration parted them." Noyes's letter clearly struck a chord, and Gates wasted no time in publishing it in the August 1837 edition of his newsletter.[19]

The public reaction was swift and severe. *The Advocate of Moral Reform*, a journal published by a New York–based women's reform group bent on eradicating prostitution, lambasted Noyes for "invading" the "domestic constitution," trampling the nuclear family in the dust while "unbridled license stalks among the ruins, smiling at the havoc she has made, and feasting on the last bleeding remnants of chastity and virtue." Noyes defended himself, both in a rebuttal sent to *The Advocate* and in the pages of his own paper, *The Witness*, with a scriptural defense of his belief that in heaven "they neither marry nor are given in marriage" and assurances that, contra Gates and his band of Christian streakers, he never intended the scheme to be tried out on earth until after the coming of Judgment Day and the resurrection of bodies. If Noyes conceived of wife swapping in heaven as theologically distinct from wife swapping on earth, however, his critics failed to appreciate the difference. In the wake of the scandal, subscriptions to *The Witness*— which had been middling at best, but which Noyes had counted on to keep himself and his fledgling kingdom of God afloat financially—came to a complete halt.[20]

Noyes was at his nadir when a wealthy young convert named Harriet Holton sent him a gift of eighty dollars that allowed him to pay off his debts in Ithaca. Over the next six months, Noyes struck up a correspondence with his admirer and, in a letter dated June 11, 1838, against all expectations, proposed marriage to this fellow Vermonter. Given Noyes's recently developed theory of sexual and spiritual communism among the saints, however, the marriage he offered was to be of no ordinary stamp. "We are already one with each other and with all saints," he specified in his letter. "This primary and universal union is more radical and of course more important than any partial and external partnerships." His object in proposing marriage was not "to monopolize and enslave her heart or my own, but to enlarge and establish both in the free fellowship of God's universal family." Harriet responded the next day, registering her shock by saying she would "as soon [have thought] of marrying the morning star" as of receiving a proposal from her Perfectionist master. Yet she agreed wholeheartedly with him that in their partnership, "the grace of God will exclude jealousy and everything with which the marriage state is defiled as we see it in the world," humbly and joyfully agreeing to the union.[21]

If John Humphrey Noyes's spiritual breadth and ardor was inherited from his mother, he had inherited from his father a canny business sense. John Noyes Sr. had made a small fortune manufacturing pot and pearl ashes for fertilizer from the burnt timber of Vermont's thick forests. Noyes's partnership with a woman who would provide him with both spiritual and financial support in his endeavor to found God's kingdom was a stroke of business genius: a quintessentially American blend of religious fervor and economic practicality that was to characterize Noyes—and his utopian undertakings—all his life.

ONE OF FREUD'S ENDURING CONTRIBUTIONS TO PSYCHOLOGY WAS HIS analysis of what he called "compromise formations." Visible in neurotic symptoms, jokes, and dreams, compromise formations testify to the creative capacity of the unconscious to take the stuff of consciousness, whether language or image, and bend it into fantastic shapes that satisfy our deepest primal urges, all the while paying lip service to the censorship of the super-ego as the representative of civilized restraint. In *The Interpretation of Dreams*, Freud gives the example of a dream he had where he had written a monograph on a certain plant and, as he looked at a colored illustration in the book, noticed that a dried specimen of the plant from a herbarium had been bound into the monograph. From his perusal of a monograph on his wife's favorite flower, cyclamen, in a bookstore window the day before to a recent conversation with a colleague named "Gardener," to a memory of a herbarium in secondary school that had been gnawed by bookworms, Freud decoded the botanical image as a displaced and condensed symbol for the bibliophilia that was his guilty pleasure.

Noyes did a fair amount of such displacing and condensing himself in working out a compromise between his intense sexual desire and his equally intense fear of female rejection and ridicule, between his deep sense of social shame and inadequacy and his narcissistic refusal to countenance sexual or intellectual competition, between a desire to serve the impulses of the flesh and a duty to follow the commands of the spirit. Ultimately, he would build a sexual, social, and theological edifice, not a brick of which was placed unless it served to buttress one or another of Noyes's psychological quirks and self-contradictions. So he would take, for instance, his fear of being the object of a critical social gaze and transmute stigma into election, the burn of shame transformed into the glow of narcissistic satisfaction at being God's chosen. He would invent a magnetic gaze that could magically flatten his competitors and, when that ceased to work, invent a world in which sexual competition itself was, just as magically, made to disappear. He would turn sexual ecstasy into a privileged mode of communion with the godhead, quite flatly refusing to admit any distinction between flesh and spirit.

Looked at from one perspective, Noyes's elaborate compromise formation, in its economy and precision, married the strangeness of a dream with the efficient beauty of a mathematical theorem. Most breathtaking of all, perhaps, was that Noyes had the wherewithal to take this delicately balanced psychic hodgepodge and materialize it into his own flesh-and-blood utopia. On the one hand, Noyes's evolving theological edifice appears an almost laughably transparent attempt to accommodate his own peculiar psychosexual needs, a structure jerry-rigged to house a fragile ego. And yet Noyes's vision of a community in which "exclusion, jealousy, and quarreling" would disappear, and all enjoy "free fellowship" in one universal family under God, oddly enough found a sympathetic ear in nineteenth-century America. At the height of his powers, Noyes would command a following of nearly three hundred souls who saw, in his vision of a golden age communitarian paradise, an attractive alternative to the stingy, competitive regime of private property and monogamy that held sway in the profane world outside their doors.

3

⤳

New Jerusalem (in Vermont)

Brushing himself off from Abigail Merwin's rejection and armed not just with the loyal support of his new wife, Harriet Holton, but also a recently acquired printing press, John Humphrey Noyes left Ithaca at the end of the summer of 1838, ready to begin building the rudiments of God's new earth smack in the middle of Putney, Vermont. But first Noyes would need to secure his troops. In addition to his wife, Noyes had already converted his fifteen-year-old brother, George Washington Noyes, and two of his sisters, Harriet and Charlotte Noyes, my great-great-great-grandmothers, to the doctrine of Perfectionism. He then consolidated his forces by handily marrying his sisters off to two recent Perfectionist converts, John Miller and John Skinner. John Miller, hailing from a prosperous family in Westmoreland, Vermont, was willing to renounce considerable business and political opportunities in order to join Noyes's ranks. John Skinner, a Quaker teacher whose family was of old New England stock, signed on to help with the printing and editing of Noyes's Perfectionist mouthpiece, *The Witness*.

With his skeptical, strong-willed mother, Noyes would wage a holy and not entirely civil battle for religious authority. A letter he wrote to his mother in February 1838 reproved her for her lack of belief in his divine commission, arguing that, by electing him His prophet, God had sanctioned Noyes to take authority over her: "So when you write me such letters as I received the other day, you must expect I shall affectionately reprove you for thinking you know more than your father," Noyer admonished her. "My child, be still. You know but little, and it becomes you to be modest." The Noyes matriarch dismissed letters from her son's acolytes aiming to persuade her that he was "the father in this dispensation, as Paul was in that of his day" and, instead, asserted that with his "lively imagination," John had somehow "imbibed the idea that he was something more than ordinary in his calling. . . . Is there anything more in him than in other great reformers, such as Luther, Calvin and Erasmus?" Happy to grant her son the status of a great reformer, Polly balked at giving him free rein as God's direct representative on earth, an entitlement even Luther had lacked the temerity to claim for himself.[1]

Eventually, outflanked by the other members of her family, Polly buckled in the spring of 1839 and published, in the pages of *The Witness*, an open confession that she accepted John Humphrey as her "teacher and father in spiritual things." But if the demon of disobedience was to pop up throughout Polly Noyes's life—she found herself time and again compelled to tell John Humphrey that "he had faults the same as other people"—she was always quickly subdued by her domineering son. And so, with his mother sidelined for the moment, and his alcoholic and aging father equally neutralized (he would die in 1841, at the age of seventy-seven), John Humphrey Noyes acceded to the unquestioned status of paterfamilias. Having set his house in order, he began to reach out to a wider circle of converts.[2]

Two earnest Christians who would prove instrumental in the eventual shape taken by the Community were my great-great-great-grandparents, George and Mary (née Johnson) Cragin. George Cragin's father had been a successful provincial businessman and politician in Massachusetts, but when the elder Cragin's concerns went belly-up in the Panic of 1819, young George was cast out into the world to earn his bread. While working as a store clerk in New York City, George fell under the spell of revivalist preacher Charles Grandison Finney. He quickly joined the reformist ranks of the Great Awakening's converted, taking a job as a publishing agent for *The Advocate of Moral Reform*, the very antiprostitution newsletter that had lambasted Noyes for the sexual theories adumbrated in his letter published in *The Battle-Axe*. Mary Johnson had been born into an august old family of Puritan descent in Maine and moved to New York City with her parents at the age of five. At eighteen, Mary adopted the role of zealous reformer: she became headmistress of a recently established "infant school" designed to care for the leagues of poor, and not infrequently homeless, children flooding the city. Petty thieves and street urchins, paupers and prostitutes were among those George and Mary served.

Indeed, it was as Mary was making her way down a New York City street with a waif in hand—one of the sooty-faced "refuse from the quays and lanes" who daily crowded her schoolroom, and whose mother had failed to pick him up at school day's end—that George Cragin first made her acquaintance. He was roundly charmed, not least by Mary's decision to cast propriety to the wind and, although it was not proper for an unchaperoned young woman to talk to a strange man in the street, to boldly accost George and enlist his help in locating the parents of her poor charge. Moved by Mary's passionate devotion to the lost child, George found himself transfixed by her peculiar magnetic power. Upon parting from her that day, he confessed that "a queer sensation came over me; . . . it seemed as though I had parted with a large part of myself or life."[3]

George and Mary had just settled down into married life when, in November 1839, Mary came across a text by John Humphrey Noyes, entitled an *Essay on Faith*, and was instantly converted to Perfectionism. Like a latter-day Esther, courageously willing to stake all for her newfound beliefs, Mary embraced Noyes's conviction "that through the power of faith a man may cast out from his nature the spirit of self" and, in doing so, become perfectly sinless. Condemnation was, indeed, swift in coming—although it would fall first upon George Cragin. Catching wind of Mary Cragin's conversion, the ladies of the *Advocate of Moral Reform* summoned George before a committee. As he stood awkwardly before the fuming matrons ranged against him in the newspaper's boardroom, "thirty pair of bright eyes scanned his figure from head to foot, as though they had expected to see hooves, and horns, and a tail to match." George was immediately dismissed from his post at the paper. Rejoicing in the persecution as a test of her faith, Mary wrote to Noyes: "Bless the Lord! On the first of December

[George] will be without money and without business. How this rejoices me!" George, less certain in his faith, was nonetheless prepared to follow his wife down whichever path she led.[4]

That path led to a ramshackle farm near Rondout on the Hudson, owned by a fellow Perfectionist named Abram C. Smith, a Noyes acolyte who, in the spring of 1840, opened up his home to the dispossessed couple. The Cragins and their infant son joined the Smith clan, including Smith's wife and four children, and the group attempted to live together on civil terms and by communal principles. In time, though, the increasing frequency of "long private colloquies" between Smith and Mary—which George Cragin had at first naively dismissed as "doctrinal discussion concerning the more intricate problems of Perfectionist ethics"—revealed themselves to be rather a full-fledged sexual affair. Smith, it seemed, had seduced Mary by convincing her that Noyes's celestial vision of spiritual wives and angel sex should be implemented on earth. Noyes eventually caught wind of the affair being bruited about in Perfectionist circles and, after severely reprimanding the couple, offered an olive branch by inviting George and Mary to join him in founding God's kingdom in Putney, safe from Smith's lascivious reach.[5]

By 1841 the stage at Putney was set with the principal actors of the drama about to unfold: John Humphrey and Harriet Noyes, George Washington Noyes, Harriet and John Skinner, Charlotte and John Miller, and George and Mary Cragin. The gathered faithful called their loose association the Society of Inquiry, and in a constitution adopted in February 1841, they declared their purpose was to "make an open and united confession of this our belief and more effectually assist each other in searching the Scriptures and in overcoming sin."[6]

This goal appears plausible enough. But given John Humphrey Noyes's repeated run-ins with scandal—both his lunatic three-week tear around Manhattan proclaiming the end of days from the rooftops, as well as his multiple brushes with Perfectionist sexual impropriety—one may well wonder why this group of socially stable and economically prosperous believers were so attracted by his doctrines. Social opprobrium and financial insolvency were, it seemed, a perfectly acceptable price to pay for a ticket on this strange train to salvation. Joined to the fact that Society of Inquiry members had to submit unquestioningly to what Polly Hayes Noyes termed, in one of her more irascible moments, her son John Humphrey's "spiritual tyranny" as Christ's representative on earth, membership in Noyes's club certainly had its downsides.[7]

But it was, perhaps, precisely Noyes's sense of unwavering self-certainty and righteousness, no matter how iron-fisted, that appealed during this era of spiritual turbulence in America. In the wake of the American Revolution and the delegitimation of official religious authority, the separation of church and state brought about what one historian has called an "explosion of cosmological speculation," a bewildering proliferation of sects and subreligions, each claiming to represent divine truth. Anyone professing a religious belief could hang out a shingle, and had the protected constitutional right to do so. Baptists and Methodists rejected the elitist Puritan belief in predestination for God's chosen few, instead promoting Jesus Christ as a personal savior for any individual soul who accepted his grace. In the opposing camp, disdaining the warm-fuzzy emotionalism of the more populist creeds, New England Unitarians bumped Jesus down a notch in the Christian hierarchy and revived the quasi-deistic notion of a watchmaker God whose existence could be fully squared with the scientific spirit of Enlightenment rationalism. Spiritual options were dizzying.[8]

No doubt in response to being set adrift in this cosmological fog, antebellum America witnessed a revival of centuries-old millennial speculations about the end of days and the coming kingdom of God on earth. The idea of the Christian Apocalypse blazingly set forth in John of Patmos's first-century Book of Revelations, which was eventually canonized in 419, predicts a mighty battle at Armageddon between the forces of Satan and God; in the end, Satan is bound (though not utterly vanquished), ushering in one thousand years of peace under the reign of Jesus Christ on earth. The millennium was to be followed by one final comeback bid on the part of the Antichrist, who would rise out of the bottomless pit to besiege God's earthly kingdom. God would handily smite Satan and his cohort with fire from heaven and send him, along with all those sinners whose names were not found written in the Book of Life, sprawling down into the lake of eternal fire. The New Jerusalem, glittering in gems and gold, would descend out of the heavens to take its rightful place on earth, and secular history would come to a close.

From the time of the earliest Puritan settlements, America occupied a prominent place in Protestant debates about divine Providence and the direction cosmic history would likely take. In his 1630 pep talk to a boatload of shivering Puritans about to cross over into God's unknown country, John Winthrop compared the group to a new Israel, a chosen people sent out into the wilderness to establish a "Shining City on a Hill" that would lead Christendom forward in its progressive march toward holiness. In the eighteenth century, the fiery preacher Jonathan Edwards's biblical typology reasoned that the millennium would come to pass in America, and even his less dogmatic evangelical heir, the reverend Lyman Beecher, used Edwards's predictions to justify American westward expansion in 1834. "All providential developments since, and all the existing signs of the times, lend corroboration" to Edwards's prediction, Beecher reasoned. The western territory, with its vast untapped land and resources, would become the very engine of modern Christendom if properly developed. "Where shall the central energy be found, and from what nation shall the renovating power go forth," Beecher queried, if not from America? America as a "redeemer nation," a light and an example to the world and foreordained as the probable site of the New Jerusalem, seized the antebellum imagination.[9]

Millennial sects of all stripes flourished in America. The English-born Quaker Ann Lee, after giving birth to four babies who died in infancy, renounced sexuality as the root of all evil, received a holy vision that God was a man-woman blend rather than a paternal father, and proclaimed that she in fact was the "bride" prophesied in Revelations and that her marriage to her male half—Jesus—would inaugurate the New Jerusalem. Another vision directed her to take a band of followers to America to build the tabernacle of God among men. Celibate Shaker communities (so called in reference to the sect's tendency to dance or shake and speak in tongues while in a state of religious ecstasy) quickly spread throughout New York and New England. Meanwhile, New York native Joseph Smith claimed that the angel Moroni had directed him to a golden-plated addendum to the New Testament buried in a dirt pile near his house and had provided him with magical spectacles with which to decipher it, to boot. The Book of Mormon revealed that God had led a group of his elect across the Arabian desert and onto the North American continent in 600 BC, upstaging Christ by half a millennium, and situating future sacred history squarely on American soil. It was here, among God's dispersed Latter Day Saints, that the New Jerusalem would take shape.

John Humphrey Noyes had his own version of the millennial timeline, and it, too, identified America as the hotspot of sacred history. The Second Coming of Christ, which so many Christians believed to be shimmering on the near horizon, had already taken place nearly eighteen hundred years before, with the fall of the Temple of Jerusalem in AD 70. Such earnest believers as Joseph Smith and Ann Lee, according to Noyes, were waiting for a train that had already left the station. At the time of the temple's destruction, Noyes believed Christ had made a brief reappearance on earth, "like a thief in the night," and inaugurated his thousand-year reign—but in heaven, not on earth. The millennium as a revolution in the spiritual and not the earthly world had come to a close roughly eight hundred years before without earthlings being any the wiser. Noyes surmised that the saints in heaven were now waiting patiently—after all, what is eight hundred years in the scheme of eternity?—for Christians on earth to prepare themselves for the final annexation of the earth by God's heavenly kingdom.

A feeling of spiritual homelessness amidst splintering sects no doubt added fuel to nineteenth-century America's millennial fire. But the millennial imagination would not have burned at quite the same white heat had it not been fanned by the massive disruptions in traditional economic and social patterns that Americans experienced as the industrial and market revolutions took off in the early nineteenth century. Rural New England during the colonial period and early Republic had been a relatively classless society; most of its citizens were independent craftsmen and yeoman farmers, knit together into small-scale economies of exchange where production and consumption were geared toward the modest goal of subsistence, not market profitability. These were communities whose members were encouraged to subordinate individual self-interest to the welfare of the group and where, as one historian has commented, "rough parity of circumstances and prospects contributed to social harmony." As industrialization facilitated the mass production of goods for a wider market, modern canals and railroads opened up the possibility of shipping and trading goods at a distance. A large-scale market system, driven by the mercurial law of supply and demand and now rooted in an impersonal cash nexus, replaced the localized, family-centered barter systems characteristic of precapitalist America. The "rough parity of circumstances" that had previously bound communities together gave way to jarring inequalities in status and fortune.[10]

Contrary to popular assumptions that the American spirit has always embodied capitalism's rough-and-tumble individualism, nineteenth-century Americans were initially horrified by the specter of individual self-seeking and competition run amok that they glimpsed in the new economic system, where, as Adam Smith had suggested, each should follow his own "enlightened self-interest" and the invisible hand of the market would take care of the rest. The bogey of market "selfishness" became a cultural byword and taboo, a threat to personal and civic virtue alike. "We call it a Society; and go about professing the totalest separation, isolation," fumed the social critic Thomas Carlyle in 1843. "Our life is not a mutual helpfulness; but rather, cloaked under due laws-of-war, called 'fair competition,' . . . it is a mutual hostility."[11]

Americans developed a number of strategies to parry these body blows to traditional premarket values. Perhaps most effective was the elaborate construction of a cult of domesticity and "true womanhood": the traditionally paternal sphere of the domus was feminized, with an angelic and self-sacrificing maternal presence now firmly in place to keep spiritual and moral order in the American home. The selfish capitalist system, and the male egotism of market relations that subtended it, could be justified so long as "women's commitment to . . . love would justify men's commitment to an unloving market," as one historian has characterized the domestic ideology of the period. Catharine Beecher, sister to the reform-minded novelist Harriet Beecher Stowe of Uncle Tom's Cabin fame, saw the woman-centered home as instrumental in balancing out the moral contamination of the male marketplace. As men toiled in the sweat of their brow to bring home earthly bread to nourish the body, women were entrusted with the care of immortal souls. The woman's "great mission," Beecher urged, "is self-denial, in training [her family's] members to self-sacrificing labors for the ignorant and weak: if not her own children, then the neglected children of her Father in heaven. She is to rear all under her care to lay up treasures, not on earth, but in heaven," Beecher lectured in her treatise on The American Woman's Home. According to the rather dubious moral calculus of domestic ideology, the

"Christian Home," animated by the spirit of feminine self-sacrifice, would offset the moral misdeeds of the market.[12]

John Humphrey Noyes agreed that the Christian home must be animated by the spirit of selflessness. But he was convinced that society's division into isolated marriage pairs and nuclear families, far from being an antidote or counterweight to human selfishness and competition, rather served to exacerbate it. The true spirit of family was inseparable from communism, Noyes argued; wife and husband "keep no account" with one another and consider their children flesh of their flesh. Why, then, Noyes pursued, should not this noble principle of sharing extend beyond the confines of the individual family? Domestic ideology, while pretending to exalt the self-sacrificing virtues of the home, was in fact a cynical bid to accommodate selfishness, not extinguish it. Only when the family principle was expanded outward to include all members united in Christ would selfishness truly disappear: in order to organize "family communism on the grandest scale," one had to "give up the old one-horse wagon . . . and go by the great railroad train that carries a meeting-house full," Noyes quipped in one of his folksy sermons.

The fact that John Humphrey Noyes's new community preached the virtue of selflessness was, then, another mark in his favor, and a particular lure to those who felt traditional community ties stretched thin by the new economic and social order. Such an expansive, egalitarian vision of community was, perhaps, precisely what Mary Cragin had in mind when she professed that Noyes's teachings had given her a vision of how one "might cast out from himself the spirit of self."[13]

Part of Noyes's plan thus included the gradual economic communization of the Society of Inquiry. The fledgling society was given a major financial push forward when, on February 5, 1841, Noyes's father settled his estate upon his eight children. The amount that fell to the four society members totaled $19,920, which, along with a $16,000 contribution from Noyes's wife and John Miller's more modest donation of $2,000, brought their total capital to $38,000. The rough equivalent of a million dollars in today's market, the society's capital provided a sound financial rock on which to build. Confident in their financial solvency, the core members of the society now admitted a swath of new recruits, bringing their total number, by March 1843, to thirty-five persons "being supported by the common purse."[14]

Official communism of property was established in March 1845, when the group signed a constitution "for the purpose of sustaining the gospel of salvation from sin and gaining the advantages of union and combined capital." Superseding an earlier arrangement that had formed a joint stock company of those members who had invested property or capital in the corporation, this new constitution made provision for two sorts of members: those who had invested both time and property, and those who had invested time only. In the case of dissolution, profit was to be divided among all members, not just in proportion to their material contributions, but also in proportion to their length of service. In addition to certificates of investment, then, the corporation also distributed time-of-admission certificates. The society was engaged on a spiritual odyssey, where a member's religious conviction and time invested counted every bit as much as his material contributions to the project.[15]

In creating a communal home of "combined capital" in which private financial holdings were dissolved, Noyes was harking back to one of the oldest myths in Western literature: the dream of a lost golden age of peace and plenty, before the introduction of law and private property. The sixth-century BC Greek poet Hesiod wrote of a "golden race of mortal men" who once lived peaceably on the earth, and "they had all good things; for the fruitful earth unforced bare them fruit abundantly and without stint." Ovid took up the theme nearly half a millennium later in *The Metamorphoses*, in the year AD 8, immortalizing the first men as a docile band of hunter-gatherers, nibbling bramble berries and acorns in communal harmony: "Needless was written law, where none opprest: / The law of Man was written in his breast; / . . . / No walls were yet, nor fence, nor mote, nor mound. . . ."[16]

Embroidering on the luminous prophecies in the Book of Revelations, Christian millennial thought of late antiquity projected a version of the pagan golden age myth into the future: a community of egalitarian peace and plenty would reign at the end of history, when God's kingdom had been established on earth. Early church fathers endorsed antiquity's vision of a communistic "state of nature," wagering that before the Fall brought sin and death into the world, Eden would have closely resembled the communitarian arcadia of the ancients. The fourth-century archbishop of Milan, Saint Ambrose, cited both the Stoics and the Book of Genesis to assert that "The

Lord God specially wanted this earth to be the common possession of all, and to provide fruits for all; but avarice produced the rights of property." In imagining this future bliss, millenarians were fond of quoting the verses from the Acts of the Apostles when, after the descent of the Holy Spirit on Jesus' followers, they forsook their private possessions: "And the multitude of them that believed were of one heart and of one soul: neither said any of them that aught of the things he possessed was his own; but they had all things in common" (Acts 4: 32–33).[17]

By the fifth century, the church began to discourage the idea that the New Jerusalem, or what Saint Augustine called "the City of God," was a tangible reality that might yet be established on earth. The Book of Revelations, Augustine determined, was largely allegorical, and the great battle between good and evil it depicted but a metaphor for the struggle within each Christian's private soul, not a call for revolutionary political action. The church's stance was that, while on this earth, we must suffer meekly the consequences of sin, including the institutions of private property and slavery, with all of the obvious injustices such institutions implied. Good Christians would receive their reward in the spiritual, not the material, world.

Still, early modern Europe witnessed sporadic attempts to bring about God's kingdom in the here and now, restoring a state of primitive communism on earth. These outcroppings of millennial zeal were more often than not quashed by the church. In 1525, the self-styled prophet Thomas Müntzer—who was later, rather improbably, resurrected by Friedrich Engels as a proto-communist martyr—led a bloody peasant revolt against the German nobility in a millenarian bid to set the lowly on high, launching a formidable verbal challenge to one of the reigning counts: "Say, you wretched, shabby bag of worms, who made you a prince over the people whom God has purchased with his precious blood? . . . If you do not humble yourself before the lowly, you will be saddled with everlasting infamy in the eyes of Christendom and will become the Devil's martyr." Perhaps not surprisingly, the attempted coup ended badly for Thomas. The troublesome prophet was captured, tortured, and beheaded, thus bringing the peasants' millennial dreams to an abrupt end.[18]

In forming their own community, Noyes and his followers had no bloody dreams of vengeance against the propertied classes; indeed, the fact that they were themselves owners of property and capital was part of what guaranteed them a measure of success. Yet in embracing communism of property, seeking to equalize the material conditions of the "high" and the "low," Noyes's Society of Inquiry was following a very old dream indeed and appealing to a deep-seated need in the American psyche. At a time when class divisions were ever shifting and financial precariousness a looming threat, those elements of the ancient millennial vision that focused on communitarian harmony—a state where grasping hunger and competition was replaced by peaceful equality—looked especially attractive to those cowed by the wolfish mien of nascent capitalism.

NOYES'S UTOPIAN ENCLAVE HAD SOME COMPETITION IN NEW ENGLAND during the heady decade of the 1840s: the sprouting of a number of communitarian experiments, largely inspired by the theories of French iconoclast and businessman-cum-philosopher Charles Fourier. Fourier located the source of all human misery in society's misguided adherence to competitive capitalism and the nuclear family as the core economic and social units of life. Human passions—in their natural state benign and constructive—had been warped beyond recognition by modern civilization, which pitted individuals and their families against one another in competitive strife. Fourier proposed that economic and social life be organized instead around a series of productive communes, or *phalanstères*. Here people of all classes would live and work side by side, eliminating the inefficiency of single-family households and the geographic divide between work and home. Fourier's system retained some basic tenets of individualism; private property was upheld, and a commune member's remuneration would vary according to his capital and skill. Yet by allowing each member to follow his individual "passional attractions" in the most efficient way possible, productivity would soar, and the commune would guarantee the spiritual and material welfare of the entire group.[19]

Fourier's secular, Enlightenment response to the ravages of industrialism pulled in its fair share of adherents in America, who saw in the Frenchman's system a way to harness the productive power of capitalism without forfeiting communal solidarity. No one did more to popularize associationism, as these alternative social models came to be called, than writer and critic Albert Brisbane, who took Fourier's social theory and packaged it for an American public. In his 1840 tract *The Social Destiny of Man; or, Association and Reorganization of Industry*, outlining Fourier's theories, Brisbane blasted contemporary labor organization as "based upon the incoherent, conflicting efforts of individuals, between whom, not only no connection and combination exist, but on the contrary, opposition and competition filled with hatred and envy." Fourier's phalanx system would harmonize and coordinate human efforts toward the greater good of the whole, replacing competition with cooperation. Brisbane went on to write a series of columns for Whig reformer Horace Greeley's *New York Tribune* in 1842–43, in which he touted the advantages of associationism and introduced the concept to a wider American audience.[20]

At the height of the Fourierist vogue, between 1843 and 1847, twenty-four communitarian phalanxes were founded across the United States. The most famous of these experiments was Brook Farm, an agrarian utopia staked out in West Roxbury, Massachusetts, by the Unitarian minister and transcendentalist adherent George Ripley. Designed as a combined working farm and school where manual and intellectual labor were equally rewarded, Ripley's bold endeavor attracted the interest of such New England intellectuals as Ralph Waldo Emerson, Margaret Fuller, and Nathaniel Hawthorne (who would give an ambivalent fictionalized account of his time at the short-lived commune in his 1852 novel, *The Blithedale Romance*). Brook Farm blended the transcendentalist belief in personal spiritual growth with a commitment to "social progress," a concept its members defined with only the broadest of strokes. In a prospectus advertising their weekly newsletter, *The Harbinger*, the Brook Farmers declared themselves "devoted to the cause of radical, organic social reform as essential to the highest development of man's nature, to the production of those elevated and beautiful forms of character of which he is capable, and to the diffusion of happiness, excellence, and universal harmony upon the earth."[21]

Noyes and his followers in Putney received a visitor from Brook Farm in 1843—a visit chronicled in the pages of the Society of Inquiry's own magazine, *The Perfectionist*—and the rival communities enjoyed civil relations, though Noyes never minced words when it came to critiquing Fourier's secular socialist model. Instead of focusing on the elimination of sin at its very root, Noyes complained, the Fourierists merely puttered about with reorganizing men's perverted social and economic relationships to one another. "We think that the Fourierists have begun at the wrong end," Noyes noted dryly in a critique printed in *The Perfectionist* in 1844. "They are trying to build a chimney by beginning at the top; and we think they will fail not because we do not believe that chimneys can and should be built, but because we do not believe that such heavy structures can be durably built on anything but a firm foundation and by beginning at the bottom." Human nature, he was certain, would never be perfected by "improving its external conditions," but only by going straight to the source of the individual soul's estrangement from God.[22]

4

Electric Sex; or, How to Live Forever

IN ESTABLISHING THE SOCIETY OF INQUIRY AS A COMMUNAL ECONOMIC unit, Noyes was no doubt influenced by the tradition of Christian social-ism, as well as by the more general fad for associationist models in forward-thinking reform circles of the 1840s. But what Noyes was after was a much more radical and, ultimately, more mystical state of union than anything imagined by early apostolic Christianity or Fourier's acolytes. To grasp his intentions we must go back to the Christian mystics and their vision of the godhead as one and indivisible, a unity in which all partial or surface identi-ties are dissolved.

In the mystical tradition, the union between Christ and his church, or between God and the individual believer, was often expressed by analogy with sexual union. In his letter to the Ephesians, Paul seizes upon the meta-phor of marriage as a fitting image for the relationship between Christ and his followers: just as man and wife "become one flesh" in marriage, so too Christ is a bridegroom espousing the church as the body of all His faithful. The twelfth-century Cistercian monk Bernard of Clairvaux elaborated on Paul's metaphor, claiming that the overtly sexual Song of Songs was a perfect allegory for the relationship between Christ and the individual soul: "No sweeter names can be found to embody that sweet interflow of affections between [Christ] and the soul, than bridegroom and bride. Between these all things are equally shared, there are no selfish reservations, nothing that causes division. They share the same inheritance, the same table, the same home, the same marriage-bed, they are flesh of each other's flesh." Bernard's sermons are stuffed with "mouth-kisses," fertile wombs, life-giving breasts ("filled with a milky richness"), and, in general, all manner of fecund flows that bind Father, Son, and church into an indissoluble union.

Noyes had the audacity (or perhaps simply the honesty) to take the mystics at their word: far from falling outside the divine orbit, the sexual organs were, in fact, "the medium of the noblest worship of God." Not just a metaphor, sexual union was a practical way for souls to bind themselves to one another in the common medium of Christ's body. The marriage law that held sway in the world, then, and the nuclear family that attended it, worked to constrict and diminish love, which in its fullness and by its very nature was expansive, rippling out in ever more inclusive circles. As the logical consequence of reading Christ's gospel to "love thy neighbor" in the most literal way imaginable, Noyes's theology quite simply refused to exclude eros as a viable channel for union with the godhead. "Love in all its forms is simply attraction, or the tendency of congenial elements to approach and become one," he mused, and sexual love was no exception.[1]

During his time in Putney, Noyes would develop an elaborate theological and biological argument that placed sexual intercourse at the very heart of Christian community. More ingeniously, he made sex the linchpin in what he theorized was humanity's progressive march to conquer death. For when the invisible world of the saints came to annex the earthly saints— that is to say, Noyes's followers—to Christ's heavenly kingdom, all of its members would enjoy everlasting life as promised in the Book of Revelations. One might believe the Old Testament God who drew forth the cosmos from the void capable of endowing His chosen creatures with eternal life by simple fiat. Yet in the spirit of Yankee self-reliance, Noyes was taking no chances: he wagered that there was a physiological mechanism involved in immortality, discoverable through patient scientific inquiry, which humans could perfect on their end in order to meet God halfway to Resurrection.

Drawing on current debates within the fields of biology, chemistry, and physiology, Noyes was able to link sex to immortality through the little-understood, apparently magical workings of electricity.

Ever since the day when, in 1780, Luigi Galvani first made an amputated frog's leg jump by connecting it to the pole of a battery (a feat his nephew had, even more spectacularly, if perhaps less tastefully, surpassed in causing the corpse of an executed convict to flinch by the same method), the mysterious link between electricity and animal energy, or what was called "animal magnetism," had become a matter of intense debate for scientists and the literate public alike. Seeking an animating force uniting the cosmos, Romantic scientists were quick to see in electricity a life force pulsing throughout creation, uniting organic and inorganic nature. Perhaps the most famous period expression of this current of thought was Mary Shelley's *Frankenstein*. Haunted by Galvani's experiment, she penned this dark romance as the story of a medical student who imparts the "spark of life" to dead matter and later discovers the jerky, lurching creature hanging over his bed, gazing at him "with yellow, watery, but speculative eyes."[2]

In opposition to the Romantics, Alessandro Volta and other scientists in the materialist camp sought to reduce electricity to a mechanical force at work in the universe, stripped of any mystical life-giving properties. Still, despite Volta's counterdemonstrations discrediting Galvani, the debate over animal magnetism would live on well into the nineteenth century, with magnetizing hypnotic treatments, healing magnets, and other electrical devices (belts, bracelets, and vests) gaining a foothold in mainstream American medical practice by the 1840s and 1850s. "The human system may be looked upon as a voltaic pile, with positive and negative polarity," commented one medical treatise from 1863, chalking disease up to a disturbance in the life force that needed to be reequilibrated. Artificial electricity—the application to the body of magnets or electric shocks—was capable of rechanneling, reorganizing, and even augmenting the human vital fluid.[3]

Toiling away in his Putney laboratory, Noyes took contemporary science, gave it a theological twist, and—like Victor Frankenstein—tinkered with the occult pathways linking matter to spirit, hoping to strike the spark of eternal life into his gathered faithful. According to Noyes, Christ possessed an "invisible energy, a battery of nervous power," and the healing power of

Jesus Christ was "a fluid which passed from him, as electricity passes from the machine that generates it." "Our life can become charged with the life of Christ, till it is magnetic like his life," Noyes elaborated. When we are open to being plugged into Christ, we receive the equivalent of "the shocks of the galvanic fluid . . . accumulating chronic magnetic power in our life, and assimilation to Christ."[4]

This life force could be passed from person to person through the exchange of words, ideas, and healing touches. But the highest form of "spiritual interchange" in the resurrected state, according to Noyes's magnetic theory, would be sexual intercourse. Man and woman, like "magnet and steel," were attracted to each other and naturally advanced to "interlocked contact." Freed from the artificial restrictions of the worldly fashion of chaining one man to one woman, the union of male and female would fold into the original God-Jesus battery, intensifying its effect. Energy begat energy, according to Noyes, and in the fullness of time, when God's kingdom was extended to earth, each individual life would be enfolded within every other, and the whole of human life enfolded into God and Christ, in a kind of nesting-doll configuration forming "one glowing sphere" and a battery of inconceivable power.[5]

Thus fused into one gigantic divine sex battery, humans would accumulate enough electrical force, according to Noyes's theory, to overcome death itself: "Victory over death," he theorized, "will be the result of an action of an extensive battery of this kind." The heat and light generated by this condensed sexual energy chain would produce a kind of temperate microclimate that would go a long way toward improving the chilling effects of disease and death. "When life shall accumulate in unity, by the centripetal force of love, till all hearts shall radiate and receive a perpetual sunshine of joy, it is not unphilosophical to believe that the substantial physical results (at least as far as health is concerned) of an *actual amelioration of climate*, shall be achieved." Warmed from the inside out by this megabattery, life would become independent of external elements and "death will lose its prey."[6]

Once these concentric nesting effects came into play, no longer would we have to eat such coarse foods as meat; light fruits and vegetables would suffice to power our energy-rich systems. Citing the work of German chemist

Justus von Liebig, who postulated that food is fuel, Noyes wrote that "the more perfectly men are in communication with the source of vital heat, and the more they are enveloped in the genial magnetism of social life, the less food, raiment, and shelter they will need. . . . [T]he grosser kinds of food, and especially animal food, will go out of use."[7]

BY ALL ACCOUNTS, THE PUTNEY GROUP HAD NOT YET PASSED OVER INTO the higher order of a fruit-and-nut-gathering existence as of the spring of 1846; they still had recourse to woolens and animal meat to fight off the lingering New England cold. Yet the sense that a warming trend—an electric "condensation of life," as Noyes referred to it—was continually knitting them closer as a prelude to God's reign on earth was certainly a factor in the Putney group's first explorations into sexual "condensation." And so, in the spring of 1846, as the days got longer and the weather balmier, the Putney group began to detect an ambient amorous energy humming in their midst.

The initial forays into multiple sexual partners were tentative and, surprisingly, did not originate in Noyes's quarter. It was George Cragin who wrote a letter to Harriet Noyes declaring his love for her as a sister in Christ; Harriet, divulging the letter to Noyes, admitted her attraction to Cragin. Noyes called a meeting of the two couples, during which not only did Harriet and George Cragin avow their love for each other, but Mary Cragin and John Humphrey Noyes did likewise. As recorded in Mary Cragin's journal, "After these avowals we considered ourselves engaged to each other, expecting to live in all conformity to the laws of this world until the time arrives for the consummation of our union."[8]

Noyes had been attracted to Mary Cragin from the time of her first arrival in Putney; later diary entries would reveal that he considered her, in the absence of Abigail Merwin, a kind of surrogate spiritual bride. A portrait of Mary Cragin that survives from the Community period shows a rather desiccated-looking woman with a tense, angular face; thin lips; deep-set eyes; and the closely combed, short-cropped hair later adopted by Noyes's female followers as a sign of their emancipation from the fashion of the world. One of her contemporaries observed of Mary that, while not conventionally beautiful, her "soft eye" and "ready smile" guaranteed that "every man who came near her fell beneath her sway." Noyes was certainly enraptured by her, imagining her, after her ill-fated dalliance with Abram C. Smith, as a Mary Magdalene figure; given Noyes's own struggles with the flesh, such an association undoubtedly marked her out as a kindred spirit.[9]

The time for the consummation of the Noyeses and the Cragins' foursquare agreement would arrive sooner than expected. One day in May 1846, as Mary and Noyes were strolling in the woods together, they were overcome by the desire to proceed to a "full consummation" of their engagement. As Noyes wrestled with his overwhelming magnetic attraction to Mary, he suddenly had a revelation about the timing of the coming Resurrection. Instead of waiting for a signal from the heavens that the merging of the invisible and visible kingdoms had commenced and that the time to break with "the laws of this world" had come, might not God be expecting the earthly saints to *initiate* the condensing action by which the final union would be achieved? Noyes called a meeting of the two couples to seek their collective opinion. "The upshot of the conference was, that we gave each other full liberty all round, and so entered into complex marriage in the quartette form. The last part of the interview was as amicable and happy as a wedding, and a full consummation soon followed."[10]

In November of the same year, Complex Marriage in the "quartette form" was extended to include Noyes's sisters and their husbands, along with another couple, Mary and Stephen Leonard, when all five couples signed a "Statement of Principles" stating that, specifically, "All individual proprietorship either of persons or things is surrendered, and absolute community of interests takes the place of the . . . property and family relations in the world." The signatories promised to be guided by God as "the director of our combinations," with a swiftly appended clause clarifying that "John H. Noyes is the father and overseer whom the Holy Ghost has set over the family thus constituted."[11]

On November 4, immediately following their solemn pledge, the couples consolidated their households, with Noyes and Harriet moving in with the Cragins in the "Lower House," and the Skinners, Millers, and Leonards taking possession of the Noyes homestead—a move clearly aimed at facilitating the smooth functioning of Complex Marriage. Mary Cragin penned a well-turned, if sycophantic, poem on the occasion of the Noyes's move:

Thou art our lover! From thy heart
A tide of living healthful love
Rolls o'er us, and makes us part
Of the blest family above
. . .

'Tis the same spirit brings you here
Brought the Redeemer from the skies.
His image doth in you appear
And this is His self-sacrifice.[12]

Whether or not Noyes's vision of sexual sharing at this early stage of his experiment involved the abolition of the taboo on incest—in other words, whether he slept with his sisters Charlotte and Harriet—is a question that has never been definitively answered. Noyes's later praise for the early Jewish practice of inbreeding—Abraham married his half-sister, according to Genesis 20: 12—indicates Noyes held a favorable view of incest, at least among God's elect, as key to promoting and purifying the group's unity. Indeed, a letter from George Washington Noyes to his sister several years later reveals Noyes once confided to him that "the fellowship of brothers and sisters is fundamental and eternal." "It is concentration," George Washington went on to quote his brother. "It approaches nearest to the fashion of God himself whose life ever turns in upon himself." But nothing in the extant record exists to either confirm or deny the practice of sex between Noyes and his siblings. If the Putney experimenters did, indeed, cross this final frontier of the incest taboo, they were canny enough to leave no written trace of it.[13]

According to Noyes's theory of "Bible secretiveness," which affirmed that certain secrets of the Resurrection were to remain hidden from the uninitiated until God should declare them ready to receive the truth, the passage into Complex Marriage was kept rigorously secret, not only from the town of Putney but also from most of the association's thirty-five members outside Noyes's inner circle. In a text entitled "Bible Secretiveness," Noyes tacitly compared his reserve on certain details of Bible truth to Jesus' practice of speaking in parables to his followers. "God does not reveal the glory of heaven to eyes accustomed only to the darkness of the world," Noyes mused enigmatically. "A premature exhibition of it would only bewilder, madden and destroy the unhappy gazers." John Humphrey and his followers were not, in other words, about to cast their pearls before swine.[14]

The core members of the association had been practicing Complex Marriage in secret for nearly a year when Noyes decided to make official the Community's status as harbingers of God's immanent kingdom. Given that he and his fellows had now flagrantly broken their marriage vows without God's having officially declared the end of days by any obvious, outward sign, on July 15, 1847, Noyes no doubt thought it prudent to clarify to his followers in the pages of their newly christened journal, *The Spiritual Magazine*, that the arrival of God's kingdom would happen not of a sudden, as traditionally predicted, but, rather, by imperceptible steps: "the evidence goes to show that the Kingdom of God will be established here not in a formal, dramatic way," he nuanced, "but by a process like that which brings the seasonal spring." On this revised view, Noyes now announced that the kingdom of God *had* begun, right in the heart of Putney: he and his cohort had been divinely tapped as the nucleus from which the universal spring of resurrection would radiate outward in a kind of chain reaction. Skirting the sexual issue, which Noyes deemed as yet too radical for the rest of the Community to handle, he anchored his prophecy instead in the miraculous healing effects that had recently been witnessed within the association. "I think there is abundant evidence, especially in the last year, that the judgment has begun. . . . We have seen that there is a power among us that can conquer death."[15]

Noyes's proof that he and his coterie were God's chosen and that the kingdom of God had already commenced was the apparently miraculous indemnity from death that the Perfectionists had enjoyed since the association's founding in 1838. Whereas the mortality rate in the town of Putney had averaged twenty-four deaths annually during that period, Noyes's band of believers had "paid no part of this tax to the king of terrors." According to Noyes, both he and Mary Cragin had been cured of life-endangering ailments through the power of faith. In his own case, Noyes had suffered since 1842 from a "disease of the throat and lungs, which deprived me of the use of my voice in public, and rendered ordinary conversation painful." Eschewing the advice of doctors, Noyes harkened instead to the voice of Jesus

Christ, who apparently counseled him personally to "neglect his disease"; as a result, "I have performed more hard labor with my tongue in the last two years, than in any other two years of my life." Mary's recurring attacks of "sick-headache" were similarly cured, and "the devil cast out of her stomach" through the power of spiritual medicine.[16]

Noyes's internal faith cures appeared to be corroborated by his miraculous intervention in the case of Mrs. Harriet Hall, a villager who, having been confined to bed for years, pled with Noyes in June 1847—right on the heels of his revised timetable for the coming of God's kingdom—to apply his healing arts to her case. Mrs. Hall, according to her own report, suffered from "dropsy"; "a serious affection of the spine" connected with "a terrible pressure on the brain"; "night sweats and hectic fever"; a "liver complaint"; "ulceration of the kidneys," ending in the sudden onset of "complete blindness." Her treatment consisted of frequent cupping. This popular nineteenth-century practice, thought to balance disordered humors by bringing blood to the surface of the skin (and, in many cases, then removing a quantity of blood through the use of a lancet), involved lighting a piece of lint on fire and placing it under a glass cup applied to the patient's skin. The heated air inside the cup produced a vacuum, sucking the skin up into the cup and pulling the blood to the surface; the inflammatory response was believed therapeutic. In addition to such traditional treatments, Mrs. Hall was under "Thomsonian treatment" for her liver complaint, a popular species of patented folk medicine based on the theory of purging toxins from the body through herbal-induced vomiting and diarrhea. Given the dismal outcomes these treatments invariably produced, it is hardly surprising that Mrs. Hall, hearing of the Putney group's experiments into "animal magnetism," should have turned to Noyes for help.[17]

Certain that the eyes of the world were trained intently upon him, Noyes declared that "from the time [Mrs. Hall] invited me to visit her, I felt myself challenged to a public contest with death." In short, John Humphrey felt the wind in his sails—what with the kingdom of God having arrived and the surge of electrical sexual energy brought on by Complex Marriage— and, sensing that through Mrs. Hall God was preparing for him a glorious triumph over his enemies, he was now ready to jump in the ring and fight it out publicly with the king of terrors.[18]

In testimony published afterward in *The Spiritual Magazine*, Mrs. Hall detailed the healing session that restored her mobility and sight, which she had been deprived of for eight long years. One imagines the scene: a darkened room, for all light was extremely painful to her, with the smallest crack of light allowed to filter in under the curtain. Wrapped in caps and flannels, heavy feather coverlets pressing on her aching limbs, the invalid lay in the bed whose restricted space had become her entire world. Hanging heavy in the motionless summer air were the acrid smells of the sickroom— the sulfurous scent of burning lint, the bitter edge of purgative herbs. John Humphrey and Mary entered the room with the firm confidence of the righteous. Mary, however, upon seeing the invalid struggle with the dark principality of unbelief, suffered a magnetic transfer of negativity from the ailing Mrs. Hall and began to descend back down to the underworld from which she herself had been so recently reclaimed. "My eyes grew dim," Mary later wrote, "so that I could not distinguish objects, and my hearing left me so that I could not hear the sound of my own voice. Still I resisted until my tongue was palsied and I did not know what I was saying. . . ."[19]

As Mary swooned in a faint, Mrs. Hall inversely felt "something good" taking place in herself, as though the spirit of unbelief that was making her ill sought refuge in the body of Mary. Noyes's electrical life-power, however, was strong enough to blast the evil spirit out of both bodies. "When I began to recover," Mary recounted, "I found myself sitting in my chair, and heard Mr. Noyes commanding me in a loud voice to look at him. The tones of his voice thrilled through me like a shock of electricity, and as soon as I looked at him life triumphed over death." All three partners held hands in a magnetic chain, and when Noyes called out for Mrs. Hall to sit up and take a seat in a chair by the window, she complied without difficulty. "Mrs. Cragin raised the curtain and let in the blaze of day. My eyes were perfectly well, and drank in the beauty of a world all new to me, with wonderful pleasure." Mrs. Hall threw off her "grave clothes" and, "in an ordinary dress, without spectacles or a vail [sic], I took my seat in [Noyes's] carriage and rode two miles, in a south direction, in the light of a midday summer's sun without the least fatigue."[20]

One can only imagine how miraculous it must have seemed to be suddenly transported from the cloistered darkness of the sickroom to the open air of a summer day. One imagines the creak of the leather seats, the sharp scent of sweat from the straining horses, the sun warming her hair. Noyes sat, jubilant, at Harriet Hall's side. Even the skeptical village doctor, John Campbell, would appear to have been persuaded by the Perfectionist miracle: "It is time for us, old sinners, to surrender," he reputedly confessed to a circle of villagers gathered in the town store one day in the wake of Harriet Hall's stunning recovery.[21]

Noyes was not so fortunate in his treatment of another ailing villager, Mary Knight, who was in the advanced stages of consumption later that same summer when her desperate father appealed to him for help. This time Noyes's patient died while nominally under his care. Noyes defended his healing record in the pages of *The Spiritual Magazine* after he was challenged by the Reverend Hubbard Eastman, Putney's Methodist minister, to account publicly for his proclaimed "miracles" (Eastman would later publish a screed against Noyes, entitled *Noyesism Unveiled*, in which he scathingly referred to him as "the great magician of Putney"). Mary Knight had simply succumbed, Noyes opined, to the power of her own unbelief, overwhelmed by the negative magnetic influence of the unbelieving friends Noyes had been powerless to keep from her bedside. Just as the Battle of Bunker Hill, though it had ended in retreat, was touted in history as a great American victory, so, Noyes grandiosely predicted, "The day will come when this first battle of faith with the terrible despotism of consumption, though it ended in retreat, will be glorified as the Bunker Hill of the Faith-Revolution."[22]

But by the fall of 1847, the tide had turned. Noyes's failure in the case of Mary Knight was followed by another public relations disaster when news of the scandalous sexual arrangements of the Perfectionist family leaked to the village. Noyes had confided to Daniel Hall, Harriet Hall's husband and, since his wife's cure, a devoted friend, the fact that he had personally broken the marriage law with at least Mary Cragin and possibly others. Hall appeared at first to accept the news complacently, but one week later he unexpectedly turned tail and went directly to the state's attorney with the damning information. On October 26, 1847, Noyes was arrested on charges of adultery by a sheepish town sheriff, clearly chagrined to be the agent, however unwilling, of the downfall of this once-sterling Putney family.

The arrest launched Noyes on a manic high. Far from deploring the revelation of his secret, Noyes exulted that the slow trajectory on which God had placed him (toward "an eminence, where I shall surely be an object of the hottest jealousy, and of course a mark for the archers") was at long last nearing its apex. Polly Noyes was away visiting Perfectionist friends in Connecticut at the time of Noyes's arrest; a letter from her daughter Harriet describes in vivid detail Noyes's eerie state of exultation upon returning home on bail: "If you have ever seen him with radiant countenance, walking with elastic buoyancy, his cane raised in a flourish, relating some glorious adventure midst shout and laughter, you have some idea of the scene. . . ." In custody for about four hours, Noyes declared smugly to the lawyers that, although the affair was in their court for the moment, "it was a controversy of principles, and would have to be settled at last by priests and philosophers."[23]

Further on in the same letter, Harriet Skinner wrote to her mother, "If you look this way now-a-days, you may conceive of us as walking unbound, unharmed in the midst of a fiery furnace, and see us not alone but the Son of God with us. . . . We walk the streets, we pursue all our avocations, compliments are passed as usual. Something inspires an awe. We think it is the majesty of truth and innocence, and a lurking fear in the people's minds that we are the Kingdom of God." Harriet refers to the passage from Daniel in which an angel of God intervenes to spare Shadrach, Meshach, and Abednego a martyr's death in Nebuchadnezzar's fiery furnace. Harriet sensed the group as hovering in the midst of an inferno, miraculously unscathed, cooled by the wing beats of a protecting angel.[24]

The Putney group's sense of exceptionalism, their conviction of being a latter-day "City on a Hill," was confirmed just a week later when Harriet again testified, breathlessly, in a letter to her mother that "miracle upon miracle" were piling up in the standoff with their opponents: "The town is in the chains of a spiritual magnetism, and with full knowledge of our principles and practice are quieting themselves as though it were said to them: 'Touch not mine anointed.'" Buoyed by John Humphrey's manic confidence in his divine commission, wrapped in the protective shield of their belief, Harriet and her fellows attributed their neighbors' pensive "quiet" to "awe," a face averted before the blaze of God's anointed.[25]

But the town's apparent quiet was just the proverbial calm before the storm. A letter from villager David Crawford to a former Putney minister, Elisha Andrews, written on November 23, 1847, refers to the "high excitement in the public mind growing out of the alleged conduct of J. H. Noyes and his followers," firmly concluding with the statement, "I think our Community are settled upon this point—that such conduct shall not continue in their midst." The prim minister replied, "How lamentable it is, that such fine talents, refined education, respectability of family, and moral influence should all be prostrated to such vile purposes," observing that it had been better "had that respectable Mansion, been scattered to the four winds of heaven, or reduced to ashes, and had the tenants been reduced to poverty" than for the family to have ended in such a state of "moral waste and desolation."[26]

By November, to remain any longer in the fiery furnace of Putney, anointed or not, appeared unwise to John Humphrey Noyes, who, having gone to Brattleboro to confer with his brother-in-law Larkin Mead, a lawyer, learned of the "possible outbreak of lynch law among the barbarians of Putney." Resolving not to return to Putney, he traveled instead across the state border to safety in Boston. A number of the association members, including George and Mary Cragin, whose arrest warrants, too, were pending, followed suit and retreated from Putney the next day. The Millers, the Skinners, and Noyes's wife, Harriet, meanwhile stood their ground to bear the brunt of the villagers' wrath.[27]

From the comfort of his position across the border, Noyes put a positive spin on the breakup, arguing that their recent separation was God's way of communicating that "our unity is not local and visible, but out of the world's reach and sight, deep in the heavens where Christ went after his resurrection. The world imagines that our Association is dissolved, but we know that our enterprise moves steadily on." It was considerably easier to be one of the saints "out of the world's reach" than one of those within its grasp, as Noyes's sister saw fit to mention in a letter to him: though Noyes had a scriptural precedent for flight in Paul's retreat before an angry mob in Thessalonika (Acts 17), "still," she chided, "we must laugh at you a little for getting out of scrapes."[28]

Eventually, although a tense truce was reached with the villagers, it was decided the best strategy was for the association to abandon Putney. And so, between the spring and fall of 1848, all of its members converged on the property of fellow Perfectionist Jonathan Burt in the rural outpost of Oneida Creek, in central New York. "Thus the Putney Community died and rose again," Noyes would write later that year in *The First Annual Report of the Oneida Community*. Under the hyperbolic flourish of Noyes's pen, the fledgling Oneida Community enjoyed no less illustrious a precedent than the Resurrection of Jesus Christ.[29]

5

Marriage Grows Complex

W HEN, ON MARCH 1, 1848, THE NOYESES AND THE CRAGINS FIRST
arrived at Jonathan Burt's home on Oneida Reserve—so called because it had been an Indian reserve until being purchased by the government
and sold off to white settlers in the early 1840s—the scene was grim. Putney
had been no metropolis, but compared with the "howling wilderness" of
central New York in the dead of winter that greeted Harriet Noyes on her
arrival at her new home, it had been distinctly civilized. Jonathan Burt and
his family occupied a modest farmhouse, while the Noyeses and Cragins set
up camp in two rough-hewn cabins that had been left by the Oneida tribe.
"There is some romance in beginning our Community in the log huts of
the Indians," Noyes commented hopefully, putting a cheerful spin on the
group's humbled circumstances.[1]

While at Putney, members of the Society of Inquiry had continued to
live in their own homes, joining the larger group for prayer and study in the
main Noyes compound during the day. But as Noyes's vision of his social
experiment developed, he came to believe it was essential to bring all members of the group to live as one family under a single roof. Current society,

with its system of isolated domiciles housing each individual family separately, only fueled "egotism and exclusiveness," Noyes argued. In the resurrected life, on the contrary, "unity of hearts will prefer unity of accommodations," he predicted. By the end of their first year in Oneida, the original Putney nucleus had expanded to eighty-four members—too many to fit into the existing structures of the original Burt dwellings. And so, during the summer and fall of 1848, the fledgling Community built themselves a proper home. "One beautiful moonlit night," one member would later reminisce, "Mr. Noyes, with the aid of the North Star, staked out the ground for the foundation walls of [their] new abode." Sixty feet long by thirty-five feet wide, the three-story building was sited on a slight elevation, with a sweeping view of the surrounding country. The Community's own carpenters and joiners constructed the house, under the guidance of architect Erastus Hamilton. Jonathan Burt ran a sawmill, and lumber was provided by the wood lots on their property.[2]

Noyes was happy enough to have a safe landing site in central New York for his displaced flock. At the same time, if he conceived of Oneida as a branch of the Kingdom of God, it was clearly not, in his mind, his Father's principal office. God's kingdom would have multiple outposts on earth, each toiling patiently away until the day when a full annexation could be accomplished. To this end, Noyes founded a branch commune in Wallingford, Connecticut, in 1851, when Perfectionist converts Henry and Emily Allen donated their property there to the cause. (While deeding the land to Jesus Christ, Henry Allen nevertheless, in a prudent afterthought, designated Noyes as the earthly executor of the property.) In the meantime, Abram Smith, Mary Cragin's erstwhile seducer, had apparently worked his way back into Noyes's good graces; in early 1849, at Noyes's request, Smith acquired a property in Brooklyn in order to start up another station for Bible Communism, as Noyes had come to call his heterodox brand of Christianity. Noyes decamped almost immediately for Brooklyn, deeming it "a more quiet place for reflection" and taking the entire Oneida printing office with him. There, he began publishing a weekly paper, entitled *The Free Church Circular*, to disseminate the good word of Bible Communism. Far from viewing his fledgling colonies as cloistered retreats from the profane world, Noyes was convinced that through the medium of the free press and modern communication networks, his vision would gradually catch fire. "We now commence a weekly paper at the center of communication," Noyes wrote in the first issue, "surrounded by radiating lines of railroads, steamers, telegraphs, and expresses." With the establishment of *The Circular*, he announced hopefully, "the Kingdom of Heaven shall [now] have a press as active as the organs of politics and commerce."[3]

Noyes's theory of magnetism was central to his proselytizing endeavors. If Jesus Christ's holy magnetism could be passed through physical contact—sexual intercourse being the most intense mode of conductivity—the spoken or written word was equally infused with electrical potential. "The contagion of God's life and righteousness passes by word[s] . . . as well as by laying on of hands," Noyes theorized. "And undoubtedly by a book or paper it might pass to a nation or a world almost instantly." As one *Circular* journalist described the process, the magnetically charged Spirit of God is always present but not always visible, just as, "hid in the bosom of the clouds that float over our heads, are the enormous and unseen forces of electricity." The Bible Communists and their newspaper, like amateur scientist Andrew Crosse and his conducting poles stretching up into the heavens, would provide the conducting wire by which "the fire and power of that Spirit would instantly fill [the nation], playing from heart to heart as lightning plays from pole to pole of an electric battery."[4]

If Brooklyn was the seat of Bible Communist theory, Oneida provided the practical workshop where Noyes's radical restructuring of family relationships was put to the test. The most immediate change in traditional social arrangements undertaken at Oneida was the institution of a "Children's House," physically separate from the main dwelling quarters of the adult members, where the young could be raised collectively by rotating teams of teachers and nurses. The Community converted one of the original houses on the property into a lodging for children aged two to twelve and another into a nursery for infants. In general, infants roomed with their mothers until the age of one and a half, when they were weaned and transferred to the Children's House. The arrangement, according to the association's *First Annual Report*, proved immensely beneficial to the "comfort and good breeding of the children" and had the added advantage of saving "the main household of the Association from much noise and confusion."

While perhaps initiated for practical purposes, this architecture of separation also served an ideological purpose: to break up what the Community members called "philoprogenitiveness," or the natural tendency of parents to favor their own children. A covetous and possessive attitude, whether toward things or persons, was inimical to the spirit of Christ. Accordingly, a report compiled for the larger Community by the "Children's Department" in August 1849 chided members for overzealous maternal attachments, affirming that "the essence of our principles is, that children cease to be private property and be property of the Association; and the true way to manage them is, as soon as nature allows, to place them under a system of general control."[5]

The First Annual Report of 1849 also contained an appendix, entitled "Bible Argument Defining the Relations of the Sexes in the Kingdom of Heaven," laying out for the first time the theological and philosophical underpinnings of John Humphrey Noyes's doctrine of Complex Marriage. Noyes drew scriptural support for the idea that monogamous marriage had no place in heaven from Christ's response to the Sadducees in Matthew that "in the resurrection, they neither marry nor are given in marriage" (Matthew 22: 30). Such a proposition was, Noyes insisted, perfectly consistent with the expanded unity of the resurrection state, in which all members become one in the body of Christ and "the intimate union of life and interests, which in the world is limited to pairs, extends through the whole body of believers." Comparing possession of persons in marriage to possession of property, Noyes argued by analogy that "amativeness and acquisitiveness are only different channels of one stream" and that only a total abolition of the spirit of possessiveness will allow a true relation to Christ.[6]

While primarily interested in grounding his antimarriage beliefs in holy scripture, Noyes was canny enough to include a section in the "Bible Argument" lambasting marriage as contrary to human nature and thus as largely to blame for the misery, vice, and illness rampant in contemporary American society. "All experience testifies . . . that sexual love is not naturally restricted to pairs," Noyes proposed. By arbitrarily yoking together unmatched pairs for life, marriage "provokes to adultery, actual or of the heart," while preventing sympathetic couples from joining in fellowship. Decades before Freud evolved his theory of the sexual drives, Noyes claimed matter-of-factly that "the desire of the sexes is a stream ever running [and] if it is dammed up, it will break out irregularly and destructively." "The only way to make it safe," he went on to suggest, "is to give it a free natural channel." Prostitution, masturbation, and "obscenity in general" were the logical result of unnaturally impeding the free concourse of the sexes.[7]

If the shift to communal child rearing met with little resistance from members (apart from the complaints of a few clingy mothers), the transition to Complex Marriage was considerably more delicate. Married couples joining the Community, in particular, had difficulty ridding themselves of what the communists called disapprovingly "the marriage spirit." "If a man comes into this Association with a wife that he has to watch and reserve from others, he has brought a cask of powder into a blacksmith's shop," Noyes explained in an address he delivered to the family a year and a half into the experiment. "It is the business of the shop to make sparks, and no wonder he is miserable." A Mr. and Mrs. Howard, for example, fell to quarreling when, shortly after joining, Mr. Howard confessed his desire to have an "interview" (the Community euphemism for sex) with another young woman. Mrs. Howard "didn't sleep for nearly a week, and cried a good deal of the time," but was finally persuaded to facilitate a meeting between her husband and the other woman, and it accordingly took place. Some were less pliant in transitioning to the new system. Mr. Seymour Newhouse, a curmudgeonly local trap maker who was an early Community joiner along with his wife, one day "gave way to his feelings and committed an assault upon D. P. Nash and Mrs. Newhouse as they were walking in the garden after meeting." Fellow member Henry Burnham was, luckily, on hand to intercede; he "drew Mr. Newhouse away, and slept with him all night" to prevent the raging man from committing any further attacks.[8]

Other men were, apparently, indifferent enough about giving up exclusive claims to their legal spouses but took exception when they perceived a competitor moving in on a sexual partner they had come to regard as their own particular "spiritual bride." Such was the case with Lemuel Bradley, who, having fallen head over heels for the sexual dynamo Mary Cragin, became apoplectic when he discovered that John Humphrey Noyes was planning to conceive a child by her and "began to act like a madman," according to one witness. Another jealous tussle recorded in the early Community correspondence involved George Hatch and John Norton, who were both in love with Noyes's niece Helen. As would become standard practice in the Community's regulation of what they called "sticky love," the lovers were separated and Helen sent to the Brooklyn branch to give George and John some time to cool off. John Humphrey Noyes penned a consolatory letter to the suffering John Norton, who had apparently become so distraught by the separation that he threatened to shoot himself. "I do not wish you to forget her, nor to love her less," Noyes coaxed. "But cannot you love her without *claiming* her, and quarreling with us and with God about her, and almost shooting yourself on her account? This is not the right kind of love." The temporary separation, Noyes advised the young man, would give him "a good opportunity to learn the great lesson . . . that God owns all things, even our sweethearts and ourselves."[9]

But if the Community used the stick a good deal in controlling sexual relations, the carrot was an equally essential part of the smooth functioning of the system. Good behavior—a member's humble and good-natured submission to the Community's rulings about sexual pairings—was often richly rewarded. Mr. Gibson Mallory, separated from his wife in a bid to cure his possessiveness, had behaved so beautifully under this trial that the association lifted the ban and permitted him to enjoy "a new honeymoon" with Mrs. Mallory (cautioning the pair, nonetheless, "not to get sticky"). Lemuel Bradley eventually managed to relinquish his exclusive claim on Mary Cragin and douse the competitive "rooster spirit" vis-à-vis John Humphrey Noyes that had for a time held sway in his heart. As a result, Noyes officially granted him liberty to sexual fellowship with Ellen and Philena Baker, two attractive young sisters in the Community. Within the sexual economy of Bible Communism, compliance had its advantages.[10]

One of the thorniest problems confronting the early Community was how to introduce virgins of both sexes into what they delicately called the "social life" of the group. Young men presented a particular difficulty, as their insatiable desire for sex made them an unpredictable force in need of serious restraint. "The transition of the young men from the hot blood of virginity to the quiet freedom which is the essential element of our Society is emphatically the difficult pass in our social experience," Noyes admitted in a letter to Erastus Hamilton in March 1850. The Community's original plan—to marry young pairs off once they were deemed sexually mature—yielded less than satisfying results. Such pairings had led to what Noyes called the "spiritual collapse" of several young wives, whom Noyes felt were not adequately protected from the "untamed lion" of their new partners' aggressive sexual urges. Another tack was tried: introducing young men to sex via the older, more experienced women. The lusty Mary Cragin, once hailed by Harriet Holton Noyes as "the mainspring of love" within the Community, was a natural candidate for the post. Yet even she struggled under the relentless ardor of the young initiates and, by the end of the experiment, was near collapse.[11]

Oneidans realized immediately that the most active sexual population were the teenage young, that they preferred to have sex exclusively with each other, and that they were the least adept of anyone at regulating their passions. In order to attain the "quiet freedom" that Noyes envisioned as the paradigm for Complex Marriage, such a volatile group needed to be neutralized. Noyes lit upon a solution in his theory of "ascending fellowship": mating the most spiritually accomplished, ergo elder, members of the group with the inexperienced young in a quasi-mentoring relationship. In September 1851, after nearly four years of complex marriage by trial and error, Noyes defined this principle in a lecture he delivered to the group entitled, "Practical Suggestions on the Subject of Amativeness." Rather than allowing the young to mate willy-nilly in "horizontal" pairings, he concluded, "in all safe, healthy fellowships the ascending fellowship must prevail."

If Oneida had abolished all material or economic distinctions among its members, it remained rigidly hierarchical in terms of what Noyes called "spiritual castes." Noyes was situated, naturally, at the apex of the spiritual pyramid, with the other members classed in descending order according to age and spiritual type and quality down to the base. The young, by virtue of being spiritually inexperienced, occupied the bottom of the pyramid. Following the new system, John Humphrey Noyes himself introduced young women to sexual intercourse at or shortly after the onset of puberty; though surviving Community records are scarce, passing references in diaries and letters suggest the average age of female induction was thirteen. Boys were introduced a few years later and had their first sexual experiences with older women, preferably past menopause, to avoid accidental pregnancies. Though

Noyes admitted that such a system of pairing old and young might be regarded as unnatural by the outside world, he bade his followers persevere, and insisted that "the time will come when . . . the idea of persons that are not spiritual embarking on the tempestuous ocean of amativeness without a pilot will be regarded as absurd."[12]

If the Oneidans were the only group in antebellum America to concretely implement a social laboratory designed to do away with the evils of monogamous marriage, they were emphatically not alone in taking aim more generally at the sacred institution of marriage in the decades before the war. Over the course of the 1840s and 1850s, everyone from feisty anarchists to committed feminists to august public intellectuals like Henry James Sr. weighed in on the tricky question of how best to reform the relationship between the sexes, which was widely acknowledged to be in crisis. Before long, the "marriage question," as social pundits would delicately refer to it, had become a national preoccupation.

As the abolitionist movement gained prominence on the national stage, reformers committed to advancing women's rights struck upon a natural analogy between the institution of slavery and the institution of marriage. Under the existing laws of coverture, a woman upon marriage forfeited her right to an independent legal identity and entered into the position of a dependent: she could neither own property nor control her wages; neither sue nor sign contracts; if she committed a crime, her husband was held legally responsible and could administer chastisement as he saw fit. In the case of divorce, a woman had no legal rights over her children. She was, as Elizabeth Cady Stanton would starkly declare in her 1848 "Declaration of Rights and Sentiments of Women," for all intents and purposes "civilly dead." As a tie that locked women into a position of legal and financial dependence on their husbands, critics thus argued that marriage differed little from the tie binding master and slave: "The rights of humanity are more grossly betrayed at the altar," Stanton commented bitterly in an 1851 letter to her abolitionist cousin, Gerrit Smith, "than at the auction block of the slaveholder."[13]

It was shocking enough to many a conservative in midcentury America that respectable middle-class women were demanding legal and economic equality within the institution of marriage. But Stanton and her crew were soon joined by—in their enemies' eyes, if not in their own—even less savory allies: a motley band of philosophers and activists promoting the outright abolition of marriage and its replacement by the practice of free love. Charles Fourier's dream of coordinating humanity's "passional attractions" in the realm of industry had been matched by his speculations about how human sexual passions could also be more harmoniously coordinated. When Albert Brisbane introduced Fourierism to the American public in 1840, he had carefully suppressed his master's sexual theories, sensing they might ruffle some puritanical feathers. But by the end of the decade, a splinter group of communards began resurrecting Fourier's vision of a sexually liberated humanity.

In 1849, Henry James Sr. published a translation of Victor Hennequin's *Les amours au phalanstère* ("Love in the Phalanstery"), a pamphlet outlining Fourier's plans for a future society no longer bound by traditional marriage constraints. James hedged his bets and, at least publicly, limited himself to a timid critique of marriage when it was not consecrated by love or a higher "spiritual union" between the partners. As a corrective, he advocated more lenient divorce laws. Still, James's perceived attack on marriage met with bitter opposition in the press and, in September 1852, led to a public dustup in the pages of the *New York Tribune*. Over the next few months, James, *Tribune* editor Horace Greeley, and philosopher Stephen Pearl Andrews sparred with one another over the future of the fragile institution, until the prudish Greeley—deeming the content of the argument too scandalous for print—finally shut down the debate.

Greeley particularly blanched at James's advocacy of free divorce, fearing total social anarchy would ensue: "Marriage indissoluble may be an imperfect test of honorable and pure affection . . . but it is the best the State can devise; and its overthrow," he solemnly predicted, "would result in a general profligacy and corruption such as this country has never known." But even James's position on the marriage question appeared lily-livered when compared with the radical proposals of Stephen Pearl Andrews, whose letters to the *Tribune* Greeley published, despite his fierce disagreement, as a gentlemanly token of his commitment to free speech. According to Andrews, the Protestant Reformation in the sixteenth century and the democratic revolutions of the eighteenth century had successfully freed individuals from religious and political tyranny. But these were mere warm-up exercises for the liberation from social tyranny that was in the works: all laws demanding conformity to a norm, including laws regulating the sexual relationships of individuals, were to disappear before the authority of the sovereign individual. Each person was to be left free to pursue his or her own happiness in peace, so long as their actions did not impinge on the happiness of fellow sovereigns. "It is an intolerable impertinence for me to thrust myself into your affairs of the heart," Andrews lobbed at his critics, "to determine for you what woman (or women) you love well enough or purely enough to live with, or how many you are capable of loving."[14]

Necessarily vague on the details of how such a stateless society was to function, Andrews drew quasi-cosmic analogies to the world of atoms and threw in, for good measure, a dash of mystical Fourierism: the natural law of the universe was to allow each particle to follow its own "natural attractions," without arbitrary interference from an outside authority, as the only way to guarantee the "harmony of the spheres." Unceremoniously bumped from the pages of the *Tribune*, Andrews would go on in 1852 to found a community of sovereign individuals, christened Modern Times, on Long Island with fellow anarchist Josiah Warren.[15]

Among those whose "natural attractions" led her to Andrews's commune was Mary Gove Nichols, a self-taught physician and circuit lecturer on women's anatomy who became notorious for informing her female audiences of a woman's right in a loveless or abusive marriage to withhold sex from her husband. Being herself a victim of an unhappy arranged marriage to a tyrannical husband, Nichols found in Andrews's philosophy of individual sovereignty a handy blueprint for liberating women from male domination. In her 1854 book, *Marriage*, Nichols rehearsed publicly the analogy between slavery and marriage that, six years earlier, Elizabeth Cady Stanton had been forced to tiptoe around at the Women's Rights Convention. Nichols challenged her so-called fellow feminists to admit to themselves that their call for independence was necessarily a call for the abolition of marriage: "Ladies of the Women's Rights Movement, you must look this question full in the face," she warns them. "When you demand Woman's Rights, you demand the abrogation of . . . marriage. When you declare independence, it is independence of man in the relation of marriage. You can have no right until you assert your right to yourselves." Marriage was the

"Bastille" of women's oppression that would have to be stormed if she was ever to reclaim her right to herself and to bestow her affections where, when, and upon whom she chose.[16]

At first glance, Oneida's sexual program as outlined in the "Bible Argument" would appear to square with many of the same sentiments animating the larger public discussion of the marriage question circa 1850. Like Stanton and Nichols, the Oneida Community also weighed in decisively on the perverting properties of marriage by comparing it to chattel slavery, printing a pamphlet entitled "Slavery and Marriage: A Dialogue" in 1850. While the Oneidans were naturally sympathetic to the antislavery cause, they felt the abolitionists' exclusive focus on the evils of America's peculiar institution left untouched the more pervasive social, economic, and sexual ills plaguing the nation. Noyes's "Dialogue" begins by presenting a heated argument between "Judge North" and "Major South" on the morality of slavery, in which Judge North's enlightened opinions clearly carry the day over Major South's attempts to bolster slavery by reference to the Bible, natural law, social order, and the supposed happiness of the slaves themselves. At this point the mediator, "Mr. FreeChurch," enters the fray and asserts that the institution of marriage is open to all the same charges that Judge North has just laid at the feet of slavery: marriage is as "contrary to natural liberty" as slavery is. Just as the slave is denied access to literacy and the Bible, so marriage locks women into following the conscience of their husbands instead of finding God for themselves. To Judge North's protest that licentious anarchy would be the result of abolishing marriage, Mr. FreeChurch responds evenly that "liberty breeds virtue" and that "free-love, or complex marriage, combined with community of property, would annihilate the very sources of adultery, whoredom, and all sexual abuse." Sexual poverty and forced abstinence, so common under the marriage system, were the true causes of sexual license; "the feeling of plenty would directly stimulate to chastity and self-control."[17]

Despite making use of the same slavery-marriage analogy that had fueled the arguments of Stanton and Nichols, Noyes's pamphlet was far from a feminist battle cry. True feminist claims, like the abolitionist arguments they modeled themselves on, borrowed from the language of contract law to assert each individual's right to "self-ownership" within contractual relationships. Worker-employer relationships and marriages that eliminated one party's freedom to contract or dispossessed one party of self-ownership were declared null and void. But Noyes, unlike Stanton, cared little for women's legal and financial subjection to men. Rather, Noyes's sympathies clearly lay with Mr. FreeChurch's when the latter asserted that in the new order women and children would no longer be financially dependent on one man but would be secured protection "by a responsible association of men," a tacit endorsement of the dependent status of women. And unlike Nichols, Noyes was blatantly uninterested in free love as a way to liberate women's desires and bodies from masculine control. Noyes essentially agreed with the apostle Paul when he declared, in his letter to the Corinthians, that "the head of every man is Christ; and the head of the woman *is* the man" (1 Corinthians 11: 3). The sole justification for the practice of multiple sexual partners was that it released the free flow of sexual energy, both male and female, that had to be communized in order to re-create God's kingdom on earth as it is in heaven. Free love as a guarantee that a woman could bestow her affections following her individual inclinations—as Nichols so ardently wished—was, in fact, the last thing on Noyes's mind.[18]

Indeed, while Noyes's unconventional positions on the questions of work and marriage often mimicked the outside world's similar calls for reform of these exploitative relationships, the liberalist argument for "self-ownership" was entirely foreign to the spirit of Bible Communism. Certainly, the Oneidans agreed, a person could not "belong" to another person: as institutions invested in the ownership of persons, slavery and marriage were both ethically dubious. But no more could a man be said to "belong" to himself. Humans were all dependents of God and achieved true liberty only by rigorously subordinating their will to His.

"There are two kinds of liberty," Noyes lectured in one of his informal sermons. The first was the liberty of independence, which Noyes characterized as the egoistic spirit of "[h]ands off, leave me alone!" The second, and higher, kind of liberty, he specified, was liberty of unity: "liberty to approach one another and love one another—the liberty of Communism." Only the second brand of liberty was worth striving for: the spiritual release that followed upon the acceptance that "I am not my own, but belong absolutely to another." To the precise extent that believers clung to the specious notion of "self-ownership" and refused to acknowledge themselves "God's property"—the precise extent that they refused to submit their individual wills to the collective good of the Community—they continued to be fettered by sin and in thrall to the devil.[19]

Nothing raised Noyes's hackles more than critics who failed to distinguish adequately between Oneida's Complex Marriage and the free love system of the Modern Times "individual sovereigns," as Stephen Pearl Andrews referred to his apostles. In truth, though Noyes's and Nichols's social critiques dovetailed in the same conclusion—the reign of free love and the liberation of humans from externally imposed law—it would be hard to find two philosophical systems more diametrically opposed as to their root principles. Nichols and her anarchist friends asserted that society needed to abolish all arbitrary, man-made laws, which everywhere hemmed and hedged man's natural tendencies, and instead give individuals license to follow the harmony of their natural attractions. Universal social harmony would reign if only all humans could learn to follow their passions naturally, wherever they might lead—precisely as the atoms of the universe, according to Stephen Pearl Andrews, must be allowed untrammeled freedom in order to ensure the "harmony of the spheres."[20]

Noyes agreed with the anarchists that a slavish adherence to the law was death. But to devote oneself to following the lawless "harmonies" of nature according to individual whim was to err in the opposite direction. For all that Oneida sought to reestablish paradise on earth, Noyes was far from believing in the pastoral fantasy of man's original innocence and goodness in the state of nature. Indeed, he took an exceedingly grim—one might even say Hobbesian—view of life in the state of nature as necessarily nasty, brutish, and short. Everywhere one looked, Noyes asserted—from the law of chemical attraction to the law of gravity—the overriding principle ruling nature's operations was the "law of attraction," a brutish "craving element" or "tendency [of things] to seize and appropriate to themselves other things." The law of attraction expressed itself, in human life, as selfishness: natural man's instinct was to ceaselessly grasp and appropriate whatever attracted him. But unlike the animal, vegetable, and mineral worlds, which were wholly subjected to the natural law of acquisitiveness, man was capable of self-restraint and the exercise of free will in civilizing brute nature—not least his own. This was, precisely, the stamp of God upon him.[21]

Noyes compared humans to an acid with a "voracious appetite for all organic substances, and [that] will destroy and consume whatever it can get at." Left in his natural state, man had just such an unregulated appetite, laying claim to and selfishly grasping whatever it came into contact with. Erecting external laws—Thou Shalt Not Kill, Thou Shalt Not Steal—was akin to placing the acid in a glass vial that would prevent it from destroying everything around it, without essentially changing the acid's internal properties. Thus, Noyes argued, man must develop within himself, and not by means of external barriers, the "conscience and discretion that will prevent its acting anywhere except where it is wanted and ought to act." Humans were neither to abandon themselves to the brute law of nature nor slavishly obey the dead letter of the law but, rather, to follow the inward law of God that they learned, through hard experience, to engrave upon their own hearts.[22]

Indeed, far from giving themselves over to human instincts in a state of nature, Oneidans liked to compare themselves to one of the most spectacular recent examples of the industrial taming of nature: the steam engine. Uncontrolled, spontaneous, romantic love—held by much of the world to be the highest form of eros—was ceaselessly denigrated in the Community press. Well-regulated eros, claimed one Community member, took the erratic force of unregulated "steam" and turned it to efficient use. "By confining and controlling steam," the author writes airily, "it is made to do a great many things, and is of incalculably more benefit to mankind, than when allowed to sing naturally through the nose of grandmother's tea-kettle." Living at Oneida was not, then, a libertine free-for-all; it meant, on the contrary, subjecting oneself to a strict regimen of introspection and self-restraint to ensure the continual, even circulation of love and of God's magnetism throughout the body of the whole organism. At the end of his "Bible Argument Defining the Relations of the Sexes in the Kingdom of Heaven," Noyes appends a nota bene, aimed directly at Fourierists and free lovers alike, limiting Oneida's liability in the case of a gross misapplication of their theory: "Holiness must go before free love. Bible Communists are not responsible for the proceedings of those who meddle with the sexual question, before they have laid the foundation of true faith and union with God."[23]

And yet for all its severity and its biblical defense of women's natural inferiority, Oneida proved itself a practical workshop for gender equality in ways undreamed of by actual feminists of the period. Its female members enjoyed a range of professional, emotional, and sexual and reproductive freedoms that would have shocked even the most ardent leaders of the nineteenth-century women's rights movement. If Noyes used scripture to confirm the spiritual inferiority of women, his quest to reform the perverted relation between the sexes that had reigned on earth ever since the expulsion from the Garden of Eden led to a series of practices that effectually liberated Oneida women from many of the strictures under which their nineteenth-century sisters in the outside world continued to labor.

Legal and religious tradition in the West had for centuries defined the chief purpose of sexual intercourse as the propagation of the species, regarding nonpropagative sexual activity with suspicion, if not moral revulsion. Having handily disposed of the institution of marriage, Noyes, in "Bible Argument," proceeds to demolish this misguided prejudice, as well. Dividing the sexual act into two branches, the "amative" and the "propagative," he boldly declares that of the two, the practice of sex for pleasure and social fellowship is unquestioningly superior to its practice for the production of children. Noyes's reasoning in this, as in his defense of Complex Marriage, is impressively wide-ranging and persuasive, drawing on physiological, economic, and religious arguments to justify his beliefs. The "Bible Argument" first draws an anatomical distinction between the organs of sexual union (the vagina and the penis) and the organs of sexual reproduction (the testicles/semen and the uterus) by way of critiquing society's indiscriminate lumping of these separate body parts together under one simplified aim. Separated from reproduction, amative sex should properly be viewed as "a joyful act of fellowship" and classed among such ordinary forms of social intercourse as conversation, kissing, shaking hands, and embracing. Indeed, Noyes foresees a day when sexual intercourse will be raised to the status of a "fine art" alongside painting and music. "There is as much room for cultivation of taste and skill in the department," Noyes exhorts, "as in any." Noyes uses the analogy of a melon to underscore his point: the seeds in the melon represent propagation, while the pulp represents the enjoyment by the person who consumes the fruit. Which is the primary? Noyes queries. "Evidently the [pulp]; for we feel that the chief end and value of the fruit is realized when it is eaten and converted to human enjoyment, even though its seeds are thrown away, and its propagative destiny is left unregarded."[24]

Metaphorically confining oneself to enjoyment of the pulp and juice, rather than meddling with the seeds, Noyes suggests, also makes good economic sense. Amative intercourse can always be chalked up under the credit column in human sexual economy, while propagative sex invariably must be accounted a debit from the collective pool of life resources. Through its reciprocal communication of vital heat between bodies, amative sex results in a surplus of life and health in its partners: "amativeness is to life, as sunshine is to vegetation," Noyes suggests. Nineteenth-century medicine believed that the too-frequent emission of one's seed had a wasting effect on male health, ultimately leading to nervous disease or death; Noyes concurs, classing ejaculation under the "expensive department" in the vital economy of sex. "If expenses exceed income," Noyes warns, "bankruptcy ensues." In order to forestall such a dire end, Noyes proposes what he calls "male continence": amative sexual activity without ejaculation. Amative intercourse that stops short of ejaculation, he insists, is every bit as satisfying, if not more so, than propagative or fully consummated coitus. Comparing the sexual act to a boat in a stream above a waterfall, Noyes argues that, through experience and training, the skillful "boatman" could learn "the wisdom of confining his excursions to the region of easy rowing, unless he has an object in view that is worth the cost of going over the falls." With his seemingly unerring instinct for awkward sexual metaphors, Noyes compares the indiscriminate emptying of one's seed into a woman to the discharge of a blunderbuss gun into a friend's face: "it is better to fire in the air," he admonishes, "than to kill somebody with it."[25]

But Noyes's unfortunate blunderbuss metaphor conveys his more serious concern about reproductive sex: if propagation could be accounted "expensive," the balance of that expense fell to women. The biggest obstacle to liberation for women, Noyes believed, was their imprisonment in the perpetual cycle of childbirth and pregnancy that robbed them of vital strength and, not infrequently, life. Indeed, it was in response to a tragic series of stillbirths back in Putney, where his wife, Harriet, lost four babies in as many years, that Noyes first developed the practice of male continence. To those who argued that withholding the seed was "unnatural," Noyes redefined the "natural" as the instinct among rational beings to "forsake the example of the brutes and improve nature by invention and discovery." One enthusiastic practitioner of male continence credited Noyes with being the greatest of all American inventors, whose discovery of this unique method of "conservation of force" was to be classed along with the discovery of the electric telegraph and the steam engine in assuring the progress of the human race and the health of women. As uncomfortable and unfulfilling as this sexual practice might have been for Oneida men, the incredible fact is that they were loyal to it. During the twenty-one years that male continence was in effect at Oneida and its sister colonies, regulating the sexual commerce of some two hundred adults, there were no more than thirty-one accidental pregnancies (or what Noyes in one communication to his flock referred to as "involuntary, unwholesome impregnation").[26]

Freed from the physical burden of perpetual pregnancy and, as well, from confinement to the drudgery of housework and childcare to which she was formerly condemned, woman could finally take her place by man's side as his true helpmeet. According to the Bible Communists, the nineteenth-century tendency to assign men to work outside, whether in field or town, while women were forced to labor within the dark enclosure of the home was an entirely unnatural arrangement. An 1856 article appearing in the Oneida *Circular* took note of a recent census published in *The Journal of Medical Reform* surveying the health of 450 married women across America; of the whole, nearly three fourths of the women were categorized as "ill," "delicate or diseased," or "habitual invalids." But sickness did not have to be the inevitable lot of women, *The Circular* journalist went on to argue. The Bible Communists were ensuring women's health precisely by sparing each woman the "drain on her life and vital energy" of involuntary propagation, as well as by affording her "an opportunity for manly labor and exercise in the open air."[27]

One of the first steps Oneida women took to liberate themselves from gender slavery was to don a new uniform free from the dictates of modesty and vanity that, in the world's eyes, served as the proper guides in women's dress. Floor-length skirts, corsets, bustles, and hoops kept women trussed up and immobile, effectively preventing them from working side by side with men. In stark contrast to a typical nineteenth-century middle-class American woman, whose coiled and piled hair could be measured by the pound and whose bustles and flounces erased any visible trace of her lower half, the Community woman wore her hair bobbed chin-length and neatly pinned; each day she donned a simple, stiff, knee-length dress with wide-legged pantaloons poking out from underneath. According to the Community, outsiders' dress and hair were "perverted by the dictates of shame," attempts to mask the feminine form and to snare women into spending the day beautifying themselves rather than engaging in activities more useful or uplifting. Free of constricting flounces and modestly attired in trousers, the Community woman was adapted to the unisex "free motion" that should characterize all "vital society."[28]

From the very outset, the Oneidans were determined to erase the arbitrary distinction between "women's work" and "men's work," public and domestic spheres, that in the outside world kept the sexes separated. In an article entitled "Industrial Marriage" that appeared in an 1854 edition of *The Circular*, one chronicler described how every task facing the Community—from clearing swamps to reaping corn to doing laundry—was accomplished in mixed teams of men and women. "The women go out and help saw and split spokes as regularly as the men," noted the journalist, and on wash-day, men cheerfully stirred the steaming vats of clothes, while women wrung them out and pinned them up to dry. An article on the same topic the following week fretted about the fact that women's marked partiality for the sewing arts, naturally regarded as "insipid and unattractive . . . [by] the more practical sex," was the last obstacle to the complete "industrial marriage" of the sexes at Oneida. The writer concluded hopefully that a growing disdain among the women for the frivolous and fancy stitching popular in mainstream American fashion, combined with the introduction of the time-saving sewing machine, would soon dissolve this remaining "obstacle to union." Only the outside world's "foolish, short-sighted sentimentality," one critic observed, led them to denounce certain occupations and amusements as unnatural to the fairer sex, whether it was "to play on the violin, or to use the hoe and rake."[29]

Nor was Oneida's desegregation of sex-specific work restricted to manual labor. The Community ruled itself by ad hoc appointed committees, which were generally staffed with both men and women. Women could be journalists, editors, typesetters, bookkeepers: they had an active voice in the day-to-day intellectual, practical, and political life of the Community largely denied their sisters in the outside world. One young woman, as reported in the in-house news bulletin, "has commenced taking lessons in dentistry, with a view to qualifying herself for service in that department." Before joining the Community, my great-great-grandmother Emily Otis expressed her desire to work in the print shop there, noting that such employment was not generally considered appropriate for women: "Father tells me that I ought to be doing something to earn my living; I told him I would like to be a typesetter but I did not expect to go out in the world and do it, as the world is now."[30]

If Noyes believed women were, spiritually speaking, naturally inferior to men, they could nonetheless give men a run for their money in the intellectual sphere. Tirzah Miller, John Humphrey Noyes's niece, took over editing *The Circular* from her aunt Harriet Skinner in 1869, the second woman to fill the post. Her uncle's hopes were pinned on her to turn *The Circular* into a mouthpiece for Bible Communism, just as the Boston transcendentalists had launched *The Dial* several years earlier to disseminate their new brand of pantheistic philosophy. *The Dial* had appointed several women to its team, including feminist Margaret Fuller as editor and Nathaniel Hawthorne's sister-in-law, Elizabeth Peabody, as business manager. Noyes abhorred the likes of Fuller, Hawthorne, and Ralph Waldo Emerson, "these Boston and German writers [who] try to influence readers with their atheism and hatred of revivals." He intended Tirzah to hone her critical skills until she could rival the transcendentalist mantra: "You must get so you can criticize Miss Peabody first. You can make a better critic than Margaret Fuller, or Miss Peabody, or Miss Q-body," Noyes coaxed his niece. In a world where work, by the middle of the nineteenth century, was being increasingly codified into a feminine "domestic sphere" and masculine public sphere, Oneida women could thus set type or hoe fields, bake bread or split logs, study Greek or write literary criticism pretty much as they chose.[31]

THE ONEIDA WOMEN'S FRUMPY BLOOMERS AND CROPPED HAIR, THE VERY symbol of the group's rejection of middle-class femininity, drew particularly vitriolic criticism from outsiders. One irate commentator who published an 1870 screed against Noyes, impressively titled, *Free Love and Its Votaries, Being a Descriptive Account of the Rise and Progress of the Various Free Love Associations in the United States and of the Effects of Their Vicious Teachings Upon American Society*, included a satirical cartoon of a male "recruit" at Oneida being ogled by its female members. The meek and bewildered prospect shrinks back in his chair as two bloomer-clad Oneida women loom over him, leering and rubbing their hands together in diabolical fashion.[32]

The most famous American portrait of Noyes as sexual grotesque, however, was penned by Henry James. In his 1886 novel, *The Bostonians*, James has a comic heyday with the fad for reform movements that swept the United States in the antebellum period, with Oneida coming in for particularly sharp treatment. Southern gentleman Basil Ransom travels to Boston to visit his cousin Olive Chancellor, who takes him to a salon where all manner of reformist types—those who "care for human progress," as Olive solemnly assures her cousin—are gathered. There he finds Mrs. Farrinder, a blowhard feminist who "lectured on temperance and the rights of women"; Dr. Prance, a "little medical lady" with an eyeglass whose feminine identity can barely be detected beneath her masculine exterior; and Dr. Seleh Tarrant, a mesmeric healer, with his beautiful young daughter, Verena, in tow.[33]

Dr. Tarrant is a composite figure, a symbol for all that is suspect and louche, according to James, in the fringe reform movements. Tarrant is, in addition to being a frequenter of "spiritual picnics and vegetarian camp-meetings," a former member of "the Cayuga community, where there were no wives, or no husbands." It is a clear allusion to the Oneida Community, and most critics have read Tarrant as a pastiche of John Humphrey Noyes, whom James publicly held in abhorrence as "simply hideous." The great entertainment of the salon is to listen to the lovely Miss Tarrant, having been put into a hypnotic trance by her father, pour forth an oration on the rights of women. Basil Ransom—already half in love with Verena—watches in horror as Dr. Tarrant performs his "grotesque manipulations" and murmurs an incantation over his daughter, who soon begins to chant a feminist oracle.[34]

James was certainly no simple moralist, and his critiques of nineteenth-century American sexual hypocrisy and naïveté are among the sharpest we have. Nor was he the only one to poke fun at the bewildering mix of fraud and good faith that characterized American "reform" culture in the 1840s and 1850s, where phrenologists and feminists, abolitionists and vegetarians, temperance activists and mesmeric healers made common cause with one another. Still, one cannot help being struck by the intensity of the sexual paranoia suffusing *The Bostonians*. The novel unfolds as a desperate contest for the virginal soul of Verena Tarrant: will she follow Olive Chancellor, her father (aka John Humphrey Noyes), and their demonic cohort of men-women down the path to perdition, or will she be reconverted to middle-class normalcy by embracing the impeccably comme il faut Basil Ransom?

In the end, of course, Ransom gets his girl. But it was precisely the inevitability of James's neat conclusion to the riddle of gender that, in their trial-and-error way, the Oneidans were attempting to open up for question.

6

The Machine in the Garden

IN KEEPING WITH HIS PHILOSOPHY THAT LIFE WAS TO BE A HEAVEN ON earth, John Humphrey Noyes initially adopted the edenic ideal of orchards as the economic engine to fuel his paradise. Oneidans had good scriptural precedent for their plan: God had seen fit to fruit the earth on day 3 of Creation, right after He had caused the dry land to appear by gathering the water into seas, even before He had created the moon and stars: "And God said, Let the earth bring forth grass, the herb yielding seed, and the fruit tree yielding fruit after his kind, whose seed is in itself, upon the earth: and it was so" (Genesis 1: 11). The rich valley where the Community lived in central New York was to be planted with fragrant cherries, plums, and peaches, its verdant hills dotted with vineyards, and the profits of the yield, joyfully gathered by all hands, would go to fund their spiritual strivings.

From the very beginning, work took on a festive character at the Oneida Community. According to Noyes's theology, the curse of labor would be magically lightened by following his resurrection plan. The enormous energy that would be released by decoupling marriage pairs and organizing the thus mingled sexes into a Christ-powered battery, he surmised, would give the Oneidans Herculean powers. "Individuals in the [new] vital society will have the vigor of resurrection," Noyes suggests, and such an arrangement would make labor sport. A notice in *The Circular* in 1852 seconded the patriarch's electromagnetic approach, arguing that the Community orchards were surrounded by a magnetism of love and that "this, together with the electrical touch of free labor, may produce results in vegetation which will astonish all previous science."[1]

Labor was "free" at Oneida, as they were fond of saying, rather than compulsory, with members gravitating toward the work to which, whether by inclination or training, they felt best suited. Frequent job rotations kept the labor from becoming monotonous. "I have been here a few days at work in the machine shop," wrote one member; "I find when I get nervous or worn out by literary confinement, that to come here and go to chiseling and filing black dirty iron . . . is better than going to [Saratoga] Springs." By disconnecting work from the "mercenary idea of doing things for pay, or making riches for [oneself]," as one member observed, all work—intellectual as well as manual—was redeemed from drudgery and restored to its original dignity. Labor, with its strong communal emphasis, was perhaps the closest thing to a sacrament that existed within Community culture. Pea picking, strawberry gathering, fence building, ditch digging: early on in the Community's history, all these tasks and more were performed by "bees," voluntary gatherings of men, women, and children to share the work and make it pass more pleasantly. "Commenced the strawberry harvest, which is always a kind of garden jubilee," records a June 1857 edition of *The Circular*. "Picked 88 quarts in a short hour after supper."[2]

In the lean early days while the communards were patiently waiting for their fruit trees to take root, they took in manufacturing piecework—braiding palm hats, sewing carpet bags—to round out the ends of the month. Members would gather, in the parlor in inclement weather, on the North Lawn in fair, to sew and weave as a group. "The Bees after dinner have been very popular," comments an article from 1855 in *The Circular*. "Elbow has touched elbow all over the parlor sometimes when one hundred needles were flying, and a bee-hive would best describe the hum and liveliness of the scene. Seasons of industrial communion they may be called, and we have found them as truly edifying and as attractive to the influx of Christ's spirit as meetings for religious communion ever were." Perhaps there was some truth to the Community's belief in a link between social magnetism and productivity.[3]

The average Oneidan's workday lasted about six hours, although sometimes less, and was remarkably varied and supple. One member's diary records a typical day in which he rose at 5:00, ate breakfast, studied the Bible (Joshua and Jericho) for a spell, then went off to milk the cows. After three hours of laboring with hammer and tongs in the blacksmith shop, "having pretty well moistened [his shirt]," he retired to his room to read Macaulay's *History of England* until the noon bell called him to dinner. Other days in the journal follow a similar pattern of work balanced by leisure and learning: loading wood, husking corn, or doing laundry punctuated by piano lessons, a forty-five-minute Greek class, and an hour of singing school.[4]

Originally, the Oneidans engaged one of their members, a horticulturalist named Henry Thacker, to aid them in their plan to create a new Garden of Eden. But while he was glad to help, Thacker warned his friends that the locality they had chosen had a singularly bad climate for raising fruit. Just a few years into their experiment, he proved himself a trustworthy prophet when the Community's "frost bitten and blighted orchards were turned into brush heaps for the fire." The canny farmer, however, had another idea. A planter by summer, Thacker was, by winter, an outdoorsman who spent his days trapping along the Calumet River. And he knew that the best traps to be had were hand-produced by a local trapper, Sewall Newhouse, who just happened to be a Perfectionist convert and member of the Community. When not engaged in the gritty task of clearing fields for the Community's ill-fated orchards, Newhouse had been permitted to continue to make his traps at the modest Community blacksmithing shop on Oneida Creek. One day, Thacker went to John Humphrey Noyes with a suggestion.[5]

"You have a perfect gold mine in that Newhouse trap," he urged the patriarch. "You can drive every other trap clean out of the market." Noyes, in his rumpled frock coat, passed a weary hand through his shock of red hair and grumbled that the Community was engaged in much more important work than gold mining. But by 1855 the Community had sunk no less than

$47,000 of their precious capital into failed fruit production; they were decidedly not making their living. And so John Humphrey Noyes agreed to give trap making a second look.

THAT SECOND LOOK WOULD PERMANENTLY TRANSFORM THE FORTUNES OF the Oneida Community. First and foremost, the decision to abandon their pastoral dream for the lucrative and expanding field of trap production put the Community on a firm economic footing, ensuring that they would not suffer the same financial rout as America's other communitarian experiments of the 1840s. Short-lived communal ventures like George Ripley's Brook Farm and Bronson Alcott's Fruitlands conceived of themselves as spiritual retreats from the base world of Mammon; they proposed to support themselves through subsistence farming and saw moneymaking as incompatible with their loftier utopian goals. Not so the Oneidans. On the contrary, after the failure of their fruit enterprise, they understood that only by winning economic success in the rough-and-tumble open market might they make spiritual inroads into the life of the nation. "Money-making is the soul of the world," Noyes once affirmed matter-of-factly. "Therefore in order to subdue the world to Christ we must carry religion into money-making." In Noyes's ambitious vision of a Bible Communist world takeover, commercial success would be the Trojan horse by means of which spiritual victory was gained.[6]

The Oneidans loved drawing ponderous, often overly labored parallels between their spiritual and financial activities. In an article entitled "Jesus Christ on Finance," a journalist for The Circular proposed that Jesus favored not suppressing the human appetite for investing capital but merely channeling it toward more secure places of deposit. "[Christ] does not condemn the treasure-seeking passion," the Christian financier insisted, "but like a wise business man who is far-reaching in his calculations, he cautions us against investing capital in treasures which can be stolen or destroyed." The writer's plug for readers to invest in the "Savings Bank of the New Jerusalem" was, however, more than just a clever literary conceit. The Oneidans truly considered that funneling one's capital into "the heaviest firm in the universe— that of Jesus Christ and Company"—was at the same time the best way to ensure material success on earth.[7]

Oneida's decision to embrace the twin dynamos of industrialization and full-blown market capitalism gaining ground in America in the first decades of the nineteenth century was by no means an obvious choice. America had been founded on the pastoral ideal of the self-sufficient yeoman farmer and the artisan craftsman. According to Thomas Jefferson's mythic vision, this boundless land of plenty had given birth to a society of independent property owners, political and social equals—a beautiful counter to the penury, inequality, and rigid class divisions characterizing Old World Europe. The misery of the emerging working class in industrialized England served as a warning against the social ills of a manufacturing economy. Reflecting on the shift toward mechanization in America marked by the outbreak of the War of 1812, Jefferson remarked ruefully, "Our enemy . . . has indeed the consolation of Satan on removing our first parents from paradise: from a peaceable and agricultural nation, he makes us a military and a manufacturing one."[8]

The market revolution that went hand in hand with industrialization received an equally tepid reception from many Americans. With its faith in impersonal, rational action and the invisible global hand of supply and demand, market capitalism appeared to strike at the heart of the patriarchal and family-based independence of the New World subsistence economy. American farmers and craftsmen were the "chosen people of God," Jefferson had once rhapsodized, who looked to their own soil and industry to maintain themselves rather than bowing to the "subservience and venality" of those dependent on a volatile market economy.[9]

Given John Humphrey Noyes's distaste for the selfish motives animating capitalism, the Oneidans' enthusiastic embrace of these new economic realities appears odd at first glance. But for Noyes, industrialization and market capitalism were not, in and of themselves, destructive forces. Rather, they were tools that could be used for good or for ill, depending on the guiding spirit behind them. The seemingly magical abundance of goods and wealth spawned by industrial production methods, and spread to the four corners of the earth through the technological wizardry of canals, steamboats, and railroads, appeared to Noyes as promises that the land of milk and honey prophesied at the end of days was now at hand.

"The spirit of selfishness—of individual gain—of strife for personal wealth—is the controlling spirit in the motives of men in this [country's] great commercial development," lamented one Oneidan on the American industrial scene in 1859. "Men are brought into contact, they meet in business relations, but they meet as integers, not as members of one another." Yet such parochial, narrow individual interests were certainly not in harmony with the expansive, inclusive thrust of nineteenth-century industry and commerce, noted the writer, where trains, telegraphs, and steam engines were racing full speed ahead to connect the globe into a single, interwoven whole. Communism, not individualism; sympathy, not strife—that was surely the direction in which progress was pushing. "Under the stimulus of love, heavenly civilization and the conquest of nature will advance at railroad speed," predicted this optimistic communist. "The oceans will be 'dotted o'er' with peaceful fleets, bound on missions of blessing. Railroads will answer them on the continents, radiating from shore to far inland, bearing burdens of life and wealth. Telegraphs will wind their electric ways over all lands and under all oceans to the myriad homes of Communism."[10]

"The expansion of business in the right spirit," noted another *Circular* journalist in 1854, "is to us a token of God's advancing conquest in the world." Unlike business enterprises in the fallen world, the "driving machinery" behind Community businesses was not moneymaking but mutual love and the desire to provide for one's brethren. The writer predicts cheerfully that, as Oneida's points of commercial contact with the outside world multiplied, "we shall expect to see one kind of business after another 'cog in' until the whole business world is won over to Christ." "As believers in a celestial railroad, as well as terrestrial ones," wrote one ardent capitalist for communism, "we opine that the former is now not only under contract, but actually in process of construction, and its route surveyed, which will run through the very heart of commercial-dom." Any trade or businesses not organized on communistic principles, or in other words not converted to the "common cause of God and humanity," was destined to perish in outer darkness.[11]

How this process of business conversion or "cogging in" was to be practically achieved remains vague in the Oneida literature. All they knew was that the current state of capitalist and industrial enterprise in America was falling ruefully short of God's plan. During the first decade or so of their communal adventure, the Oneidans saw it as their duty to reform the inequalities of class and capital that, by pitting individuals against one another in what they called the "grab game" for economic spoils, forever hindered true community. "We look upon it as our mission to break up the system of hireling poverty and overgrown capitalism, that every where affects the industrial world, and to saturate society with a taste for better relations," wrote one earnest Community commentator in 1854. Rather than factories and wage labor, Oneida proposed the industrial model of the "working school." Even without reading Marx, the Oneidans surmised the deep injustice situated at the heart of the capitalist transaction: surplus value, or the process by which the factory laborer consistently produced more value than he was compensated for through his hourly wage. "We know of a carpet-bag manufacturing company who . . . pay poor women . . . an average, perhaps, of three cents per bag, while they themselves make probably an average profit in selling of fifty cents per bag," explained one armchair Oneidan economist. "The result is that the many live poor, work hard, and have little time for education; while the capitalists pile up riches."[12]

The solution was not, however, à la Marx, to expropriate the means of production from private individuals and put them into the hands of the state. To effect an "equal distribution of capital or profits" among all members of a society, the Oneidans suggested, or to otherwise wrest control of production away from those most skilled in running businesses and making a profit was a grave error. Under Noyes's peculiar brand of communo-capitalism, captains of industry would continue to control the means of production but would simply cease to exploit labor. The master would "do no injustice to his brother, who also will stop quarreling with his natural subordination, because his own inspiration lets him sympathize with his inspired captain." The entire capitalist pod would function as one extended family and the master would make of his workshop "at the same time a church and school," devoting himself "not to making money for himself and his own little family, but to enriching spiritually and with physical comfort, the whole of his working school."[13]

But in order to turn trap making into the financial gold mine predicted by Henry Thacker, Oneida would have to drastically increase its output. With Noyes's blessing, the Oneidans set about regularizing and improving what up to that point had been a one-man cottage industry of trap making, with Sewall Newhouse handcrafting each and every trap. Among Oneida's members was a backwoods Mainer named John Hutchins who had been hunting and catching animals since he was a boy of ten. By the time he joined the Community, Hutchins estimated that in his lifetime he had caught 100 moose, 1,000 deer, 10 caribou, 100 bears, 50 wolves, 500 foxes, 100 raccoons, 25 wildcats, 100 lynx, 150 otters, 600 beavers, mink and marten by the thousands, and muskrats by the ten thousands. Up until this time, Newhouse had confined his trap making to one size of trap, known as the "Number 1 Newhouse," suitable for catching midsize creatures like mink and otters. Now, in order to expand market share and meet the increased demand for traps, Hutchins and Newhouse set about testing traps in larger sizes geared toward catching deer, moose, and bears. Hutchins was expert at knowing what opening of jaws and strength of spring was required for different animals; his encounters with otters, for example, had taught him that these animals, though small, were incredibly muscular and strong and demanded a trap to match.[14]

Consummate perfectionists, Newhouse and Hutchins undertook a series of painstaking tests and experiments to determine such things as the appropriate length of spring, the strength of spring, and jaw width for each of their specialized traps. Theoretical laboratory work was not enough; only once the traps had been proved effective in the wild would the pair authorize manufacture for sale. The problem was that trap making was labor-intensive. Each trap had to be cut, forged, beaten, coiled, and tempered by hand; "it was," one later commentator noted, "hammer and tongs from beginning to end in making the Newhouse Trap." Tempering the trap springs was a particularly grueling job. Each spring had first to be held in a vat of oil until hardened, then dipped in melted lead until the right resiliency (or "temper") was obtained, which was determined by wiping a grease rag over the hot spring until a certain flash of metal, well-known to the practiced eye, indicated that the spring was ready. Newhouse was able to manufacture between one and two thousand traps a year single-handedly. But this would hardly do if trap making was to become the main economic support of the Community.[15]

In 1855, seeking to cut costs, John Humphrey Noyes decided to consolidate two of the satellite communes the Community had, up until this point, tried to maintain in Brooklyn and Newark. This had the added advantage of bringing a group of trained machinists from the Newark branch commune up to Oneida, where they agreed to put their heads together to speed up trap production. The first invention to result from these new arrivals was a power press that would cut the iron and steel to the various lengths required by the springs and jaws. After making visits to hardware factories throughout New England in 1856, expert machinist Leonard Dunn returned to design a machine that could wrap the steel lengths into coils, bypassing the sheer toil of hammer and sledge ("ding dong from morning to night") that had previously been required in forging the springs. The next breakthrough, also the brainchild of Dunn, came in the tempering of the springs. Instead of holding them in the melted lead by hand, thus producing a few hundred springs in a day's work, Dunn designed a revolving tempering oven that would temper between eight thousand and twenty thousand springs in one batch. The only work required was filling and emptying the oven and tending the fire. Community members toiled cheerfully at the shop amidst the punch and clang of the presses, the scent of the wood-fired tempering oven, the hiss of molten metal plunged in oil.[16]

Despite the shift to mechanized labor that came with the trap factory, Oneidans saw no reason to avoid applying their arcadian work festivals to the job of punching iron just as naturally as they had once gathered strawberries and pieced together straw hats. Not even reports of the horrors of the factory system plaguing England could chill the Oneidans' ardor for their expanding enterprise. The spectral, dirt-smudged faces of factory waifs that haunted Charles Dickens's novels were not Oneida's reality. For their workers, engaged in what they called "industrial communion," the ping and clang of machinery symbolized not misery, but a bright future of progress; not dehumanization, but shiny traps by the thousands and profits to match. Even the very young were enlisted in the production process. "A flock of the children went over to the trap shop this morning to put their little fingers into the pie there," recounts one member of a trap bee in 1867. "It was very inspiring. They did good service, assorting pieces from the foundry to the amount of fifty or sixty hundredweight." Tiny Tims these children of Oneida were not.[17]

The Oneidans, whose numbers by 1860 had swelled to 250, used part of their hard-earned profits to build themselves what came to be called the "New House," a replacement Mansion House more than double the size of their original dwelling. In the spring of 1861, once the earth had thawed from the bitter winter, ground was broken on the project. A main brick building, three stories high, forty-five feet wide, and sixty feet long, was to be joined by an equally sizable north-jutting wing, with an eighteen-foot-wide, four-story tower rising up triumphantly at its northeast corner.

The New House was designed solidly, if not extravagantly, with all modern comforts; a commentator for *The Circular* reviewing the new building praised the light-filled meeting hall and the "taste and nicety with which the German artists executed the work of frescoing the room" with allegorical figures of Justice, Music, Astronomy, and History. The official opening of the New House, on February 20, 1862, was attended with toasts and festivities befitting the christening of this "small branch of that great heavenly Community, of which Paul and Peter and John and Mary, the apostles and faith-heroes of all time, are the glorious center," as John Humphrey Noyes's younger brother, George Washington Noyes, commented in a toast.[18]

With the success of their trap manufacturing, the Oneida Community believed that they had finally broken through the third and penultimate link in the great "chain of sin and death" that, according to Noyes's theology, held humans captive. Having first freed humans from sin, and then having restored proper sexual relations, the Oneidans had now overcome the burden of oppressive labor. In its place, they had substituted the principle of "heavenly industry" along with what they called "Free Labor": energizing, noncompulsory, unisex, and rotating work that kept the industrial mechanism joyfully spinning without the dreadful fear of poverty or the soul-deadening effects of exploitation.[19]

THE ONEIDANS WERE NOT ALONE IN PONDERING HOW BEST TO ORGANIZE labor under the new regime of market-driven industrial production. By the 1850s, Thomas Jefferson's original vision of America as an agrarian economy, content with the self-sufficient model of the family shop or farm, was becoming unrecognizable. Under Jefferson's ideal, hired work, or labor for a wage, was viewed as degrading, insofar as it rendered the worker dependent on his employer and deprived him of the freedom and self-ownership white Americans held to be the basis of civic and political personhood. (Black slavery was an accepted economic fact of life that, because blacks were not legally considered persons, fell entirely outside the sphere of such tender moral and political considerations.) But by 1860, the number of wage earners in the country for the first time surpassed the number of the self-employed. "Hired labor," as a class, found itself ideologically homeless in a nation dedicated to the ideal of economic independence.[20]

It would fall to the Republican Party in the 1850s to rescue wage labor—what they euphemistically christened "Free Labor"—from the stigma of economic dependence and transform it, instead, into a legitimate step on the proverbial road from rags to riches that increasingly came to embody the American dream. "Our paupers today, thanks to free labor, are our yeomen and merchants of tomorrow," asserted *The New York Times*; and in 1859 Abraham Lincoln, in a speech to the Wisconsin State Agricultural Society, famously denounced the misconception that a wage laborer was "fatally fixed in that condition for life." On the contrary, any American with a bit of grit and thrift could lift himself up out of the hireling class into the class of property owners. The wage system could not be faulted for those who remained trapped at the bottom, Lincoln insisted; in a foretaste of the social Darwinism to come, such a fate was due to either "a dependent nature which prefers it, or improvidence, [or] folly" on the part of the individual worker. The traditional stigma that attached to the hireling—that of being an economic dependent, without property—was magically lifted by liberalism's credo that a man naturally owned property in his labor, which he could sell for the best price offered on the open market. The labor-capital relation was no longer framed as a relation of subservience, but, rather, as a contractual agreement between autonomous actors.[21]

Free labor had its critics, notably among those who feared that what they called "wage slavery," by analogy with black chattel slavery, would destroy America's traditionally classless society and push the country down a slippery slope toward the retrograde European caste system. The Catholic reformer Orestes Brownson articulated one of the most cogent attacks on the hireling system, describing the wage relation as "a cunning device of the devil for the benefit of tender consciences who would retain all the advantages of the slave system without the expense, trouble, and odium of being slaveholders." The Oneida Community, which abhorred American society's cult of ruthless moneymaking and individual autonomy, could not have agreed more heartily. In this spirit, Noyes's right-hand man, William Woolworth, followed up on George Washington Noyes's 1862 Mansion House dedication toast with the suggestion that, in addition to being a consecrated outpost of the primitive church on earth, the new Mansion House be regarded as a monument to "Communist Free Labor." Woolworth's moniker was a conscious critique and reframing of the Republican Free Labor mantra, suggesting that neither Southern slavery nor the Northern hireling system was ethically viable: "The North may abolish Slavery at the South, and substitute the hireling system, . . . but this will not be the end," he concluded. "[T]he leaven of Free Labor has been put into the world, is at work, and will spread through the whole mass, to supplant the hireling system, whether North or South."[22]

THE IDYLL, HOWEVER, WAS NOT TO LAST. THE COMMUNITY'S MODEST blacksmithing shop soon proved much too small to handle the volume of traps demanded by the booming market. And so, drawing upon their ever-widening profit margin, in 1865 the Oneidans completed construction of a large trap factory at Willow Place on the Sconondoa Creek, a mile or so distant from the Community, which could house the operation's expanded infrastructure. Along with trap making, and in order to offset the occasional drops in demand that inevitably plagued the trap market, the Oneidans also took up the manufacture of silk machine "twist," or thread. The invention of the sewing machine had revolutionized the clothing industry, and by manufacturing spools of silk thread, Oneida could help keep the country's sewing machines profitably spinning.

As was his habit before undertaking any new manufacturing venture, John Humphrey Noyes sent out an advance party of scouts to research the industry. While Oneida's enterprising machinists set out for New York and Newark to acquire castings to forge their own silk machinery, another party, headed by my great-great-grandfather Charles Cragin and two young Community women, Harriet Allen and Elizabeth Hutchins, managed to convince a prominent silk twist manufacturer in Willimantic, Connecticut, to take them in as apprentices and teach them the tricks of the trade. There were several steps in the process of producing machine-ready spools of thread: the skeins of raw silk needed first to be reeled and cleaned, then "thrown" or twisted, and finally dyed and wound onto bobbins. Though done on machines, all of this work required human hands at certain points along the way—preferably the small, nimble hands of young women and girls.

Elizabeth Hutchins wrote back to the Community after her first day at the factory as a silk cleaner, explaining how the thread was mechanically transferred from one spool to another by first passing through two small blades, so that any rough areas or knots would be cut out. The resulting break in the thread needed then to be retied by a worker's patient hands. "The work is not at all difficult," she reported; "One person can attend a good many spools, when the silk is good." All the same, Elizabeth and Harriet clocked a ten-and-a-half-hour day—standard fare for a woman textile worker— "standing all the time, only seating ourselves on an old box that stood near, occasionally, for a little rest." The machinery made so much noise that the workers were effectively prevented from talking, and by noon of her first day, Elizabeth admitted, "I felt so tired I didn't know how I should get through the day." Still, Elizabeth rallied and completed her three-month internship, returning to Oneida to teach other Community members the craft. By the summer of 1866, the Oneida silk machinery was up and running.[23]

Ladies' fur stoles, capes, and caps dominated the front pages of fashion magazines at midcentury, with the demand for velvety animal pelts seemingly inexhaustible. Within a year of its launch, Oneida's high-quality machine twist was the bestseller on the market, and the Perfectionists did all they could do to keep pace with the ever-changing shades of silk required to match the seasonal vogues. Machine-twist sales rose so steadily that, in 1869, they bought an old spoon factory in Wallingford and fitted it up, too, with silk machinery to supplement the Willow Place output. The Oneidans might snub their noses at the soulless materialism of the rising middle class outside their doors, but they were growing rich off the fashion follies of their compatriots.

As their industries took flight, it became clear that the Oneidans would no longer be able to supply the necessary labor from among their own numbers. Maximizing their capital investment and securing a steady market share in these volatile commodities was going to require more than the four-to-six-hour shifts that they had agreed upon as providing optimal spiritual and physical benefit to their members. It would require the Oneidans to dip into that indefatigable and endlessly renewable resource that they had, for so long, resisted: wage labor.

On paper, the Community valued the dignity of all work. "He is the truest gentleman who is capable of doing the most useful things," observed one literary man who found it invigorating occasionally to swap brainwork for the gritty atmosphere of the machine shop. But even the Oneidans, when the opportunity presented itself, jumped at the chance to recuse themselves from the more menial and drudgelike of tasks. The Community began to dabble in wage labor in 1861, when they hired local masons and carpenters to build the New Mansion. By 1863, they were taking on domestic help, as well: "a couple of young colored women from the vicinity" to aid in the laundry. The Community members who had, formerly, fully manned the machinery in the trap shop and silk works began to fall away. By 1867, all of the assembly-line jobs in the silk-twist and trap factory were filled by "hirelings," local outsiders specifically engaged for the task. By 1875, Oneida employed over two hundred hirelings in its various industries.[24]

Half of the hirelings were "silk girls," most of them mere children between the ages of ten and sixteen. Adopting the same schedules and pay scale as the Northeast's burgeoning textile manufacturing industry, the Oneidans had the silk girls working the same grueling ten-to-twelve-hour days that Elizabeth Hutchins had experienced during her brief stint at the Willimantic machine-twist factory. The girls were hired and fired at whim, according to the shifting seasonal demands of the market. The Oneidans, to be fair, were attentive to the problem of "how to work [the girls] economically and yet not oppressively," but their solution—to give the girls fifteen-minute recreation breaks at 10 A.M. and 4 P.M.—hardly appears lavish.

The silk girls' relentless work schedule stood in stark contrast to the Community members' participation in the machine-twist enterprise. The final step of the silk processing—winding the thread onto spools for sale—was transferred to the Mansion House premises, where Community members took turns manning the machines. One amateur Community journalist con-

ducted an interview with a group of Oneidan women assembled in the spooling room in 1869, inquiring as to their daily work schedules. "At ten o'clock
I sit down at one of the spooling machines, where I work till twelve. In the
afternoon I study, sew, or recreate until supper time," volunteered one young
worker. "I spool till noon. In the afternoon I go to school till four," offered
another eager silk spinner. "You see [their] lot is not a hard one," commented
the beaming journalist. "There is one thing I like about our silk-spooling
business, and this is, it gives light, pleasant employment to such a variety of
persons," raved one woman who felt blessed to be able to put in a few hours'
productive labor toward the communal fortunes. Middle-class wives in the
outside world, this commentator went on to observe, were debarred from
working with their hands by bourgeois demands of delicacy, much to their
detriment: "An hour or two a day of escape from the routine of household
cares to some pleasant and profitable form of productive labor," she lectured,
"would be a better diversion to the mind, and a more wholesome tonic for the
whole system, than a trip to Saratoga [Springs]." Convinced that middle-
class women would benefit from an occasional vigorous round of silk winding, this commentator nonetheless remained silent on the one hundred or
more working-class women and girls who toiled patiently at their posts in
Oneida's factories for ten hours a day—with little chance of a trip to the
bracing waters of the Saratoga spa to replenish their energy.[25]

As conscientious capitalists, the Oneidans sought ways to accommodate
their workers comfortably and, within reason, to better their lives. But the
obvious disparity in the Community literature between how they talked about
the scope and prospects of hired workers' lives and how they talked about
(and took for granted) the scope and prospects of their own lives is at times
almost painful to read. In tackling the thorny problem of how best to get
large numbers of workers lodged near the factories, the Community debated
a hotel-style boardinghouse versus providing tenant houses for individual
families. The former, it was argued, could be a profitable enterprise: they
would house workers and "sell the board thus provided, just as we would sell
any other commodity, . . . calculating on making a fair profit on an investment." But the tenant houses also had their benefits: given lodging, the hireling families would "in the course of time raise up scores of children to be
made available at an early age for our businesses," following the system

devised by "the large Factory Villages of New England." A similar anecdote is captured in an 1867 entry in *The O.C. Daily*, where my great-great-
grandfather Charles Cragin was reported to be looking for four or five more
girls to hire in the silk works. "He thought it more profitable to hire girls
from twelve to sixteen years, as they did not require as high wages as women,
and for the work wanted, girls could do about as much as women."[26]

In 1859, a Community idealist had been able to lambast the market economy as it functioned in the outside world for bringing men into contact as
"integers"—faceless numbers, calculations on a ledger—instead of as united
"members of one another." Yet once they made the shift to wage labor, one
observes only the thinnest of distinctions between the proverbially greedy
factory owner's crass calculations as to the life span, reproductive capacity, and
muscle power of his workers and the Community's similar calculations about
how to competitively price room and board—in other words, how to squeeze
the most labor out of every dollar.

The Community literature on labor relations in the 1860s and 1870s
presents a fascinating portrait of an ideology stretched to the breaking point
by its internal contradictions. In *The Circular* of this period, for every article
recommending that the capitalist values of thrift and economic self-interest
should guide Oneida's transactions with the market, there appears an equally
earnest plea that the Community's original communistic principles be extended to include their factory workers. Thus one anonymous commentator
on what the Oneidans called, in 1867, "the Boarding Problem" resurrected
the Community's original model of the "working school" to argue that worker
boardinghouses should not only provide food and shelter but also educational opportunities to the "better class, lovers of improvement," who would
thus seek admission to Oneida's factories "as the best place for laying an educational foundation." The Oneida factory worker was both an integer on a
balance sheet and a perfectible child of God, both an impersonal cog in the
machine of Bible Communism and a member of the body of Christ waiting
to be brought into the fold.[27]

One image from the period shows a line of silk girls outside the brick
factory. Their faces are blurry in this sepia-toned print, but one can make
out the identical calf-length dresses, white stockings and brown boots, and
crisp white aprons tied around their waists. On the end of the line there is

one tiny girl without an apron; her hand is raised to her mouth in a curious gesture of apprehension—or perhaps she is just scratching her chin. What strikes one in her figure is the smallness and delicacy of her limbs and the awkward, unsprung energy of childhood. In the summer, the silk girls were allowed to go bathing in the creek three times a week as recreation. They would wade into the cool stream—the more exuberant racing into it, splashing, in a "joyous rush," according to one Community observer—and, for the space of half an hour, the elemental sun and water must have softened the roar of the machinery, soothed their cramped and calloused hands.

AS THEIR FACTORIES SWELLED WITH THE RANKS OF THE GROWING WORKing class, Oneidans retreated into the relative comfort and leisure of their home. The Oneidans were, in fact, soon indistinguishable from any other upwardly mobile middle-class American family engaged in manufacturing: their own rise in the world was bought at the expense of a servant class, a tireless cadre of both domestic and factory wage laborers whose rigorous separation from and subordination to their propertied employers greased the wheels of the capitalist machine.

"My father's rich, you bet he is!" yells Randolph Miller, the younger brother of the eponymous heroine in Henry James's 1878 novel, *Daisy Miller*. The daughter of an unnamed manufacturing magnate hailing from Schenectady, Daisy is only one of a host of characters in James's novels, all more or less tragic, who make their fortunes along the Erie Canal during the Industrial Revolution. Schenectady, Albany, Rochester, Buffalo—along the main streets of these former metropolises, now struggling rust-belt towns, one can see today the mansions of a vanished class. The magnificent houses that salt and iron, textiles and flour built in the booming last decades of the nineteenth century persist as eerie reminders of more prosperous times. When it came to making their social mark, the Oneidans proved little different from the Daisy Millers in the profane world surrounding them. As soon as they could afford it, they, too, built themselves a brick, ivy-covered mansion worthy of their dignified station in the world.

There was active debate among Community members as to what style the 1861 New House should be built in. Gothic was the prevailing taste for "country manors," but ever since the 1850 publication of Andrew Jackson Downing's influential tome on the art of domestic architecture and landscape gardening, *The Architecture of Country Houses*, the Italianate-villa style had been gaining popularity. Downing's treatise suggested that the "taste" and order displayed in the shaping of the middle-class home and its natural environs directly reflected its inhabitants' level of Christian civilization. "So long as men are forced to dwell in log huts and follow a hunter's life," Downing warned readers in his foreword, "we must not be surprised at lynch law and the use of the bowie knife." "But, when smiling lawns and tasteful cottages begin to embellish a country, we know that order and culture are established."[28]

The middle-class home in Victorian America held an almost sacred position in the popular imagination. Within its walls, strict conformity to a set of rules guiding everything from interior decorating to how to serve a cup of tea to proper leisure activities guaranteed a world in which Christian self-restraint and gentility were bulwarks against social anarchy. Given their rather unorthodox definition of what constituted an ideal Christian "home," Oneida's enthusiasm for such guides to middle-class taste and civilized standards appears at first paradoxical.

Landscape gardening, in particular, became a matter of lively interest to Oneidans. In 1862, their resident gardener, Alfred Barron, wrote a series of articles for *The Circular* about the landscaping arts; his essays drew heavily on Downing's ideas about virtue and the American home. Barron begins his series by contrasting two kinds of homes: the landscaped and the neglected. Which home would the "Christian educator select as the home for his children and charges," Barron queries: that which "stands upon an emerald green lawn, perfect and velvety," and where a tasteful choice of trees are surrounded by "a path glid[ing] in gentle sweeps and undulations like the rich curves of a beautiful woman," or a home situated on a "trampled piece of earth" and which serves as a "common ground to . . . children, poultry, cattle and dogs"?[29]

The aesthetic ideal of the lawn as an artificially smooth and evenly grassed surface originated as a landscaping fad with the eighteenth-century English aristocracy. Having the leisure and manpower to cultivate a lawn was in itself a mark of class elevation, and as lawns became easier to create and maintain—the first lawn mower was patented in 1830—the middle class eagerly adopted the style as a badge of gentility. A smooth lawn was thus, according to Downing and Barron, the first order of business in creating a tasteful setting for one's home. By the end of the summer of 1862, under Barron's careful guidance, Oneida was on its way to reaching this benchmark of middle-class respectability. "Our new lawn, for the first time close shaven, begins to have the carpet feeling and finished reflection which is required," enthused a reporter for *The Circular*. The grounds had been planted with clusters of trees, "with an eye to judicious arrangement," and "notwithstanding the lack of shade, which only years can supply, [the lawn] with its paths and verdure pleasantly environs our Community dwelling."[30]

One of the advantages of the new lawn was that it allowed Community members to engage in croquet tournaments, a leisure activity (also imported from England) that spread like wildfire throughout America in the 1860s. So popular did croquet become as a middle-class pursuit that *Godey's Lady's Book*, a monthly magazine designed specifically to guide anxious women through the perilous maze of middle-class etiquette, published a set of rules for this fashionable new game and included a croquet outfit among its fashion plates. Community photographs from the 1860s and 1870s routinely portray groups of men and women artfully arrayed on the Mansion House lawn, croquet mallets in hand, with the handsome redbrick ancestral home towering impressively in the background, proper as any newly minted bourgeois mansion in a Henry James novel. For all their short-cropped, bloomered women and scandalous sexual practices, the Oneida Community had become, by the most bizarre of twists, full-fledged members of the emerging American bourgeoisie.

7

Sticky Love

JESUS DIDN'T MUCH LIKE LAWYERS. HE WAS PARTICULARLY CRITICAL when it came to the rule-obsessed Pharisees, who measured holiness by how closely one hewed to the outward letter of the law. "Now do ye Pharisees make clean the outside of the cup and the platter; but your inward part is full of ravening and wickedness," Jesus admonished a gathered group of Pharisees and lawyers (Luke 11: 39). The apostle Paul pushed the spirit of antilegalism even further, affirming that, "All the law is fulfilled in one word, *even* in this; Thou shalt love thy neighbour as thyself" (Galatians 5: 15). Law, Paul thought, had been necessary to regulate a formerly unregenerate humanity, but the redemption promised by Christ dissolved all legal distinctions through the unifying power of love. Circumcision of the spirit replaced circumcision of the flesh.

John Humphrey Noyes and his followers fully embraced the Pauline spirit of antilegalism, and the Oneida Community, accordingly, had no written constitution or formally articulated laws. Humans and God, in Noyes's view, were not separate contracting parties in a legalistic covenant but, rather, permeable, linked units composing a divine whole. He envisioned the self not as cut off from other selves but as an empty vessel joined to other vessels in the body of Christ, through whom divine love flowed impartially and evenly, as in a single body. Law, Noyes thought, presumed the existence of separate persons whose conflicting interests stood in need of arbitration. Love, on the other hand, dissolved persons in Christ, which was why the reign of love that Noyes and his followers instituted at Oneida obviated, at least in theory, the need for law. At Oneida, the goal was to realize this dissolving effect to the fullest: one did not merely *love* one's neighbor; one *became* one's neighbor through the body of Christ.

In seeking to explain his new vision of the relationship between individual and community, Noyes relied on scientific analogies drawn from the fields of chemistry, physics, and biology. His favorite metaphor compared the church to a battery: God, Christ, and humans were connected and vivified through the flow of a divine, electric love fluid, and its even distribution throughout all parts of the body was key to attaining the perfection of the resurrection state. "Faith is the wire coil which connects us with God, the great electric, life-giving power of the universe," mused Noyes's sister Harriet Skinner. "All the world needs for its perfect regeneration is the free and perfect flow of the spirit of God, magnetizing the hearts of men."[1]

Avid students of the biological sciences, the Oneidans were equally fond of digestion metaphors. "The method by which we approach God and become assimilated to him, may be illustrated by the process of digestion," writes one solemn theorist in *The Circular*. "We take food into our stomachs in a crude and perhaps hard state. Then commences a process [that] reduces it to a pulp. It is only when changed to this condition that it is capable of being made a part of the body. Just so, it is needful that we should be softened before we can become a part of the body of Christ." Inevitably, what jammed the circuit or, depending on which metaphor one chose, gummed up the divine intestines was the hard knot of individual selfishness: those secret, wayward desires and impulses, harbored by each of God's frail creatures, that resisted submission to the collective good.[2]

From the Community's very beginnings at Putney, Noyes put into practice an internal regulating mechanism he called "Mutual Criticism." As a theological student at Andover, he had joined a club called the Society of Brethren, composed of seminarians planning to devote themselves to foreign missionary service. The society developed the habit of submitting one another's characters to moral criticism as a means of purifying themselves. Each in turn was confronted with an exhaustive list of his faults and failings as drawn up by the other members of the group; the target of criticism was to receive the appraisal in complete silence, without offering a rebuttal of any kind. (Two of the group's original members, Noyes wrote wistfully in later years, were eaten by cannibals "on an East Indian island," an event that may or may not have been a consequence of trying to introduce Mutual Criticism among the natives there.) In any case, Noyes judged the procedure instrumental for regulating Community life, and thus he introduced it as a routine practice first at Putney and, later, Oneida.

Criticism at Oneida was, for the most part, freely requested by individual members who felt themselves in need of spiritual cleansing, "perhaps several times in a year or even as often as once a month," according to one member. Occasionally, criticism was imposed as a curative for bad behavior on the part of members who refused or were unable to self-correct. The Community established a revolving "Criticism Committee," whose members were changed every three months. Anyone who desired a good bout of bracing criticism could submit himself to the standing committee. The criticisms were apparently quite open, with any member who felt that he had something useful to contribute to the character portrait free to join in. In some cases, the criticisms even took place during the daily Evening Meeting in front of the entire assembled Community.[3]

No personal fault, no tic or mannerism deemed noisome to communal harmony, was too small to escape the microscope of criticism. Members were criticized for being brazenly insubordinate to their "ascending superiors" or for laughing too freely and loudly; for having too quick a temper or for failing to correct a pigeon-toed gait. One contrite soul felt compelled to take out a blurb in the *Oneida Daily Journal* thanking a recent criticism committee for curing him of the "coughing principality"—a ticklish throat that had, apparently, been a source of particular irritation to his mates. The Oneidans were remarkably literal in imagining their souls as falling prey to the foibles and follies of sin. Earth, heaven (where the 144,000 saints of the primitive church resided), and Hades, Noyes's name for that hazy land of the as-yet-unresurrected dead, formed three separate but continuously interacting realms that were filled with shades and demons, "powers and princi-palities," spirits both benign and hostile. Bad behavior was pictured as the consequence of a "bad spirit" or dark "principality" perched, toadlike, on the shoulder of the sufferer; members prayed for God to send them a "good spirit," or a "soft spirit," to wipe out the darker tendencies of their natures. The Oneidans developed a shorthand vocabulary for spirits and principalities that were particularly common or bothersome: excessive attention seek-ing, or what they called "the prima donna spirit"; hypochondria, labeled "body tending"; the tendency to become too attached to a particular lover, or "stickiness."

Criticisms were not wholly negative, but judiciously larded with praise, in order to counteract the naturally demoralizing effect of having one's charac-ter flayed before a live audience. "Criticism should carry no savor of condem-nation," Noyes wrote in a pamphlet the Community published dedicated to their critical practice. "There should be discrimination between the spirit that is on a person, or his superficial character, and his heart, where Christ is." Jessie Catherine Kinsley, who was born into the Community in 1858, later re-corded her feelings of tearful "mental chaos" upon leaving a criticism session: "'I am certainly a fool,' self-deprecation would clamor. . . . 'Perhaps what Miss Chloe says about my temper is true, too.' 'But, oh! How glad I am George M. said that there was *no lack of desire in me to do right*. Yet how *can* I be as good as I want to be?'" Another earnest soul, coming out of a criticism so extensive that it required eighteen handwritten pages to record, protested to John Hum-phrey Noyes that, in spite of it all, he was a good citizen. "Yes," Noyes replied, "[a]nd don't you know that in a spring freshet there is always a lot of flood wood— don't be discouraged." Criticism humbled the spirit but at the same time instilled hope that the crooked could someday be made straight.[4]

A typical Oneida criticism was, then, a curious hybrid institution: a mix-ture of town meeting and exorcism, legal deposition and group therapy. The notes taken on the occasion of a criticism of James B. Herrick, in 1866, are particularly illustrative of the aims of Mutual Criticism. Herrick was living partly in the Community at the time of the criticism and partly in New York City with his wife and five children, who, despite his best attempts at persua-sion, remained unconvinced of Noyes's mission. Noyes himself opened the session with the caveat that, "in criticizing Mr. Herrick we are to assume that whatever he may be individually, he stands in such connection with the world that in a certain sense he represents a portion of it." The fact that he spent so much time outside the Community, compounded by "the amount of worldlings he has to contend with," was assumed to entail a certain unavoidable contamination. The task of the Community was to "cooperate with God in purifying him" of society's dross through a brisk, critical scrubdown.

Mr. Herrick was, in some respects, a "beautiful member of Christ's body," as two panelists kindly observed. However, the body of Christ was being "crippled" in Mr. Herrick by the "great marriage principality [which] got possession of him" through his ties to his wife. Herrick's selfish refusal to sacrifice himself wholly to the Community was identified as his principal shortcoming (except for one rather cranky panel member who kept emphasizing a tendency to tell boring anecdotes as Herrick's chief social sin). "There is a part of you that is not communized," Noyes chided, "that is not obedient to the Community Spirit." Mutual Criticism sought to ferret out the secret recesses of both body and soul that remained outside the healthy circulatory loop of the larger Community, dissolving every particle of the self into the living unity of the whole.[5]

To "communize the self," to borrow Noyes's phrase, was the extraordinary task Oneidan men and women set for themselves. In reading the official Community literature, as well as private diaries and letters, one moral failing in particular surfaces again and again as being stubbornly resistant to the process of communization: sticky love, or sexual possessiveness. These sticky attachments to individual lovers blocked the circulatory works of the Community body by obtruding a toxic, indigestible ego (or pair of egos) into the free-flowing stream of universal love. Two women whose letters to each other record the challenges of communizing the self—and in the process eradicating sticky love—were Beulah Hendee and Annie Hatch. They shared their trials and joys and, more crucially, a lover, whom they struggled to make into a bridge, rather than a barrier, to their union in Christ.

BEULAH FOSTER HENDEE, BORN IN LEXINGTON, NEW YORK, ON FEBRUary 18, 1847, was a young woman decidedly alone in the world. Her mother had died giving birth to her, and her father had, in turn, abandoned her. She had been brought up by a family named Hendee, who reportedly mistreated her; after that, she moved in with her aunt, Candace Bushnell. Beulah was an attractive, delicate-looking young woman, with clear, sad eyes; a straight nose; and a pouty mouth that had just the faintest hint of an underbite. Those acquainted with the facts of her love-starved youth could be forgiven for detecting a remoteness in the girl's portrait, a sadness in the wispy, close-cropped hair and dark ruffled dress. Nor is it surprising, given her lack of strong family ties, that she readily consented when her aunt, a fervent Perfectionist convert, urged her to join the Oneida Community in 1864, when she was seventeen years old.

Beulah found in Annie Hatch a fast friend and confidante. Annie's portrait shows a woman more robust than the fragile Beulah, with handsomely chiseled cheekbones, a confident gaze, and the hint of a smile playing over her lips. A Community "lifer" (she had been brought to Oneida with her family at the age of five) and older than her friend by five years, Annie undoubtedly helped the young Beulah negotiate the daunting complexities of the Oneidan sexual system. In August 1878, Annie Hatch left Oneida to live for a time at the branch commune of Wallingford Community; though the evidence is sketchy, it is possible that the departure was meant to cure Annie of her unhappy involvement in a "sticky" relationship with a recent joiner named Arthur Towner, who eventually seceded from the Community. Indeed, Beulah's first letter to Annie exhorts her to "forget these things that have troubled your heart and look for that peace and happiness that cometh like a thief in the night."[6]

Annie's departure left Beulah bereft and Dorothea, Beulah's two-year-old daughter, quizzical as to where "Aunt Annie" could have disappeared: "Where is Annie[?] . . . All gone . . . ," wrote Beulah to her departed confidante on August 3, mimicking the infantine logic of her child. "Should think you would feel bereft without your Pythias—or Damon—whichever one she was," quipped one of Beulah's friends upon Annie's departure, comparing the friends' steadfast love for each other to the iconic friendship of Greek myth. "I do," replied the chagrined Beulah.[7]

Annie's coach to Wallingford most likely carried another passenger Beulah was sad to see go: John Sears, an earnest machinist who was being sent to

Wallingford to help with the silk manufacture and who had been Beulah's lover. If one is able to read between the lines of the ever-encrypted references to sex in the Oneida letters, Beulah and John had begun their affair two years earlier at the Community's vacation beach house in Connecticut, nick-named Cozicot. A note from John to Beulah in May 1877, as he revisited the scene of their love, commemorates the event: "I did think of you, and last June, a great many times when I was there, I went and sat in your stone seat southwest of the house where you and I sat and talked on the 16 of last June. And you put some roses in my notebook. I looked around for some roses, but could not see any as it was too early for them." The romantic inter-lude of the stone seat and the roses was fondly recalled in John's letter, and John and Beulah kept up their friendly romance over the next two years. A note from John upon his arrival in Wallingford registered the loss he felt on leaving Beulah back in Oneida, noting that he "misses [her] ever and ever so much." But Beulah had, perhaps without even knowing it, already turned her romantic sights elsewhere.[8]

Before Annie's and John's departure, both Beulah and Annie had under-taken to follow a course of French lessons with James W. Towner, a dash-ing newcomer who had joined the Community along with twelve followers in 1874 (and who was, coincidentally, the father of Arthur Towner, the ob-ject of Annie's misplaced affection). "I ran away from the Children's House this afternoon long enough to recite my first French lesson," Beulah re-ported to Annie in her letter of August 15. "As a friend I have ceased to be afraid of him, but as a teacher I stand somewhat in awe of him."[9]

Beulah was right to be intimidated by Mr. Towner. Originally from Willsboro, New York, Towner bounced around from state to state before finally landing in Oneida in 1874. His impressive if somewhat eclectic résumé included studying theology in Ohio; passing the bar exam in Iowa; losing an eye in the Civil War as a soldier for the Union army; and dabbling in a free love experiment that had sprung up, and then collapsed, in Berlin Heights, Ohio. His portrait reveals a man with a close-cropped beard star-ing directly into the camera—no demure three-quarter angle for him—with searing blue eyes of an almost uncomfortable intensity. His lofty white fore-head would have denoted, in the phrenological idiom of the time, a strong intellectual tendency. His was a philosopher's mind, which he put to work writing a series of articles for *The Circular* in 1875, picking quarrels with the skeptical philosophy of Hume and Locke and arguing for the precedence of belief over reason. He had, in other words, the kind of worldly experience, authority, and gravitas that inspires a student's awe.

Annie and Beulah quipped back and forth in their August letters about their relationship to "Jacques," as they agreed to refer to their French teacher, engaging in a sort of three-way epistolary flirtation in which the couplings pivoted dizzyingly back and forth among the possible permutations, not unlike the proverbial shell-and-pea game. Towner was planning to visit Wallingford in September, and Beulah used her correspondence with Annie as an erotic chip in the game she was playing with him: "Mr. Towner says I may tell you anything I like from him but I told him I should be careful considering that he is coming there before long and might possibly inveigle you into showing him what I had written," wrote Beulah. Invoking the titillating secrets women share in their private correspondence, Beulah tempted Jacques to think of himself as a prized object of the friends' daily gossip, all the while suggesting she had secret thoughts about him she would not want him to discover. Annie and Beulah's confidential letters gave Beulah a means of upping the sexual tension with her would-be lover, shutting him out playfully from the secrets women share and stoking his curiosity as to her true feelings toward him.[10]

At the same time as Beulah invited Annie into a teasing conspiracy against their erotic adversary, she also hinted at a possible romantic liaison between Annie and Jacques: what would "inveigle" Annie to share Beulah's letters with him, if not a shift in erotic allegiance away from her female confidante and toward a male lover? In her conversations with Jacques, Beulah again triangulated her relationship with her tutor by invoking Annie's superior linguistic talents and setting up an unspoken sexual competition for Jacques's attentions between the two women: "I said 'Annie won't have to be drilled in pronouncing,' but he said 'Wait till I get there and see'—So you had better look out, and be thankful that you have me to warn you." Beulah teasingly provoked Jacques to compare the talents of his two students, all the while presenting herself to Annie as the coy go-between in her as-of-yet unconsummated rapport with Jacques. Beulah functioned by turns as Jacques's lover, his matchmaker, and his teasing (possibly lesbian) adversary in a game where eros could move in many different directions at once. "Jacques has been here playing Cribbage. I mean to ask him to carry the cribbage board when he goes and teach you the game," Beulah wrote to Annie, cribbage having become a metaphor for the three-way sharing of affections.[11]

By Beulah's epistle of September 4, the relationship with Jacques had flowered and, presumably, culminated in an "interview" between teacher and student. In the face of Jacques's impending departure for Wallingford on September 15, Beulah's letters take on a slightly anxious, or at least wistful, tone as she imagines her new lover and Annie resuming their "French lessons" in her absence. "Jacques will call you his best pupil I know, especially after he has been down there to attend to you," Beulah wrote to Annie, and one detects—beneath the flattery and playful matchmaking—an unconscious anxiety that Jacques may, indeed, find Annie a "better pupil." Beulah and Jacques even undergo a mock "break-up" prior to his leaving, which allows Beulah both to test Jacques's love while at the same time giving him generous leave to take another lover. "I tell JWT that I shall neither write to him or you while he is there or send any exercises, and he on his part threatens to turn me out of the [French] class," Beulah wrote Annie. Neither threat would come to fruition, but here Beulah both enlists Annie's help in keeping her purchase on Jacques's affections while at the same time giving her friends freedom to love. "You won't sympathize with him, will you," she coaxes Annie. "I won't be turned out of the class, but I am quite sure that neither of you will have the time—if you have the inclination—to attend to either my letters or exercises."[12]

As if sensing the uncommunized note of competition she had injected into the relationship, Beulah immediately reversed herself and urged Annie to spend a weekend with Jacques at Cozicot. "To have him go to Cozicot with you would be next to going there with him myself," she confided. In a gesture typical of the communists' romantic dealings with one another, Beulah generously extended her relationship with Jacques to Annie, picturing herself and her friend as interchangeable units of Christ's body. Annie's sexual experience with Jacques would flow into and amplify Beulah's own love for him, folding all three into the glowing love sphere John Humphrey Noyes imagined as the very shape of heaven.[13]

One senses in the letters both Beulah's ambivalence about sharing Jacques's love with another woman and an anxiety that she might lose Annie to her friend's budding romance with the French tutor. Despite the Community's ruthless regulation of sexual "stickiness," intense platonic affection between members of the same sex tended to escape criticism and, indeed, was frequently imagined in romantic terms. Neither same-sex eros, it should be noted, nor its possible consummation ever arises in the Community literature—presumably because John Humphrey Noyes's theory of magnetic male and female poles rendered such an arrangement anatomically as well as theologically unthinkable. Nonetheless, there is a way in which the universalization of eros as the key tenet of Community doctrine lent all relationships—sexually consummated or not—an aura of romance and longing.

On one sultry afternoon, Beulah felt compelled to write to Annie: "It is so dreadfully hot. . . . Everything is so sticky—I'm sticky, too, to you—everlastingly so." "I have all at once become unappeasably hungry for you, and what am I to do?" Beulah wrote in another plaintive missive to her friend: "Why, I feel like a lover to you—and yet you are so far away." The day after Annie's departure for Wallingford, Beulah had compared herself to Adam having woken absent one rib. Beulah felt Annie's absence as an almost corporal loss; one wonders whether, through the shared medium of Jacques's body, she might not reclaim her lost part. "[You] won't become so absorbed in your French as to forget Sister Beulah," she wrote coaxingly to her friend soon after Jacques's arrival at Wallingford. "I shall want to hear from you." Whether or not their "sticky" love was ever physically consummated, Annie and Beulah may have imagined a kind of vicarious erotic experience facilitated by their common lover, Jacques.[14]

With Jacques safely ensconced at Wallingford, Beulah detected a change in Annie's letters, an uptick in her mood. "I can see from your letters that your heart is getting comfort and peace. You will find the 'true pitch' about love I'm sure," she wrote encouragingly. The "true pitch" was probably a reference to Noyes's affection for musical metaphors in speaking about getting into the right relationship with God. "We are like a piano with many strings sounding high and low," Noyes once wrote in a sermon entitled "First Love," and "the question is how to keep our attention on the key note

[of] the voice of God in the heart." The question of what—or who—was affording Annie this sudden spiritual guidance in matters of love was, however, left untouched between the two women, at least in the extant correspondence.[15]

By the end of October, Jacques was back at the Oneida Community. The letters from this period reveal that Beulah was now under an interdiction from seeing him. While we don't know the details of the decision, Annie's letter to Beulah of October 25 indicates that Beulah had been judged "ensnared" in sticky love—and that Jacques had been judged "proud" and in need of learning more "about himself and Community principles" before he could appropriately associate with Beulah again. "Your last letter did give me a good understanding of the 'case' as it stands—and I don't see as you can do better than to submit" to the injunction, wrote Annie sympathetically to her friend. Jacques was, with his "proud," "intellectual," and "upright" character, undoubtedly deemed by Noyes or a criticism committee to be a bad influence, drawing Beulah away from God into man worship. Beulah recognized that she had ceased to "set the Lord always before her" (Psalms 16: 8), as the psalmist recommended, and that she had given in to idolatrous love. "This has been different from any experience I ever had in my life. I never had my heart so ensnared before. I thought I had suffered before, but never like this. I had such confidence in JWT that I gave him my heart without reserve."[16]

As would often happen in cases of sticky-love injunctions, John Humphrey Noyes invited Beulah into his sexual orbit in order to reteach her the higher, non-idolatrous way to love. On New Year's Day they shared an oyster stew together and Beulah confided to Annie, "New Years I celebrated with him another way—I need not tell you how." The renewed magnetic sexual contact with Noyes seemed to be doing the trick of unsticking Beulah's heart. "It is a matter of great thankfulness to me in this trial that my heart is so warm and loving toward JHN," Beulah wrote to Annie. "He feels like a lover to me; and I had a sense yesterday that that is just the way he feels toward God. It is a feeling no different from that we have toward our dearest lovers, only far more intense. When I get that in my heart toward God I shan't have any more trouble about love. I shall think first of God, then will come perfect liberty," she penned hopefully. Noyes may well have given Beulah the advice he had, one year earlier, dispensed to his niece Tirzah Miller, where again the notion that God love is the most ecstatic and intense of emotions was meant to coax lovers away from their sticky, egoistic attachments: "[Noyes] said I must get my affections into such a state of obedience to God that I should let my heart out to someone, and then take it in again instantly at the word of command, just as the dancers obey the call of the manager. . . . [H]e said if I could get this obedience to God, I could love more intensely than now."[17]

Meanwhile, crisscrossing in the mail with Beulah and Annie's missives, were those between Beulah and her Cozicot lover, John Sears, with whom she remained in regular contact throughout her Towner affair. John was smitten with Beulah, and her wrestle with Towner, as well as her sexual rapprochement with John Humphrey Noyes, clearly tried his soul. Community members referred to sexual relationships by the general term of "experience," encompassing all that this word connotes of learning and trial, of failure and progress, insofar as mastering special love was critical training for coming into a right relationship with God. In his October 9 letter to Beulah, John admitted to being "hungry to hear from [her]" and missing her "ever and ever so much," but not to being unhappy, as God had "arranged our experience just before I came here, and . . . [it] has made me more softhearted and humble than any experience I ever had before, and I shall have to thank God and you for it." Relationships were intended, at their best, to lead members to "softheartedness," by which the communards meant a lack of stubborn egoism and cheerful obedience to the spirit of community and God. If, in his October letter, John thanked Beulah for helping him soften his heart, in a November letter to Annie, Beulah wrote of Towner's contrary refusal to achieve soft-heartedness, to relinquish his pride and become "communized." "He thinks he is all right, but God can show him and melt his heart," she wrote hopefully.[18]

Beulah reported her sexual rapprochement with Noyes to John. Just as Beulah had tried to have a soft heart toward Jacques and Annie—viewing all three as connected in an ever-expanding chain of love—so John expressed an expanded sense of fellowship for both Beulah and Noyes through their triangulated sexual union. "I am very thankful that you have got so near Father Noyes and it does my heart good to have you write about him, for it draws me nearer to him, and makes me feel thankful and happy. How I should like to see him: I would give him a good hug and kiss and it would do me ever so much good." The medium of Beulah's love brought him into closer connection and brotherhood with the Community at large, and in particular with Noyes: "I do not have any fears but that you will love me enough and I do want you to love me ever so much, for I do you; and I love Father [Noyes] too. I am glad that he has fallen in love with you so that he can sympathize with me, for I have fallen in love with you too." John and "Father" Noyes's shared love of Beulah brought them into a vibrating chord of sympathy with one another, an expanded fellowship that carried with it its own unspoken erotic dimension.[19]

Still, reconciling himself to Beulah's sticky liaison with James Towner and her renewed position as Noyes's lover had its moments of difficulty for John Sears. "I have sometimes asked myself if you would have got back so near to Father as you are now if I had been at Oneida instead of Wallingford," he wrote in a January 12 letter to Beulah. "I do not know as I can answer the question but I do know that I should have tried to help you back." Despite his best efforts at viewing himself as a bridge in Beulah's journey closer to God, John's letter closed on a melancholy note, a well of sticky sadness, the source of which he leaves her to divine: "But dear Beulah my heart is too full to write more and there is a great bunch that keeps rising up in my throat and the tears will flow in spite of me so that I can hardly see to write. Ever Yours, John." Despite his earnest desire to be "a good soldier and be loyal . . . to Christ and Mr. Noyes," John's uncontrolled tears testified to the trials of communizing oneself and the resistance of the body to ridding oneself of all selfish impulses.

Ironically, given Beulah's and John's individual struggles against special love at this time, it was precisely the lesson of universal love, "communism of heart," that Annie had forced herself to learn in the course of her sexual rapport with Jacques during September and October. For on December 12, the pregnant silence between the two women on the question of Jacques was broken, as Annie confided to Beulah her "experience" with the charismatic French tutor. During the two months that he had lived at Wallingford, Annie confessed, Jacques had taught her the secret of unselfish love, how to channel the potentially unsettling, and sticky, power of eros into the expanded peace of agape: "I do not prize his friendship so much for the mere pleasure of loving and being loved . . . but for the effect it has had of awakening my heart anew to Communistic love," Annie explained in her letter. "When he came here, my heart was shut up and I felt as though I never wanted anything more to do with men sexually—and it was all I could do to be even friendly to them." Jacques slowly "let me feel that I had a heart and gave me new courage to let it be warmed and melted," such that, by the time he left, Annie found herself truly in love with him. "But the best thing was, that I found my heart warming and enlarging toward all the brothers here—and my heart has been filled with a desire to seek unselfishly to please those around me, even at the sacrifice of my own tastes and inclination. I feel that God has the first love of my heart, and it is my earnest prayer that He will keep it." Annie's bout of sticky love led her to recommunize herself, enthroning God as "first love" of her heart.[20]

Towner was less helpful, however, in aiding Beulah to conquer her sticky love for him. In fact, in a desperate bid to hold on to her affection, Towner threatened her that Annie would break with her if Beulah refused to stay loyal to Towner in the face of Noyes's imperious interference. When Beulah confided her fears to Annie, the latter assured her that her friendship was worth a thousand Towners. Annie passionately defended their relationship against the incursions of "man-love," or the sexual love she had learned now to use as a vehicle for approaching God and expanded fellowship in Christ's body: "I am glad you wrote just how you felt, and am grateful to you for your deep, sincere love for me. That certainly is more gratifying to me than to know that any man loves me, and be assured that Jacques or any other man shall not separate our hearts. . . . If you could only see me you would know that I should be faithful. It seems cruel to have love of man come in and separate two women—and God helping me, it shall never be." Tired, perhaps, of the ceaseless emotional ups and downs of her relationships with male lovers, Annie pledged her loyalty to Beulah as an anchor whose love would hold her fast. "Do you know," she wrote reflectively to her friend a few years later, "and it is not flattery nor imagination, that you seem nearer to my heart than anyone on earth, and I think I love you more than anyone else?"[21]

By January 1879, in addition to her renewed sexual relationship with John Humphrey Noyes, Beulah was engaged in a budding romance with Alfred

Barron, the Community gardener. The triangle originally joining Beulah, John Sears, and Noyes in the aftermath of her Towner affair was now giving way to a happier triangle linking Beulah, John, and Alfred. As her love for Alfred blossomed, Beulah got word from John that he was planning a return to Oneida from Wallingford. Having learned to place God at the center of her affections, Beulah was certain her heart had room for both men. Always conscious of themselves as links in an infinitely expandable emotional chain rather than as isolated objects of a single desiring gaze, Alfred and Beulah jointly pledged to open their hearts to John when he returned: "Alfred said the other day that he would make me all happy," Beulah confided to Annie, "so that John could enjoy me when he came back."[22]

SUBMITTING ONESELF ENDLESSLY TO MUTUAL CRITICISM AND SEPARATING oneself again and again from sticky attachments were clearly excruciating experiences for Community members. One star-crossed tale of sticky love that became immortalized in Community lore was the affair carried on between my great-great-grandfather Charles Cragin and a young woman named Edith Waters. Mary Cragin's magnetic son, Charles, came of age in the Community in the 1850s and 1860s, and he was beloved by many young Oneida women. One of his lovers, Edith Waters's best friend, Jessie Kinsley, would later describe Charles Cragin as "alive with quick intuition, vivid, clear-thinking, strong, unselfish, filled with subtle thought for others." Having completed his degree at Sheffield Scientific School at Yale, Charles served the Community first by starting up the machine-twist business and later by overseeing experiments in "scientific farming" and animal breeding at the Wallingford Community. He was brooding and intense in his work; his passion was photography, and, in an old barn on the Wallingford property, he set up a studio and darkroom, where he delighted in taking portraits of his friends.[23]

The whole time he was at Wallingford, Charles Cragin suffered from bouts of malaria. On Christmas Day 1877, he took to his bed; his health deteriorated rapidly, and he died several days later. Edith Waters, barely twenty years old, followed him to the grave a mere six months later, a victim of consumption. Like many Community members, Charles had been an avid diarist. There is no record of who recuperated his diaries or of who saw fit to report them to the Community higher-ups as rife with unrepentant expressions of sticky love. However it transpired, Charles's diaries, filled with what Jessie Kinsley recalled as "wild and strong" declarations of his undying love for Edith, were read aloud in Evening Meeting as examples of precisely the kind of selfish, exclusive attachment that the Community worked to combat. Even those most committed to the Community ideal of selfless love, including Jessie Kinsley, were horrified by the public exposure, instinctively feeling it to be a desecration of something that should have remained private. In a letter written to her daughter nearly forty years after the event, Jessie Kinsley is literally at a loss for words to describe the experience. "This must be a simple narrative. I am not the one to write of things so complex, which I look back upon through the years with mingled feelings of pain and wonder, admiration and regret." Surely, for all their earnest belief in the principle that private feelings had to be communized, the Oneidans must have struggled with doubts on this point. Were there no private griefs, no wild elations, no dark nights of the soul that a heart could claim for its own? Was everything, then, the common property of Christ's body?[24]

And yet ridding the heart of sticky love could be exhilarating as well as excruciating. Every religion contains within it a kernel of mysticism: a conviction that beyond or beneath the immediate reality of the self as separated from others, and separated from God, there exists a plane where the many become one. Early Christian hermits wandered into the desert, where, alone and face-to-face with God, they discovered the peace—*quies*—that comes with losing the petty cares of the individual self and dissolving into a larger whole. "Rest," the twentieth-century mystic Thomas Merton once observed of these proto-monks, "was a kind of simple no-whereness and no-mindedness that had lost all preoccupation with a false or limited 'self.' " The Oneida Community had evolved their own method of achieving Merton's negative state of selflessness; they imagined it as dissolving the self into "the Spirit of Truth."[25]

"There is nothing more exhilarating than that electric union between our spirits and the Spirit of Truth," John Humphrey Noyes wrote of the experience of Mutual Criticism. "If we are members of Christ—one with his righteous, glorious life at the center—criticism does not touch the real *I*."

The experience of love was the same: if one was true to its spirit, the individual lover became a vehicle for union with God, not an idolatrous end in itself. As Jessie Kinsley, no simpleminded cheerleader for Bible Communism, observed of her youth in the Community, "I wonder if there was not an afflatus, renewed through criticism (criticism that was almost always upbuilding rather than destructive) that made us go beyond ourselves—our natural selves—and took from us the desire for selfish *rights*."[26]

At its best, the Oneida Community's practice of Mutual Criticism, and its mortification of sticky love, kept alive in its members a keen sense that they were participants in a more elemental unity that transcended their limited, finite existence as individuals. The banal weight of daily cares—of stinging jealousies and clutching desires and gnawing regrets, creeping in their petty pace from day to day—was burned off in the pure fire of universal love. But at its worst, the Community's ruthless dedication to communizing the private life of its members could, quite literally, turn to nightmare.

8

Brave New World

TIRZAH MILLER LIKED TO HAVE SEX. A TYPICAL ANECDOTE FROM THE diary of this niece of John Humphrey Noyes and member of his exclusive inner circle recounts an impromptu romantic encounter with her on-again, off-again lover James Herrick. One day, while wearing his favorite white dress ("he calls me his little bride in it"), Tirzah and Herrick were caught during a rainstorm in the Community business office. "There was a wonderful glow and ache between us," Tirzah later rhapsodized in her journal. "We seemed all aflame. We hurried to the house, and then he wanted me to come to his room. Ecstasy."[1]

Tirzah was by many accounts the most sexually sought-after woman in the Community. That she was a "powerful social magnet," as one Community elder commented of her, there can be no doubt. Tirzah's diary is littered with bewitched men, broken hearts, and sulking lovers caught in the snares of sticky love. The most glowing testimony to Tirzah's sexual magnetism comes from John Humphrey Noyes himself, who saw Tirzah as both a sexual and a political ally within the Community. With his unswerving instinct for coining awkward sexual metaphors, Noyes once commented to Tirzah that women's differing degrees of prowess in bed resembled the difference in music produced by "a grand piano and a ten-penny whistle." Tirzah's own efforts in the arena of making "social music" he categorized as "sublime." Coming from a man who saw sexual ecstasy as a path to achieving union with the godhead, this was high praise indeed.[2]

The fact of Tirzah Miller's libido being in permanent overdrive was a lucky thing for John Humphrey Noyes. For, beginning in 1869, he had chosen Tirzah to be the cornerstone of an ambitious new plan he was hatching for the Community: a eugenics experiment, whereby the highest spiritual members would cross-breed to produce a new race of super-Perfectionists. After twenty years of struggling to achieve perfection through the labor-intensive processes of Mutual Criticism and self-discipline, perfection would now be "fixed in the blood," blueprinted at the cellular level.[3]

Noyes's bold experiment, the first (if not the only) practical eugenics trial in America, was different, it should be said, from the garden-variety eugenics societies that would spring up in the early decades of the twentieth century in England and the United States. For groups like the British Eugenics Society and, in the United States, Charles Davenport's American Breeders Association, the goal was always the rather pedestrian one of preserving Anglo stock from contamination by the lower classes and races. Under the misleadingly mild motto that "Eugenics Is the Self-Direction of Human Evolution," the International Eugenics Conferences held in New York in 1921 and 1932 favored immigration restriction and forced sterilization to weed out genetic undesirables. The English biologist Julian Huxley, for whom Noyes was a great inspiration, held slightly more enlightened views, and in a 1936 lecture he championed eugenics as a way to prepare humanity for the advent of a pacifist-socialist world state in which the capitalist vices of selfishness and greed would be bred out of human DNA. But for sheer chutzpah, it must be said, Noyes outdid any of his successors in eugenics: he believed humans might be bred for nothing less than immortality. But, as with all creatures that fly too close to the sun, those who participated in Noyes's experiment were destined to singe their wings.

A TYPICAL DAY IN TIRZAH MILLER'S LIFE READS, FROM ONE PERSPECTIVE, like an advertisement for the freedom offered women by Oneida's social system. As a writer for and editor of *The Circular,* Tirzah would spend the morning in the library working on an article to be published in her paper. Scribbling and erasing, she would labor on the piece until pleased with its rhythm and flow. Passing by the Children's House, she would then take her son George (a product of her union with her uncle George Washington Noyes) out for a romp in the Big Hall; they would prattle and play with each other until lunchtime, whereupon she would dutifully deposit him back with his caretakers.

As a mother, Tirzah had stopped rooming with George when he turned one and a half, the customary age at which children were weaned from their mothers and transferred to the Children's House to be raised communally by a group of specially selected Community members. If Tirzah found herself missing her son once separated, there is no record of it in the diary; in fact, to the contrary, her liberation from childcare duties appears to have given her free time to pursue aspirations as a writer and as a pianist that were of some importance to her (not to mention her near-daily trysts with Community men). One journal entry has Tirzah passing an afternoon practicing the piano with Henry Hunter in preparation for a Community concert. Later that evening, having fallen under Tirzah's magnetic spell, the love-struck Henry— seventeen years Tirzah's junior—passed by her room for a spontaneous "interview" in which he "threw aside his almost supernatural self-control, and kissed and embraced me ardently. We had a delightful time." Because Henry had been trained in *coitus reservatus,* Tirzah could enjoy the sex for itself, without worrying about unwanted pregnancy.[4]

According to the handful of recorded accounts by members who grew up in the Community, the "Children's Department," as they referred to their communal child-rearing project, raised its charges with a mixture of discipline, love, and scientific efficiency. Although the system was flexible, the basic structure of the Children's Department invariably comprised a "Head" and between six and ten helpers, who by turns fed, clothed, exercised, and educated the children. While the head of the department was usually a man (William "Papa" Kelly was at the helm for much of the department's existence), there were always one or more "Mothers" appointed as adjuncts to fulfill the maternal function in the absence of the birth parents. The children's indoor amusements were simple but ample: they made scrapbooks and played cards; read books and painted pictures; stacked blocks and built mazes of wooden runners for rolling marbles, toys fashioned for them especially by an accommodating Carpentry Department.

Just as the adults had their Evening Meeting, so the children met each day at 5:30 for a reading from the New Testament, a recitation of the Lord's Prayer, and a round of "Confessing Christ"—the closest the Community came to having its own institutionalized liturgy. As one memoirist recorded later, "We children said, 'fess Christ' or 'fess Christ a good spirit' without clear understanding but with firm confidence that we were in some way acquiring merit," as well as "getting into good relations with a dimly sensed heavenly hierarchy." The children were made aware, without any overt program of indoctrination, that their Community occupied a special place in God's kingdom and that "outsiders" should be regarded with the pity appropriate to the unenlightened and the unsaved. Their elders were "in possession of truths not vouchsafed to the rest of the world," noted one Community child of the ambient sense of election with which he was raised.[5]

Community children learned early on about sticky love. In their case, it was called the "spirit of partiality" and referred to two playmates' preference for each other's company to the exclusion of others. Two boys growing up in the Children's House in the 1870s, cousins Pierrepont and Dick Noyes were inseparable and frequently found themselves sentenced by Papa Kelly not to speak to each other for several days. The cousins worked around the injunction by forcing a younger boy to act as a translator between them, a serviceable if cumbersome way of remaining faithful to the letter, if not the spirit, of their punishment. Just as their parents were expected to parcel out their love equally among the Community's members, so the younger set were taught from an early age to honor the golden rule: peacemaking, "turning the other cheek," and equitable and even-handed treatment of others.

Natural and sentimental stickiness of parents for their children had always been rebuked by the Community. "Philoprogenitiveness," Oneida's neologism for excessive parent-child affection, was regarded as a particularly serious violation of the spirit of equality essential to maintaining the harmony of the group. Those who couldn't restrict themselves to sensibly limited visits with their children were often slapped with a one-week separation penalty. Even those diarists inclined to be most generous toward the Community that raised them found this Community discipline, in retrospect, a heartbreaking ritual. Pierrepont Noyes recalls the "petting and peppermints" he enjoyed during his afternoon visits with his mother, Harriet Worden. "I often wept bitterly when the time came to return to the Children's House," he mused, and "I remember my mother's terror lest my crying be heard . . . [depriving] her of some of my regular visits." Corinna Ackley Noyes records an equally wrenching scene. After suffering through a period of enforced separation from her mother, Julia Ackley, the young Corinna one day caught a glimpse of her parent passing through a hallway near the Children's House. "[My mother] knew—what I was too young to know— that if she stopped to talk with me another week might be added to our sentence. . . . Hoping, I suppose, to escape, she stepped quickly into a nearby room. But I was as quick as she. I rushed after her, flung myself upon her, clutching her around the knees, crying and begging her not to leave me, until some Children's House mother, hearing the commotion, came and carried me away."[6]

For every Tirzah Miller, who appeared to enjoy the liberty from maternal cares that the Oneida system afforded her, there was a Julia Ackley or a Harriet Worden who suffered keenly under the Community's draconian policy regarding sticky love. The Oneida Community was quick to remind such women that the system was in their best interest and that they foolishly flew in the face of science and women's liberation in clamoring for more contact with their children. A letter of "apology" written by Julia Ackley to the Community on an earlier occasion when sticky love for her daughter had gotten the best of her, this time when little Corinna was six months old, has the eerily scripted, hollow quality of a confession at a Stalinist show trial. And it clearly reveals the ideological line the Community tended to take in such cases: "I now realize, as I did not before," Julia confesses, "that the old way of each mother's caring exclusively for her own child, begets selfishness and idolatry and in many ways tends to degrade women. The new system works very well in every respect."[7]

Despite its deep ambivalence about women's liberation as a whole, the Community was keen to take credit for its progressive sexual policies as a great leap forward in the emancipation of womankind, using them as evidence that the Oneidans were on the cutting edge of social science compared with the outside world and its antiquated system of uncontrolled reproduction and maternal drudgery. It was precisely under the mantle of progressive "science" in opposition to the "sentimental" dictates of society regarding women and marriage, in particular, that Noyes would promote his eugenics program in an 1872 pamphlet, *Essay on Scientific Propagation.* Citing Plato, Charles Darwin, and Francis Galton as his scientific predecessors, Noyes hazarded that, genetically speaking, "spiritual proclivities . . . are as transmissible as the speed of horses" and that any society claiming to found itself on scientific principles would have to admit at its base the vital importance of "the scientific propagation of human beings." Noyes coined his own term for this ambitious project: *stirpiculture,* from the Latin *stirpes,* or "race."[8]

Yet Noyes's supposedly enlightened project, promoting itself as the latest branch in a scientific tree that counted such luminaries as Charles Darwin and Gregor Mendel, was wedded to what must surely be a contender for the prize of most preposterous hereditary theory in the history of nineteenth- and early-twentieth-century eugenics (which was, of course, awash in preposterous genetic theories, including Charles Davenport's belief in the existence of a specific gene for "shiftlessness" that would neatly account for the physical and moral inferiority of the lower classes). John Humphrey Noyes's original conviction that, in their highest state of perfection, human beings would become immortal was rooted in his electro-spiritual theory of the soul. Death would be vanquished and immortality gained once the flow of electric love juice from Christ's divine battery had achieved unobstructed equilibrium throughout the nervous fibers of each and every member of His universal body. After immersing himself in the study of genetics, Noyes came to the conclusion that, along with red hair or muscular legs, electrical-spiritual conductivity was another trait that could be passed on through the blood.

God had been the first scientific "herdsman" of humans, Noyes opined, breeding the Jewish nation from Abraham through Christ to be a race of divine superconductors. Abraham, Moses, Christ, and Paul had functioned like divine telegraph stations, uniquely primed to receive and transmit God's messages. This state of nervous refinement was the result of following "a course of close culture"—in other words, Jewish inbreeding. Like a magnifying glass focusing the sun's rays into a concentrated point of heat and light, inbreeding had intensified the "central nerve-region of the body" among the Jews, making them, spiritually speaking, the "most perfect race in history." As opposed not only to the claim of French Emperor Louis-Napoléon that the Latin race would conquer the earth, but also to Britain's confidence in the genetic superiority of the Anglo-Saxon upper class, Noyes suggested that "the typical man who is to head the race [of the future] is a compound of the Yankee and the Jew." The Jews, as representatives of true religion, would be combined with "invention, enterprise and capacity for progress," which were characteristics of the Yankee temperament, to forge the "Yanko-Jew," "the winning candidate for leadership of the world."[9]

Fancying himself the apostle Paul's spiritual descendant and a latter-day superconductor in the divine electrical network, Noyes claimed to be in direct telepathic communication with the spirit of Paul and would often sequester himself from the Community to enter into silent converse with him. What better way, then, to increase human chances for immortality than by mating Noyes with himself? From the Putney group's earliest forays into Complex Marriage, Noyes had been obsessed with what he called the "centripetal force of love," a mystical vision of the godhead as a unity turned endlessly in upon itself. The sexual union of brother and sister—for which Noyes found scriptural precedent in Abraham's marriage to his half-sister, Sarah—was the very type and symbol of such a "turning in."

In a conversation Noyes had with his brother, George Washington, in September 1869, Noyes revealed that he viewed "the fraternal relation [as] the true radix of society" and that it was Oneida's destiny to break down "the last citadel of social falsehood, which forbids the union of brothers and sisters." Anticipating Freud's famous declaration in his 1919 essay "The Uncanny" that even our most innocent visions of "home, sweet home" always hark back unconsciously to a desire for the mother's genitals, Noyes insisted that it was only by "going home"—sexually and reproductively speaking—that spiritual and biological perfection could be attained.[10]

In 1869, on the eve of the stirpicultural experiment, Tirzah Miller recorded in her diary a conversation with her uncle in which Noyes outlined his plans for "going home" by proposing that she bear him a child. "He said he believed it to be his duty, and he had considerable curiosity to see what kind of a child we should produce," Tirzah observed. Though Tirzah already had one child by Noyes's younger brother, George Washington, John Humphrey suggested that "to combine with me would be intensifying the Noyes blood more than anything else could do." In fact, Noyes contemplated having children by Tirzah and her sister Helen (both of them his nieces), as well as by Constance Bradley Noyes, his daughter.[11]

In the end, despite Noyes's evident enthusiasm for the idea, the surviving documents provide no evidence that such sister-brother or father-daughter unions were ever consummated at Oneida. The closest the Oneidans would come to breaking the incest taboo, at least on the record, was their open practice of "avunculate unions" between uncles and nieces. While no doubt frowned upon, if not illegal, in nineteenth-century America, avunculate marriage had for centuries been standard practice among European royal houses, who seized upon this apparent loophole in Leviticus 18 whenever it suited their geopolitical ambitions. Avunculate marriage bordered on, but did not expressly violate, the taboo on incest.

Still, following his own precepts of "breeding in and in," Noyes fathered ten of the sixty-two Community children born during the eugenics trial between 1869 and 1879, while another nineteen were his blood relatives. An impressive 50 percent of the newest generation of Oneidans had Noyes blood running through their veins. The Noyes patronymic proliferated among Community offspring; family trees sprouted in increasingly bizarre, stunted, and inwardly folding shapes as cousin crossed with cousin, niece with uncle. In Edgar Allan Poe's story "The Fall of the House of Usher," Roderick Usher and his twin sister, Madeline, are the only remaining scions of an ancient house that, the narrator suggests, had inbred itself into such a state of febrile precariousness that the slightest outside breath threatened to bring the whole edifice crashing down. The story is cluttered with mirrors, doublings, and claustrophobic images of entombment, eerie symbols for a family turned dizzyingly in on itself. The narrator watches in horror as Usher descends into madness: this, Poe warns us at the outset of the tale, is a house and a family with no exit.

From his youth Noyes had displayed an uncanny ability to devise complex theological and social systems that he claimed were grounded in divine inspiration but that were also remarkably effective at meeting his peculiar psychosexual needs. The genius of Noyes's theory of spiritual wives and, later, Complex Marriage was that they both fulfilled a spiritual urge many Americans felt at midcentury to purge themselves of market-bred selfishness, *and* they guaranteed that Noyes could enjoy sexual liberty with as many spiritual wives as he chose (including those, like Abigail Merwin, who were already taken) without guilt or competition. Stirpiculture was act 2 in Noyes's ongoing quest to shore up his fragile ego, as well as to solidify power over his followers, whom the paterfamilias, as he aged, no doubt felt slipping from his grasp. Whether, in the last decade of the Community's existence, Noyes's reason was indeed "teetering on its throne" like that of Roderick Usher is open to debate. What is certain is that for the full ten years between the inauguration of Oneida's breeding program and the dissolution of the Community in 1879, the patriarch held firm in his creepy vision that immortality could be gained only through a kind of mystical Noyes parthenogenesis. For all of its scientific pretensions, Oneida's experiment in stirpiculture, as narrated in private diaries by its participants, presents a dark, at times sinister, tale that is at stark odds with the triumphant march toward truth and progress it imagined itself to be.

STARTING IN 1869, NOYES THUS CALLED UPON HIS CONVERTS WHO "LOVED truth" to put his genetic theories to the test. Stirpiculture was inaugurated with great solemnity when fifty-three young women signed agreements pledging their loyalty to Noyes in his choice of "scientific combinations," and, in addition, they made the following promise: "That we will put aside all envy, childishness, and self-seeking, and rejoice with those who are chosen candidates; that we will, if necessary, become martyrs to science, and cheerfully renounce all desire to become mothers, if for any reason Mr. Noyes deem us unfit material for propagation." Thirty-eight men signed a corresponding document, offering themselves as "servants of the truth" and "true soldiers" in Mr. Noyes's battle for genetic perfection. Couples who wanted to try for a child applied to the Community's central committee; as per the signed pledges, Noyes was the final decider on the suitability of each suggested combination. Out of fifty-one applications, nine were vetoed as "unfit," while forty-two were approved. The Community took into consideration spiritual, intellectual, and physical qualities in its reproductive selections, as indicated by a leather-bound ledger in the archives whose pages are divided into three neat columns, under which the candidates' credentials were to be recorded.[12]

Within a year of the inauguration of the stirpicultural program, three babies had been born and five more were on the way; an article published in *The Circular* on June 13, 1870, predicted "not less than a dozen" new members before the year was out. The clinical nature of Noyes's "scientific combinations" was depicted in a satirical cartoon that served as the frontispiece to John B. Ellis's 1870 *Free Love and Its Votaries; or, American Socialism Unveiled.* In the cartoon, Community men and women slide ballots into a box marked "yes/no" while the anxious couple being voted on await their fate in the wings, all under the watchful eye of Noyes. The caption: "Ratifying the Choice of Affinities." These jabs at Noyes's genetic laboratory were not misplaced; Oneidans also held a weekly "weighing-in" of the babies on the stage of the Big Hall, performed to the strains of the Community Orchestra, where they scrupulously recorded the vital statistics of their newest, and presumably more perfect, members. Stirpicults furnished a favorite subject for Community photographers, who, fueled by a sense of their historic mission as breeders of supermen, shot image upon image of ruddy-cheeked children, pulled in wagons or standing in clusters around the Mansion House grounds.[13]

Tirzah Miller's diary, which she kept on and off between 1868 and 1879, gives us an intimate and at times searing glimpse inside the life of one woman caught up in the political and emotional turmoil of Noyes's stirpicultural experiment. Tirzah was a key member of Noyes's "inner circle," a tight group composed mostly of the original Putney settlers and their children: Noyes and his wife, Harriet; his sisters Charlotte and Harriet, along with Harriet's husband, John Skinner; and George Cragin. (Mary Cragin had died, tragically, in a boating accident in 1851.) These members kept a fairly tight rein on Community affairs, despite their democratic habit of power sharing via the Community's innumerable "committees." The children of the original Putney pod, who came of age in the early 1860s, enjoyed key positions within the spiritual and intellectual Community hierarchy. Tirzah, Helen and George Miller, and their cousins Joseph Skinner and Theodore Noyes (John Humphrey's only surviving son with Harriet), as well as the Cragin boys, George and Charles, were all advantageously placed. The boys had been sent off to Yale in the 1860s to undertake engineering and medical studies, a step Noyes saw as increasingly vital to the Community's project of fusing science and religion. The triumphant scholars returned to the Community as credentialed scientists and doctors, poised to take their place as leaders of the next generation. While the women were not sent away for formal studies, Helen Miller became a bookkeeper, and Tirzah inherited Harriet Skinner's plum position as editor of *The Circular*. The second-generation Putneyites were thus invested with substantial intellectual and social capital within the nominally egalitarian system that reigned at Oneida.

Tirzah's absolute obedience to Noyes's quixotic, and at times outright cruel, demands when it came to her participation in the stirpicultural program is disturbing but not, perhaps, surprising. Tirzah had everything to gain by believing in the system she had been taught to think of as her birthright. Tirzah's biological father, John Miller, had died when she was just a baby, and by Tirzah's own admission, her uncle had quickly stepped into the role of father surrogate, making him "the only father I have known since childhood." When coupled with the fact that Noyes also acted as Tirzah's "first husband" when she reached puberty, initiating her into sexual life at Oneida, the young woman's overdetermined fealty to this Freudian father-husband loses some of its mystery. Although a casual conversation between Noyes and Tirzah in January 1869, on the cusp of the stirpicultural experiment, suggested that she should be free to choose the fathers of her future children, such was not, in fact, to be the case. Tirzah was far too politically useful to Noyes to be left to her own devices, and Noyes would, accordingly, choose her mates for her. Not surprisingly, the shady politics of power consolidation would trump scientific suitability at every turn.[14]

When Tirzah's diary opened in 1873, she was struggling with a sticky attachment to Homer Barron that John Humphrey Noyes—with whom, the diary suggests, Tirzah had sexual relations as frequently as once a week—was seeking to cure her of. While Noyes gave her the go-ahead to practice her piano alongside Homer for the Community Orchestra, her secret wish to have a baby with her musician-lover was clearly out of the question. Tirzah confessed her frustration at the injunction, especially once she heard that her sister Helen had been granted permission to conceive a child with her once-sticky paramour Frank Wayland-Smith. "My first feeling on hearing about Frank and Helen was, that I didn't see why H[omer] and I couldn't as well as they," she grumbled. But before going to bed that night, Tirzah had managed to get herself into the "right spirit" and was "determined to do my duty fairly, and expect God's blessing either way."[15]

That duty would appear in the form of John Humphrey Noyes's sudden and, in Tirzah's words, "stunning" command that she immediately start trying for a baby with Edward Inslee, a prominent member who had lately been tempted by thoughts of leaving the Community. Edward was one of the master machinists who had migrated from Newark to Oneida when the Community consolidated its branches in 1854, and he had been instrumental in getting the silk and trap machinery up and running. From an economic and practical point of view, Edward was a proverbial pillar of the Community. Rumors of Edward's possible defection sent ripples throughout the Community, and Noyes believed he might be able to lure the doubter back to the fold by proffering his niece in exchange for loyalty. On May 4, Tirzah recorded this request with all the nonchalance of one who was, indeed, determined to do her duty "either way": "J. H. N. told me this evening that he sent Mrs. Ackley to [Edward] to propose to him to have a baby by me. . . . I see no reason why it should make any difference to me." In offering up Tirzah to Edward, John Humphrey was essentially dangling the Community's prize possession, sexually speaking, before the apostate's eyes.[16]

Edward took the bait. "He was pleased, he said, and overwhelmed, and said he didn't deserve it," Tirzah recorded of Edward's gushing reaction.

One week later, he and Tirzah submitted to the stirpicultural ceremony in which the kneeling couple had a blessing pronounced over their heads: "Our Father, on these two who kneel, / Our blessing with thy blessing seal; / And grant in coming joyous days / A noble child may lisp thy praise." Tirzah was reconciled; Edward, over the moon; and Noyes, relieved at having found such a quick fix for one believer's faltering faith. But not everyone was so pleased with this neat resolution. Fuming in the background of the blessing ceremony was Homer Barron, who couldn't seem to soften his heart enough to give Tirzah up to God. Tirzah would spend the next six months seeking to pacify Homer, who confessed he was "inclined to think his lot a harder one than ever man was called to bear" and that the trial would "kill him."[17]

As her intimacy with Edward intensified, Tirzah's special love for Homer diminished, a fact that she captured in a poignant image recorded in her May 15 entry. "Curious phenomenon," she penned. Upon looking through a sun-filled window earlier that day, Tirzah's gaze fell upon Homer's figure outside. "Old hat pushed tightly over his brows, hands on hips. Gazed a moment. The image remained like a sunspot on the retina for ten minutes afterward, growing fainter and fainter, but the exact outline of my friend." As Homer receded into the background, Edward rushed in to fill the vacant psychic and emotional space. "Is it possible that there should be a sensation in the womb the very next day?" Tirzah queried in her journal the morning after sleeping with Edward for the first time. By November 1873, Tirzah was pregnant with Edward's child; she felt her "love and respect for him grow continually." No sooner had she fallen out of sticky love with Homer than she found herself right back into the thick of it with Edward Inslee.[18]

John Humphrey Noyes was, as usual when it came to Tirzah's love life, quick to react. Furious about the "marriage spirit" that had possessed the couple ever since the conception, Noyes told Tirzah that he had "sworn in his heart that he would have the use of [her], and he was not going to have his plans about [her] frustrated any longer by stirpiculture or special lovers." Reasserting his claim on her, Noyes went so far as to demand that, as soon as Edward's baby was born and her health permitted, Tirzah should be "ready at the earliest to try with him." "He said he did not know but he should have more than one child by me," Tirzah reported, and the young acolyte's pleasure at being thus singled out is palpable. Redoubling his attacks on Edward for the dual crimes of unbelief and, now, sticky love, Noyes forbade his seeing Tirzah.[19]

Edward was initially compliant. When he was informed that an impromptu rehearsal of the Community's string quintet—of which both he and Tirzah were members—had been called, he discreetly sent his regrets via George Cragin to the rest of the group. "He says he is not at liberty to associate with the pianist at present," the messenger reported. To which Francis Wayland-Smith—who was notorious in the Community for his own prolonged struggle with a sticky attachment to Tirzah in his youth—replied, "How natural that sounds! . . . I have been in that situation toward this very pianist for the greater part of my natural life."[20]

Joking aside, Edward was not able to maintain such a light spirit toward his lover and child to be. Edward initially attempted to funnel his love into a more communal channel by sleeping with Harriet Worden—a development Noyes could not refrain from sharing with Tirzah, as if to cauterize the open wound of her sticky love for Edward—but eventually the ousted lover began petitioning Noyes for renewed contact with Tirzah. A volley of letters back and forth between Noyes and Edward bickering over his right to see the mother of his child ended in a brutal slap down: Noyes prohibited Edward not merely from talking with Tirzah, but from even *looking* at her until he could learn to properly soften his heart. Noyes proposed that his right-hand man, Francis Wayland-Smith, step in temporarily as Tirzah's "husband" to sleep with her and minister to her for the remainder of the pregnancy. Noyes felt confident that Wayland-Smith had successfully conquered his youthful stickiness to Tirzah, and his absolute loyalty to Noyes— he had been brought to the Community as a young child by his widowed mother, the fatherless boy adopting Noyes as a paternal surrogate—made him a safe bet in guarding Tirzah's sexual neutrality.

On April 20, 1874, Tirzah gave birth to an eight-pound, eleven-ounce baby boy, whom she and Edward named Haydn in deference to their favorite composer. Edward and Noyes continued to spar bitterly over the next year and a half, chiefly over how much access Edward was to be allowed to Tirzah and his infant son. But by the fall of 1875, Edward had suffered all he was going to take and definitively took his leave of Oneida. He

sent word to Tirzah, via James W. Towner, that he desired her to sign papers releasing him of all financial or legal obligation toward her and
baby Haydn. "I thought this would kill me," Tirzah recorded on September
1, "and I almost drew back; then I did it as I would put my head on the exe-
cutioner's block, or as Queen Elizabeth signed the death-warrant of her
favorite Leicester."[21]

Tirzah's tortured love for Edward strained her duty to the Community
and to John Humphrey Noyes to the breaking point. But, in the end, she
made her choice. She sought to staunch her grief at losing Edward by getting
into "more fellowship" with Noyes: "I wanted to open my life to him as to a
surgeon's knife," she recorded in her diary. The first "cut" Noyes proposed
was that Tirzah shut off all communication with baby Haydn, as he was
"the link between [her] and Edward" and thus a distraction to her quest to
reintegrate herself into the Community. The second cut involved inoculating
Tirzah, and the Community at large, against Edward Inslee by changing his
child's name from Haydn to Paul. "He said the name 'Haydn' was a symbol
to him of Edward's idolatry towards music, and had always been distasteful
to him on that account," Tirzah explained in her diary. Tirzah complied,
citing "excellent spiritual reasons" for the linguistic exorcism and claiming
that "[i]t will be a great help in separating both him and me from the associations of spirit connected with his father."[22]

Within two months of Edward's departure, Noyes had already drawn
up a list of six "scientific" contenders for the role of impregnating Tirzah for
the third time—an announcement Tirzah greeted with a characteristically
cheerful vow to be "thoroughly scientific" in abiding by Noyes's final selection. But Tirzah's heart never healed from her break with Edward, and clo-
sure was made more difficult by the fact that, like a ghost compulsively
revisiting the grounds of its former life, Edward continued to write letters to
Noyes requesting a visit with Tirzah and once even made an unannounced
visit to Wallingford hoping to wrest a glimpse of his former family. Noyes
stuck fast to his initial decision to refuse Edward any contact with his wife
and son. Almost three years after Edward's defection, in the spring of 1878,
Tirzah recorded a vivid dream she had had the night before. She was attending a meeting in the Big Hall and, after sitting down, discovered to her
surprise that Edward was seated directly in front of her. "By and by I leaned

forward, and whispered: 'Edward!' He turned instantly, his eyes meeting mine and melting into the humid expression of unutterable tenderness which I remember so well." For the remainder of the dream, the two lovers wandered endlessly throughout the Mansion House "trying to find a room where we could talk without interruption," Tirzah recorded—a fitting metaphor for the ruthlessly interrupted nature of her relationship with the father of her child.[23]

Despite the name change aimed at severing young Haydn/Paul from the evil principality of his father, the little boy was a constant reminder to Tirzah of what she had lost. "Paul stood looking out my window today at the tulip tree which is in blossom, and said 'Mamma, when my own papa comes, won't you ask him to climb that tree and get me one of those pretty flowers?'" But, like his mother, Paul's contact with Edward was limited to the fleeting glimpses that he caught of him in dreams. "I dream about my own papa all the time," Paul sighed to his mother one day. "You mean you see him?" Tirzah pressed. "Yes, ma'am."[24]

SHARP AS NOYES'S SPIRITUAL KNIFE CUT IN THE CASE OF TIRZAH MILLER, it would slice others more deeply yet. Tirzah was, after all, a Noyes and, as such, a genetic front-runner in the stirpicultural game. What of those excluded from the genetic pool of winners? One of these was Victor Hawley, a timid, thirty-year-old dental assistant and a man desperately in love.

The photographic portrait of Victor Hawley preserved in the Mansion House archives shows a serious man, his full, dark beard peppered with blond streaks; his cheeks sharply cut; his eyes a pale blue, almost white against his pupils. His left eye catches the light, lending it an eerie blankness. There is a certain emotional blankness, too, in the journal Hawley kept between 1876 and 1877, the entries conveying the minutiae of his day-to-day life with an almost mechanical simplicity, from the hours worked each day to a dry recapping of the tasks he completed. "JO [Job Office] 6 ½ printing Bill Heads & Statements 1500 for Oneida and 1000 Office sheets," reads one record of a dull day spent in the Community printing office. As the journal opens, Victor is working as an assistant in the dental office as the Oneida Community's unofficial anesthesiologist, administering cups of brandy to the patients as they await their turn in the drilling chair. A less charitable commentator reading Victor's entries might say that the numbing effects of his trade must have worked their way into his soul.[25]

Yet a more careful look reveals a rather different portrait—one of transparent intensity and emotional turbulence. The source of Victor's passion, revealed soon enough in the pages of his journal, is his love affair with fellow Community member Mary Jones. Not in the least adept at expressing his feelings in words, Victor expressed his tears, pains, and joys with Mary largely in simple unpunctuated phrases, frequently falling into romantic clichés that muffle the authenticity of his plaints: "Oh my aching heart has no rest," he recorded simply on May 12, 1876, with no further attempt at elaboration. One must look beyond the repetitive and often numeric character of his notes on her subject ("She slept 2 ½ hours here last night," he records with statistical zeal) to discern the emotion very much behind them. Victor and Mary's love affair was nothing if not piquant, a heady mixture of love and compromise, fierce loyalty and bitter betrayal. Indeed, the lover of nineteenth-century melodrama will find nothing missing in this improbable and moving tale.[26]

When he began his diary on January 1, 1876, Victor was nearing the end of a two-month enforced separation from Mary, a penalty for their overly exclusive attachment to each other. Applying to Tirzah Miller as his go-between, Victor pleaded that he had faithfully abided by the Community's judgment for "two months and 8 days"—the numeric precision is in this case touching rather than simply numbing—and requested permission to see Mary again. Permission granted, he had "a ½ hour talk with Mary after dinner and [felt] far better" afterward.[27]

The joy of their reunion, however, was to be short-lived. On January 6, Victor floated the idea of having a child with Mary to Mrs. Dunn, a Community stalwart, who replied that "she did not think a combination was good between us . . . as Mary's mind was affected." Mary was known within the Community as being "baby-mad"; bitterly disappointed upon giving birth to a stillborn child a year earlier, her unholy haste to conceive again was seen by the larger Community with a disapproving eye. Despite Mrs. Dunn's rebuff, Mary and Victor continued to meet and, in blatant opposition to the Community's wishes, secretly "pray God give us a baby." Two months later,

Mary heard a rumor that "there were a number of people trying" to conceive. This time Victor appealed their case directly to William H. Woolworth, Noyes's appointed substitute as "father" of the Community during Noyes's absences from Oneida. Even a vaguely supportive, if ultimately noncommittal, letter from John Humphrey Noyes sympathizing with Victor's paternal wishes was of no avail. Four days after he made his application to the central committee, Victor received a note back from Mr. Woolworth: "[F]olks here . . . would like to have you gratified and yet the inordinate & unsanctified desire [for a child] especially on Mary's particular, makes folks hesitate & shrink from the consequences."[28]

While not definitively refusing Victor's request, Woolworth's note was nonetheless deeply discouraging and clearly suggested the line the Community meant to take in his case. Not even the young man's brothers, Alfred and Roswell, who staged an intervention to coax Victor away from Mary, managed to alter his course. One day, on checking his mailbox, Victor found a folded note hidden in its recesses. Given the fact that his petition was still up in the air, one can imagine his anxiety mixed with impossible hope on seeing his name scrawled across the envelope in Mr. Woolworth's hand. He unfolds the stiff white paper, his heart in his throat. In the instant just before he reads them, Woolworth's looped letters must seem full of promise. But within a second, all hope has been dashed.

"The committee decidedly disapproved of our having a baby," he recorded grimly in his diary that evening. In true nineteenth-century form, Victor took to his bed, unable to eat, and expressed in his body what his limited emotional vocabulary was unable to convey: "I am weak in every bone [sic] I can hardly crawl around."[29]

Then, on April 10, the impossible happened: Victor's father came to inform him that Mary had been instructed to try for a baby with Mr. Leonard. She was scheduled to leave the next day for the Wallingford Community in Connecticut, where the conception would take place. Victor was permitted a forty-five-minute visit with Mary the evening of her departure. In their last moments together, Mary confessed she had decided to "stick to the community"—including its directive that she have a child by another man—but that "still she loved [Victor] same as ever."[30]

One can feel the agony of her choice; loving Victor, she still grieved for the child she had recently lost and ached for another chance at mother-hood, even if it meant conceiving with a man she didn't love. In short, the Community had forced her into a devil's bargain. The shattered Victor put on a brave face. "I gave her a cologne bottle an orange & locks of hair. Parted with good feelings & love for those were happy moments & I tried to keep bright for her sake we eat an orange to gether [sic]." The following morning, Victor watched as the coach pulled out and away from the Man-sion House. "I watched the team as it left and the whistle blew for meeting as they disappeared . . . for W.C."[31]

Mary mounts into the Community carriage to begin the long road to Wallingford. The clip-clop of the horses' hooves is in her ear as the sun rises on the green Oneida hills rolling by. She has a lock of Victor's hair stored safely away in her traveling case. Spiritualists say that touching a lock of hair from the loved one's head can bring separated lovers closer together, bridg-ing space and time such that the experience of one becomes suddenly vivid for the other. And then there is the bottle of cologne. Will she wear the perfume for her "interviews" with Mr. Leonard? Even now, her fingers are fragrant with the peel of the orange she shared with Victor an hour ago, the sweet scent fading yet persistent, not unlike heartache itself.

VICTOR SLOWLY CONVALESCED FROM THE ATTACK OF SICKNESS THAT struck him the evening he received Mr. Woolworth's crushing note. As part of his cure, he took to having a daily Turkish bath, dutifully recording the time spent and water temperature in his journal entries. "T.B. 10m hot r 18 m at 170 °," he noted on Sunday, April 30. At times he felt an almost super-natural sense of closeness to Mary, imagining his physical malaise as a sym-pathetic response to some suffering she was undergoing hundreds of miles away: "A hard headache . . . Perhaps Mary is unwell [sic] the feeling came over me during meeting that she was & that that was why I felt so."[32]

One day, as he was distributing type in the printing office, a friend deliv-ered a note to Victor that had arrived that evening from Wallingford. After reading Mary's letter, which revealed that she "fe[lt] the separation keenly," he could hardly hold the little metal letters, his hands "tremble[d] so." As soon as he was free, Victor quickly penned a response and spent the next week anxiously awaiting Mary's reply, when, like a bolt from the blue, even this lifeline of words with his beloved was cut: he received a directive from Mr. Noyes forbidding him to correspond with Mary. This was too much. Victor promptly revolted and asked Mary to leave the Community with him. Although at first she agreed, sending word to that effect to Victor via his father, she soon balked and begged him to remain in the Community with her. Reluctantly, he agreed.[33]

As the spring advanced, Victor sought distraction from his pain by throwing himself into pursuits as an amateur naturalist. He collected beetles and butterflies; his friend Cornelius was also teaching him how to stuff birds for botanical displays. He took lessons from Cornelius in how to skin the birds and, whenever he was out of doors, hunted for interesting avian specimens to bring back for his friend: "I sat in the summer house when I started for the house I saw a male and female red throated Woodpecker I shot them for Cornelius with his pocket gun;" "After dinner got a Purple Grackle's nest and blew the eggs." And Victor pursued his own botanical interests on the side, documenting and labeling his beetle collection: "After dinner I went down and set up the names that I have been verifying of my Coleoptera [sic]. I worked till meeting & after meeting till 2 o'clock in the night & finished them." He helped Mr. Warne make an insect case for the schoolroom, pinning the specimens under glass. By fixing the natural world, in all its beauty and complexity, under the hush of glass, framed and pinned and preserved forever, Victor must have found, in the still beauty of his craft, a certain solace from the relentless turbulence of his emotions.

But what Victor managed to push beneath the surface during the day only returned at night with redoubled vividness. With Mary gone and all correspondence with her blocked, Victor suffered in his dreams: apocalyptic visions of solitude, waste, and catastrophe. He dreamed of snowdrifts, ice-choked rivers, train wrecks, all with Mary's "thin and down cast face," Mary "dressed in black," floating like an afterimage in the middle of the scene. "I dreamed that the cars were going by and one was off from the wheels & the rest of the train went on & left it," Victor recorded on June 15, a scarcely veiled symbol for his feelings of abandonment by Mary. Or again, later that summer, "I was . . . by a roaring river where many were carried down among cakes of ice [George E. Cragin] & I were trying to pull away some cakes that were nearly crushing a fine young woman she said don't kill me we said we will save you & George E lifted her in his arms and disappeared down the torrent." "I dreamed that my brothers killed someone & I buried them in a snow drift." Victor's dreams were filled with frozen bodies, disappearing or disappeared—bodies hidden, crushed, saved, killed. One can feel the conflicted core of his psyche frozen by rage and despair both.[34]

And then, one day, news: Mary was back from Wallingford.

Victor and Mary met in front of the Children's House, of all places. She was two months pregnant—not by Mr. Leonard, as originally ordered, but by Noyes's eldest son, Theodore Noyes, a "scientific" combination specifically (and, one imagines, strategically) engineered by John Humphrey himself. "Will they tear the hearts out of both of us?" wondered a benumbed Victor.[35]

Mary was sick almost continuously during the first months of her pregnancy. Victor tended to her as if he were the father of the child, bringing her grapes, sage tea, porridge—whatever she might keep down. He put hot cloths on her head and rubbed her temples; he massaged her stomach to soothe the vomiting. They had "connection" several times, which Victor noted always made her pains go away. Surely the disappearance of symptoms was a sign of magnetic equilibrium and, consequently, divine benediction. Health meant one was in good communication with Christ, and Victor relayed these stories of sexual healing with obvious relish, as vindications in the face of continuing Community criticism of his and Mary's love.[36]

Through the chill months of January and February, Victor and Mary entered into a comfortable domestic routine. In the evenings, Victor cooked her oysters and eggnog, which he brought to her room; afterward, they sat together quietly while Victor wrote in his journal and Mary sewed a gown for her baby. The baby had started to move, and together they put their hands on Mary's belly to feel for the kicks. "I lay down on her bed for an hour last night after meeting with my hand on her I felt the baby move 3 or four times after she went to sleep & the night before I felt it 10 or 12 times before I went to sleep."[37]

But, once again, their domestic peace was to prove short-lived. On April 5, Theodore Noyes arrived from Wallingford; as if in lockstep response to the appearance of the patriarch's son Mary and Victor found themselves once again under community censure. Victor stayed away from Mary for one week before applying to Noyes's sister Mrs. Skinner for permission to see her again. Mrs. Skinner refused, claiming "she was afraid my influence would be bad for Mary & draw her down into a sickley [sic] state." In direct contradiction to Victor's belief that his continuous contact with Mary had brought about a magnetic improvement in her health, the larger community judged Victor's brooding spirit to be an "evil principality" on Mary's weakness.[38]

In the midst of this turmoil, Victor developed a toothache and went to have his tooth pulled. "I took gas the first breath I could taste it & the third I felt at the bottom of my lungs & the fourth or fifth I felt a slight prickling sensation down my legs to my toes & every thing seem dark & I was asleep." The warm blanket of oblivion settling into the grooves of his brain, the pain in his tooth, and then the pain in his heart slowly released their pinching grasp; Victor allowed himself to let go, the forgetfulness total, consciousness numb, not unlike the frozen bodies of his nightmares.[39]

On June 22, Victor felt the baby's heart and counted its beats: 109 beats per minute. He listened to Mary's heartbeat over the baby's, following the complex weave of pulsing blood. That night at 11:00 he went out to get some leaves for his silkworms and glimpsed a light in Mary's room. It was a clear June evening, warm with the stirring quickness of summer, the scent of blossoms on the air. The sap was running thick in the leaves Victor snapped off the tree on the North Lawn.

Later that morning, at 4:00, Mr. Herrick woke Victor, pulling him up out of his dreams: at 2:10 that night, Mary had given birth to a plump, seven-pound baby girl, stillborn.

"I did not sleep anymore," Victor wrote.[40]

9

Twilight of the Gods

I t was the spring of 1865 and Theodore Noyes, a student at Yale's medical school, was following his professor around during patient rounds. "Case 2," he marked in his notebook; "Small girl—5 yrs.—abnormal discharge of urine too frequently—nervous temperament, mother thinks it hereditary," he jotted down. The doctor provided no diagnosis—perhaps the combination of nerves and heredity was thought diagnosis enough—but instead prescribed a course of treatment for "general health," duly noted by Theodore: a dose of cinchona, a homeopathic preparation made of tree bark, and a "wine glassful infusion of bitter orange peel" daily.[1]

Theodore was one of twelve promising young Oneida men who had been sent off to Yale in the 1860s, some enrolling in the medical school and others in the newly founded Sheffield Scientific School, one of the first institutions of its kind in the United States, supplementing the traditional liberal arts curriculum with courses specifically in the sciences and mathematics. Though recognizing the risk he was taking in allowing the new generation such unprecedented contact with outsiders, Noyes, like many nineteenth-century Americans, was confident that the exciting new vistas opened by science would only confirm the truths of revealed religion. Science and religion would work hand in hand in humanity's progressive march toward perfection. Beginning in 1865, the pages of *The Circular* were peppered with periodic reports from the New Haven students documenting their medical and engineering adventures. Theodore Noyes and George Cragin reported attending Dr. Flint's invigorating lectures (where they watched their mentor vivisect pigeons to demonstrate the effect of removing various portions of the brain); they regularly attended dissections, amputations, and surgeries (during one of which the medical team sought to reconstruct the nose of an unfortunate woman who had had her appendage bitten off in a drunken brawl). Noyes senior hopped eagerly onto the scientific bandwagon, explaining the part medical physiology would henceforward play in Oneida's overall resurrection plan. Claiming that Oneida had pushed as far as it could in terms of securing humanity's salvation from sin (its Perfectionist phase) and perverted economic and sexual relations (its communist phase), Noyes proposed that Oneida's true destiny was to achieve "Anastatism," or a fully realized resurrection state. Oneida was slated "to develop not only Anastatic Theology and Sociology, but finally an Anastatic Physiology, or, if you please, an Anastatic school of Medicine." Having vanquished the blights of sin and marriage, Oneida could now take a crack at curing the world of death and sickness.[2]

Theodore, John Humphrey Noyes's eldest son and the only surviving child of the five he had sired by Harriet Noyes, was generally recognized to be the leader of the young generation. He was highly intelligent, with a keen, critical mind, and of the same intellectual bent as his father, if less pugnacious in the assertion of his ideas. Corpulent, with flashing black eyes and a handsome dark beard, Theodore was, also like his father, something of a ladies' man and a great favorite among the young women in the Community. Among his sweethearts was his first cousin Tirzah Miller, in whom, expert lover though he may have been, he met his match. His love letters to her from New Haven are, by turns, tender and reproachful. In one letter he taxed her with being "intentionally cruel" to him during her fellowship with another member, William Hinds, though as a good communist, trained to avoid the snares of special love, Theodore was piously "conscious that the discipline did him good."[3]

Theodore Noyes must have been something of an enigma for his Yale classmates. Medicine was just beginning to gain social cachet as a recognized profession in the 1860s; its eager adepts were filled with a sturdy nineteenth-century faith in science mixed, no doubt, with a healthy dose of the ambition to gain a foothold in the Victorian social hierarchy. As a free-loving communist, Theodore was, among this set, a square peg in a round hole: by day, rubbing shoulders with his colleagues as they furiously scribbled notes in anatomy lecture and, by night, penning love notes by lamplight to Tirzah in his modest scholar's quarters.

John Humphrey was passionately attached to the idea that Theodore should succeed him as leader of the Community. Yet as every student of history knows, succession can be a bloody business. And so it would prove at Oneida.

BY THE EARLY 1870S, JOHN HUMPHREY NOYES'S CONFIDENCE THAT BIBLE Communism could be dipped in the acid bath of science without getting burned was being tested. He was not alone; beginning in the years following the end of the Civil War, the conflicting claims of religion and science fueled nationwide debate. The radical evolutionary theory proffered in Darwin's 1850 *On the Origin of Species*, though slow to take off, began to gather a loyal following within American scientific circles and universities in the 1860s. While some men of science stonewalled against this obvious affront to the biblical account of Creation, proclaiming it tantamount to atheism, others found in evolution confirmation of their more liberal Christian theories about the progressive perfection of the human race. Charles Loring Brace, a leading social worker and reformer of the period, reread Darwin as an aid to, rather than a thorn in the side of, the Christian march toward improved humanity. "For if the Darwinian theory be true, the law of natural selection applies to all the moral history of mankind, as well as the physical. Evil must die ultimately as the weaker element, in the struggle with the good." John Humphrey Noyes echoed Brace's progressive reasoning in his own 1872 *Essay on Scientific Propagation*; stirpiculture was, precisely, the "scientific" application of Darwinian evolutionary principles to the moral improvement of the human species.[4]

Eventually, evolution was packaged and sold to a more popular audience. Such widely read magazines as *The North American Review, Popular Science Monthly,* and *The Atlantic Monthly*—all three of which Oneida received regularly in its library—reserved ample space in their columns for discussions of biological evolution and its latest offshoot, Herbert Spencer's application of the principle of natural selection to man's social and cultural development (what would eventually take on the name social Darwinism). A genial, watered-down version of evolution even found a voice in the pulpit. Boston minister Henry Ward Beecher, dubbed "the most famous man in America," preached the absolute compatibility of evolution and the theistic "argument from design," proclaiming himself a "cordial Christian evolutionist."[5]

One book that made the rounds among the younger generation at Oneida in the 1860s and 1870s was the anonymously published *Vestiges of the Natural History of Creation.* This proto-Darwinist treatise on the evolution of life on earth takes the reader on a dizzying journey back in geological time, tracing the eventual emergence of the human species to "the unpretending forms of various zoophytes and polypes" embedded in the earliest layers of the earth's crust. Still, having to reckon mollusks as our biological avatars was somehow not a barrier to this doughty author's belief that man had been created in God's image. The author of *Vestiges* airily attributes evolution to the intelligent design of a benign creator and appoints the human species undisputed ruler of all animate creatures.[6]

But other veins of scientific thought and skepticism circulating in American intellectual circles during this period were more difficult to square with the existence of an all-knowing creator God. French philosopher Auguste Comte developed a theory he called "positivism," which held that all humans could know of the world was external phenomena and the scientifically derived laws guiding their behavior, never the underlying essence, or "true," nature of things. The primitive belief in God (or gods) as higher powers controlling the movements of the universe would eventually be surpassed by faith in the scientific method as the only reliable way to interpret experience. In Comte's generally skeptical system, which flourished in American universities during the 1870s, John Humphrey Noyes's claims to divine inspiration as God's spokesperson on earth were so much mumbo jumbo.

This strain of skepticism eventually came to permeate the heart of Oneida's young generation. In 1871, a small coterie of "positivists," led by Daniel Bailey, Theodore Noyes, and my great-great-grandfathers, Charles Cragin and Joseph Skinner, began to form at Oneida. Called out by John Humphrey Noyes for spreading a "narcotic [influence], dulling the spiritual sense" among the Community's youth, Daniel Bailey admitted that for several years he had been laboring under a "crust of heathenism"; he would eventually leave the Community in 1872.[7]

More disturbing, however, was the possible defection of those closer to Noyes's inner power circle: his nephew Joseph Skinner, the only son of his sister Harriet, and his own son Theodore. Joseph was the first to balk publicly. Despite several desperate attempts on the part of Community criticism committees to convert him back into a believer, on April 10, 1872, Joseph left the Community. At that night's Evening Meeting, Noyes's terse announcement of his nephew's departure left no question as to the patriarch's displeasure. "In consequence of abandoning himself to science and to Daniel Bailey, Joseph had become substantially a Positivist. The unbelieving spirit over him gave way more or less at times but returned, and finally could not live in the atmosphere of the Community."[8]

Entries in my great-great-grandfather's diary following his exodus— since he had taken his engineering degree at Yale, he chose New Haven as a reasonable landing place—record a young man adrift in an unfamiliar world. While a student in residence at the Sheffield Scientific School, Joseph had been a happy enough visitor in that world; but now that he had become a permanent resident, he felt baffled. His first order of business was to find employment, and through his old Sheffield contacts he was offered work assisting a professor in "making calculations for a statistical atlas for the government, and in drawing maps." "Thus, just one month after leaving the O.C.," he writes with justifiable contentment, "I got the first definite promise of having something to do to earn my bread and butter by." At other times, his diary reads like the notes of an inquisitive visitor to another planet, as he records his observations of "outsiders" and their alien rituals: "One evening not long ago, passing on the Green, I saw a gathering in front of Trinity Church. It proved to be a wedding party. I went into the church and witnessed the ceremony, it being the first time that I ever saw a wedding."[9]

Theodore Noyes managed to hold out a bit longer. But a little over one year after Joseph Skinner's defection, in July 1873, Theodore admitted that he too had concluded that he was an agnostic, if not an atheist, and that he could no longer believe in his father's divine commission. To his father's great chagrin, Theodore decided the only honest option was to leave the Community, at least for a trial period. And so, with fifty dollars in his pocket, Theodore took the train for New York, his father's parting words to him—that he "hoped he would come back"—resounding with a kind of elemental and tragic simplicity. "No one," Theodore had replied, with equal poignancy, "could wish he could be changed more than he."[10]

The separation was of short duration, in the end. "Home and the love of friends," the estranged Theodore wrote to his mother, "are the best things we can have." Within a week, Theodore pleaded for readmission; while his religious beliefs remained unchanged, his week of soul searching had convinced him that he was, in truth, a committed communist and that the Community offered the best environment for him to live out those social ideals. He suggested to his father the extraordinary proposal that the Community adopt a nonsectarian policy, in which religion would be entirely a matter of individual conscience, as a means of "sav[ing] the coming generation, for they *will* think." This was too much for Noyes, who responded that there could be "no hope of the unity which is essential to Communism without agreement in religion." Theodore was finally readmitted, on the condition that he "come with an honest wish and purpose *now* to go through the [conversion] which you admit is possible in the future and which is an inexorable necessity if you are ever really to rejoin the Community."[11]

John Humphrey Noyes had a plan that he believed might win some converts among the young agnostics to his cause. Spiritualism—the belief that certain gifted mediums could, in a state of altered consciousness or trance, make contact with dead spirits—was a popular fad in the 1870s, with séances held in parlor rooms across the country and mediums drawing crowds at top entertainment venues. The habit of talking with the dead had begun humbly enough, in 1848 in Hydesville, New York, in the house of a Methodist farmer by the name of John D. Fox. It suddenly happened one day, in this small hamlet, that a series of unholy rapping sounds were to be heard in any room of the house occupied by Fox's two teenage daughters, Margaret and Kate. The rapping ghost had the uncanny ability to answer questions using an agreed-upon number of taps, by which means the girls divined that the poor haunt was the ghost of a murdered peddler buried in the cellar of Fox's home. Abandoning the house, the frightened family found that the ghosts followed them wherever they went and, in fact, demanded, via raps, that the girls start giving public demonstrations (and charging admission). Spiritualism was born.

Noyes recognized in spiritualism a homespun version of the spirit talk he had been practicing ever since first receiving messages from the invisible world of the primitive church in 1834. The spiritualist's belief in the material reality of the spirit world—of "ghosts thick as puddings," as Noyes phrased it—offered him an opening gambit for the so-called positivists. For spirit contact was not just entertainment, it was an object of scientific study, as well. No less eminent an intellect than Harvard philosopher William James took the phenomenon of spirit contact entirely seriously in his writings on the science of consciousness. While he and his colleagues at the London Society for Psychical Research found a fair amount of quackery in their investigations into practicing mediums and clairvoyants, they persisted in believing that spirit contact was, in principle, scientifically possible. They imagined the medium's consciousness as a kind of wireless telegraph—a radio avant la lettre—that could tune into the brain waves of departed spirits and translate their messages for the living. By 1870, rapping had become hopelessly outmoded, rather like Sumerian cuneiform; the more sophisticated modern spirits communicated either verbally, by ventriloquizing the medium, or via automatic writing, where a pen placed in the medium's hand would unconsciously scribble messages from the dead. The "sitters" at a séance—those who came to contact their dead loved ones—would pose questions to the medium and receive spoken or penned responses.

The particular spirit occupying the medium's body at any one time, called the "control," would relay messages from the clustered masses of the dead who, like the shade of Odysseus's mother in Hades, were unable to make contact with their loved ones on their own. One particularly effective medium William James discovered was named Leonora Piper; in the trance consciousness, Piper's body was taken over by a control calling himself Dr. Phinuit, a self-appointed guide to the spirit world who claimed to be able to speak for many of the sitters' relatives. The dead were an orderly bunch, generally speaking, and usually waited their turn to speak through the medium one by one. Occasionally there was some line cutting, however, and on at least one occasion, Dr. Phinuit and another spirit got into a scuffle over who would control Mrs. Piper, leading the disgruntled spirit to scribble an insulting message to Dr. Phinuit and resulting in a "struggle in Mrs. Piper's organism" for control of her writing hand.[12]

John Humphrey Noyes, capitalizing on spiritualism's scientific pretensions, encouraged Theodore to make a full investigation into the topic. Theodore and Francis Wayland-Smith paired up to spend the next year traveling around the country to visit famous mediums and bone up on the voluminous literature concerning contact with the spirit world. Theodore stocked the Community library shelves with tomes on mediums, mesmerism, and theories of immortality, while Francis Wayland-Smith wrote a series of articles for *The Circular* in 1874, entitled "Controls," in which he reinterpreted revealed religion in the quasi-scientific terms of spiritualism, attempting an official fusion of science and religion of the sort John Humphrey had hoped for. Citing the Hebrews and Greeks, in his first article, as cultures convinced of the reality of supernatural influences on humans, Wayland-Smith denied the very existence of free will and claimed, instead, that "the only scope which is given to our free-will and independence is to choose what invisible control we will live under": Christ or the devil. The modern spirit medium, buffeted about at the whim of the different controls taking charge of her consciousness, was merely an exaggerated image for the Christian, who must make a careful study of the invisible forces motivating his behavior at any one time and choose wisely among them.[13]

If invisible spirits from the other side could be said to be our primary controls, Wayland-Smith did not want to exclude the very real magnetic influence that our fellow mortals have on us. When one is with a "strong, magnetic man," Wayland-Smith theorized, "you are very apt to feel, think and talk as he does, or as he wants you to; and when you go away and meet another such, you may feel, think and talk in a very different way, and that within the same day." Wayland-Smith warned his readers to be mindful of the way spirits dominating others could affect them in a "secondary way," through the medium of the other's consciousness. "If A. is under a certain spiritual control, his friend B. may be said to be under the same control in a secondary way. . . . For that reason B. ought to regulate his intercourse and fellowship with A. by very much the same principles that he would apply to primary controls." The Community system of Mutual Criticism worked as efficiently as it did, Wayland-Smith avowed, precisely because it helped the criticized member identify negative controls, whether primary or secondary, and labor against them while striving to become more receptive to Christ's beneficent influxes.[14]

Francis Wayland-Smith, with his enthusiastic belief in the healing power of "ice and strong criticism" as a means of casting out devils and curing diphtheria, was undoubtedly a more doctrinaire follower of Noyes's theology than the medically trained Theodore. Nonetheless, after a year of soaking in spiritualism, Theodore made an official statement to the Community in March 1875 of his "reconversion" to a belief in the spirit world. "I think there is conclusive evidence of the existence of a spiritual world, inhabited by spiritual beings," he avowed. "I think it extremely probable that these beings have lived as men and women in this world. The question of spirit identity I do not think fully settled, but our continued existence in the spiritual world seems to me a fact, and furnishes a satisfactory ground for action. I think I believe it as fully as anyone in the Community." As tepid an endorsement of his radical theology as this may have sounded, Noyes took his son's words as sufficient support to propose that, while he was away at Wallingford, Theodore be appointed to the position of "Father" of Oneida—a kind of training position for the ultimate post of Community leader that Noyes envisioned for his son. The Community took up the question with great gusto and debate but, ultimately, at the end of six days of discussion, voted in the negative.[15]

Reasons for the vote of no confidence varied from person to person. Some thought it unseemly that Noyes should be setting up a dynastic empire. In her journal, Tirzah Miller railed against the idea of an "aristocracy of blood" forming in the Community as antithetical to the very spirit of Christianity and communism. "One of our dominant ideas is that the natural should be subjected to the spiritual—that the Community has a right at any time to step in and set aside the natural when it interferes with the spiritual. We are taught to consider the children as belonging to all the Community with equal claims on our love. Why should not this doctrine be applied to the Noyes children? Is not Mr. Noyes as likely and even more likely to transmit his spirit to those who have adopted his faith than to those who are of his seed?" As Noyes's niece, Tirzah candidly admitted that her own position within the Community had been artificially elevated: "I am conscious," she mused, "that I myself have in the past held a position which I by no means merited."[16]

Theodore's reply to his rebuff by the Community was even-handed and civil, carefully defending his competence for the job while graciously accepting the will of the majority: "The Community certainly need fear nothing from my ambition. I am not too humble to say I cannot do a thing when I think I can, but I certainly grasp at nothing but a place in the hearts of the whole Community." Noyes was not done prodding his son forward to leadership of the Community, however. By 1877 the patriarch, at sixty-six years old, was feeling his age. Increasingly deaf, he suffered as well from a recurring throat infection that prevented him from talking above a whisper, making him ineffective as the leader of Evening Meeting. The time was ripe, then, to act upon the question of a successor.[17]

This time around, Noyes left no doubt as to who would have the final word in the matter. On May 17, 1877, he addressed the Community in a speech claiming his absolute right to determine his successor, noting that he had been called to leadership "not by vote of the members but by the will of God" and, as such, could rightfully "dispose of the government of the Community" as he saw fit. Putting a positive spin on Theodore's apostasy, Noyes hailed his son's temptations as rigorous spiritual "training" for leadership, not unlike his own New York experience some forty years earlier: "He now believes in the spiritual world, in Providence and in inspiration, and I have evidence that he is inspired by the same control that has carried me through my career." Noyes was using the vocabulary of spirit controls that by the end of the 1870s had become the lingua franca of the Community, lessening the pain of the transition by asserting that the same "control" that had inspired Noyes since his earliest election as God's chosen medium would continue in charge under Theodore's reign. Cowed, perhaps, by the divine right being asserted, the Community rubber-stamped Noyes's proposal that Theodore should be appointed Noyes's successor. In a letter of thanks to the Community the day following his appointment, Theodore made a plea for unity in the great weaving together of science and religion that he saw as the primary goal of the Community moving forward: "I think we can all take hold in unity for the pursuit of truth in the great circle which embraces Spiritual-ism, Christianity, Communism, stirpiculture, and science of every kind," he reassured them.[18]

During his investigations into spiritualism, Theodore had worked closely with my great-great-grandmother Ann Bailey Hobart, a gifted spirit medium described in Francis Wayland-Smith's journal as "the strongest woman we have" in the Community. The two began an intense and, ultimately, turbu-lent love affair. Theodore accordingly appointed her the general woman su-perintendent at Oneida, a politically sensitive position previously held by Noyes's sister Harriet Skinner. As "mother" of the Community, Ann was to act as the women's confidante in sexual matters, as well as to keep unofficial tabs on which men and women were pairing off for interviews. One of Ann and Theodore's first items of business was to put some order into sexual relations at Oneida, for the old custom of having the "invitations given by responsible women," Theodore observed, "[had] passed away and such matters are often arranged with personal friends." The ruling duo revived the original system, whereby all invitations would pass through a number of vetted older women, who would duly record them and turn the records over to Theodore once a week (on Sundays). This sexual bookkeeping was not the only matter Ann and Theodore took in hand. At several Evening Meetings, Theodore chided Community members on their lack of public spiritedness, claiming that not all members were pulling their weight in the matter of job rotations. "There are some among us who suffer from what is no more than laziness. I do not feel like mincing the matter at all," he asserted, announcing that he would start keeping statistics in order to chart each member's productivity.[19]

Perhaps as a result of their attempts to tighten the reins in the sensitive areas of love and work—activities whose "great regulator," Theodore de-clared rather sententiously, must be "walking in the light"—dissatisfaction with Theodore and Ann's joint rule emerged almost at once. This took the extraordinary form of a rumor buzzing around among the rank and file that the pair was planning "to establish themselves with a few favorites in a villa overlooking the Hudson River . . . [and] govern the Community by means of administrative reports, rescripts and regulations." Theodore, caught up in his work charts and sex logs, was accused of the "spirit of legalism," a clumsy overfondness for rules and regulations when organic grace, or an inspired group consensus on the right course of action, was the Community's preferred mode of governance.[20]

Such centralized mechanisms of control were fine and well so long as John Humphrey Noyes held his flock contained under his magnetic influence, with his will alone accepted as the final and unquestioned arbiter in matters of dispute. Within this enchanted circle of his influence, there could be debate and questions, discussions and votes: democracy aplenty in the day-to-day running of Community life. Noyes was a remarkably supple sort of autocrat. But Noyes's once-potent mantle of sexual and political authority was fading fast, and Theodore, despite his charm and intelligence, was woefully unable to fill his father's shoes in this respect. Mandates regulating the private life of work and the affections that would have been eagerly accepted as wholesome discipline for the soul under the senior Noyes's command became, in Theodore's hand, the dead letter of an empty law—not inspiration but simply drudgery. The communal fantasy of a kingdom ruled by whimsical, autocratic proxy exacerbated the general sense of panic and confusion that members felt in the vacuum left by Noyes's gradual retreat into old age.

Ann Hobart was an ambitious woman; her brother Daniel Bailey, the positivist agitator who had left the Community in 1872, once said of her, " 'You will find her out; she has got her eye on being the head of the Community.' " Jealous of Theodore, Ann was accused of abusing her position as Community "mother" by manipulating interviews to exclude him from having any sexual partners beside herself. If we accept her brother's assessment of her character, part of Ann's effort to gain control of the Community also involved the rather risky strategy of sinking Theodore in his father's estimation; in one explosive episode, she went to the elder Noyes directly and angrily denounced Theodore as being false to Community beliefs, in particular male continence. Noyes saw the ploy for what it probably was—an attempt, born of jealousy, to undermine confidence in Theodore's leadership—and confronted Theodore about his less-than-loyal helpmate. But the son stood stubbornly by Ann's side, making an elaborate argument drawn from his spiritualist philosophy that, being as sensitive a medium as she was, Ann had fallen under the control of bad spirits and should thus not be held accountable for her critical outbursts. She was also, according to Theodore, under the control of *his* spirit, passively channeling his own ambivalence about Bible Communist orthodoxy. The fault was his, not hers; she was merely the impersonal conduit through which Theodore's internal doubts manifested themselves. "Instead of using her as a lever with which to work on each other," Theodore suggested to his father, they should "send messages of peace and concord across her."[21]

Noyes did not buy Theodore's explanation for Ann's destructive behavior. Instead of Ann's being a helpless medium channeling Theodore's criticism of certain facets of Community doctrine, Noyes determined that Theodore's apostasy had, in fact, its very beginnings in his connection with Ann, whose own "unbelief and irreverence" had originally infected Theodore and caused him to depart from his father's path. Ann Bailey's father, Seba Bailey, Noyes asserted, had been a powerful agent of diatrephiasis in the Community, a pseudo-scientific neologism Noyes invented to describe "the preeminence mania, or the Who-shall-be-greatest mania" that occasionally made the rounds at Oneida. According to this interpretation, Ann, under the negative control of the "Bailey spirit," had hijacked Theodore's soul; far from holding her under his own influence, Theodore was himself in the destructive grip of Ann's unbelief. Unable to come to an agreement with his father on the question of Ann—and, more specifically, who had hypnotized whom—Theodore resigned leadership of Oneida in January 1878. His ill-starred reign had lasted less than seven months.[22]

WHEN THEY HAD FIRST MOVED TO THE HOWLING WILDERNESS FRONTIER of Oneida Creek in 1848, John Humphrey Noyes and his band of Perfectionists had been in the vanguard of national movements that questioned the sanctity of marriage and the nuclear family. Feminists, free lovers, and anarchists had all worked, in varying ways and with varying degrees of success, at reforming traditional monogamy. But by the early 1870s, the national sentiment on questions of marriage had dramatically shifted. Moral conservatives were circling the wagons in defense of marriage and the nuclear family.

In 1873, Anthony Comstock, who had been appointed as a special agent for the New York Committee for the Suppression of Vice, delivered a trove of obscene materials—playing cards with pictures of naked ladies, contraceptives, salacious novels—to the United States Senate chambers with the goal of having legislation passed to limit their circulation and thus combat "a virus more destructive to the innocence and purity of youth . . . than . . . the most deadly disease to the body." Congress complied, passing the nation's first antiobscenity law on March 3, 1873. What came to be called the Comstock Law prohibited the circulation by U.S. mail of all obscene materials, including information regarding contraception and abortion. It also gave postmasters the right to inspect mail and seize suspicious material. Ever prudent, Oneida responded by cutting out all reference to their birth control practices from their publications and by ceasing to print and distribute Noyes's popular essay *Male Continence*.[23]

But Comstock was not done with his crusade against obscenity. Increasingly, he saw the free love movement propagating a breakdown in the American family. In 1872, Henry Ward Beecher, America's preeminent Protestant minister, was accused of committing adultery with his best friend's wife, Elizabeth Tilton. The titillating news was leaked to women's rights and free love advocate Virginia Woodhull. Woodhull was outraged that Beecher, who had publicly condemned her for her open advocacy of free love, was practicing free love in secret, and she published the story in her New York City newspaper, *Woodhull and Claflin's Weekly*. Seeing his opening, Comstock swooped in and personally arranged for Woodhull's arrest and imprisonment on charges of distributing obscene material, thus inaugurating a spate of attacks on free lovers under the Comstock Law. But the Beecher-Tilton affair, as it soon came to be called in the press, was just getting started. Tilton's husband charged Beecher with adultery, and the subsequent trials of Woodhull and Beecher led to a media feeding frenzy. While Woodhull was released on a technicality and Beecher's trial resulted in a hung jury, the national dustup served as a lightning rod for religious and moral crusaders across the nation. Oneida could hardly escape being caught in the net of the "moral belligerence" that, as historian Nancy Cott has argued, was the prevailing atmosphere surrounding questions of marriage in the 1870s.[24]

Oneida's own nemesis appeared in the person of John Mears, a Protestant minister from nearby Hamilton College who was enraged by the "systematic concubinage" being practiced at Oneida. Heartened by a recent decision handed down by the courts in *Reynolds v. the United States* that gave Congress the power to criminalize bigamy in the Mormon territory of Utah, Mears wrote a screed in *The New York Times* on April 10, 1879, in which he excoriated the New York senators and representatives in Congress for opposing Mormon polygamy in Utah while countenancing Oneidan Complex Marriage at home. In short, the ambient national mood boded ill for the Oneidans' unconventional definition of what might constitute a family.[25]

With the dismal collapse of Theodore's regime in January 1878, John Humphrey Noyes effectively resumed control at Oneida. Rife with internal dissent, the community braced itself for the onslaught of the local clergy under Mears's zealous command. Several restless voices within the Community, among them James Towner and the more staid William Hinds, had formed themselves into something of an opposition party; they were "strongly advocating a representative government," according to the diary of Francis Wayland-Smith, a Noyes loyalist. William Hinds, more accommodating than the rough-and-tumble Towner, wrote an article in *The American Socialist* (the new, more "scientific" journal replacing *The Circular*) entitled "Democratic Theocracy," in which he delicately suggested that a nation could transfer its sovereignty to God but "would still be left to manage its municipal affairs by some form of political mechanism." Rather than electing a single ruler or legislative body to rule, Mr. Hinds proposed to let "a periodical paper be established as the sole medium of proposing, discussing, and recording laws. . . . [T]he whole people [would resolve] themselves into a permanent legislative convention." Noyes responded to the article tersely, claiming that those discontented with his administration were agnostics who did not "have any idea of annexation to the Kingdom of God," while those members who still believed in the immanent presence of Christ in the world were "contented with the liberty they [had]" under Noyes's scepter. Noyes was not about to buckle on the central question of God's preferred form of government: benevolent theocracy, not democratic self-rule, was the only way a heavenly kingdom would hold together.[26]

Tired, emotionally bruised, and increasingly isolated, Noyes did not escape that perennial temptation of crumbling dictators: paranoia. Like a beleaguered Macbeth, Noyes lashed out at his own Macduff, Francis Wayland-Smith, for an article the latter had written in the same issue of *The American Socialist* in which Hinds's article appeared, speculating on the viability of various forms of world government. Reading into its assessment of republicanism a veiled criticism of his own autocratic authority, Noyes held firm to his belief in his absolute right to rule. "I have not been put into my present position by the members of this Community," he protested to Wayland-Smith, who recorded the conversation in his diary. "The real stockholders in our institution are the men and women of the invisible world. They have built up the Community and it is to them that I am accountable. I am resolved not to relinquish one iota of the authority they have given me."[27]

The situation at Oneida had reached the point of a standoff, with Hinds and Towner holding steady on one side, and Noyes, "more and more autocratic and secretive," according to Wayland-Smith, refusing to give an inch. Wayland-Smith's journal entry on June 9 continues: "I wish I could make a complete pen-picture of the state of the O.C. at the present time. It is in the strangest condition imaginable. The disaffection continues and spreads. . . . There is a great deal of uneasiness and anxiety among the thinking classes. All are waiting for something decisive to happen."[28]

And then, something decisive did happen: early in the morning of June 22, 1879, John Humphrey Noyes slipped out of the Mansion House into the still-black dawn, mounted a waiting carriage, and fled to Canada, pleading he was forced into the move by his imminent arrest at the hands of New York state authorities. Just a day earlier, the *Syracuse Standard* had carried an article whose headlines no doubt spooked Noyes: "The Oneida Community. Another meeting of the Central New York Committee. The leading communist, Noyes, to be arrested. Legal proceedings to be commenced. Testimony being taken which stamps the Oneida Community as far worse in their practices than the polygamists of Utah."[29]

In retrospect, arrest would have been unlikely. There was not a clear legal case against Noyes, for one thing. And, Mears's righteous zeal notwithstanding, Noyes and his followers enjoyed widespread support in the region: with the Community's successful business ventures propping up the local economy, their immediate neighbors looked upon them kindly and turned a blind eye to their sexual eccentricities. But Noyes, sounding not unlike the panicked heroine in a nineteenth-century sentimental novel, would record his flight as a hair's-breadth escape at the hands of his enemies. When he finally crossed the Canadian border, "I was dreadfully hungry for rest and my heart took a great swallow of it," he was later to reminisce, though one cannot help wondering whether his extraordinary fatigue had been triggered not so much by his grueling journey as by the agonizing odyssey of his slow fall from power.[30]

Noyes's sudden decision to desert his flock stunned the Oneidans, but this was, after all, part of a well-established pattern with Noyes. Once upon a time, Noyes had mastered his rejection at the hands of Abigail Merwin by concocting an elaborate theological fantasy that made her his spiritual wife. Later, he had mastered his rejection at the hands of the Putney natives by fleeing to the central New York wilderness. Now, thirty years into his fragile truce with reality, John Humphrey Noyes found himself face-to-face with a rejection he could not master. And so he bolted.

THE TWILIGHT OF THE GODS—THE DEFEAT OF ONE GENERATION OF KINGS by their usurper children—is a staple human fable. The Norse Ragnarok saga predicts the death of the old gods and, after trial by fire and water, the renewal of the earth. Richard Wagner wrote this scene of divine immolation into his Ring cycle: Valhalla goes up in flames at the end of *Götterdämmerung*. And in "The Fall of Hyperion," John Keats imagined the psychic pain of the tumbled Titans, evoking "grey-hair'd Saturn, quiet as a stone," whose solemn figure awes Hyperion:

> *Saturn is fallen, am I too to fall?*
> *Am I to leave this haven of my rest,*
> *This cradle of my glory, this soft clime,*
> *This calm luxuriance of blissful light,*
> *These crystalline pavilions, and pure fanes,*
> *Of all my lucent empire?*

Slowly, almost imperceptibly, the gods of Science and Doubt had toppled Oneida's pantheon of powers and principalities, the gleaming saints of the primitive church, and Saint Paul himself, all once so crisp and clear in their regnant majesty. John Humphrey Noyes's complex cosmos faded until its lineaments must have appeared to former believers with the flickering indistinctness of an afterimage. Forty years earlier, Noyes had taken up the Lucifer-like task of transforming the world into a kingdom of love, on earth as it was in heaven, with himself at its glorious center. On June 22, 1879, he was, at last, expulsed from his lucent empire.

10

Things Fall Apart

WITH JOHN HUMPHREY NOYES IN ABSENTIA (INCONGRUOUSLY "FISH-ing on the St. Lawrence in Canada," according to a journal entry by Francis Wayland-Smith), rumors at Oneida sprang up like wildfire, including the old saw that Noyes had once again appointed Theodore in charge of the Community (which turned out, once again, to be pure fantasy). Evening Meetings continued, tense but moderately civil. Noyes's sister Harriet Skinner noted that a passage from the Bible read in meeting the day following Noyes's departure particularly captivated the audience, with the recent "experience of the Community [giving] a new meaning to every word": *"Behold, how great a matter a little fire kindleth! And the tongue is a fire, a world of iniquity: so is the tongue among our members, that it defileth the whole body, and setteth on fire the course of nature: and it is set on fire of hell."* (James 3: 5) The tongue was indeed a fire; the backbiting and infighting, whispered accusations, and panicked rumors in the wake of Noyes's waning leadership were consuming Oneida.[1]

A scramble to fill the power vacuum at Oneida ensued, with Noyes loyalists closing ranks against the "proponents of anarchy," as Wayland-Smith termed them, opposition leaders James W. Towner and William Hinds. Though a staunch Noyes supporter, Wayland-Smith, who had collaborated professionally with Hinds as coeditor of *The American Socialist*, stepped into the role of mediator between the two warring parties. On June 25, 1879, Wayland-Smith wrote in his journal that he had had a sincere discussion with Hinds on the current political situation, during which he had clarified that while he "agreed with [Hinds] that the government of the Community might be made more representative to advantage," Hinds's method of going about it—bypassing Noyes altogether and "inaugurat[ing] a revolutionary movement"—was ill-advised and that the real way to accomplish change was to do it in collaboration with Noyes. Wayland-Smith believed that, having lost confidence in the founder, the "true and honorable way for [Hinds] was to leave, and not stay here and imperil our home by starting a revolution." To which Hinds replied, rather testily, that Wayland-Smith would be "grey as a rat" if he were to wait for any compromise to come from Noyes and that he fully intended to stay and "make such changes as he [thought] desirable" to the governance of the Community. A house divided if ever there was one.[2]

In Noyes's absence, the Administrative Council, consisting of members drawn from both the loyalist and opposition camps, was named and voted in. What the Hinds-Towner party demanded was, first, a measure of egalitarian, representative government in the running of the Community. In a list of "suggestions" drawn up by Hinds and submitted via Wayland-Smith to Noyes, suggestion number 3 proposed that the "question of Mr. Noyes's successor in the presidency" be subject to a vote by "all covenanted members" of the Oneida Community. This was a direct rebuff to Noyes's claim that he had the right to appoint his own successor.

If a more democratic distribution of political power was key to the Hinds-Towner reforms, of equal if not primary importance was the demand for the decentralization of sexual control in the Community. The right of "first husband"—the right to introduce virgins into Complex Marriage—had from the very beginning of the Community been Noyes's chief prerogative. For years, Noyes's unquestioned control of the Community's sexual relations helped keep a lid on sexual rivalry among the male members. Indeed, as Theodore Noyes would later explain, without his father's sexual dominance holding the Community together, the center would not hold. "To get at it, you must realize that the government of the Community was *by* complex marriage," Theodore claimed. "Much has been said about mutual criticism and in itself it certainly was a very powerful force in favor of law and order," he conceded. "But all moral government, no matter how benign, in the end has to look to penalties for its enforcement. The power of regulating the sexual relations of the members, inherent in the family at large and by common consent delegated to Father and his subordinates, constituted by far the most effectual means of government." His father, Theodore suggested, "possessed in a remarkable degree the faculty of convincing people that the use of this arbitrary power was exercised for their own good, and for many years there was very little dissatisfaction and no envy of his prerogative."[3]

Since 1877, in tandem with his efforts to install Theodore as his successor, Noyes had also taken to designating proxies, chosen from among his coterie of loyal insiders, in the matter of sexual initiations. He no doubt did so with a view to ensuring a smooth transfer of power—both sexual and political—from one generation to the next. But in opening up the possibility of distributing sexual spoils to men other than himself, Noyes opened to increasing questions his unilateral right to control the Community's flows of desire. According to Freud's anthropological fable in *Totem and Taboo*, primeval human society was ruled by one dominant male, or father figure, who allocated all the females to himself. One day, the envious brothers of the primal horde rose up, killed the father, and ate him. At Oneida, the father had been killed—at least symbolically—and now the sex-starved brothers were waiting in the wings, itching to move in.

Suggestion number 8 on Mr. Hinds's list was, then, an explicit demand that individual preference be given free rein in the matter of Complex Marriage: "[E]very member is to be absolutely free from the undesired sexual familiarity, approach, and control of every other person." In other words, Noyes's de facto control of who slept with whom, along with the general rule of ascending fellowship, by which the sexual lives of the younger members, in particular, had previously been controlled, were to be completely abolished in favor of individual preference. "The new rule is that there shall be no compulsion," wrote Francis Wayland-Smith, reporting on July 19 to Mr. Noyes, "and any considerable amount of moral suasion is construed as compulsion. I doubt if it would be proper under this new rule to do more than suggest to the young certain desirable lines of conduct." But Wayland-Smith saw that such a system would either "plunge [the Community] into marriage" or dead-end in an anarchic state of free love. "Now I see clearly that unless the young of both sexes are trained and controlled substantially as you have trained and controlled them in the past, our social system must eventually go down," he wrote. "And what troubles me is that I do not see how any other man or committee can hope to succeed with them on our system."[4]

Harriet Skinner told Noyes in a letter that she deplored the "awful state of disrespect and rowdyism" into which the young had fallen, which she attributed to having "separate[d] the girls from you and the ascending fellowship, and letting the young of both sexes run together without so much as a word of reproof." While she was somewhat heartened by the action the new governing committee was taking to "get . . . up a machine to bring them to order," she lamented the turn away from the reign of grace to the reign of law and the system of compulsion that was being substituted as a "schoolmaster" for the youth.

Theodore Noyes, for his part, was less sanguine yet as to the ability of "communism of the affections" to survive the shift in regimes. Ever the philosopher, he argued that through "experience and action of forces going on for thousands of years," outside society had worked out the best system for regulating the sexual passions as far as a monogamous model was concerned. Communism, on the other hand, was "a new form of society" that was best regulated according to the unique system that Noyes had pioneered. "Now that your system [is] departed from," Theodore reasoned in a letter to his father, "we are on a sliding scale that will certainly land us in the order outside. There is no stopping place—no modified form that will work."[5]

There were now three parties forming within Oneida. The loyalists wanted communism with Noyes at the head; the opposition wanted communism sprinkled with a dose of democracy and increased sexual freedom, without Noyes at the head. The emerging third party, led by Theodore Noyes and Francis Wayland-Smith, continued to support Noyes, but its adherents were pragmatic enough to admit that his reinstatement as head of the Community was unlikely. Yet without Noyes at the helm of the ship and the rule of ascending fellowship in place, all sanction for Complex Marriage would disappear, leading the Oneidans to fall into a state little better than the "free love" from which they had for so long strived to separate themselves. The lesser of two evils, this party believed, was to settle for some form of traditional monogamy; as Harriet Skinner reasoned, "I had rather have legitimate marriage than Berlin free love," referring contemptuously to Berlin Heights, the free love commune in Ohio of which James Towner had once been a member. Wayland-Smith was clear on the point as well, writing to Noyes, "I prefer the idea of cooperation and familism to communism in legality and subsequent shipwreck. . . . Do you not think that if you should withdraw your sanction from our sexual practices until such a time as your influence and authority should be restored, it would have a wholesome effect? I do."[6]

The young people within the Community tended to side with Wayland-Smith's option to restore monogamy—but not from any particular loyalty to Noyes or hope that his "influence and authority" might one day be restored. Rather, they feared that should the Community break up, the women in particular would be cast adrift in a hostile world, without a mate to act as "a guardian and provider and husband," a role the Community currently filled. Having imbibed positivist ideas, and with faltering faith in Noyes's divine commission, the young Oneidans were quite simply trying to hedge their social bets against the possible dissolution of the Community. "The young people as a class, and some of the older ones, are free to speak of their preference for a more limited sexual fellowship than Mr. Noyes has always advocated," Wayland-Smith observed in his diary. "The more bold and ultra of them coolly declare in favor of a monogamic relation." Wayland-Smith immediately divined the source of such a sentiment. Complex Marriage and stirpiculture had created an almost dizzyingly complicated family structure, in which a single woman often had children by several different men, and men had fathered children by multiple women. A Community breakup and ensuing efforts to patch together traditional nuclear families out of such a jumble would render Oneida's failure "the most dismal and heart-rending one in the annals of communism," Wayland-Smith commented soberly.[7]

From his exile in Canada, John Humphrey Noyes remained in constant epistolary contact with Wayland-Smith and other supporters of the newly formed "third party." Together, they drafted a resolution proposing that Complex Marriage be suspended and presented it to the Administrative Council for consideration on August 20, 1879. Finding themselves blind-sided by this sudden tack toward traditional marriage on the part of Noyes acolytes like Theodore, Harriet, and Francis, the Towner-Hinds party objected vigorously to this trend away from the communism of affections and attempted to take the moral high ground on the continuation of Complex Marriage, quoting Noyes himself on the subject and thus appearing the true loyalists to the original cause: "I received the Social Theory of our founder because I was convinced that it is a natural and legitimate outgrowth of Christianity," argued Hinds, "[and that] communism of the affections [is] as much a principle of Christianity as communism of property. If it can be shown to be a truth which can be properly put in practice only under a par-ticular person's supervision, then we might as well abandon its practice at once and in fact ought never to have entered upon its practice. . . ." Hinds attempted to paint Noyes as having shamelessly backtracked in his theology, abandoning a key component of the Bible Communist creed simply in order to maintain power.[8]

Crushing his opponents no doubt played a part in Noyes's reversal on the question of Complex Marriage. But in truth, the new "communism" advo-cated by the opposition party resembled Noyes's communism in name only. Writing to Harriet Skinner, Noyes maintained that "just as every good thing has its counterfeit," so true "unity of life" was mocked by the hollow shell of communism put forth by the Hinds-Towner party. These calculating people, he charged, saw "a great advantage in communism of property and com-munism of sexual privileges while they have no idea of communism of the heart," which, he asserted, could "exist only by grace through faith in the blood of Christ identifying with God." True communism entailed a delib-erate subordination and cutting off of the self to serve ends of the whole, while the Hinds-Towner party was attempting to artificially yoke principles of individual rights and democratic decision making to the communal enterprise.[9]

The Hinds-Towner "bill of rights," as Noyes loyalists took derisively to calling the opposition party's original list of suggestions to reform the community, substituted an individualistic and republican form of government for theocratic communism. Community, according to Noyes, was an organic entity that took its directives from God via his own divine inspiration. As in a living body, God's energy was infused throughout the whole cell structure of the Community, and the individual was nothing without the energy links to its source and fellow cells. The Community was not, in short, a cluster of separate individuals that decided policy by the rule of the majority. The will of the Community was immanent in the group, a mystical emanation of the whole; it was not the cold result of a legalistic vote, the counting and tallying of separate wills one by one.

The basis of the split tearing apart the Oneida Community was thus nothing less than a fundamental disagreement about how to define the scope and status of the self within the group. The liberal-democratic political tradition operating in the "outside world" took a rights-based approach to the social contract. Individuals were, ipso facto, free and equal under the law—although, in practice, natural inequalities in the distribution of talent and character led to vast disparities in individuals' social and economic fates. The radical economic individualism of the market revolution had rallied Americans behind this definition of the autonomous, free-willed individual as the basic unit of society. In the sweeping reconceptualization of "work" and economic relations that followed the abolition of slavery, the ideology of contract-based "free labor" rushed in to justify the existence of growing class divisions within industrial society. According to this vision, both the workplace and the polity were composed of free, contracting agents following their own self-interest in the open market, with only themselves to blame for economic failure.[10]

Oneidan communism had never held any truck with rights-based individualism, and the pages of its journals are filled with eloquent and repeated arguments for what Oneidans called an "organic" rather than rights-based society. In a mystical article written for *The American Socialist* in May 1879, Theodore Pitt, serving as a mouthpiece for Noyes himself, explained how the classical liberal notion of an unconnected "individual" was an illusion: "Every individual stands in a universe of life, and every pulsation of his existence impresses its record on the material and spiritual atmospheres which surround him. . . . Every fact, both in the natural and in the spiritual world,"

he intones, "proclaims that we are 'members of one another.'" In another re-
lated essay, subtitled "The Socialism of Jesus," Pitt argued that a Christian
community was not an assemblage of contracting individuals but a body;
governed not by law but by life: "Jesus found a company of men and women
who received him, and with whom he could come into organic relations. He
became to them a radiant center. . . . The organic bond of that society was
not law—it was life: the new divine-human life that was in Jesus." "Unquestionably there is a true individualism," Pitt admitted, throwing a sop to the
hallowed American value of individual liberty. "But it is one which recog-
nizes the sacredness of its organic connections."[11]

Other Community writers expressed the difference between organicism
and contract by invoking "chivalry" and "honor," rather than "law," as the
binding principles in any true community. "Communism abstains from
law, and puts all relations on the ground of honor, or Christian charity,"
George Washington Noyes wrote. The Christian knight acts to help all who
need his aid, not because he is contracted or constrained to do so, but because his obligation to the social whole of which he is a part and his abnega-
tion of selfishness in consequence of this duty lead him to do it naturally.[12]

"God is no respecter of persons," Peter tells us, but instead has his eye on
the whole united body of his children. But by the 1870s, as the Community
was unraveling, the idea of an organic society based on such mystical notions
of shared "life," chivalry, and honor, rather than the hard-edged calculations of contractual obligation, had begun to seem hopelessly romantic.
The communitarian ventures of the heady 1840s, utopian efforts to provide
a cooperative countermodel to the rising economic and social isolation of
market man, had all ended in failure. Yale sociology professor and proto-
libertarian William Graham Sumner, in his 1883 essay, *What the Social
Classes Owe to Each Other*, lauded America's break with the "sentimental
relations which once united baron and retainer, master and servant, teacher
and pupil, comrade and comrade" and their replacement by a "society based
on contract [as] a society of free and independent men, who form ties without favor or obligation." The "poetry and romance" of sentimental ties between people is lost in the rational rule of contract, Sumner conceded, and
may be lamented by "humanitarians, philanthropists, and reformers." Yet,

according to the ascendant philosophy, only a stoic embrace of contract could guarantee "the self-reliance and dignity of a free man." From within the cocoon of the Oneida Community, Towner and Hinds had absorbed *l'air du temps*, and they now sought to inject communism with a healthy dose of liberal self-reliance.[13]

John Humphrey Noyes's August 20 proposal to the council that the Community suspend the practice of Complex Marriage pulled the rug out from under his opponents. Noyes further weakened the opposition by reminding Community members to take heed of the looming threat of a legal attack on Oneida from Reverend Mears and his followers. A recent court decision that had criminalized Mormon polygamy was an indicator of which way the wind was blowing politically concerning marriage, and the only way to safeguard the Community's continued well-being was to abandon the offending practice of Complex Marriage altogether. Uniting all parties by conjuring up the fearsome image of their common enemy, the courts and clergy who were even then organizing their forces for attack, Noyes sought to "persuade with voices of thunder and entreaty to every man, woman and child to seek harmony to hold together, and keep that great machine—the business organization which shelters and feeds them—going with unfailing momentum." Under Noyes's new plan, marriage was to be permitted, subject to application and approval by the Administrative Council, but celibacy was to be preferred as closest in holiness to Complex Marriage.[14]

Noyes had outfoxed his opponents. No one with a heart could look in the eyes of Oneida's vulnerable women and children—adulteresses and bastards, all, by the outside world's cold estimation—and vote for anything that might imperil their continued protection within the bosom of the Community, "a mother whose care and brooding they will bewail with many and bitter tears, if they ever lose it," Noyes pleaded. Better for the Oneidans to give up their position on Complex Marriage than risk the continued existence of the Community itself. "The adherents of the different social arrangements can respect and tolerate each other on Paul's principles . . . and all work together to make a happy home, to get out of debt and to make money, not to multiply our indulgences, but to support missionaries and multiply communities." A nostalgic return to early Community days, when the sacrifice of selfish pleasures for the well-being of the whole was counseled, Noyes's proposal was admirably belt-tightening. At the same time, the plan was full of Yankee verve and optimism, looking forward to increased profits and multiplied communities.[15]

The plan was presented before the family, and a vote taken. When Noyes's proposition for celibacy or marriage was called, all stood except for William Hinds. Not a soul stood for the opposition position of continuing Complex Marriage, not even Hinds himself, who explained his abstention: "I could not do anything which might be interpreted as approving the introduction of marriage into the Community: and I did not vote against the proposition because I was not prepared to say its plan is not, under all the circumstances, expedient."[16]

At ten o'clock, then, on August 28, 1879, Complex Marriage came to an end. Most ushered in the change without fanfare. Francis Wayland-Smith, for instance, passed the day leading up to the moratorium quietly with Cornelia Worden, the mother of his son Gerard. Others kept up a more frantic pace in saying their sexual good-byes. Tirzah Miller, according to her diary, had sex with James Herrick in the morning, Erastus Hamilton in the afternoon, and Homer Barron in the evening in a frenzied last hurrah before the iron curtain of monogamy once again descended.

The American Socialist's September 4 issue announced the departure, presenting it as a victory for Oneida insofar as it proved the sincerity of their original project: "[T]heir present course in giving up that phase of their communal life which has caused offense [proves] that the Communists have not been the reckless bacchanalians a few have represented them," the editorialist wrote. "The truth is, as all the world will one day see and acknowledge, that they have not been pleasure-seekers and sensualists but social architects, with high religious and moral aims." In no way admitting defeat for their program, they simply posited that, having found that the conditions in America were not sufficiently ripe for a "social system so much in advance of existing civilization," they had seen fit to suspend it; "its endorsers and advocates can safely commit its claims to the civilization of the future." Always with a keen eye on their public image, Oneida spun its bitter internal dissent, and consequent tactical retreat on the question of Complex

Marriage, into a sign of the organization's continued vibrancy and moral superiority. But this fragile peace was not to last.[17]

Noyes had been clear that under this new regime, celibacy was to be preferred to marriage. But the minute Complex Marriage was dissolved, the young people of Oneida started a rush toward matrimony that quite dismayed both the opposition, who seemed bent on holding out for some sort of magical reversal that would reinstate sexual communism, as well as Noyes loyalists, who saw it as an unwholesome inrush of the "worldly" spirit. The first application for marriage came before the Administrative Council from F. A. Marks and Martha J. Hawley. The council judiciously ruled that the couple should wait for one month from the day of the application, to allow time for "the discussion of objections" to the union. Sensing the council's cool attitude toward matrimony, two days later Alfred Hawley and Elizabeth Hamilton bypassed official channels altogether and penned a quick note to the council on September 2: "Wishing to be married elsewhere and as quietly as possible, we take this occasion to inform you that it is our intention to do so without further delay." The council expressed their "strong disapprobation" of the couple's renegade action, but the tone had been set: the "individual sovereigns," as Noyes rather snippily referred to the opposition party by reference to the Modern Times free lovers, were taking matrimonial matters into their own hands, council or no council. Harriet Skinner compared the marriage fever to "a kind of baptism," as if the young people were impelled by an "irresistible power" in their rush to monogamy, presaging disconsolately that "it looks as if marriage would eat up Communism."[18]

Young mothers who had borne children out of wedlock, not infrequently to men already legally married to other women, might be forgiven their haste to secure for themselves a husband, given the increasingly shaky foundations of the Community. One such woman was Beulah Hendee, who had a daughter, Dorothea, by John Humphrey Noyes. Having begun a romance with Alfred Barron just before the dissolution of Complex Marriage, and knowing that marriage with the already-married Noyes was not a possibility, Beulah's letters to Alfred betray her anxiety to see herself legally attached to her lover. Just days after Complex Marriage ended, Beulah, who had gone to Wallingford for the fall, heard rumors that Alfred planned to marry a woman named Elizabeth, by whom he had a daughter. "I hear from various sources that you have declared your intention of marrying at no distant day. . . . Is it true dear? Tell me. I did not believe it. I thought you would tell me if you had such a plan. . . . The terrors of this new situation come upon me with an overwhelming force." Under the specter of this uncertainty, her nights were filled with anxious visions: "I dream about you every night," she confessed to Alfred. "Last night I thought I was following you all about trying to get a chance to talk with you but was hedged about with all sorts of obstacles. What a tightening sensation there was around my heart all the time."[19]

Beulah's panicked letters crossed in the mail with Alfred's own ardent declaration that the rumors of his intention to marry were correct—but that he planned to wed Beulah, not Elizabeth. "You have given me a happiness that I never expected God would give me in this world," Beulah sighed with relief in her missive of September 7. The couple was not out of the woods yet, however. As loyal Noyesites they dutifully awaited the approval of their leader, and then of the Administrative Council, before proceeding to a union. Noyes's approval came via his sister Harriet Skinner, in a letter that arrived at Oneida on November 27, 1879, recording his own personal pleasure at the prospect of Alfred and Beulah's union, but also the "public good" that would be secured should the couple "contribute several children to the Community." Noyes still had his stirpicultural eye on the prize of breeding good stock. But the Administrative Council had their doubts as to whether communism's ends were best served by a love match between Alfred and Beulah, which appeared to favor "sticky love" over Alfred's duty to the mother of his child. "They have been discussing our case in Council and yesterday they appointed Sarah Dunn and Mr. Burnham to find out what Elizabeth's real mind is and whether she is going to oppose [us] or suffer unduly," Alfred wrote on December 9. "We may have to wait some for Elizabeth to get some new work of grace in her heart," he gently warned Beulah. For her part, Beulah lamented the next day, "[M]y nerves [won't] stand much more."[20]

In the end, Elizabeth was, apparently, soft hearted enough to assent to Alfred's union with another woman and, on December 12, Beulah Hendee and Alfred Barron were quietly wed in the Mansion House. "In the face of such triumphs of love and softness of heart, who can doubt the perpetuity of the Community spirit?" Beulah exulted. "I can see the meaning that God had in this new departure, which at first seemed a move toward the world and its spirit. All these wrenchings and agonies are going to work for Communism," she wrote optimistically, "for real softening and purifying of heart, and brotherly love will grow. Exclusive love is not going to be the thing gained, but enlargement of heart."[21]

Seeking to preserve as much of the Community philosophy as possible within the changed context of marriage, John Humphrey Noyes suggested in November 1879 that the stirpicultural project begun in 1869 continue unabated, according to a new plan he called "Circumscribed Marriage." Regarding the stirpicults as "the capital which we have accumulated in our experiment of Complex Marriage," Noyes suggested in a letter to the Community that they place themselves under "a rule of persuasive grace and home loyalty that as our children grow up their marriages shall be kept, so far as it lies in our power, within the [Community] enclosure" in order to ensure the purity of the germ strain already attained through the first generation. For current Community couples, it was, Noyes continued, "our highest duty to God and man to propagate as fast as we can." But the opposition refused to give the green light for Circumscribed Marriage as the new social policy to be adopted. Convinced that it would only exacerbate the rush to marriage, and petulantly adamant that the stirpicults were no superrace but, rather, "only an ordinary lot" not much worth propagating, William Hinds and his cronies quickly put the kibosh on Noyes's sunny prospects for intensified inbreeding within the Community.[22]

These objections notwithstanding, such cooperative inbreeding would have been a logistical challenge in any event, given the civil war now splitting the Community down the middle between what Francis Wayland-Smith called the "Townerites," on the one hand, and Noyes supporters on the other. Over the next eight months, squabbles between the two parties broke out at every turn, from petty accusations against William Kelly, director of the Children's Department and a Noyes acolyte, that he had forbidden Townerite and loyalist children to play together, to more serious accusations, such as William Kelly's counterassertion that James Towner was surreptitiously gathering evidence from disgruntled members in order to bring a lawsuit against John Humphrey Noyes for sexual impropriety. In a long paper addressed to the Community on June 18, 1880, Judge Towner protested his innocence, declaring himself the victim of vicious Noyesite rumormongering. Theodore Noyes weighed in on the debate, declaring that "whether Mr. Towner had done what Mr. Kelly supposed or not, there certainly was some ground for the feeling among Mr. Noyes's friends that there was danger of his being accused by persons in the Community." Theodore claimed he had, in fact, been told directly that there were "persons in the Community [who] stood ready to accuse [Noyes]" of sexual impropriety. Kelly eventually had to publicly apologize to Towner for his unverifiable accusations. Still, the threat rankled, and it revealed that the opposition was holding fast to the charge against Noyes of "sexual impurity and harmful and demoralizing practices in [his] dealings with the young women and girls," as Francis Wayland-Smith had written some months earlier in his diary. The situation was dire.[23]

On July 18, 1880, a solemn resolution was presented to the family at Evening Meeting and adopted: "Whereas great differences exist in the Community and many think there is little prospect of securing upon our present basis the internal harmony essential to the peace and prosperity of the Community; and whereas the continuance of the existing condition of things will seriously imperil the financial condition of the Community," they resolved to appoint a commission to the task of studying "what changes, if any, in our present arrangement are . . . necessary to enable us to continue our communal organization in peace and good order" or, this being found impossible, "to further consider and report upon what basis other than communism our relations as a business organization can, in their judgment, be best conducted."[24]

The commission's first report was sobering. "We have now no government worthy of the name," Francis Wayland-Smith recorded. "The Council is a failure. The young people do just as they like." "Our own members are . . . no longer industrious," he continued later in the same report; according to his diagnosis, they saw no object in hard work "while the earnings and profits are controlled by others." Without an entrepreneurial stake in advancing the company's earnings, members simply relaxed into living comfortably—Wayland-Smith would say shiftlessly—off the fat of the Community. In a last-ditch attempt to inject a boost of individual entrepreneurship into the Community economy, both Theodore Noyes and William Hinds had earlier offered modified privatizing schemes, such as increased individual "appropriations" (annual allowances to be spent as members saw fit) and a plan to fix a set number of work hours required of each Community member with overtime wages being paid. Suspicious of the "privateering" aspect of the new proposal, Noyes had nonetheless, with characteristic flexibility, been game to try it. Indeed, reconciling private economic resources and communism might be less difficult than it looked at first glance; the "true" communists, Noyes suggested, by funneling their private shares into a Community treasury or by starting missions abroad, would "in a short time either convert the Individual Sovereigns or bury them out of sight in the wealth and blessings of communism." In Noyes's optimistic vision, the two parties—communists and individual sovereigns alike—could enter into "a friendly and fair competition to test the question of whether communism or individualism is the best system for education and happiness."[25]

Alas, such free-market sops to the opposition did nothing to reduce the acrimony rife within the Community. The commission's report made it clear that the only solution to the stalemate was a financial parting of the ways. And so a joint-stock proposal was placed on the table, turning the Community into a corporation that would pay shares to its holders, once and for all dissolving financial ties between warring members. On August 31, 1880, an "Agreement to Divide and Reorganize" was presented to the family at Evening Meeting for approval, and, the following day, 203 members signed it into effect. The Oneida Community now became, officially, the Oneida Community, Limited.

The agreement allotted all signatories shares of stock in the new company according to a division plan to be voted upon by them. In the end, the plan adopted granted one half of the total number of shares to members in proportion to their original monetary contributions to the Community, while the remaining half were distributed according to length of membership. In dividing up the shares, provision was made for "certain aged and invalid members of the Community," who, in lieu of stock, would receive lifelong pensions. "Suitable annual appropriation for the support and education of every child now born and belonging to members of the Community, until they become 16 years of age" was also granted, and signatories were given preference in employment in Community industries and habitation of Community dwellings. In a clause that would become central to the management philosophy of the succeeding corporation, the agreement specified that, "in order to make the dividends of the new Company as large as possible, we agree to do all we can both as stockholders and (if elected) as Directors, to keep the wages paid to officers of the Company, to Superintendents, agents, and other employees as low as is found consistent with the most efficient management."[26]

The Community's industries—upon whose profits the 203 souls who had signed the "Agreement" would henceforth depend—had evolved over the years. Trap making was still the principal moneymaker for Oneida Community, Limited, or OCL, followed by the silk business. The Community still carried on a small but profitable fruit-canning enterprise on the Mansion House grounds. The greatest shift in their economic composition had been the addition of iron spoons to the Community's roster of manufactures. In the 1870s, the Wallingford Community property, located on the Quinnipiac River, had housed a 150-horsepower plant and factory that were sitting idle. My great-great-grandfather Charles Cragin had been appointed head of "scientific" cattle breeding on the Wallingford farm. One day in the early summer of 1877, as he sat on the bridge gazing down at the water rushing downstream to power the Wallace tableware factory a quarter of a mile below, he was struck by an idea: "'Why couldn't we make spoons as well as Wallace?'" he wondered. "Here was the power and the empty factory only waiting for someone to start a busy hum of our own."[27]

Cragin jumped right to it: in traditional Community fashion, he sought out an industry specialist, a spoon man who had previously worked for the Hall and Elton silverware company, to help him design the necessary machinery. By June, the once-abandoned factory was fitted up and ready to produce "one thousand gross per week of ungraded tinned iron spoons." Laboring day and night in the swampy malarial woods of Connecticut, Charles Cragin was struck down with fever and ague just as the spoon business was getting started. He died on January 2, 1878. Myron Kinsley took over as superintendent of the business, which turned a tidy profit. After the transition to joint stock, Kinsley took advantage of the opportunity both to escape the malarial morass of Wallingford and to relocate the spoon business nearer John Humphrey Noyes in Canada. In September 1880, Oneida Community, Limited—much to the chagrin of the Townerites, who saw in this move a calculated political attempt to shift the company's center of power closer to the deposed "king bee"—signed an agreement with the Niagara Falls Hydraulic Power Company to lease power, land, and buildings for their spoon factory on the banks of the Niagara Gorge.[28]

FOR A COMMUNITY THAT HAD, FOR THIRTY-TWO YEARS, LIVED ACCORDING to the credo "each according to his ability, each according to his need," dismantling communism into tidy individual entitlements was tricky business indeed. The new, gerrymandered family units moved into new, gerrymandered clusters of rooms in the Mansion House. The space that had previously belonged to all was now divvied up and rented by the square foot. Under the Community ethos, such private property as each individual had need of— clothing and a modestly furnished bedroom—had been disbursed by the even hand of a central committee. Each adult member received, in addition, a small sum of money annually to cover the incidental expenses that might arise should he or she happen to travel off the Community premises. Personal possessions outside of these bare essentials were roundly regarded with suspicion.

At one point in the 1860s, spooked by a sense that a spirit of "private speculation" had broken out among the young, the Oneidans appointed a special committee to investigate the issue. Of particular concern, according to the committee's findings, was the growing fad among the boys to acquire pocket watches, which they guarded jealously and refused to consider communal property. "It seems that we are expected to give to the Community our time, our passions, and all our property—with the exception of watches," the report commented sardonically of the recent fetish for timepieces. "The desire to carry a watch is perfectly natural and good in itself," the committee conceded; when it becomes an idolatrous object of fashion, however, then "it is the duty of the Community and all interested to crucify this spirit."[29]

With the passage of the joint-stock resolution, such scruples disappeared overnight. All the Mansion House furnishings, from straw-tick mattresses to pots and pans, were gathered up and priced; each member was permitted to appropriate thirty dollars' worth of items. The rest was auctioned off and, as one commentator would later reflect, many felt "a certain novel elation in thus wielding, for the first time, the age-old power of money." As if overcorrecting for their years of communist sharing, the newly separated households clung to their private property with an odd tenacity. "It was difficult to borrow a hammer," one man reminisced about early postbreakup days. And it was said that anyone who borrowed so much as a pin from a neighbor was punctual in returning it.[30]

Following the same logic, the directors of the new Oneida Community, Limited, closed the communal dining room and set up an à la carte restaurant in its place, where each item would be assessed at its precise value: butter pats, one cent; pancakes and syrup, five cents. When the new restaurant opened, the former communists marveled at "the ambitious worldliness of the new rooms," with food kept hot in bright copper steam chests and the walls painted "a luxuriant, unspiritual shade of green," as one member later recalled. Yet despite such early enthusiasm for the perks of capitalism, communist habits were slow to fade. Under the Community system, each member had worked earnestly according to his individual talents and capacities, whether that meant washing dishes or superintending the trap shop, and all had enjoyed an equal share in the collective wealth. Such a radical egalitarian instinct was tough to shake: under the new system, the superintendent of the restaurant was paid the same salary as the newly elected president of OCL.[31]

Despite the existence of a spiritual caste system within the Oneida Community, the material equality of its members had been an article of faith. No one member—up to and including John Humphrey Noyes himself—enjoyed access to more or better resources than any other. At the breakup, this artificial bubble of equality vanished overnight. Stock shares provided former Community members with annual payouts, and stipends helped in the support of children. But the economic fortunes of the ex-members varied widely, depending on such factors as how much money or property one's family had contributed upon joining the Community and how well-connected or engaged in the Community's manufacturing ventures one had been. For women—who, despite the Community's lip service to gender equality, had never penetrated into the upper echelons of business management—much depended on how they made out in the marriage lottery by which couples were patched together at the end of Complex Marriage.

Though there remain few personal accounts detailing this liminal period in the Community's posthistory, the general state of disintegration during the period immediately following the breakup must have been disheartening. Harriet Worden, one of the unfortunate women left at the breakup without a husband, who had three young children by three different fathers, records her sense of gloom in an 1880 diary entry: "The New Year has begun and we now bid adieu to communism. . . . [A]nd we enter 'O.C. Limited' with all its terrors," she wrote in her journal. "I have no pleasure in the contemplated change—instead, my outlook is not especially cheering." Harriet eventually moved her children out of the Mansion House to cheaper quarters in the worker village near the trap factory and sold books door to door to round out her meager income.[32]

Her sister, Cornelia Worden, by contrast, fared much better. Two months after the dissolution of Complex Marriage, Cornelia wed Francis Wayland-Smith, the father of her second stirpicultural son (the first had been fathered by Theodore Noyes). Wayland-Smith had been a central member of the Community administration, and at the breakup he moved easily into a position as superintendent of the Hardware Department, which oversaw the trap business. With his accumulated capital he was able to purchase a farm near the Mansion House in which to raise his family, and the Wayland-Smiths settled into a comfortable bourgeois lifestyle, complete with house servants. (In a candid diary entry, Cornelia recorded of one particular servant that she was "a good natured soul . . . [but] she does not make my bed at all well.")[33]

Another tale of two sisters is equally illustrative of the disparate and, at times, arbitrary economic fates handed out at the breakup: that of Annie Hatch and her stepsister, Jessie Baker Hatch. During the final years of the Community, Annie's true love was Myron Kinsley, the able manager who had taken over as superintendent of the spoon business at Wallingford when Charles Cragin died. A staunch Noyes supporter, Myron had been single-handedly responsible for arranging the leader's midnight departure for

Canada and remained one of Noyes's chief confidants throughout his exile at Niagara Falls. Jessie Hatch, sixteen years Annie's junior, was born to Catharine Baker Hatch and John Humphrey Noyes in 1858. At the breakup, Noyes, wishing both to see his daughter well married and his right-hand man equipped with a good and loyal wife, decided to kill two birds with one stone and proposed a marriage between Jessie and Myron, although the two barely knew each other and were separated by an almost twenty-five-year age difference.

Annie Hatch graciously ceded her cherished lover to her younger sister; she was never to marry herself. Annie wrote a letter to Jessie expressing her hearty consent to her sister's marriage to Myron, although in a follow-up missive to Beulah Hendee, on December 28, 1879, Annie admitted to some ambivalence: "I feel real reconciled to [Myron's] marriage—but I wonder how I shall really feel when it is done. I trust God about it," she confided to Beulah. As a single woman alone in the world, Annie had few options but to stick with the Oneida family. At the breakup, she moved to Niagara Falls, where she rented modest rooms with her half-sister, Mary Baker Hatch, another Community woman who had been left without a husband by the debacle of Complex Marriage's end. The pair eked out a modest income working at the Oneida spoon factory.[34]

Jessie and Myron Kinsley also moved to Niagara Falls so he could continue in his position as superintendent of OCL's tableware division. The couple built themselves a mini–Mansion House, a cheerful redbrick villa in the Italianate style with an impressive tower and cupola. Initially, Jessie had some trouble assuming the proper cultural and social attributes of a bourgeois matron. "You cannot imagine me as I was then," Jessie later wrote in a memoir addressed to her daughter Edith. "I was most unsophisticated and green. Our hired girl, Maggie, was often imagined by strangers to be the mistress, because she wore fine clothes and had assurance. I would always forget to use my money, which I then handled for the first time." Jessie and Annie remained close until Annie's death in 1906, with Annie even moving into the Kinsleys' homestead for a period of time, but the class divide separating the two sisters was stark: one, a factory day laborer; the other, the leisured wife of a successful industrialist.[35]

Bible Communism as a binding element also largely vanished, although some ex-members—notably, controlling members of the OCL board of directors—held fast to the spiritualist beliefs current during the last decade of the Community. The board conducted séances after John Humphrey Noyes's death, during which the patriarch's ghost reportedly disbursed financial advice via a medium. Other ex-members tried, and largely failed, to find a comfortable spiritual substitute for Bible Communism in mainstream Christian denominations. Both Francis and Cornelia Wayland-Smith experimented with different faiths. They found Roman Catholicism intolerable, a religion where "priestcraft, and all its senseless mummeries, still rule"; Protestant sects were little better, their church services "theatrical and repetitious," lacking true feeling.[36]

In Noyes's cosmology, Hades—the underworld where the phantom dead awaited resurrection at the end of days—was the most dismal of all dwelling places: a dark, sleepy limbo vastly inferior to the lively movement and action of the living on earth. Caught somewhere between the old world and the new, between a need to forge new beliefs and a tenacious desire to hold on to the past, the survivors of the Oneida shipwreck in these early years must often have felt a certain sympathy for the residents of that gloomy, twilight realm of shades.

NOYES LIVED OUT HIS FINAL YEARS IN NIAGARA FALLS IN A HOUSE HE called the Stone Cottage, surrounded by a loyal coterie of followers and steady stream of visitors from his previous life in Oneida. Throughout the slow unraveling of his life's work at Oneida, and up until his death in 1886, Noyes remained oddly cheerful and detached. In fact, true to his lifelong habit of self-invention, once in Canada he declared himself to be under a "new control." This time, the spirit guiding him was not Saint Paul but a sweet, undefined feminine presence; he wavered between identifying it as the spirit of Queen Victoria; her daughter Princess Louise (who had moved to Canada in 1878 as wife of the governor general); Mary Magdalene; the Virgin Mary; or "some higher and unknown seraph representing all of these." He felt, in any case, "a sense of having passed from the cold, harsh, masculine control of the Yankee Principality to a vast Motherly Empire, ruled by a loving woman whose social nimbus carries a feeling of family and home along with her morning drumbeat around the world."[37]

Psycho-biographical interpretations of Noyes's shift from his lifelong patriarchal fixation to this sudden vision of the British Empire radiating maternal, queenly warmth are all too tempting. Chased out of the primal horde by his sex-starved brothers, bruised by the rough assertiveness of the individual sovereigns' masculinity, perhaps Noyes found such notions of healing maternal warmth all he could cope with psychically. Having been dethroned by what he called the "bald republicanism" of the likes of James Towner and William Hinds, Noyes sought succor in what his friend and fellow political tactician Theodore Pitt called "the sweetness and glory of loyalty, of reverence for authority, and that organic unity which give to society a center and win hearts to a common love and subordination" to be found under the British monarchy.

Noyes's dreams of empire were to have one final act. Undertaking a boat trip from Niagara Falls to Ottawa in July 1880, Noyes's right-hand man, Theodore Pitt, became seasick and vomited his dentures over the side of the vessel. On arriving in Ottawa, he sought the services of a dentist, Doctor Martin, to replace his lost teeth. Dr. Martin, as it turned out, was also the royal dentist and had recently treated Princess Louise. The fast-thinking Pitt took advantage of this providential concatenation of events and penned a letter to the princess to be delivered in person by the good doctor.

In the letter, Pitt informed the princess that she had been selected by Providence to be the medium for the immanent kingdom of Christ that was coming to join itself to the British Empire. "In the great coming Confederation of the English-speaking people, around the English Throne and into one grand world-surrounding empire—an event and achievement which must come if Christian civilization is to be saved, and the kingdom of heaven established in this world—you may perform a great and glorious part," Pitt enlightened the monarch, "as a medium and representative of the spirit of reverence and loyalty." (Surprisingly enough, the princess responded to Mr. Pitt via her courier, acknowledging receipt of the letter and thanking him for his "many kind wishes.") Noyes, thrilled with Pitt's royal contact, wrote breathlessly to his sister in Oneida that "there are many signs that the center of [my] 'control,' so far as it has relation to Geography, has passed from the United States to Canada—from Oneida to Niagara Falls," and that it "assumes the tone of Internationalism." Oneida was small game compared to the Christly world-state Noyes contemplated in connection with the royal house of Saxe-Coburg-Gotha. But this grander vision was never to come into proper focus, let alone find its realization on earth.[38]

John Humphrey Noyes died in his bed at the Stone Cottage on April 13, 1886. His son, the heir apparent who had, in the end, failed so utterly in his mission to carry on his father's spiritual dynasty, was by his side. The last word to pass the lips of the tumbled patriarch, dreaming even in death of miraculous resurrections, was "Theodore."

11

Selling Silver

IN 1877, PIERREPONT B. NOYES, THE SEVEN-YEAR-OLD STIRPICULT SON of John Humphrey Noyes and Harriet Worden, was walking home from the trap shop one day, pleased because Jack McQuade, the husky Irish foreman with the red mustache and a wad of chewing tobacco always lodged in his cheek, had taken the time to show him the workings of the trap-making machines. Suddenly, a mob of "Turkey Street" boys, the sons of the Irish laborers who manned the trap shop, came running down the road, swearing wildly and shaking their fists at him. "Bastard!" they called. "God-damn goody Community boy!" Such was Pierrepont's first real introduction to "outsiders," and, to the sheltered little utopian that he was, they seemed devilish indeed.

The epithet regarding his parentage was no doubt an unfamiliar term to young Pierrepont. But he couldn't have misread the contempt in the gang's dirt-streaked faces or their glee at being able to taunt the "goody-goody" for his clan's departure from the ways of the outside world. And he would find out soon enough what the offending term meant.

As he would later record in his memoir, Pierrepont's earliest memories

JOHN HUMPHREY NOYES

When she gave birth to her son John Humphrey in 1811, Polly Hayes Noyes prayed that he might become a "minister of the everlasting gospel." Thirty-seven years later, her prayer would be answered, after a fashion: John Humphrey Noyes founded the Oneida Community, blending an ethic of total selflessness, communism of property, and free love into one of the most baroque interpretations of Jesus' "everlasting gospel" ever attempted on American soil.

As he aged, John Humphrey Noyes became increasingly deaf; he also suffered from a throat ailment that prevented him from presiding at Evening Meetings. Noyes's attempts in the 1870s to appoint his son Theodore as his heir, despite the latter's avowed atheism, led to widespread discontent within the wider community.

HARRIET HOLTON NOYES

John Humphrey Noyes was living in Ithaca, New York, and on the verge of bankruptcy when a wealthy young convert and fellow Vermonter, Harriet Holton, sent him eighty dollars to pay off his debts. Noyes responded with a proposal of marriage, to which Harriet readily consented.

HARRIET NOYES SKINNER

Noyes's younger sister was his most fervent, if not fanatical, supporter up until the day of his death in 1886. When her son, my great-great-grandfather Joseph Skinner, lost faith in his uncle's divine commission and left the Community in 1873, Harriet shunned her only child rather than prove disloyal to her cherished brother. Noyes was, according to a family letter, "the one great love of her life."

JOHN LANGDON SKINNER

This young teacher of Quaker background brooked extraordinary family opposition to join Noyes's fledgling Society of Inquiry in 1839, where he helped edit and publish the group's journal, *The Witness*. In 1841, Skinner was tapped to marry Noyes's sister Harriet.

MARY CRAGIN

Of blue-blooded New England origin, my great-great-great-grandmother Mary Cragin (née Johnson) was one of Noyes's first converts, and his first partner in the experiment in "Complex Marriage" undertaken by the Putney group beginning in 1846. When Mary died tragically in a boating accident several years later, Noyes was inconsolable.

GEORGE E. CRAGIN

When George Cragin's father, a prosperous Massachusetts cotton manufacturer, went bankrupt in 1827, young George was left to shift for himself. He settled in New York City, where he discovered the fiery new religion being preached by Charles Finney and fell in love with Mary Elizabeth Johnson. The two were married in 1833 and joined Noyes's Putney group in 1840. George struggled with, and never entirely reconciled himself to, Mary and John Humphrey Noyes's intense sexual and spiritual affinity.

BEULAH HENDEE

Orphaned early in life, Beulah Hendee joined the Oneida Community at the age of seventeen in 1864. The file of more than one hundred letters she exchanged with her friend Annie Hatch records the painful, yet at times spiritually rewarding, emotional struggles members faced in ridding themselves of "sticky love," the Oneidan term for overly exclusive sexual attachments.

JAMES W. TOWNER

James Towner was a latecomer to Oneida, arriving in 1874 after a stint at a free-love commune in Berlin Heights, Ohio. Detractors would later allege that he had come to Oneida with the express purpose of wresting control away from the aging Noyes. When internal tensions began to shake the community in 1878, Towner was the first to form a vocal opposition party whose aim was to depose Noyes and establish increased sexual and political democracy within the community.

TIRZAH MILLER

One of the most sexually sought-after members within the community's system of Complex Marriage, the libidinous Tirzah was John Humphrey Noyes's niece and a member of his trusted circle of counselors. Her diary chronicling her participation in Noyes's eugenics project—she would give birth to two "stirpicults," by two different fathers—is a harrowing and often dark account of the inner power workings of the Community in its final decade.

THEODORE NOYES

Theodore, John Humphrey Noyes's first son and the only surviving child from his original marriage with Harriet Holton, was early on tapped as Noyes's successor at Oneida. But as a medical student at Yale in the 1860s, Theodore had absorbed the skeptical atheism of modern science, rendering him remarkably ill suited for the job. Theodore's unbelief, and Noyes's stubborn insistence on instituting him as his rightful heir in spite of it, foreshadowed the Community's eventual dissolution.

FRANCIS WAYLAND-SMITH

Francis came to the community with his widowed mother when he was ten years old; John Humphrey Noyes acted as a father-figure to the boy. As Noyes's power waned in the 1870s and a fierce battle for control of Oneida's sizable assets ensued, Wayland-Smith was able to broker a workable if tense truce between the "Noyesite" and "Anti-Noyesite" parties. On September 15, 1880, 199 Oneida members voted to pass an agreement turning the Community into a joint-stock company.

CHARLES CRAGIN

In 1877, while sitting on the banks of the Quinnipiac River, my great-great-grandfather had the inspiration to start manufacturing silverware at Oneida's branch commune in Wallingford, Connecticut. The silverware plant joined the Community's other manufactures, which already included canned fruits and vegetables, silk thread, chain link, and animal traps.

SKETCH OF THE 1851 MANSION HOUSE

According to John Humphrey Noyes's doctrine of "Bible Communism," all Community members were to be housed under one roof as an extended family. "Unity of hearts will prefer unity of accommodations," he lectured his flock. The original Mansion House erected in 1848 was a modest three-story building housing eighty-seven members. By 1851, membership had expanded to more than two hundred, prompting the addition of two extensions and an adjacent wing.

MANSION HOUSE (VIEW OF EASTERN FRONT)

As their businesses prospered, the Oneidans improved and added to their original dwelling. The "New House," an Italianate mansion constructed in 1862 following the latest taste in bourgeois country houses, gave the radical commune a veneer of middle-class respectability. By 1878, the Oneidans were comfortably housed in a 93,000-square-foot compound.

MANSION HOUSE (VIEW FROM SOUTH LAWN)

COMMUNISTS AT LEISURE

The Oneida Community faced constant criticism in the press for their unconventional sexual practices. Satirical cartoons portrayed Oneida women in their signature "pantalets" and short-cropped hair as wild, sexually predatory, and de-natured females. The Oneida Community countered, in part, by photographing their members in decorous bourgeois poses: women's gazes modestly averted, while their male counterparts, holding themselves at a respectful distance, removed their hats in deference to their feminine companions.

BEAR TRAP

One of the Oneida Community's early joiners, Seymour Newhouse, was a blacksmith who made a living manufacturing animal traps. With the help of expert machinists, starting in 1855 the Oneidans expanded and mechanized their modest trap-making shop. Newhouse had previously been capable of forging 1,500 handcrafted traps a year; by the early 1860s, Oneida's blacksmith shop was turning out an average of 45,000 traps annually.

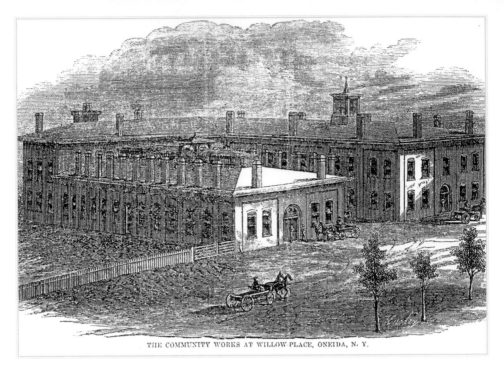

ENGRAVING OF WILLOW PLACE FACTORY

By 1866, the Oneidans had built a factory on the nearby Sconondoa Creek and were churning out 275,000 traps a year, becoming the largest trap manufacturer in the United States. A wing of the Willow Place building was devoted to another budding industry, the manufacture of silk "twist," or thread for sewing machines. While in the early stages these line jobs were largely filled by Community members, the Community increasingly turned to outside "hirelings," or wage labor, to fill unskilled positions. By 1875, the Oneida Community employed two hundred hirelings in assembly-line jobs.

"SILK GIRLS"

Among the hirelings Oneida employed were a substantial group of local girls and young women between the ages of ten and sixteen referred to as "silk girls." Their nimble little fingers were perfectly suited to the task of tying up broken thread ends when the spinning silk snapped, and the Oneidans were able to pay them substantially less than their adult counterparts. Because Oneida's ideology was theoretically opposed to wage labor, the community's increasing reliance on hirelings during the last decade of its existence placed its members in an uncomfortable—if not outright hypocritical—position.

"STIRPICULTS" IN A WAGON

In 1869, Noyes announced the launch of an ambitious new project by which the Oneidans would selectively breed amongst themselves with the aim of producing a physically and spiritually improved race of super-humans. On the eve of the initiative, fifty-three Oneida women of child-bearing age signed a pledge that they would "become martyrs to science, and cheerfully renounce all desire to become mothers, if for any reason Mr. Noyes deem us unfit material for propagation." In all, sixty-two "stirpicults" were born between 1869 and the dissolution of Complex Marriage in 1879.

GROUP OF STIRPICULTS, 1892

As arguably the world's only living specimens of a sustained trial in "scientific" breeding, Oneida's stirpicults were of interest to a growing community of social scientists and biologists committed to studying, and if possible implementing, eugenic programs at the turn of the century. Dr. Anita New-comb McGee, a gynecologist and medical anthropologist, conducted an 1891 study of the stirpicults from which she concluded that these unique products of "artificial selection" boded well for the future of race betterment: "The boys are tall," she recorded admiringly, "broad-shouldered and finely proportioned;" the girls "robust and well-built."

PIERREPONT B. NOYES

The stirpicult son of John Humphrey Noyes and Harriet Worden, Pierrepont was nine years old when the Community disbanded in 1880, leaving his single mother to raise three children by three different fathers. Haunted by the "ghost of illegitimacy," Pierrepont worked relentlessly to succeed in business. In 1895, as the Oneida Community Limited was foundering under incompetent leadership, Pierrepont was appointed superintendent of the silverware business. By 1910, the company had become one of the most recognizable silverware brands on the American market.

1903 ADVERTISEMENT

In 1900, Pierrepont Noyes determined that Oneida Community, Limited, should concentrate on producing a single product line. Machine twist, canned fruit, and eventually traps were sidelined as the company poured all of its resources into manufacturing plated silverware. Early advertisements appealed to the penny-wise middle-class consumer seeking better quality for a lower price, which Oneida promised to deliver with a special "triple-plate" technology that set it apart from its competitors.

A BEAUTIFUL OLD AGE IS ATTAINED BY

THE ONEIDA COMMUNITY

TRIPLE PLUS PLATE SILVER TABLE WARE

Superior in use to Sterling Silver, and in its old age will still be as bright and beautiful as the Solid Service.

The ONEIDA COMMUNITY QUALITY Silver-Plate Table Ware is durable, of elegant pattern and beautiful finish. It has the heaviest ornamentation, and in this respect is an almost equal counterpart of Sterling Silver. The famous AVALON pattern of the ONEIDA COMMUNITY is recognized as the most refined and chaste produced. The moderate price of the ONEIDA COMMUNITY Triple-Plate Plus enables it to take the place of the inferior plated ware, sold under fancy names, at fancy prices.

A Guarantee Bond good for 25 years with every piece of ONEIDA COMMUNITY Triple-Plate Plus Silver Table Ware.

Since 1848 "the ONEIDA COMMUNITY *quality*" has been recognized as the best. Their canned and preserved fruits, vegetables and jellies are recognized as this country's finest—their sewing and embroidering silk, the dealer will tell you, have no equal. Their Silver-Plate Table Ware has won the approval of the discriminating public.

Ask for the illustrated story about the ONEIDA COMMUNITY, Booklet F. It tells the story of their early struggles and their success in making a beautiful garden spot out of a dreary wilderness.

A Baby Silver-Plate Feeding Spoon of the famous ONEIDA COMMUNITY Triple-Plate Plus will be sent prepaid on receipt of fifty cents. A useful article and an elegant gift.

ONEIDA COMMUNITY Silver-Plate Table Ware can be found at most good dealers. If not at yours, write us, and the address of the nearest dealer will be sent.

ONEIDA COMMUNITY, Kenwood, N. Y.

COMMUNITY SILVER ADVERTISEMENT (1912)

Originally trained as an oculist, stirpicult Berton "Doc" Dunn abandoned doctoring to join the Oneida team as advertising czar in 1904. Dunn's early ads showcased Oneida silverware by placing it against elegant lace backdrops in skillfully photographed, full-page ads. Dunn culled his lace samples from fine arts museums and the choicest European lace shops in order to imbue Oneida's product with an air of Old World aristocratic grace.

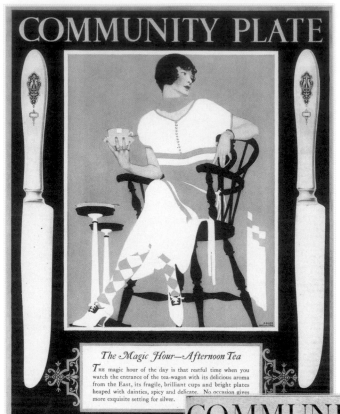

The Magic Hour—Afternoon Tea

THE magic hour of the day is that restful time when you watch the entrance of the tea-wagon with its delicious aroma from the East, its fragile, brilliant cups and bright plates heaped with dainties, spicy and delicate. No occasion gives more exquisite setting for silver.

COLES PHILLIPS
ADVERTISEMENTS

Coles Phillips was a New York illustrator who, as his wife quipped, "made his reputation as a painter of pretty girls." In the first decades of the new century, Phillips's trademark beauties graced the covers of *The Saturday Evening Post*, *Good Housekeeping*, and the *Ladies' Home Journal*. Berton Dunn hired Phillips to design Community Plate ads in 1911. Elegant and alluringly aloof, Phillips's pinup girls were key to Oneida's sales strategy: sell silver by tapping into American women's dreams of class distinction.

Silverware of Quality

BACK HOME FOR KEEPS (1945)

Oneida Limited converted its factories to produce materiel for the war effort in 1942 but wanted to make sure it maintained its prominent place as America's best-loved silverware company in the meantime. Their answer to this conundrum was the spectacularly popular "Back Home for Keeps" ad campaign designed by BBDO executive Jean Wade Rindlaub in 1942. Appealing to Americans' patriotic stirrings as well as to nostalgic images of home and hearth, Oneida received hundreds of thousands of mail requests for poster-sized copies of its ads not only from pining stateside wives but from homesick soldiers stationed abroad, as well.

THIS IS FOR KEEPS

Ring the bells of Christmas . . .
for a beautiful bride . . . and beloved Community,
first choice for holiday entertaining.
Community has true distinction of line,
richness of ornament, finely balanced beauty.
Community . . . *lifetime* Community . . .
is thoughtfully overlaid with extra silver
for *longer* wear at special wear points.
And a dinner service for eight places
at distinguished jewelers everywhere
starts as low as $53.50. (No federal tax.)

Community
THE FINEST SILVERPLATE

*CORONATION

*LADY HAMILTON

*MILADY

If its Community . . . its correct

TRADE MARKS OF ONEIDA LTD.   COPYRIGHT 1948 ONEIDA LTD.

THIS IS FOR KEEPS (1948)

When the war ended, Oneida Limited shifted seamlessly to advertisements depicting cheerful young brides and grooms dedicated to re-establishing traditional pre-war gender roles centered on a submissive housewife and bread-winning husband. Despite the fact that the war had freed up the labor market and given women an unprecedented taste of economic and social independence, Jean Wade Rindlaub's studies confirmed that marriage and family remained the ultimate dream for young American women. Oneida rode the trend, convincing brides-to-be that no true home would be complete without a set of Community Plate silver shining on the sideboard.

of growing up in the Children's House were sweet, as sweet as the fragrant pink applesauce from the fruit of an Early Joe tree that he recalled eating out of a homemade tin cup in the East Room as a baby. In the "vivid green and sunlit yellow summers" the children played at croquet and at chasing after squirrels and butternuts and birds' nests; in the "white world" of winter, they "rolled immense snowballs, or played fox and geese in the field." Papa Kelly, the superintendent of the Children's Department, was loving, if strict, and taught the children, as their primary lesson, to turn the other cheek in their dealings with one another ("we never spoke of fighting, always 'quarreling'").[1]

The vague outlines of a world beyond the Community walls hovered on the edges of the children's vision: a world populated by "hired men" and "outsiders," strictly off limits to the children, and where the studied hypothesis that "hired men spit brown and outsiders spit white" was perhaps the closest Pierrepont would get to penetrating the mysteries of their universe and its inscrutable class distinctions. Yet, from the beginning, the "outside" exerted an almost hypnotic hold on the young boy's imagination, if for no other reason than that Ontario and Western freight trains thundered past the edges of the Mansion House grounds, giving the impression that "everything [out] there was immensely bigger and more powerful than in our world."[2]

"Outsiders know more than our folks," Pierrepont insisted in scrappy debates with his more devout companions. One early morning, he was out on the South Walk and saw the sun rising in a blaze of gold and crimson glory. "Lucifer, Son of the Morning!" exclaimed his poetic older half-brother, Theodore, who happened to be walking by at that moment. Though Pierrepont soon learned that Lucifer was not a good god, he did—just for a moment—compare his glorious new idol to the "hallowed but . . . somewhat drab gods of my father's Pantheon—Christ, Paul, Principalities and Powers" and "longed to ride in the chariot with Lucifer." That young Pierrepont found in the rebel angel a more compelling hero than Jesus Christ was an early sign of his inquisitive and risk-taking spirit.[3]

By 1878, the winds of dissension were beginning to blow in the Community, catching Pierrepont and his mother up in their gusts. Harriet Worden was a devout Bible Communist and until the end of her life a firm believer in Noyes's divine commission; Noyes was, after all, the father of her son. But

Noyes had always suspected her of an independent spirit; her maternal uncles, the Cook brothers, had been successful lawyers, puffed up and worldly, and all the suggestions made to her during Mutual Criticism had made acerbic reference to the "Cook Spirit" in her. Moreover, as a close friend of Mr. Hinds and Mr. Towner, the two mainstays of the anti-Noyes faction, she was jealously excluded from the "loyalist" camp, a rebuff Pierrepont felt keenly. As the Community spiraled into dissolution, the young boy, neither Noyesite nor secessionist, neither Community nor "outsider," found himself essentially stripped of a social identity.

Following the breakup, his mother, who had had three children by three different fathers, was left without a husband. And so, with the protective walls of Bible Communism in ruins around them, the nine-year-old Pierrepont was left to brave the icy winds of social opprobrium alone. Along with his half-brother Ormond and half-sister Stella, Pierrepont moved into an apartment with their mother on Turkey Street near the trap shop—the home of the very Irish toughs who, several years earlier, had taunted him. His mother sold books door to door to round out their meager yearly payouts from the Community while, to add a few dollars a month to the family income, Ormond worked in the trap shop and Pierrepont labored part-time for a carpenter.

Pierrepont sought to exorcise the "ghost of illegitimacy" by throwing himself into his carpenter's work, identifying a path to acceptance in the outside world through sheer physical toughness. On one occasion, Pierrepont and a fellow journeyman carpenter, Owen Morrison, were working on the roof of a house under a beating noonday sun when, suddenly, Pierrepont blacked out, succumbing to the heat. Any physical discomfort, however, was fully recompensed when he overheard Owen speaking of him: "I told Pip not to work so hard; he's a good boy—a good boy, but he doesn't know when to quit." In time, Pierrepont's addiction to physical prowess as a means of proving his worth would give way to more intellectual aims, and a burning desire to attend college replaced his carpenter dreams. But whether the goal in question was building a brick-and-mortar chimney or conquering Virgil's *Aeneid*, Pierrepont was propelled by an indomitable drive: the inescapable feeling that, as a social outlier, he must never quit. In his memoir, Pierrepont would later write of this period of his life, "Recognizing that my technical illegitimacy could not be helped, I decided to bury the past in a successful future. . . . I became possessed by a towering ambition to try my mettle in a struggle with the hostile world."[4]

In 1886, a generous hundred-dollar yearly supplement from his "Uncle" Abram, the father of his brother Ormond, allowed sixteen-year-old Pierrepont to attend Colgate Academy and then Colgate University as an avid classics and mathematics student. But when his mother fell gravely ill in 1891, he dropped out of school to nurse her and, upon her death, decided that, rather than returning to school, he would try his fortunes working for OCL along with his half-brother Holton Noyes (thanks to his father's disproportionate representation within the stirpicultural experiment, Pierrepont had no fewer than twelve half-brothers and -sisters). Holton and Pierrepont moved to Niagara Falls, where Oneida's silverware and chain factory were now located, taking up jobs in the chain department and in the administrative offices, respectively. Lodging in the Stone Cottage across the border in Canada where their father had lived out his final years, Holton and Pierrepont worked grueling ten-hour days at the factory and nourished ambitious young hopes for getting ahead in the business.

Drawing on the young man's mathematical prowess, Pierrepont's supervisor asked him to work out a cost-accounting system for the plant's manufactures. Most of the foremen cooperated in providing him with the facts and figures he needed to implement his new system. But one ornery foreman with a profitable outside business selling hooks that he bought from the company refused to provide the information Pierrepont needed. A little sleuthing soon revealed that the foreman was buying the hooks for 30 percent less than it cost Oneida to manufacture them, thus making a tidy profit on the deal. A cold war ensued between "the dishonest and the lazy-minded members of the staff" and Pierrepont, who insisted on cleaning up corruption among the employees in the company.[5]

But OCL's management expressed little interest in the young turks and their business counsels. By 1892, the control of OCL had shifted over to a group of retrograde spiritualists, old-time Community men who believed the best way of formulating a business strategy was to consult the spirit of John Humphrey Noyes via séances. The spiritualist "party," as it came to be known, was led by Community stalwart Theodore Pitt, who claimed that

Noyes—from the other side of the grave, no less—had tapped him as a successor in business and spiritual matters. "On the 21 of [April], eight days after his death, Mr. Noyes came and manifested his presence to [me]," Pitt recorded of his initial interview with the departed patriarch. "Well, Pitt," Noyes's shade supposedly said, "I want you to understand that you are my man yet. . . . I was not able to carry through the whole work on which I was engaged, I went as far as I could in my environment and limitations, and as far as Christ had planned for me to go. I had to lay down the work then and come here. You must take the work up and carry it out to completion. I rejoice that it is your lot to do what I could not do, and finish the work."[6]

Though the outlines of "the work" to be done remained vague, Pitt was convinced—and managed to convince a fair number of postbreakup followers—that he had been invested with Noyes's mantle in guiding OCL. Not least among his efforts to gain a following was a forty-one-page letter he addressed in 1888 to George Noyes Miller, John Humphrey's nephew and the leader of an antispiritualist faction that had sprung up among the younger generation. In the letter, he sought to prove his spiritualist credentials by detailing an interview he had held with the spirit of Mary Magdalene back in 1853. ("It was in June of 1854 that I first became conscious of Mary's personal presence," mused the would-be successor. "The one among the white-robed throng whom my soul was learning most deeply and passionately to love came to me . . . [and] my body thrilled with her wondrous magnetism.")[7]

With the directorship in hand and a spiritualist majority of five out of nine seats on the board of directors secured, Theodore Pitt seemed unbeatable. So when pressure was applied to Pierrepont and Holton to join the spiritualist ranks, the two found themselves on the horns of an awful dilemma. Should they stay with Oneida and remain loyal to their father's project, albeit now in less than competent hands, or should they make a clean break and set out on their own? Leaving, indeed, seemed the only rational option. And so, on April 1, 1892, Holton and Pierrepont found themselves on a ferry from Weehawken bound for New York City. Pierrepont's memoir records the metropolis glimpsed through the magic lens of youth: "New York, shadowy, inscrutable, reflecting in the clouds the brilliance of its night life . . . drawing every moment nearer. . . . [T]here, under those glowing clouds, lay the fairyland of opportunity."[8]

Having sold some inherited shares of OCL stock along with their bicycles, the two fortune hunters planned to use their scant pool of capital to make a killing on Wall Street. Like two characters out of a Horatio Alger novel, Pierrepont and Holton shared a room for twelve dollars a week. Armed with a bagful of charts and graphs, they spent their days in a broker's office, watching the tape and trading, and their evenings anxiously calculating profits and losses down to the last cent. But the age-old dream of turning mud into gold soon ran its course, and the boys recognized that they would need to find paying work.

As luck would have it, Pierrepont and Holton's first cousin George Miller was working as a traveling silverware agent for Oneida. He owned a warehouse in the city and made the boys a proposition. He would sell them Oneida silverware products at wholesale prices, and they could try their hand at selling them to small stores and restaurants around New York. Trading in their stock-market charts and graphs for bags of silverware samples, Pierrepont and Holton were about to join the ranks of that great American fraternity, the Order of the Salesman.

The archetype of the salesman occupies a unique place in American mythology. As an up-and-at-'em go-getter, brimming with confidence and optimism and displaying an even-handed sociability toward all comers, the salesman epitomizes America's preferred image of its national type: democratic, ambitious, positive. At the same time, the salesman has always shared a certain affinity with the confidence man, that liminal trickster figure whose shadowy image haunted the pages of every middle-class youth's advice book in antebellum America, the "man on the make" who preyed on naïfs freshly arrived in the city. The term "confidence man" was coined after the 1849 arrest of one William Thompson, whose grift was to strike up conversations with strangers on the street in New York City, eventually asking them if they would have enough confidence to allow him to hold their watches for a day. Confidence (and gold watch) in hand, Thompson walked away from his marks laughing.[9]

In antebellum America, the ominous specter of the confidence man betrayed America's collective anxieties about an uprooted and increasingly mobile system of social relationships. The middle class distrusted these lone wolves, ambitious young men who, cut loose from traditional family and communal ties, flocked to the cities to try their fortunes. The psychological coin of the day—mesmeric "influence"—gave rise to urban legends of crafty seducers who could lead the unwary down the path to perdition. But by the 1890s, the prevailing opinion had switched, and the confidence man enjoyed a kind of cachet as a cherished American type, revered for his exuberance and his ability to "win friends and influence people," as Dale Carnegie's self-help bible would later phrase it.

Starting in the 1890s and throughout the first decades of the twentieth century, salesmanship manuals sprang up like mushrooms, each claiming to hold the keys to success in selling and touting the very methods of seduction (now dignified as "suggestion") and influence that, a half century earlier, would have raised not a few disapproving eyebrows. In his 1911 manual, *Influencing Men in Business: The Psychology of Argument and Suggestion*, Walter Dill Scott discredited the traditional view of man as being influenced by reason, countering that, on the contrary, on the merest hint of suggestion, "the American public have come to believe . . . that Ivory soap is 99 44/100 per cent pure [and] . . . that the Gillette [razor] adds to the sum total of human happiness." He concludes the obvious application to business: "If we can give a man any sort of an idea it is not necessary to convince him of the truth of the idea if we can keep conflicting ideas from arising in his mind." The textbook for the YMCA Standard Course in Salesmanship similarly noted, "The mind can hardly be said ever to choose what it will believe." The successful salesman effects a Svengalian substitution of his own will for the will of the client. "You become a will *for* the man," promises the textbook, while "he completes the act you have commenced as though your will were indeed his own. In many cases he really thinks it is." Obtruding oneself (or one's product) onto the psychic screen of the client was the critical first step to making a sale; clinching the prospect's hypnotic confidence in the inevitability of the salesman's will was the next.[10]

It was just as this heady atmosphere of mental maneuvering and derring-do within business circles was catching on that Pierrepont Noyes would, on a fine spring day in 1893, gain his first taste of being a salesman. Silverware satchel in hand, he took to the streets. One day, after being roundly refused by restaurant after restaurant up and down Third Avenue, Pierrepont had the idea of taking what he knew to be the salesman's most annoying trait—

his persistence—and turning it on its head. Upon receiving the usual "not interested" from a restaurateur named Mr. Bortel, Pierrepont "instantly . . . showed exaggerated symptoms of diffidence and indicated immediate retirement," saying he would leave his card and call another day instead. But in reaching into his bag to get his card, "with the sudden rapidity of a magician, I produced this package [of spoons] instead of the card. Before Mr. Bortel had time to resent my importunity, I was orating at full speed ahead, holding the spoons under his nose." Pierrepont's psychological bait and switch worked, and he was soon making out an order for three dozen teaspoons, two dozen tablespoons, and two dozen forks and knives. Of course, not all sales were so easy, as when one thick-chested, red-faced proprietor of a seafood restaurant leaped across the counter with oyster knife in hand and chased Pierrepont down the street. But Pierrepont's natural irritation at being beaten, and his bull-like "determination to break through the stone wall of opposition," almost always carried the day. "I aimed to cover every street in New York which sheltered a restaurant," he would later reminisce of his peddling days.[11]

In their spare time, and when they felt business was good enough that they had a few quarters to spare, Pierrepont and Holton would play a round of pool at a billiard parlor on 116th Street. Their fellow patrons—confidence men and gold-brick artists of every stripe—were cordial enough, teaching the boys massé and carom shots and adding a "touch of romance" to their weekly nights out. The trust-building techniques of the con men, if not their actual swindles, commanded a kind of awed reverence from the novice salesmen. "I do not regard salesmanship as a form of confidence game," cautions William Morey Maxwell in his 1919 manual, *The Training of a Salesman*. At the same time, he admits, "I can't refrain from comparing . . . [the] salesman to the confidence man who says: 'I don't care who he is, or what he is; if he's got the money, I'll try to hook him.'"[12]

And then something happened that, by complete happenstance, drew Pierrepont back into the inner orbit of Oneida that he had so recently vowed to quit. Pierrepont's uncle Abram, needing to take a one-year leave of absence from his position as minority leader of the OCL board of directors, urged Pierrepont to take his place. The spiritualists were still in command, locking down company decisions with their invariable 5–4 vote on the board of directors, and by 1894 OCL "was sinking into a morass of elderly incompetence," Pierrepont would later note in his memoir. The company continued to maintain its diversified mix of products, from silk to traps to canned vegetables. But the burgeoning silverware factory, accounting for one half of OCL's total revenue, was now being egregiously mismanaged by the elderly directors. Between the declining quality of the silverware itself and one employee's corrupt sweetheart deals with Oneida distributors, which was siphoning off profits, the Niagara plant was rotting from the inside.

Pierrepont accepted his uncle's offer. As a fresh new voice on the board, Pierrepont knew that times were changing, that "mass production was taking the place of the little factory on the mill stream." His constant heckling of the spiritualists' incompetence and superstition over the course of the following year's board meetings managed to reinvigorate the fighting spirit of the minority. By November 1894, feeling the wind in his sails, Pierrepont decided to launch a campaign to wrest the company away from his séance-consulting elders at the upcoming January board election. Pierrepont's goal was to put the company back into the hands of vital, youthful men, rather than allowing it to be run through the spurious ghostly pronouncements of his dead father.[13]

With a solid cohort of other antispiritualists, Pierrepont set himself the task of contacting every single holder of Oneida stock to gain their proxy vote for his party. By the day of the election, no stone had been left unturned in their campaigning efforts. One of the chief supporters of the minority, Noyes loyalist Myron Kinsley, drove his horse and buggy into the village to consult with a local businessman who owned a considerable chunk of stock and who had previously always sided with the spiritualists. But by the time Myron found the august stockholder in the village tavern, another minority supporter had already gotten to him and convinced him to swing his vote to Pierrepont's party. Hopping up from his chair, he pointed at Myron and shouted, "No, sir—spirits can't can corn—not by a damned sight they can't! There's the man that's got my proxy, and he's going to keep it!"[14]

Voting stretched far into the night, and when the votes were finally tallied on the following morning, the minority had won by a sixteen-share margin in an election where nearly twenty-four thousand shares had been voted. Pierrepont, at the ripe age of twenty-four, was elected the new superintendent of the Niagara operations and the de facto head of OCL. "Your father's hand is in this," intoned one of John Humphrey's erstwhile allies to the newly tapped leader. "You think you decided the issue yourself . . . [but] your father inspired you." John Humphrey Noyes had believed we were connected to heaven by myriad little spiritual wires, through which communication between departed spirits and earth could take place. To be inspired was to receive a divine telegraph from the other side. Whether he felt himself telegraphically connected to his father's spirit or not, Pierrepont had nonetheless discovered that blood was thicker than water. Despite his contentious relationship with the Oneida Community, in the end it was home.[15]

Yet even after his easy glide over into an executive position, Pierrepont never for a moment lost his scrappy salesman's spirit, and he applied it to his new post with excellent results. One popular marketing technique in the late nineteenth century was the use of gifts or premiums as a reward to loyal customers; the fledgling Wrigley's gum company, for instance, had contracted with an Oneida competitor to offer a free butter knife or sugar shell spoon to its frequent buyers. One day in 1898, a telegram landed on Pierrepont's desk from Wrigley, asking, "Where is the hundred gross of butters and sugars you promised?" The telegram had mistakenly been addressed to Oneida, rather than the rival silver manufacturer who actually had the commission. But Pierrepont lost no time. Within hours he was on a train to Chicago and early the next morning popped up in Bill Wrigley's office, fresh-faced and ready to offer his services. "From that day until Wrigley died, I had all his silverware premium business," Pierrepont would later write with satisfaction.[16]

By 1900, OCL was thriving. Still, Pierrepont worried that depending on dexterous salesmanship for revenue, given the economy's unsettling ups and downs, was too shaky a foundation for the company. Oneida needed to create a recognizable identity, a cultural brand for itself: one that would be so popular with the buying public and would generate such a volume of sales that it could guarantee revenue in good times and in bad. Pierrepont settled on silverware as the most promising field for both growth and security. Oneida's locally canned fruits couldn't compete with the new mass-production corporations, whose sheer volume and geographic reach allowed them to offer the same products for a fraction of Oneida's price. If silk thread was the largest of the Oneida businesses, it was also the least profitable, the price of raw silk being so high that the margin on return was minimal. Traps and chains were profitable enough but had a limited consumer base. Only silverware could offer the kind of market scope and margin for expansion he was looking for.

In order to overhaul Oneida and forge the company silverware into a recognizable nationwide brand, Pierrepont knew he would have to assemble a team of expert businessmen, salesmen, financiers, and marketers—and the first place he thought to recruit was from among the now far-flung ranks of his early stirpicultural brothers. Many stirpicults had left Oneida with their families at the breakup. Some had gone to college; others were pursuing successful business careers in New York City or elsewhere. With the decrepit spiritualists sidelined, a host of young and energetic stirpicults were ready and eager to join Pierrepont in rebuilding the Oneida Community, Limited. Not surprisingly, those invited back, for the most part, all bore the names of families who had been on the Community A-list during John Humphrey Noyes's reign: Wayland-Smiths and Skinners; Allens and Kinsleys and Noyeses. In this second, secular iteration of the Oneida Community, the inner power circle uncannily reproduced itself.

The problem with Pierrepont's ambitious branding scheme was that the market was already monopolized by well-established silver trademarks—so well established that even well-wishers, upon hearing of Oneida's plans to break into the silverware market, taxed the plan with being "brave but suicidal." Pierrepont glimpsed an opening, however. The upscale sterling market, limited by nature, was already amply covered by the old silverware companies, certainly. But middle-class and younger consumers, unable to afford the high price of sterling, were looking for quality plated ware, and the market for this demographic was quite plainly underserved. Silverware makers offered these down-market buyers cheap single-plated ware or triple-plated ware at triple the price. Triple-plate was a notorious underseller. As one young clerk in a jewelry store pointed out to Pierrepont with some perspicacity, both single- and triple-plate were manufactured in the same stale patterns, and "ladies would not pay a big price for patterns their hired girls might buy at a fraction of the price."[17]

The plated ware being offered housewives in 1900 was of a hopelessly outmoded stamp, with frumpy florid Victorian motifs, akin to "hoop skirts and poke bonnets," and in no way keeping step with the evolving fashions of the times. It was clear: if Oneida could produce a high-quality triple-plated ware to rival sterling, but in distinctively chic patterns that would set it apart from the hired girls' silver, they might have a chance with the young, middle-class housewife aspiring to keep up with the Joneses. The company had no designers at that point, so Pierrepont went to his die makers and concocted a pattern of his own: "I showed [them] a spoon whose top I liked, another whose side ornaments seemed to fit with that top, and still another whose contour might lend itself artistically to a combination of the first two." And so was born the "Avalon," named for the misty, apple-treed island of Arthurian legend. So much for distinguishing triple-plated ware from the hired girl's humble eating utensils. The middle-class housewife could now slice her pot roast with the Avalon, imbibing medieval romance with every bite.[18]

But there was another reason triple-plate was a poor seller: those who could already afford to pay the high price of triple-plate would scrimp and save a little more to purchase sterling. Pierrepont, in consultation with Oneida's head plater, realized that the bulk of the cost of the spoon was already expended before it was ready for plating; keeping it in the silver bath until it had received a thicker coating would not add a proportionate amount to the cost of the final product. There was no reason, then, not to plate their silverware even more thickly than their competitors, offering better than triple-plated silver at a bargain price.

Pierrepont was convinced that the only way to create steady sales in the modern marketplace was through the power of advertising, creating an Oneida brand so recognizable and seductive that consumers couldn't help buying it. As a crackerjack salesman, Pierrepont knew a thing or two about the power of suggestion, and what was advertising if not suggestion on a grand scale, saturating the consumer psyche so thoroughly with images of the product that he would dream of it in his sleep? Pierrepont set himself, and the Oneida team, the not inconsiderable task of conquering the American subconscious.

So in 1901, placing their implicit trust in Pierrepont's instincts that mass advertising was the royal road to increased sales, the board voted the company an unheard-of budget of five thousand dollars to experiment with advertising. Early ads for Oneida triple-plate focused on the quality of the silverware and the fact that it wouldn't thin out, no matter how rough-and-tumble the treatment. They concocted a "wear-test" machine, a large spinning wheel whirling horizontally above a platform covered in pieces of wood, iron, and cloth. Eight spoons were hung from the arms of the wheel and dragged over the abrasive surfaces turn after turn until a spot was worn through on the back of the spoon's bowl. "We published the result in miles," Pierrepont later remembered, and "our competitor's spoon ran much fewer miles."[19]

In keeping with the tentative early phases of the advertising business as a whole, whose golden future was then but dimly glimpsed, the 1901 magazine advertisements were typically text boxes crammed with lettering, touting the quality and value of the product, and serving mostly as crib sheets for the agents. "Whenever a prospective customer permitted, the salesman read it all impressively to him," Pierrepont explained. One ad showed a photograph of the sterling shell of a plated spoon cut in half, with the caption, "If you could take out the metal filling of a Community Silver Spoon, the pure silver remaining would be almost heavy enough to eat with." In short, the early Oneida ads had all of the clunky, homespun didacticism of what today would be the equivalent of an infomercial.[20]

Text, however, could never compete with the image, concluded Berton "Doc" Dunn, Pierrepont's stirpicultural contemporary, who was appointed advertising czar for the company in 1904. And Dunn realized that while the durability of the silverware was certainly of some concern to consumers, such practical considerations paled in comparison to how the silverware *looked*. "The thing that matters to people of the class to which we were appealing . . . is chiefly how it looks," he explained in an interview with the advertising magazine *Printer's Ink*. "Is it pleasing, graceful, distinguished? Has it a well-known name?" The power of suggestion worked most forcefully through the eye, Dunn knew, and his first idea was to take out full-page ads on the theory that such a commanding space would make the reader sit up and take notice. Reducing text to a minimum, Dunn decided to showcase large-scale photographs of the silverware itself, attractively positioned on elegant lace backgrounds. Dunn selected only "the finest and most distinguished examples of lace" to offset the silver, carefully avoiding anything "that savored at all of *popularity*."[21]

Dunn looked far and wide in museums, antique shops, art galleries, both at home and in London, to cull the finest lace patterns for his ads. The Metropolitan Museum of Art even lent him priceless laces for his silver still lifes. "I was after not merely the finest designs in lace, but those that were the most appropriate for the different patterns of silver," Dunn would later record of his early forays into advertising. "We were appealing, you must remember, to the women, and women know lace." When lace appropriate to a particular silver pattern couldn't be found, Dunn commissioned an artist to develop a prototype and then had it executed by a Fifth Avenue lace shop. No expense was spared in surrounding Oneida silverware with that aura of genteel Old World elegance longed for by every middle-class housewife.[22]

At the same time as Dunn was developing his lace fantasies, stirpicult Grosvenor Allen, who manned the design department, realized in 1904 that Oneida needed a new pattern—and they needed it fast. Their competitors in plated ware had recently brought out a floral pattern, and so, in consultation with American sculptress Julia Bracken, Grosvenor created Oneida's "Flower de Luce" design, the company's first big seller. At once easy to pronounce and enticingly foreign—tinged with aristocratic echoes of royal fleurs-de-lis—the pattern was an immediate success. In 1910, after ten years of careful research and armed with an advertising budget pumped up to a gargantuan thirty thousand dollars a year, Oneida appeared to have hit the marketing mother lode. Community Silver was making a profit the first time, taking its place as the principal earner for OCL.

Dunn's finest hour was yet to come, however. Having successfully imbued the Oneida name with an aura of exclusive chic in the imaginations of American housewives, he now sought to cast his advertising net even wider. "Men," Dunn mused, "while not actually buying the silver, usually *help* buy." To appeal to this target audience of wage-earning husbands—the million or more male readers of *The Saturday Evening Post*—a new tactic was needed, trading in the sober distinction of antique lace for "snappy, up-to-date stuff." Dunn imagined drawings of chic couples in domestic settings chatting casually about silverware, "pictures of 'nice people,' the kind who 'belong,'" Dunn specified, "combined with light dialogue." In 1911, Dunn contracted with popular society illustrator Coles Phillips to draft some copy for him. "Are your pink ears listening, Betty?" queries a "nice"-looking young man in shirtsleeves reclining in an armchair in one 1911 advertisement. "Yes indeed," answers a lithe young beauty, lounging casually on the arm of her husband's chair and running her fingers through his hair. "Will they hear something nice?" These quirky, relaxed portraits of the fashionable silver-buying set were an immediate hit.[23]

Phillips went on to design an iconic line of advertisements for Oneida, each featuring a woman in the center, a prototype for the modern "pinup" girl. The established conventions for representing women in illustrated magazines and advertisements at the time was the "Gibson girl," named for the illustrator Charles Dana Gibson. While retaining certain elements from Victorian stereotypes, such as the vogue for ample hips and busts, Gibson's sketches superimposed a springy litheness suggestive of youth and the period's more permissive view of female athleticism (female tennis and cycling were in vogue at the turn of the century, as was swimming). Confident, stylish, occasionally standoffish toward the opposite sex, the Gibson girl nonetheless remained safely anchored in traditional feminine roles. She was, in other words, decidedly not the "new woman," threatening the status quo by, among other illicit activities, seeking the vote.

Coles Phillips thus inherited a well-established feminine prototype whose contours he could gently push into a more independent, daring feminine figure. In the critical early stages of this remaking of the American woman, which would culminate a decade later in the controversial figure of the flapper, Oneida played a key role. Oneida eschewed their competitors' reliance on august images of authority to sell silver (one particularly cloying ad by their competitor, Rogers Brothers, displayed an ample-bellied, white-whiskered grandfather sanctimoniously passing down his sterling to his daughter, with the caption, "Some gifts never grow old"). Instead, Oneida anticipated the anything-goes cult of youth that would dominate the next several decades and fashioned their advertisements to match.

Perhaps the distinctive feature of Coles Phillips's silverware ads for Oneida was their conspicuous lack of silverware. One particularly popular campaign featured a sketch of a beautifully gowned young woman staring into a silver chest, rapt in the face of her treasure. The silver itself was no more than a tantalizing flash of light within the somber ark that held it, leaving everything to the imagination. A 1917 ad in this style displays a woman walking toward the left panel of the frame, arms fully extended in front of her, holding at shoulder height her blue-velvet-lined case of silver. Though her dimpled, bare arms link her to a vanishing era where embonpoint was the fashion, her delicately revealed ankle, rakishly bobbed hair, and diaphanous dress make her enticingly, even shockingly, modern. Silhouetted against a sylvan tapestry in the background, the model, with her flowing robe and transfixed, worshipful gaze, resembles a pagan forest goddess, a tree nymph, more than a flesh-and-blood woman. Oneida silver, the ad seems to suggest, is primal, hypnotizing: every woman's dream.

Other ads repeated the formula, in each case displaying bobbed beauties in various states of rapture and adoration before their chest of silver. A hand posed lightly on the breast, as though the silver had taken one's breath away; an avid gaze leaning into the mysterious depths of the chest; in one case, a woman literally kneeling, hands clasped, before the magical box. Nor were the quasi-religious references, whether to temple or to holy ark, misplaced: these ads were essentially a recasting of religious wonder. In all the ads, the exact object of this reverence remains brilliantly vague. Is it the silver itself, the ancient lure of that which shines and glistens? Is it social respectability, the satisfaction of knowing you've impressed your guests with the perfect fish knife? Is it the maternal ideal of hearth and home and nurture represented by a fork and spoon? Or is it the intimacy of a woman alone with herself, a woman face-to-face with an unspecified "chest of dreams"? Only she who risks a look inside the ark might tell.

THE ONEIDA COMMUNITY, WHICH HAD PRIDED ITSELF ON EMANCIPATING ITS members—and its women, in particular—from the chains of social competitiveness and fashion, had been reborn from its ashes by cashing in on these very same middle-class fantasies in its twentieth-century female consumers. As the money-mad decade of the 1920s rolled out, Oneida's ads appealed in an ever more unabashed manner to American consumers' aspirations to class distinction and chic. In a 1928 ad in *The Saturday Evening*

Post, two cool turbaned flappers at a restaurant idly apply lipstick while their waiter serves tea. The caption warns, "Look at your silver—your guests do." "Women of position today are unwilling to use make-shift silver . . . dessert forks for salad, or teaspoons for oranges," another sententious magazine ad lectures. "Fashion in table service today requires that each course, each dish, have its appropriate silverware." Oneida specifically engineered the names of its silver patterns to conjure up aristocratic fantasies in class-obsessed consumers. From the art deco "Deauville," named for the tony French seaside resort, to "Coronation," timed to coincide with Edward VIII's ascension to the English throne in 1936, starry-eyed housewives were captivated by Oneida's tantalizing promise that they, too, could aspire to aristocratic distinction, all by plunking down some money at a jewelry store. (The fact that, instead of taking the throne, Edward abdicated it in order to marry the decidedly middle-class Wallis Simpson was, apparently, an irony lost on American consumers.)[24]

Oneida went further, seeking royal celebrity endorsements to vend its wares. Princess Margrethe of Denmark, upon marrying her cousin Prince René de Bourbon in 1921, received a gift of Community Silver from her brother, and Oneida made hay of the occasion. A 1926 advertisement featured a grandly outfitted bride, staring dreamily at a bouquet of flowers in her hands and with one delicate white-slippered foot resting on a brocade pillow at the base of her throne. "When a Princess Weds," the caption reads, what does she receive? A "magnificent cabinet" of Community Silver. Whereas Oneida Community women had been freed from a slavish devotion to fashion and material wealth, the better to focus on increasing their spiritual riches, their heirs now relied on the calculated nuances of social class and its material milestones in order to keep their coffers full.

This concession to worldly values was, apparently, a sacrifice the Oneida family was willing to make in order to keep itself afloat. Under the auspices of the newly solvent company, and with so many of the former stirpicults having returned home from their far-flung business ventures to set down roots, the 150 or so members of the Oneida family were looking at a friendly future. They christened their new community Kenwood. Something of a cross between an enormous family and a small village, the one hundred plus descendants who continued to live, quasi-communally, in and around the Mansion House constituted a curious sociological phenomenon. The stirpicults, all born between 1870 and 1880, began to marry around the turn of the century. To a surprising extent, they married each other—and their children did the same—creating an almost impenetrable maze of blood ties across generations. For three full generations the entire "family" lived and worked within a stone's throw of one another and referred to one another as cousins, uncles, and aunts—generally with some degree of genetic reliability.

The Mansion House's small rooms had been gerrymandered together to create what might be loosely called "apartments" (although in the railroad setup of the Mansion House's rooms, getting to one's apartment often entailed walking through someone else's private space—an invasion no one blinked twice at). The apartments lacked kitchen amenities, so everyone took meals together in the first-floor dining room. As had been the case during Community days, a cadre of outside "hirelings"—cooks, dishwashers, waitresses, gardeners—catered to the family's daily needs. When an individual family grew too big to be lodged commodiously in the Mansion House's cramped apartments any longer, they would build a house on a plot of land, leased from OCL, never privately owned, across the country road from the Mansion House.

As families began to build private houses around the Mansion House, the expanding village of Kenwood reflected the community's commitment to finding a delicate balance between the claims of the individual and the welfare of the whole. "Our present society," a family member once observed, "seeks the utmost freedom of individual initiative and development compatible with those principles of organization to which we are committed." Each separate home was "the product of its possessor's tastes and desires" but built "in the closest possible association to that central building [the Mansion House] which stands as the bond of union."[25]

Perhaps the most telling sign that Oneida had been reborn from its ashes was the enthusiastic resurrection, in 1908, of a bimonthly journal dedicated to chronicling the life of the family and the larger OCL community. *The Quadrangle*, named for the courtyard at the center of the Mansion House where residents gathered to chat in the shade of a tulip tree, was consciously designed as a successor to *The Circular* and *The American Socialist*. "Among associated persons interchange of thought contributes to harmonious progress; and knowledge of events carries sympathy and understanding among all interested," Stephen Rose Leonard explained in the first issue of the magazine. "Also, among associated persons, a record of ideas and events is of interest, or even importance, to their successors." With precisely the same sense of historical mission that had energized their grandparents, for whom "the business of publication was of prime importance," Leonard notes, the third generation of Oneidans were keen to chronicle for themselves and for posterity this latest phase of their communal enterprise.[26]

12

Survival of the Fittest

Iⁿ 1895, Pierrepont stopped by the home of a company worker, a capable and loyal hand at the polishing wheel who had been badly injured at work. Upon seeing the squalid living conditions of his employee—who, along with his wife, father, and four children, occupied a small three-room hovel—Pierrepont experienced what he would later call a "spiritual conversion" that kindled in him a commitment to abolish poverty among the employees of the Oneida Community, Limited.[1]

Pierrepont's conversion was timely. Just one year before, the country had been rocked by the Pullman Strike, when George Pullman's railway-car workers walked off the line to protest brutal wage cuts without corresponding cuts in rent on their company-owned homes or prices on staples at the company store. Union leader Eugene V. Debs's freshly formed American Railway Union called a sympathy strike among its members, the first of its kind in the United States; for the space of a week, from June 26 through July 3, the country was effectively paralyzed as railway workers across the nation refused to operate trains employing Pullman cars. When it became clear that the mail was no longer being delivered, federal troops were called in, the movement quashed, and Debs jailed for disobeying a court injunction against the strike.

But despite this tidy victory for the Gilded Age capitalists, change was in the air. Debs would emerge from jail six months later a converted socialist, a copy of *Das Kapital* under his arm, and harboring a plan to mobilize the country's working class against the all-powerful enemies of labor. In 1904, Debs would run for president on the Socialist Party ticket, determined to emancipate the working class from wage slavery, that "inhuman traffic in the brains and blood and bones of human beings." From a membership of ten thousand in 1901, the Socialist Party skyrocketed to eighteen thousand members by 1912, with hundreds of elected public officials and more than three hundred periodicals devoted to its cause. The "labor problem," as some squeamishly referred to it, was not about to disappear.[2]

Socialism was not a new idea at the time of Debs's arrest in 1894, and certainly not new to Pierrepont Noyes, whose father, in 1873, had written *History of American Socialisms*, cataloging the dozens of utopian communities that had popped up in the social and religious ferment of America in the 1830s and 1840s. But the tenor of Debs's socialism was quite different from the bookish, bucolic communes documented by John Humphrey Noyes. After the wave of European working-class revolutions in 1848, Marx and Engels's "scientific socialism" trickled into the United States through the pages of Horace Greeley's radical reform newspaper, the *New York Daily Tribune*. According to Marx and Engels, utopian socialists of John Humphrey Noyes's ilk, while well intentioned, had come on the historical scene too early. Predating the apotheosis of capitalism in the mid–nineteenth century, they remained trapped within the quaint bourgeois ideology that maintained that social progress would come by cultivating virtue in the individual rather than through structural reforms of the capitalist mode of production. Not simply one choice among others, socialism, according to dialectical materialism, was a historical necessity, as impassive and inevitable as the law of gravity.

But the claim that class warfare, rather than the individual soul, was the linchpin of history had never sat well with John Humphrey Noyes or his fellow utopians. "We fully believe that the grand objects before [labor] will be obtained, not by agitation, not by strife, not by legislation, not even by cooperation; but by such radical changes of character as can be effected only by the grace of God," opined a Community editorialist in an 1871 issue of *The Circular*. In his aptly titled essay "The Socialism of Jesus," Noyes acolyte Theodore Pitt remained skeptical of the socialist tendency to beatify the working class. Unless "individual hearts have been touched and impregnated with the life and spirit of Jesus," he averred, the average workingman was "just as selfish, sensual, materialistic" as was the workingman "by the Sea of Galilee, at Corinth, Ephesus, and Rome, eighteen hundred years ago." Righteousness inhered in one's character, not in one's allegiance to a particular class.[3]

Thirty years later, as the reality of organized socialism pressed closer, Francis Wayland-Smith corroborated Pitt's point. His 1907 pamphlet, *Shall We Choose Socialism?*, asserted that the "tyrannical dictations of the labor unions have come to be as great an abuse as the grasping monopolies of the rich." Until individual souls could learn to root out selfishness, he concluded, no economic system—feudal, capitalist, communist, or otherwise—would ever produce a regenerate society. Heaven on earth would work itself out, not on the godless terrain of dialectical history, but through the medium of the converted soul.[4]

In his 1906 paean to the working class, *The Jungle*, Upton Sinclair drew a clear distinction between these two brands of socialism—utopian and scientific—with a clear sense that the latter was in the ascendant. The novel follows the declining fortunes of a Lithuanian immigrant, Jurgis Rudkis, who, brutalized by the Chicago meatpacking factory where he works, slowly discovers socialism as the only path to salvation. The final chapter of the novel describes a socialist soirée in which Mr. Lucas, a former itinerant evangelist and "a mild and meek-looking little gentleman of clerical aspect," faces off with Nicholas Schliemann (aka Marx), a former professor of philosophy who "understood human institutions, and blew them about," in his systematic analysis of the ravages of capitalism, "like soap bubbles." Sinclair's novel ends with the recently converted Jurgis and the rest of the party faithful gathered in a meeting hall, listening breathlessly to telegraphed election returns, dreaming of the ultimate victory of America's outraged workingmen.[5]

Pierrepont rigorously rejected Sinclair's socialism, along with his confidence that overthrowing the capitalist mode of production would magically end human misery. "Absolute equality—the dream of Socialism—has been declared impracticable by political economy, undesirable by philosophy, and utterly condemned by history," Pierrepont noted in a 1909 article for *The Quadrangle*. Instead, he remained faithful to his father's millennial vision of a world of justice wrought through love: selflessness was not only the highest virtue but a practical path to personal happiness and economic success. At the same time, Pierrepont and his Kenwood contemporaries had abandoned any organized form of Christianity. They were now for the most part agnostics, if not atheists; their new religion, if they had one, was OCL itself. And so, in a brilliant psychological campaign, the charismatic Pierrepont managed to take his father's model of a selfless, mystical Christian community of God's elect and translate it, point for point, into a program for secular salvation and peaceful coexistence between the classes that had become the burning social question of the day.[6]

When John Humphrey Noyes had founded his Society of Inquiry in Putney in 1834, America could still be considered partly a "classless" society. The "middling sorts" counted among their ranks merchants and businessmen, yeoman farmers and artisan craftsmen. In seventy years, all that had changed. The artisanal class sunk into the ranks of the working class as the distinction between manual and nonmanual labor hardened into a clear class marker. By the time the Community folded in 1880, the Oneidans had passed definitively into the station of the propertied middle class. Pierrepont's genius was to take the classless vision of Christian brotherhood imagined by his father and remake it for a world in which class divisions were a stark reality. Within the Kenwood family, failure to value the greater good of the whole above selfish, private interests did not betoken a failure of godliness so much as a failure of character and, perhaps even more critically, a betrayal of one's class honor. If the Kenwood society was no longer bound together by a belief in their role as God's chosen in ushering in the millennium, they were firmly convinced they were to play a providential role in leading America's propertied class to a peaceful resolution in the looming confrontation between labor and capital.

When news of John Humphrey Noyes's unconventional sexual practices first leaked to Putney villagers in 1847, his sister Harriet had interpreted the town's hushed response as a token of their awe in the face of God's elect, comparing herself and her companions to Old Testament characters Shadrach, Meshach, and Abednego who, in the Book of Daniel, emerged unscathed from Nebuchadnezzar's fiery furnace: "If you look this way now-a-days, you may conceive of us as walking unbound, unharmed in the midst of a fiery furnace, and see us not alone but the Son of God with us. . . . Something inspires an awe. We think it is the majesty of truth and innocence, and a lurking fear in the people's minds that we are the Kingdom of God." Kenwood's denizens regarded themselves and their family enterprise as endowed with no less sacred a mission than that of their ancestors. OCL was a providential company, a voice in the wilderness, a modern-day chosen people "walking in the midst of the fire" of social discord unharmed.[7]

PAYING THEIR WORKERS WAGES SLIGHTLY ABOVE THE MARKET RATE, OR IN any event above the rate at comparably sized factories, was Oneida management's first pledge of commitment to overcoming the divide between labor and capital. Next was the establishment of a "bonus wage," whereby wages were adjusted in order to keep pace with the rising cost of living. Oneida also evolved what was termed a "contingent wage," which was essentially a manner of profit sharing. At the end of each business year, up to half of the earnings of the company (after paying out taxes and dividends) were paid out to the employees. Because workers saw that the company's profit was returned directly to them in the form of wages, the contingent wage gave a stiff boost to worker morale and trust. Business historian Esther Lowenthal wrote approvingly in her 1927 study of Oneida's labor policies that workers were "more careful in their use of material, more sparing in the use of heat and light, less destructive generally." Finally, the institution of a service wage, which increased wages incrementally with length of service, decreased turnover.[8]

One of the most interesting choices Pierrepont made in structuring the new company was to insist that, in times of austerity, when wage cuts were necessary, OCL would cut deepest at the higher levels of management. In 1914, following a lean year, all management personnel accepted a 10 percent cut in their pay until the financial situation improved in 1916. In 1921, more serious economic difficulty brought correspondingly deeper cuts: Pierrepont halved his salary, while the directors of the various OCL departments accepted a one-third reduction in salary. Pierrepont's insistence that management not only share but also, in some cases, personally shoulder a large percentage of the austerity measures required by lean financial times convinced workers that the company was genuinely interested in their welfare.[9]

In addition to giving workers a stake in the company's success by tying their wages to profits and length of service, OCL management took pains to secure dignified living conditions for the factory hands, encouraging home ownership by selling the workers cheap land to build on and advancing affordably financed loans. "Before we are ten years older," Pierrepont proclaimed in a 1913 speech to the Oneida management, "before we are 5 years older—I believe we shall feel a little ashamed if each employee who is honest and efficient cannot own his own home if he wants to." In the heart of Sherrill, the newly created worker village, the company constructed a new school, a "high street" shopping block, a community center, and recreation fields that they heavily subsidized, providing its employees with "good, clean amusements and all kinds of athletics, picture shows, lectures, bowling, baseball, [and] football." Oneida also matched the amount of money collected in Sherrill school taxes each year, securing not only "a high school equipped with the most modern requirements" but also "a well-trained staff able to prepare students for the college entrance examinations." When a trade-union organizer paid a visit to OCL workers in 1915 to see if he might find there fertile ground for forming a union, he left mystified: at Oneida, he had found nothing but contented workers and an honest "business policy carried out by men who put the man and woman ahead of the dollar."[10]

Pierrepont's new operating plan, or "Industrial Socialism" as he christened it, resembled reform efforts undertaken by dozens of other companies across the country in the critical first decade of the twentieth century that came to be known under the general term of "welfare work" or "corporate welfare." Profit-sharing and stock-holding plans were not uncommon tactics by which management sought to convince workers that they were partners in a joint enterprise, where profit for one meant profit for all. Opening up possibilities for home ownership, through advantageous loans and wage garnishing, was another avenue management hoped would turn workers away from revolutionary grumbling and, instead, give them a clear stake in keeping the wheels of capitalism greased.

Organizing structured opportunities for outdoor athletics, so as to draw workers away from the temptation to drink and dissipate themselves in other thriftless forms of consumption, was another popular tactic. Management at some of America's canniest industries even attempted the psychological sleight of hand of mixing in upper- and middle-class sports—rifle clubs and horseback riding—with the more plebeian activities of billiards and boxing in order to convince workers that they, too, at least in their leisure time, were capable of upward mobility. In her paean to Oneida's labor policy, historian Esther Lowenthal noted with pleasure that one of the most popular worker's clubs in Sherrill was one devoted to the suitably genteel occupations of stream stocking and game propagation.[11]

At a time when capitalists all over the country were scrambling to stymie socialist agitation and to prevent the federal government from stepping in to regulate labor relations, Pierrepont's efforts to uplift the workers in both their work and private lives, all the while instilling the good capitalist values of thrift, teamwork, and perseverance, were far from revolutionary. What was original was Pierrepont's conscious decision to engineer a state of "semi-socialism," as he called it, among the propertied class. This design for the good society rigorously rejected both working-class socialist calls for shared ownership and middle-class industrialist materialism and entitlement. Rather, Pierrepont insisted that the owners of capital remained true to their class dignity only by accepting to live modestly and in terms of relative economic equality with one another and with their workers.

The years immediately following the breakup had demonstrated to the Oneida communists, in a particularly dramatic and bruising way, how pitiless the free market could be in distributing economic fortunes. Some ex-communists, through a combination of luck and skill, rose to the top of the financial food chain, while others—particularly unwed mothers with children to provide for—found themselves nearly destitute. From the very beginning of his takeover of OCL in 1895, Pierrepont had been clear-eyed about how best to structure the company in order to preserve the Kenwood family's fragile sense of unity. The first step was to establish a relative economic parity among its members while expunging any vulgar taste for the accumulation of wealth and the competitive material displays that were its natural consequence. The OCL and its managing family, the Kenwood clan, would work tirelessly "to replace that selfish, pitiless personal ambition, so long recognized as the only practical agent of human progress, by an equally potent ambition for the welfare of all; and to find in Brotherhood that happiness so vainly sought by the world in the pride and luxuries of wealth."[12]

In order to institute this ethos, OCL established a maximum and a minimum for management's incomes: "a maximum which puts it out of the power of any member to get rich, and a minimum which insures against poverty. Between these two every grade of efficiency is recognized in fixing salaries." In his 1909 speech at the Annual Agents' Banquet, Pierrepont quipped, "Let all abandon hope of getting rich who enter here," adapting the legend scripted over the entrance to Dante's hell. "We will have no rich and no poor," Pierrepont went on to lecture. He insisted he was not aiming at absolute equality—which would be perhaps as disastrous financially as it would be impossible to achieve practically—but at "a reasonable equality, an equality which will allow us all to live together as brothers."[13]

John Humphrey Noyes had always distrusted democracy, and his heirs were equally wary of democracy in its more populist, rabble-rousing form. Polite, top-down "consensus" was more to their taste. Pierrepont once described the Oneida Community as an association in which "300 people got away from the squabbles of majority rule, the tyranny of unbridled power, or the anarchy of no rule, and lived happily and successfully for over thirty years on the basis of unanimity." If anarchy and tyranny were obviously undesirable forms of government, democracy was little better. Pragmatically speaking, absolute democracy made no sense. To give the workingman, whose talent lay in his hands, a voice in the management of a complicated financial mechanism like Oneida Community, Limited, bucked both common sense and financial prudence. But rights-based democracy was just as philosophically distasteful to Pierrepont and his cohort, insofar as it assumed that the base unit of society was the free individual, each pursuing his own selfish, private interest. Democracy's constant clash of wills, ultimately carried by the majority, had the advantage of preventing tyranny, certainly, just as the founding fathers had calculated. But it could never achieve the higher ideal of pacific, selfless agreement. Only brotherhood, where the social bond was forged not through a legalistic grasping after individual rights but through love, might yield a perfect society.

Pierrepont's uncle George Washington Noyes had written an 1875 screed against the spirit of legalism inherent in most social contracts, insisting that true communism "abstains from law, and puts all relations on the ground of honor, or Christian charity." Thirty-five years later, Kenwood residents still held fast to their ancestors' model. When asked to describe the special nature of Oneida Community, Limited, as a social and business organism, Pierrepont responded that "we are a body of people having a community not of goods or of government, but a community of aims," where membership in the society was not to be gauged by vote or by right, by birth or by petition, but by what Paul would have called "circumcision of the heart." One could count oneself a member of the mystical corporate body of Oneida to the precise extent that one had managed to subordinate one's private interests to the welfare of the whole. "In your own heart is the test," Pierrepont once observed, "and by a careful inventory you can find out just how much of a member you are."[14]

But if the Kenwood family and their workers lived in a state of relative economic equality, the descendants of John Humphrey Noyes's bold experiment made no pretense that men were socially, intellectually, or even politically equal. Pierrepont's insistence that men should learn to live together on terms of "reasonable equality" had nothing to do with the self-evident truth that all men were created equal; such philosophical niceties were of little interest to him. Rather, Pierrepont believed that the propertied class should strive to achieve "reasonable equality" with its workers because honor and decency demanded it. As survivors of the brutish struggle for existence, they were morally bound to extend chivalrous compassion to the losers. "When we are prosperous we must sit right down and raise our men's wages without reference to whether we are forced to or not," he insisted. Pierrepont had a horror of labor unions, not because he dreaded their demands, but because the very notion of being forced to wrangle over reciprocal rights and duties in the public forum was an insult to his class honor. Having been blessed by culture and inheritance with the virtues of "altruism and self-control," as one descendant described the qualities required of the ruling class, the members of Kenwood society were invested with the unique responsibility to create a more equitable distribution of the spoils.[15]

Natural equality was a fiction; the kind of economic parity achieved among the OCL community, workers and management alike, was a radically unnatural state, one that could only result from evolution's winners being sufficiently gracious to grant it. Referring to his father's spiritual vocabulary of ascending and descending fellowship, by which the higher would draw the lower up to their level, Pierrepont accused socialism of acting from the wrong end of the hierarchy. Having been initiated by the have-nots, instead of "start[ing] at the top and work[ing] downward," socialism's failure was certain: "If the experiment is forced on the country all it can possibly mean is the pulling down of the prosperous to the level of the needy, and this, as always, would involve the latter in worse and worse conditions—never a pulling up of anyone." Men were as "unlike as goats and lions," Pierrepont once mused to his cousin Edith Kinsley, who jotted down the saying in her diary. To achieve the good society, what was needed was not "to educate the minds of the goats and turn them into competing lions," but to "educate the hearts of the lions" so that they would compassionately refrain from killing the goats.[16]

That Pierrepont and the rest of the Kenwood family should treat the idea of natural equality with skepticism was nothing exceptional in early-twentieth-century American thought. The English biologist-cum-sociologist Herbert Spencer applied Charles Darwin's theory of evolutionary adaptation to the development of human societies, postulating that only the fittest individuals and, by analogy, the fittest societies would survive the natural struggle for existence. Spencer's conservative social theories hit a chord in America when his works traversed the Atlantic in the 1870s and 1880s, where liberal economic policies had created a "gilded age" of spectacular wealth inequalities that begged explanation. Spencer's most avid fans, including Yale University professor William Graham Sumner, deplored the "humanitarian" turn taken by nation-states in the wake of the eighteenth-century revolutions and their misguided call for the recognition of natural human equality. Modern governments and their egalitarian policies of assistance to the

poor, Sumner argued, worked directly against evolutionary progress by artificially propping up the weaker members of the species. "Nature's forces
know no pity," Sumner opined, and nor should the state: as a scientific enterprise designed to guarantee the unimpeded functioning of free market
individuals, sentiment was completely foreign to the state's operation. Spared
their natural fate of swift elimination by the sentimental modern state, the
unfit were thus left free to propagate in ever-greater numbers.[17]

Andrew Carnegie's 1889 essay, "Gospel of Wealth," fully conceded Sumner's point that handing out money willy-nilly to the poor was improvident
and that giving a quarter to a begging indigent was likely to "work more
injury than all the money which its thoughtless donor will ever be able to give
in true charity will do good." Like Sumner, Carnegie was rigorously opposed
to "public charity," or state intervention to meliorate the inevitable inequalities generated by competitive capitalism. Yet even Carnegie stopped short of
Sumner's endorsement of an all-out abandonment of the underclass. According to his philosophy, the best that could be done was for the rich man (by
which he meant the evolutionarily "fit" man) to dole out his money privately
to elevating public institutions—libraries, schools, museums, parks—so that,
moving at the geologic pace proper to social evolution, nature's losers might
one day be made more equal (or at the very least, in the interim, more
civilized).[18]

Other scientists and philosophers stumped by the puzzle of inequality
would light upon a different solution: the scientific regulation of reproduction,
or eugenics. Human inequality was written in the genes, and any attempt to
foster evolutionary progress had to start at the cellular level. From English
utopian socialists to prim American conservatives in the pocket of Gilded Age
millionaires, eugenics as an antidote to social ills appealed across the political spectrum. As a product of the only extended eugenics experiment ever
attempted, Pierrepont and his fellows at Kenwood were of obvious interest
to eugenics enthusiasts. In his autobiography, Pierrepont recounts the story
of a dinner party he attended in London in 1910 hosted by H. G. Wells;
George Bernard Shaw was also at the party. During the dinner, Mrs. Shaw
stumbled over a question she wished to ask Pierrepont and was quickly aided
by her more socially adept husband: "We should both like to know whether
you were born under the old Oneida Community system? Were you what

your father called a 'stirpicultural' child?" Candidly replying that he was, indeed, a "stirp," a product of his father's breeding experiment, Pierrepont was met with a torrent of questions from the fascinated guests.[19]

Wells, Shaw, and Charles Davenport, the father of American eugenics, all made pilgrimages to the hallowed site of John Humphrey Noyes's eugenics experiment during the first decade of the new century. All were keen to glean lessons from Kenwood on the possibility of social engineering being accomplished through scientific breeding. Both George Bernard Shaw and his fellow Englishman Julian Huxley saw scientifically driven reproduction and socialism as complementary doctrines. Under the current capitalist system, humans were divided up into segregated classes with little to no reproductive interaction. Such a social arrangement was an obstacle to genetic progress, as it prevented the genetic front-runners in each class from combining forces. In George Bernard Shaw's 1903 play, *Man and Superman*—inspired, in part, by the "experiment at Oneida Creek," as Shaw referred to it—the protagonist, John Tanner, writes a "Revolutionist's Handbook" arguing that eugenics requires social equality in order to get results: "To cut humanity up into small cliques, and effectively limit the selection of the individual to his own clique, is to postpone the Superman for eons," reads Tanner's list of revolutionary tips. "Not only should every person be nourished and trained as a possible parent, but there should be no possibility of such an obstacle to natural selection as the objection of [the marriage of] a countess to a navvy or of a duke to a charwoman. Equality is essential to good breeding."[20]

Shaw's penchant for flamboyant satire in advocating his political beliefs made him an unreliable spokesperson in the view of the eugenics movement's more fervent supporters, who (as is so often the case with the zealous) lacked a sense of irony. More to their taste was Julian Huxley, who constructed a remarkably humorless argument against the "competitive and individualist system based on private capitalism" as inherently dysgenic and predicted that, once society had equalized the social and economic conditions of rich and poor, we would be able to reliably separate the genetic wheat from the chaff and breed our way to a utopian socialist world state. A true eugenics program would inevitably have to involve a revolution in sexual mores, by which the "amative" and the "propagative" functions of sexual intercourse (to quote John Humphrey Noyes's original distinction

Male Continence) would be rigorously separated from each other. Men and women could pursue their individual desires in any direction they wished as far as "amative" sexual intercourse was concerned, so long as, reproductively, they sacrificed personal inclinations "on the altar of the race" in order to forward the collective progress of "social salvation."[21]

Charles Davenport, perhaps the most influential advocate of eugenics on this side of the Atlantic, had no such visionary dreams as animated the English Fabians and was decidedly not of socialist leanings. Having studied engineering while in prep school, Davenport brought a mathematical zeal to his later studies in biology. In 1904, with a grant from the newly created Andrew Carnegie Institution in Washington, Davenport established a station for the "experimental study of evolution" at Cold Spring Harbor on Long Island. Applying the hereditary theories of Gregor Mendel to the heritability of eye, hair, and skin color in humans, Davenport was soon eager to test his theory that character traits were as genetically determined as eye color. He sent out hundreds of surveys to medical, mental, and educational institutions across the country asking for detailed family trees of their clients and inmates. On the basis of the data collected, he concluded that a whole host of character types—from the "feebleminded" to the criminal, the alcoholic to the pauper—were inherited conditions.[22]

Davenport discovered that when it came to underwriting scientific research that would track race degeneracy back to its (inevitably lower-class) sources, America's financial elite had deep pockets. Generously funding the establishment of a Eugenics Record Office in 1910 were, first, the railroad heiress Mrs. E. H. Harriman and, later, John D. Rockefeller. Davenport hired teams of young researchers, biology students fresh out of the finest colleges, and sent them into the field to study albinos, the Amish, the insane, the feebleminded, and juvenile delinquents, among other populations. The resulting data was compiled on three-quarters of a million filing cards stored at Cold Spring Harbor, endowing the eugenics movement with a scientific archive that would lend it weight and authority in the eyes of the public.[23]

In his 1911 book, *Heredity and Eugenics*, Davenport explained the elements of the new science of heredity and pointed to its practical applications in the fields of immigration and population control. In his preface, in a reactionary riff on the Declaration of Independence, he states the eugenic fact that will guide all his analyses: "the fundamental fact [is] that all men are created *bound* by their protoplasmic make-up and *unequal* in their powers and responsibilities." His book is studded with images of slack-jawed, in-bred families whose general unfitness for life is meant to speak for itself, jux-taposed with dizzying black-and-white Mendelian diagrams demonstrating the scientific inevitability that "the children of two feeble-minded parents will be defective" and underscoring "how great is the folly, yes, the crime of letting two such persons marry." Pauperism and criminality are chalked up to genetics, as well, supported by a diagrammed family tree demonstrating the fatal transmission of the gene for "shiftlessness" from one generation to the next.[24]

The Kenwood family sympathized with the spirit of justice animating the English socialists but took issue with more than a few of their revolu-tionary goals. It might be true, as Huxley and Shaw postulated, that vast pools of genetic gold were destined to remain untapped under the rigid capitalist class system, but Pierrepont was not interested in tinkering with the basic capitalist method of distribution in order to hunt inequality back to its roots. Pierrepont always shirked the title of "reformer," insisting in his autobiography that at Oneida they had "aimed only to work out [a] . . . more equitable distribution . . . in our own little industrial island." "We were not revolutionists, lawless or otherwise," he cautioned. Social responsibility re-mained a matter of personal culture, not a matter for institutional or legisla-tive action.[25]

H. G. Wells recognized as much when he paid a visit to Kenwood and later wrote about it in his 1906 book of essays, *The Future of America.* Pierre-pont, with boyish enthusiasm, showed his guest all over the factories, in-cluding the trap works: "He showed me photographs of panthers in traps, tigers in traps, bears snarling at death, unfortunate deer, foxes caught by the paws." While Wells struggled to block the grisly images from his mind, he tried Pierrepont on the subject of politics, or collective action—and got pre-cisely nowhere. A "sense of the State," apparently, fell entirely outside his sphere of operation. "All his constructive instincts, all his devotion, were for Oneida and its enterprises. America was just the impartial space, the large liberty, in which Oneida grew, the Stars and Stripes a wide sanction akin to the impartial irresponsible harboring sky overhead." In Wells's clever allegory, Pierrepont remained blithely blind to the systemic nature of capitalist exploitation, accepting the inevitable existence of crushed paws on a global level as long as Oneida, "his own little industrial island," remained true to its chivalrous ideals.[26]

Charles Davenport's visit to Kenwood in 1912 seemed to make more of an impression, warranting a little blurb in the December issue of *The Quadrangle* by Tirzah Miller's daughter Dr. Hilda Herrick Noyes. Davenport gave a résumé of the eugenics movement to his audience and spoke of its vital importance to the United States' national interest, estimating that "over one-fifth of the State's funds are required to support [America's] ever increasing army of defectives." He noted that American philanthropists had taken a keen interest in his work, having "gotten tired of giving to homes for cripples and aiding paupers." Dr. Noyes closes her article with the rather stunning conclusion that the most important event to have transpired in 1912 was neither the election of President Woodrow Wilson nor the sinking of the *Titanic* but the sum total of the moments in which each young man asked for a young woman's hand in marriage, thus determining the protoplasmic fate of America.[27]

Davenport's message resonated with other leading members of Kenwood as well. *Quadrangle* editor Stephen Leonard published a rather testy critique of socialism in a 1909 issue of the magazine, arguing that "it may be as hopeless as bailing the ocean to expect by beneficence to control human misery before first controlling human existence and human folly," by which he euphemistically referred to birth control. "Among human beings, each family is responsible for its own existence, makes no voluntary effort to match supply and demand, or to reproduce with the best inheritance, and is its own master when indulging in human folly. This irresponsibility entails competition and survival of the fittest." Properly directed reproduction, not government handouts, was the key to solving social ills.[28]

Hilda Herrick Noyes's brother George Wallingford Noyes concurred, claiming that socialism's argument that the poor masses should replace the few rich in charge of the means of production missed the crux of the labor-capital crisis. The modern revolution would be a struggle to secure not the means of production but "an equal diffusion of the altruistic qualities of character." The good society would not be achieved through welfare work, since such imprudent spending only dissipated society's resources "in the impossible attempt to secure the welfare of the morally unfit." Curtailing reproduction of the "morally unfit" (who were, of course, almost universally to be found populating the dregs of the underclass) was the key to social justice. Just as evolution had begun by securing a race of human beings strong enough to survive physically, so in its advanced stages evolution had to be steered in the direction of developing the social virtues of "altruism and self-control" if the human race was to prosper.[29]

A decade later, in 1921, George Wallingford Noyes joined Hilda Herrick Noyes to give a joint paper at Charles Davenport's Second International Eugenics Conference in New York City, held in the hallowed halls of the Museum of Natural History. After opening remarks by the museum's president, Henry Fairfield Osborn, no less a personage than Major Leonard Darwin, Charles Darwin's son and the president of the British Eugenics Education Society, would kick off the proceedings with a lecture titled "The Aims and Methods of Eugenical Societies." Railing against environmental reformers whose efforts had not advanced humanity one mote since ancient Greece, Darwin suggested eugenics as a "new method of striving for human welfare" and closed his piece with the specter of "national deterioration resulting from the unchecked multiplication of inferior types." The proceedings—nearly a thousand pages of them—included papers from the anodyne to the chilling, from a plodding genetic exposition of "Variations in the Jimson Weed" to a phrenological disquisition on the "high degree of complexity" to be found in the cranial sutures of the European race as opposed to "relatively simple" skull sutures of Hawaiians and American Indians.[30]

The talk Hilda and George delivered, "The Oneida Community Experiment in Stirpiculture," provided a brief overview of John Humphrey Noyes's project and hazarded some speculations as to the superior health and mental cultivation of the stirpicults compared to a nongenetically culled population. "The Oneida Community was a product of successive unconscious group selections," the paper suggested, beginning with the English Puritans. The New England pioneers were a particular group selected from among the Puritans; the religious revivalists were a subset of New England pioneers; the Perfectionists, who believed in the possibility of freedom from sin, were a subset of the revivalists; and, finally, the Oneidans self-selected from among the Perfectionists as a group who "believed in the necessity of human leadership as an auxiliary to direct divine guidance." Establishing the heritability of such key physiological and temperamental traits as physical hardiness, longevity, native intelligence, leadership, and faculty of agreement, the paper went on to establish (with the aid of voluminous and tedious comparative charts) the apparently superior health, intelligence, and lifespan of Oneida's genetically selected stock.[31]

A general survey revealed that the fifty-eight products of the stirpicultural experiment experienced a markedly lower death rate compared to the average American population, or just 13.3 percent of the expected national death rate (that one of these casualties was "run over by a railway train" raised no suspicions, apparently, as to the victim's native intelligence). In addition, "No deaf and dumb, blind, crippled or idiotic children were ever born in the Community"—certainly a eugenic badge of distinction not to be overlooked. By 1921, among the fifty-two survivors of the fifty-eight stirpicultural births, "there are only two cases of sub-normal development": a man fifty years of age who had "since birth shown a partial lack of muscular coordination, caused probably by cerebral hemorrhage during delivery." The man's mental capacity, however, was "normal," the paper hastily added, and he had "always been able to support himself by his own labor" (to avoid any suggestion that an Oneida descendant might suffer from that most grave of Davenportian sins, a genetic propensity to shiftlessness). The second, a man forty-five years of age, having suffered a blow to the head as a child, was "slightly sub-normal mentally," though still industrious and "physically well-developed."[32]

Anita Newcomb McGee, a gynecologist and amateur anthropologist, noted in her 1891 study of the stirpicults that, in addition to their physical vigor and stature, they were intellectually superior to the stock they had come from, Oneida males having been largely drawn from the class of mechanics and farmers. She goes on to note the attainments of the eldest sixteen stirpicults, who counted among their numbers ten clerks and foremen working for the Community industries; one medical student; one law student; two college undergraduates, one of them a math whiz; a musician of unusual talents; and one (disappointing) mechanic, "the only one engaged in manual labor," she concludes apologetically.[33]

Ultimately, despite Hilda Noyes and G. W. Noyes's academic tinkering with the question of scientific reproduction, neither the socialist vision of a genetically engineered peaceable kingdom nor Davenport's dream of wiping out America's "army of defectives" appealed to Kenwood sensibilities. Nature, as John Humphrey Noyes had always maintained, was a brute struggle to the death, pitting selfish individuals against one another. To accept this state of existence impassively as a natural law by which society was to be ordered, as suggested by William Graham Sumner, was to descend to the level of brutes. Nature had to be tamed, pruned to follow a higher law. In 1912, my great-great-grandfather Theodore Skinner published an essay in *The Quadrangle* comparing the Kenwood family to a tree carefully pruned and grafted by a master botanist. Filled with eugenically tinged language, the article suggested that the Oneida Community descendants needed to exercise caution in selecting new "scions for grafting," in order to ensure that Kenwood would "receive foreign matter into our living organism and convert it into living tissue, harmonious and integral with the original stock." "We must only graft with scions of like characteristics, capable of absorbing and assimilating our sap," he warns.[34]

But Theodore Skinner's ideal of grafting the family with scions of "like characteristics" did not rely on a literal or biological notion of purity à la Davenport. His idea was that only by blending with stocks that shared Oneida's original values would the Kenwood family continue to thrive as a unique bio-philosophical unit. Kenwood's "natural fruits" were not to be accepted as good in themselves, according to the inherent purity of their genetic sap, but only insofar as they conformed to the higher moral principles of self-control and selflessness that had been guiding the Oneida enterprise since its founding.

At the 1910 Agents' Banquet, Pierrepont addressed rumors he had heard running through the larger Oneida organization that there existed some kind of "secret" society at the heart of Kenwood, a special clique to which only the elect were admitted. Pierrepont denied the existence of any such secret society, proclaiming that one was a "member" of Kenwood to the precise extent that one had learned to sacrifice individual desires for the common good of the whole. "He who is absorbed by [these common aims], who devotes his life to them, is a full member," he assured his audience. "In your own heart is the test and by a careful inventory you can find out just how much of a member you are."[35]

Perhaps. But it also helped to have one of a dozen last names: Noyes, of course, but also Miller, Skinner, Cragin, or Leonard (the original founders); Wayland-Smith or Allen or Kinsley (loyal supporters during the breakup); or any one of a number of other families who had pledged their loyalty to the tribe by marrying within it. (These marriages among stirpicults and their children were known in Kenwood as "inner-inners," to mark them off from "inner-outers," where members had introduced "foreign sap" to the Oneida tree by marrying outside the genetic pool.) One's position within the Kenwood hierarchy was determined by a combination of factors, including how far back one's family had joined the Community (was one descended from founders or "joiners"?), relative purity of descent (was one an "inner-inner" or an "inner outer"?), and one's family's degree of loyalty to Noyes during the turbulent breakup. Despite Theodore Skinner's claim that character, not blood, determined the shape taken by the Kenwood family tree, this unspoken lineal calculus would generate relatively fixed social outcomes— generation after generation—with the unwavering predictability of a Mendelian chart.

The pages of *The Quadrangle* are filled with chatty gossip columns narrating the lives of the inner-inners: their marriages, their travels, the exact location of their apartments within the Mansion House. "On September twentieth, 1928, Prudence Skinner and Robert Wayland-Smith were married in the Mansion House hall at high noon," reported a bubbly correspondent for the journal. This wedding between Wayland-Smith and Skinner was the apotheosis of what John Humphrey Noyes had once called "circumscribed marriage," his hopeful bid to conserve the genetic gains of stirpiculture beyond the breakup by encouraging community inbreeding. In my grandparents' union, the entire Putney nucleus—the Noyes, Miller, Skinner, and Cragin lines—was miraculously reunited. "[The bride's] gown was of white tulle embroidered in silver and gold, her veil of white tulle fastened with orange blossoms, and she carried white Madonna lilies," notes the breathless *Quadrangle* correspondent; the ceremony was attended by an unsurprisingly homogeneous crew of Cragins, Skinners, Wayland-Smiths, Noyeses,

Allens, and Kinsleys. "Bob and Prue are to live in an apartment on the third floor of the New House, in the Mansion," the journalist informs her readers, and confesses that she can barely wait to "pounce upon them for a grand tour of inspection the minute the wedding presents are installed."[36]

In 1896, OCL commissioned a golf course to be built for the use of its executives, and the sport soon became the central hub around which Kenwood society revolved. In the 1920s, a series of portraits of key executives in the Oneida hierarchy appeared in *The Quadrangle* under the title "Community Album," where, in addition to a roster of professional accomplishments, such clubby details as each man's prowess on the links were duly recorded. "Something should be said about Lou's golf," quips the author of a portrait of my great-grandfather Louis Wayland-Smith, then the vice president and treasurer of the company. "Take my advice and don't bet him a nickel on any one-shot hole."[37]

Not all descendants, however, made it into the Kenwood society pages. Martha Hawley Straub was born in 1900, the daughter of Roman Hawley, the granddaughter of Victor Hawley and Mary Jones—the couple Noyes had denied permission to procreate during the stirpicultural experiment. The entire Hawley family—Victor, his two brothers, and his parents—had sided with the opposition party during the breakup, and some of the family had even followed James W. Towner when, in 1881, the latter picked up stakes and led a group of ex-Oneidans to settle in Santa Ana, California. Victor and Mary were married right before the breakup, and against all stirpicultural expectations went on to have five healthy children of their own. Victor's granddaughter Martha was growing up in Kenwood, a child of nine or ten—contemporary with Pierrepont's three children and my grandparents—when the great debates about socialism and equality were being buffeted about at the agents' meetings.

In 1992, my father interviewed all the surviving local descendants of the Oneida Community; the nonagenarian Martha Hawley was among his interviewees. On the tape, my father questions Martha about how she remembers the "stirp" generation, in particular Pierrepont Noyes and his wife, Corinna Noyes, also a stirp and John Humphrey's niece (Pierrepont and Corinna were, in the stirpicultural tradition, first cousins). Martha remembers him as a "strong character" and his wife, Corinna, as "a wonderful woman." Then she goes on to specify: "To me she may have been just slightly aloof but that was because probably I was younger . . . and I didn't know her on a social basis because my mother and father were not socially involved here at the Mansion." Martha fumbles around for a delicate way of discussing what was still, in her generation, essentially a caste system among Kenwood families.

When Martha was a child, her mother (an outsider married in) worked in the Mansion House laundry and the kitchen, as both a cook and a dishwasher. She took the young Martha to work with her, where she remembered taking naps in the large laundry room among the washing tubs. "Everybody that lived here had their laundry done" by her mother. My father asks: "What did your mother say about the Mansion House and working here and the people here?" Martha replies tentatively: "I hate to be negative but my Mother instilled in me the thought that we did not belong." Then, a bit further on in the tape, like a child, she hedges: "Maybe I shouldn't even say this out loud." One can sense Martha's reluctance to question the genetic status quo in the hesitancy with which she addresses my father on the tape. He, after all, is the descendant of stirps; his father and grandfather had distinguished themselves as treasurers of the company; he is, in short, the sterling Kenwood stock that Martha is not.

My father, however, presses her. Finally, she talks: "My mother, having worked here in the Mansion House, I think perhaps she was looked down upon because she was a servant say and, therefore, there was one group of girls, my contemporaries, I started out being good friends with one of them but then in later life, later teen years, I don't know whether they just weren't allowed to play with me because my mother was in the position she was in or what but I always felt that."

At last, when her mother's varicose veins became too painful for her to work any longer, Martha went to work in her place in the Mansion House kitchen. "I would come down early in the morning and toast was made in the broiler. You would have to come down about quarter to seven, heat up the broiler, and then when the people would come in I would make their toast."

At this point on the tape Martha's memory is jarred. "Oh," she says dreamily, "I remember Josephine Noyes."

Apparently, Josephine Noyes had liked her graham bread cooked to a crisp—"I had to cook that very, very slowly for her and very, very brown," Martha remembers without a trace of irony in her voice. "That was her desire, to have it that way."

13

"The Strike of a Sex"

MARTIN KINSLEY, NAMED VICE PRESIDENT FOR NEW DEVELOPMENTS of OCL in 1924, once observed to his wife, Edith, that Oneida's most meaningful accomplishment was not the making of silver but the making of men. "Yes," he mused, "building men has been our most important product." Kinsley's insight pierced deeper than he knew. When he took over the company in 1895, Pierrepont Noyes had sought to rehabilitate his father's vision of a socialist utopia to fit the capitalist realities of the twentieth century. As for the Oneida Community's sexual theories, they were quite obviously outside the realm of rehabilitation. And so, stripping his father's legacy of anything that touched, even lightly, on the question of sex, Pierrepont proceeded to package up the rest into a socially acceptable mixture of masculine chivalry, Yankee business sense, and Christian charity (with some tantalizing ads of pretty flapper girls thrown in for good measure). That was a story that would sell spoons—as Pierrepont, with his keen advertiser's eye, was quick to recognize.[1]

For Pierrepont's mission was not only firmly to establish Oneida Community, Limited, as an economic powerhouse and a leader in the field of industrial relations; he also, less overtly, sought to replace the topsy-turvy gender dynamics that held sway under his father with a more stable, and ultimately more conventional, model at Kenwood. While sexist in his theology, John Humphrey Noyes had nonetheless granted women in the Community a remarkable amount of freedom, from their eligibility for "brain" work, for which the outside world deemed them unfit, to their relative freedom to control their reproductive lives. As a result, critics had always targeted the Oneida Community as a devilish cauldron of gender anarchy and sexual perversion. One particularly vitriolic report published in 1870 portrayed Oneida's women as grotesque, pants-wearing half men, leering at desexed prospective male converts or, in one telling cartoon, throwing snowballs at one another in a series of contorted, suggestive poses, like a nineteenth-century girls-gone-wild fantasy. Oneida was a place where, decidedly, men were not in control and where gender boundaries were dangerously fluid.

Pierrepont's anxiety and Kinsley's comment were to some extent prompted, no doubt, by what historian Michael S. Kimmel has identified as the "masculinity crisis" of the turn-of-the-century American male. Panicked at the specter of vote-seeking viragos in the public square, and convinced that white-collar jobs pushing paper behind desks betokened a loss of red-blooded vitality, white middle-class men sought to reboot American masculinity with a shot of physical toughness and rugged individualism. The Victorian model identifying masculinity with genteel self-restraint risked tipping over into effeminacy; the ideal man, according to the new model, had somehow to tap back into the virile, prehistoric energy of his primitive ancestors in order to put civilization back on track.[2]

Teddy Roosevelt's famous 1898 charge in the Battle of San Juan Hill during the Spanish-American War set the tone for manliness at the turn of the century; indeed, the soon-to-be president, throughout his eight-year command in the White House, never tired of speechifying about the virtues of physical courage and athletic prowess in the making of real American men. While "rich boys" were once condemned to indolent effeminacy by the customs of their class, the surge in popularity of athletic sports, Roosevelt noted in his 1900 essay, "The American Boy," was unquestionably responsible for an uptick in American manliness among the ruling classes: "Nowadays, whatever other faults the son of rich parents may tend to develop, he is at least forced by the opinion of all his associates of his own age to bear himself well in manly exercises and to develop his body—and therefore, to a certain extent, his character—in the rough sports which call for pluck, endurance, and physical address." The image of the rugged athlete on the field became the very type and symbol of the honorable man in the public arena, he "whose face is marred by dust and sweat and blood," who never shrinks from doing "the rough work of a workaday world" in pursuit of a worthy cause.[3]

Pierrepont had an ideological ally in the process of recasting the Oneida image and, with it, the parameters of Kenwood masculine identity: his son-in-law Miles E. "Dunc" Robertson, who took over from him as president of Oneida in 1926. Together, the pair forged a masculine ideal that was equal parts competitive vigor and manly self-sacrifice. Dunc Robertson had been born into a prosperous farming family that had fallen on hard times during his childhood, and he prided himself on his ability, from an early age, to contribute financially to his family's well-being. In this he followed Pierrepont, who had similarly faced a hardscrabble childhood and had labored at carpentry to help his impoverished mother make ends meet. Dunc worked to pay his way through Syracuse University, where "he was on the football team and captained the track team," as his 1948 biographer, by way of vouching for his character, felt compelled to mention. After graduating, he took a job at Oneida and became a crack salesman for Community Silver. Selling was in itself a sport, an "exhilarating struggle," as Pierrepont once referred to it, to assert oneself, no longer on the athletic field, but in the rough-and-tumble world of the marketplace. Dunc felt it to be so and, once he had passed over to management, recalled his days as a rookie salesman with fond emotion. "You never forget the excitement of your first sale," he reminisced in his letters, comparing retired salesmen to penned horses, restlessly pacing the sides of the corral, anxious to breathe once again the invigorating air of the open plain.[4]

Business was competitive sport, but, at the same time, Dunc Robertson held himself to a nobler standard than base moneymaking. A letter he wrote to his young brother-in-law Pierrepont "Pete" Trowbridge Noyes—then a fledgling salesman for the company—reveals the depths to which Dunc had imbibed the Community commitment to self-restraint. "The measure of greatness is not money or affluence," he lectured his friend. "Rather, generally speaking these are the measures of small tight minds." And he went on to give a disquisition on the virtues of selflessness in the pursuit of one's profession that would have made John Humphrey Noyes himself glow with pride. "As you climb," he advised the boy, "you will be surprised to find that the number of people for whom you are responsible continually multiply and if you are the man I know you to be, self will almost be forgotten in the larger problem." In his own case, Dunc detailed, he was responsible for 2,350 employees and their families—roughly "9,000 mouths which must be fed, backs which must be clothed"—and another thousand stockholders who depended on quarterly dividends. "What part has self in that problem?" he queried solemnly of his protégé. At times, he suggested, "even an absolutely impersonal attitude must be maintained because for the good of the larger whole you must hurt a smaller part, and to the end that group success should come, you must be impervious to personal criticism." Dunc was clear-eyed, selfless, rugged, loyal: everything Pierrepont felt a Kenwood man should be.[5]

But the corollary of Oneida's "making of men" involved the explicit unmaking of women: exorcising the ghost of female equality, whether sexual, physical, or intellectual, and putting woman firmly back in her place as man's domestic helpmate. In a June 1917 entry in her diary, Edith Kinsley recorded some candid sociological observations about the Oneida descendants under the heading "Kenwood Mores." As opposed to the old Community's emphasis on women's emancipation from childbearing and housework, Kenwood had returned to traditional gender roles with a vengeance. The habit of granting women full suffrage, as had been the case in Community days, Kinsley noted, "is quite abolished; it is lost. Women are inferiors, dependents. They take small part in business and cannot intrude with equality into sports."[6]

Sports had, in fact, become an integral part of the Kenwood cult of masculinity with the construction of a golf links adjacent to the Mansion House in 1896. Kinsley noted that playing golf was an essential part of men's business, "a happy combination of work and play, shared responsibility and pleasure which promote and express . . . a brotherhood of interests more basically important than salaries or dividends." A Kenwood man who did not play as well as work was not part of the gang and was considered something of a misfit. "Either he is throwing sand in the machinery, lying down on his job, or is just 'a sissy,'" Kinsley observed of those disinclined to sport. Holding important business positions within the company was no alibi for failing to partake in golf; even those in key managerial positions, were they to fail to show up on the links, were "excluded from the Gang, the very core of brotherhood." The emphasis on physical sport was matched by a suspicion of intellect and art. "We are frugal readers nowadays and, except for business thinking, frugal thinkers," remarked Kinsley. There was a taboo against the discussion of ideas in Kenwood circles, and "straight intellectuals" or artists were looked upon with some skepticism, arts and intellectualism both being considered "somewhat 'sissy.'"[7]

Kinsley recorded a keen observation once made by her cousin Kenneth Hayes Miller, an artist who lived in New York City and who thus, as an official practitioner of a "sissy" occupation, took a certain critical distance on Kenwood culture. "The attraction felt between Kenwood men is unconsciously more basic than any attraction felt towards women," Hayes ventured. If homosexuality was taboo among Kenwood males, Hayes suggested, a fervent culture of homosocial kinship nevertheless prevailed. Men were brothers in arms on the competitive field of sport and in the dog-eat-dog world of the marketplace, and such shared experience created a bond of intimacy no woman would ever understand. Kinsley assented heartily to her cousin's insight: "This may be true and the society be Greek in this respect; that is, Kenwood women may occupy much the same place as Grecian women in civic life," she mused. "At any rate," she went on to note, "the more important function of woman [in Kenwood] is child-bearing."[8]

If Edith and Martin were comfortable with Pierrepont's conscious reforms of gender roles at Kenwood, not all of the descendants bought the party line quite so wholeheartedly. One pair of dissenters was Hilda Herrick Noyes and George Wallingford ("G. W.") Noyes, children of the infamously lusty Tirzah Miller, and half-siblings. Hilda was born in 1878 under the stirpicultural program to Tirzah and James Herrick. She eventually married her cousin John Humphrey Noyes II. After attending the Women's Medical College in New York City and the Syracuse University Medical College, where she earned her degree in 1901, Hilda became one of the first practicing women doctors in central New York and an outspoken proponent of the American eugenics movement in the 1910s and 1920s.

G. W. Noyes, eight years Hilda's elder and the son of Tirzah and John Humphrey Noyes's younger brother, George Washington, was a studious sort who followed in the intellectual footsteps of his father. George Washington had been a mere fifteen years old when the prophet converted him to Perfectionism in 1838; he was a frequent contributor to *The Circular* up until his death in 1870, writing eloquent glosses on the finer points of John Humphrey Noyes's theology. G. W., whose father died the year he was born, inherited not only his father's love of ideas but also his loyalty to the cause of Bible Communism.

In 1884, Tirzah sent fourteen-year-old "Georgie" to Niagara Falls to live with John Humphrey Noyes. Despite the collapse of his kingdom, Noyes continued to preach to a small but loyal family following during his exile in the "Stone Cottage" from 1879 until his death in 1886. The impressionable young George was an immediate convert. "We have a real revival move here," G. W. wrote to his cousin Pierrepont in 1884. "Father Noyes says we ought to testify in such a manner as to let folks know which side we are on, and I want every one to know that I am on Jesus Christ's side, and am going to follow Mr. Noyes forever." "I had rather hear [Father Noyes] talk than to read the most interesting novel in the world," a rapt G. W. confessed in an 1885 letter to his mother. When his beloved uncle died on April 13, 1886, G. W. was by the patriarch's side. G. W. was, consequently, one of John Humphrey's favorite nephews. "My father would have swapped all his sons for one-half of George," Theodore Noyes once remarked jokingly—or tartly, depending on how one reads it—of his younger cousin.[9]

Though intimately woven into the community through ties of blood, neither G. W. nor Hilda could be considered, strictly speaking, part of the Kenwood inner circle, the "Gang" described by Edith Kinsley in her journal. The bespectacled, alpha-female Hilda kept obsessive health records of each family member as part of her eugenics research, and her outspoken references to the old Community sexual practices—once, when describing a friend who was particularly wide-ranging and generous in her affections, Hilda observed that "she would have made a great Community woman"— caused others to "shy at her," as she once admitted. G. W., for his part, had a curious and suspiciously "sissy" hobby: as if taking up where his father had left off as the official hagiographer of John Humphrey Noyes, G. W. spent all of his off hours writing history books about his uncle. In fact, he retired as vice president of Oneida Community, Limited, in 1920 in order to devote himself to his research full-time.[10]

Of all the descendants, G. W. was especially well placed to chronicle his uncle's life. When John Humphrey Noyes fled to Canada in 1879 and feared the Community's papers might be seized by authorities and used in court against him, he ordered that the whole mass of documents—thousands of pages of letters, diaries, journals, and records—be delivered to him over the border, where they would be safe from prying eyes. On Noyes's death in 1886, the cache of documents passed to Theodore Noyes and, upon the death of the latter, finally settled on G. W. His uncle's papers couldn't have found a more appreciative home. G. W. built a room-sized, fireproof locked vault—eight by eight feet—in his home across the road from the Mansion House in which to store his archive.

G. W. cut a strange figure against the practical, hardheaded business ethos that now dominated the family. Puttering about his dusty papers, immersed in the quaint world of a bygone era, he was no doubt looked upon with some bemusement by his relatives. In 1923, he published *The Religious Experience of John Humphrey Noyes*, a detailed narrative of his uncle's spiritual odyssey, collated from Noyes's personal letters and journals. By 1925, he had completed a second manuscript, this one laying out, in meticulous detail, the Oneida family's early experiments in moving from monogamy to Complex Marriage, or "a second volume dealing with Mr. Noyes's social career," as he described it euphemistically to a friend. G. W. had distributed copies of the manuscript to forty of his family members to get their reaction. This loyal descendant's sympathetic treatment of his uncle's radical views on the relationship between the sexes, as well as his candid discussion of the Community's practice of *coitus reservatus*, flew in the face of Kenwood's prudish return to traditional gender roles. And this, as might be expected, was where the trouble all started.[11]

TO BE HISTORICALLY ACCURATE, THE TROUBLE PROBABLY STARTED MUCH earlier: on the day in 1872 when John Humphrey Noyes first published his pamphlet essay *Male Continence*, advocating *coitus reservatus* as a means of birth control. Once humans learned to accept the legitimacy of the amative function, or nonreproductive sexual intercourse, Noyes argued in his audacious pamphlet, women would finally be free from the slavery of perpetual pregnancy, and the human race could reproduce intelligently rather than at the brutal whim of nature.

Noyes's contemporaries found the practice of *coitus reservatus* unnatural and suggested that it led to impotence in males, sterility in females, and nervous disease in both. To disprove these myths, Theodore Noyes published a "Report on Nervous Diseases in the Oneida Community" in 1875 as an appendix to Noyes's pamphlet *Scientific Propagation*. After making an elaborate tabulation of all the cases of nervous disease documented in the Community, Dr. Noyes concluded that no correlation could be drawn; "the body of men and women in the Community who have practiced male continence longest and most continuously, are scarcely touched in the above list of subjects of nervous disease . . . and many enjoy better general health than ever before." As for the quality of the male sperm at Oneida, Dr. Noyes tested it under the microscope and claimed confidently that, "as far as abundant and active zoosperms are evidence, we have retained our natural powers in nearly every case, including those up to 65 or 70 years of age."[12]

An even more thorough investigation was undertaken in 1877 when, at Theodore Noyes's invitation, Syracuse gynecologist Dr. Ely van de Warker examined a representative sample of thirty-four Oneida women to determine if the Community's unusual sexual practices had deleterious effects on their health. Though he declined to defend male continence, declaring it an "evasion of the legitimate, physiological sexual relation," his scientific findings led him to conclude that this method of contraception could not be proven to be a "disease-producing cause" in women.[13]

Van de Warker's admission that he could find no proof of a causal connection between birth control and ill health in Oneida's members was an anomaly; the mainstream American medical establishment in the last decades of the nineteenth century, and well into the twentieth, was consistently anti–birth control in its outlook. Fusing moral and medical arguments, these doctors offered hard scientific evidence for the deleterious effects of contraception on human health, thus appearing to corroborate its sinful nature: according to Boston gynecologist Augustus Kinsley Gardner, condoms were not only "bulwarks against love" but prone to causing painful lesions on the genitals. Bucking nature inevitably led to physical degeneracy.[14]

With the passing of the Comstock Law in 1873, contraception would, quite literally, go underground in America. A handful of vocal opponents continued to advocate for its legalization, as a matter both of women's rights and of the right to free speech—and not infrequently with tragic results. Ezra Heywood's decision to publish advertisements for contraceptive syringes in his free love journal, *The Word*, led to no fewer than three arrests and trials; in 1890, he was sentenced to and served two years hard labor for his flouting of the Comstock Law, dying soon afterward. Ida Craddock, the first woman admitted to the University of Pennsylvania in 1882 (but whose actual enrollment was blocked by the board of trustees), went on to write several sex manuals with titles ranging from the self-consciously hygienic (*Right Marital Living*) to the opaquely spiritual (*Psychic Wedlock*). When Anthony Comstock personally pursued her arrest and conviction on charges of distributing obscene literature in 1902, Craddock committed suicide rather than face a five-year sentence in federal prison.[15]

But the first widely publicized challenge to Comstock's stranglehold on free speech came in 1914, when Greenwich Village bohemian and anarcho-socialist Margaret Sanger published a pamphlet entitled *Family Limitation*, giving graphic descriptions of a variety of contraceptive techniques. Sanger's pamphlets provoked her indictment under New York's antiobscenity laws, but the true test came when Sanger opened a family planning and birth control clinic in Brooklyn in 1916. Convicted of violating the state's law against distributing contraception, Sanger appealed and won a historic victory when, in 1918, Judge Frederick E. Crane of the New York Court of Appeals ruled that contraceptives could be legally distributed if under the direction of medical doctors.[16]

While Judge Crane's decision did nothing to decriminalize the distribution through the U.S. mail of contraceptive devices or even written mention of contraceptives, his concession to allow doctors to dispense birth control marked a turning of the tide in the American politics of contraception. Sanger was canny enough to realize that, by converting white, male establishment doctors to the cause of contraception, the birth control movement would be granted the medical-moral legitimacy it required in order to advance its aims.

And indeed, by 1918, the issue of birth control had spread beyond Sanger and her small circle of radical activists to become the pet cause of a handful of committed medical men who insisted that birth control—and the "obscene" topic of human sexuality in general—was not a matter of private vice or virtue but fell under the purview of medicine and public health. Through the voices of these men, the American medical establishment for the first time placed its moral authority behind the separation of sex from reproduction that, since John Humphrey Noyes's time, had been the dearest wish of birth control advocates of all political stripes, from social-purity reformers promoting "voluntary motherhood" to socialists seeking to relieve working-class poverty to feminist sex radicals claiming a woman's right to sexual pleasure.

One of these activists was Dr. Robert Latou Dickinson, the chief of obstetrics and gynecology at Brooklyn Hospital. Dickinson sought to wrest the issue of birth control away from the disreputable fringe radicals with whom it had been associated and bring it, instead, under the legitimate umbrella of medicine and scientific study. It was 1923; he had just been made director of the newly created Committee on Maternal Health, a rather euphemistic title for what was essentially a research institute devoted to investigating issues of contraception and fertility. Here, Dickinson hoped to gather and collate clinical data on contraception from private doctors and hospitals in order to give a patina of medical legitimacy to the once-taboo subject. It was while at the CMH that he first caught wind of the Oneida Community.[17]

It is possible that the Oneida experiment came to Dickinson's attention originally as the subject of fellow gynecologist Anita Newcomb McGee's 1891 paper in the journal *American Anthropologist*, entitled "An Experiment in Human Stirpiculture." In the summer of 1891, Dr. McGee had interviewed a number of ex-communists from Oneida, including William Hinds, James W. Towner, James Herrick, and Theodore Noyes, on the topic of John Humphrey Noyes's eugenics project. She published the results, making only passing reference to the method by which the Community had "controlled" reproduction, focusing instead on the incredible hardiness of the stock obtained from the experiment. But in an unpublished talk she had delivered in Philadelphia before a medical society in 1896, Dr. McGee gave a painstakingly detailed description of sexual life at the Oneida Community, with particular focus on their practice of *coitus reservatus*. In 1924, she sent a copy of this paper to Dr. Dickinson. Here, Dickinson thought, was a gold mine of precisely the kind of information he needed in order to pull together some hard statistics about the feasibility and practicality of contraception.[18]

While Dickinson may have first learned of Oneida through the published medical studies of his fellow gynecologists van de Warker and McGee, it is equally likely that he stumbled across the doctrine of male continence through his contacts in the twilight underworld of the New York birth control movement. For among this group of radical feminists, anarchists, and free lovers, John Humphrey Noyes enjoyed something of a cult following as one of the unsung founders of the birth control movement. Alice B. Stockham, who began her career as a "medical medium" curing illness through a combination of magnetism and trance, became a vocal birth control advocate and even founded a press in order to circulate essential reproductive information and "ensure that no girl . . . go to the altar of marriage without being instructed in the physiological function of maternity." Stockham's 1896 pamphlet, *Karezza: Ethics of Marriage*, urged male continence in order to "control the creative power," drawing explicitly on the theories of that "distinguished minister," John Humphrey Noyes.[19]

Despite the Kenwood family's efforts to repress the "social theory" of their ancestors, pockets of resistance remained among the descendants. In 1890, Tirzah Miller's brother George Noyes Miller published a feminist pro–birth control novel entitled *The Strike of a Sex*, with Alice Stockham's press. The book went on to become a bestseller, with thirty-five thousand copies sold in America and Europe, a sequel to which appeared in 1895. In the preface to the 1891 fourth edition of his novel, Miller revealed that he had been inundated by letters from grateful women readers when the book first appeared. "The whole world is plainly in travail to lift the primeval curse of brutalizing labor from man," he observed. "But the just, at least, are beginning to perceive that the primeval curse must also be lifted from woman."[20]

Borrowing the theme of labor unrest to presage dire consequences if women were not granted freedom to control their reproduction, *The Strike of a Sex* narrates the trials of a futuristic city where the women have gone on strike, removing to separate quarters and refusing to further participate in the domestic contract until the men agree to relieve them of the "fearful treadmill of enforced maternity." Thanks to the ingenious Dr. Zugassent, who discovers a method by which men and women might "enter into the joys of marriage without ravaging each other like wild beasts," the human race is saved and Eden restored. The miraculous means of avoiding conception is, of course, left up to the reader's imagination, as Miller no doubt wished to avoid prosecution under antiobscenity laws. In a 1915 series of informative pamphlets on birth control methods, Margaret Sanger would lump together Noyes's male continence, Stockham's "karezza," and Miller's "Zugassent's Discovery" under a single heading, lauding this method of sexual intercourse as a way to transform the "exhaustive, abrupt fertilizing function [of sex] into a quiet magnetic charm, producing health and increased happiness.[21]

However he caught wind of the Oneidans, in 1925 Dr. Dickinson decided to reach out to the Community's descendants to see if they might be willing to aid him in his research. His gamble paid off. George Miller had died by 1925, when Dickinson first made contact with Kenwood, but in Hilda Noyes he found a very willing interlocutor. In a letter he wrote to her in January 1926, Dickinson suggested that "as part of our [Committee on Maternal Health] study of fertility and sterility the Oneida Community naturally comes in for report" and that the Community's practice of gathering minute clinical information on the health of its members would be of particular use in blasting the public's misconceptions about the negative health effects of contraception: "the medical reports secured toward the end of the Community experiment that show the fine physical condition of the members of that Community constitute perhaps the largest single series in the way of clinical evidence concerning one method of contraception."[22]

In February 1926, Dr. Dickinson paid a visit to Kenwood, and he and

Hilda entertained a cordial correspondence over the next several months. Hilda wrote expansively to Dr. Dickinson about her hopes for harnessing contraception to the goal of eugenics, or race betterment. "The need for cutting off defective lines is coming to be understood and appreciated," she observed bluntly in a 1920 article published in *The Journal of Heredity*. But not enough had been done, she argued, in the way of increasing the propagation of superior stocks. Thinking Dr. Dickinson would be a natural ally, Hilda confided to him her pet project of convincing life insurance companies to underwrite the genetically fit and thus encourage them to reproduce. Instead of paying subscribers when they died, insurance companies should pay select subscribers each time they injected a shot of their superior DNA into the national gene pool. Dickinson put her in touch with a friend of his in New York at Metropolitan Life, who was "very enthusiastic" about her plan to "investigat[e] . . . the mental, moral, and physical heredity and status of applicant[s] to determine the quality of their risk."[23]

But a letter to Hilda written on September 24 suggested that Dickinson wasn't getting exactly the kind of information he had hoped from his Oneida contacts. "I am glad that the Metropolitan Life statisticians speak to me so warmly of your study of the stirpiculture children. . . . But you can appreciate that it does not strictly belong to our program," he wrote in a gentle attempt to steer her away from her eugenic hobbyhorse. "On the other hand," he continued coaxingly, "data concerning coitus reservatus, and particularly well accredited case histories, are of importance to us."[24]

The "case histories" in question were under lock and key in G. W.'s archive; these Hilda was unable to deliver. But what she could and did deliver was an interview, toward the end of September of that same year, in which she gave up a host of insider information on the sexual life of her parents and grandparents, which Dickinson then meticulously recorded in a typewritten transcript of their conversation. What proportion of Oneida males, in their practice of *coitus reservatus*, were "untrustworthy"? he queried. "They were called 'leakers,'" Hilda offered candidly, "and ran in one family. The menstruating women declined them and those who had quick or uncontrolled emissions had to take women past menopause." Dickinson's next two questions stop the reader in her tracks, not only by their complete irrelevance to the "scientific" study of *coitus reservatus* he was purportedly undertaking but by the utter franchise with which Hilda, this earnest statistician and proponent of "scientific propagation," met them: "Were the women satisfied? Was their orgasm produced?" and, finally, "[Were there] postures directed or discussed?" Hilda allowed that her husband had, indeed, even after the breakup of the Community, been instructed as to the most felicitous sexual positions: "wife on side—upper thigh bent—husband enters from rear."[25]

Dickinson's momentary lapse into the territory of sexual autobiography makes more sense when we understand that, since the beginning of his practice, the good doctor had been living a kind of parallel life as a sex researcher, taking down detailed sex histories of his female patients and, even less orthodoxly, devoting a portion of his sessions to sketching their genitalia (the art of sketching had been his passion ever since he was a child). By the end of his career, Dickinson had collected more than 5,200 sex histories. He had a pet theory that women's varying sexual response was a function of physiological differences in their genital anatomy and was determined to prove it by producing and cross-referencing detailed sketches and, later, photographs of thousands of vulva.

Dickinson's dual aims in interviewing Hilda Noyes reveal the conflicted identity of the birth control movement of the era. While many birth control proponents of a conservative stripe supported "social hygiene" in order to protect women's health, combat male lasciviousness, or promote eugenic reproduction, another branch of the procontraception movement was motivated by different aims: a liberal if not anarchist desire to liberate sexual desire from repression. The discipline of "sexology," a mixture of the biological and the sociological sciences, had come to prominence by the early years of the new century, with a cadre of influential European medical men championing its cause. Havelock Ellis was among the first doctors-philosophers to argue that sex was not simply an anatomical and biological function, but a pattern of behaviors with complex psychological and sociological determinants. Ellis shocked the world with the 1897 publication of a medical textbook, *Sexual Inversion*, which offered a dispassionate, scientific study of homosexual behavior and declined to attribute it to anatomical or biological disease.

Ellis's resolutely unpuritanical approach to studying sex in all its dizzying diversity was seconded by Freudian psychoanalysis, which in the first two decades of the new century took the American neurological and psychiatric establishment by storm. Although hotly contested, at least one faction of American psychologists and doctors supported Freud's claim that liberating the sexual drives—not repressing them, as most proponents of nineteenth-century Victorian morality asserted—was the key to achieving psychic and physical health. "Civilized" codes of sexual repression, and a fortiori American Puritanism on questions of sex, led to neuroses, Freud's research seemed to indicate—and a coterie of liberal intellectuals and activists—including Margaret Sanger and Robert Latou Dickinson—were inclined to agree.[26]

In running the Committee on Maternal Health, Dickinson may have been trying to wrest contraception out of the hands of disreputable anarchist radicals and place it under the aegis of sound health policy. As he once urged his fellow doctors, "[Let us] take hold of this matter and not let it go to the radicals, and not let it receive harm by being pushed in any undignified or improper manner." But it is clear that Dickinson's own interest in the topic stemmed not just from a concern for women's physical health but from a fascination with, and apparent devotion to, women's sexual pleasure.[27]

Such a prurient interest in female sexuality, and in separating the procreative from the "amative" functions of intercourse, was by now not something the Kenwood crowd particularly cared to discuss. Women were for "child-bearing," as Edith Kinsley had concisely phrased it, not for emancipating. But beyond this, Pierrepont and his associates were no doubt uninterested in the fringe machinations of those doctors and political radicals seeking to push against the legal and moral tide of anticontraception feeling that still held sway in the American consciousness. Kenwood mores and OCL advertisements converged in their commitment to women as docile, limited creatures best dedicated to the concerns of hearth and home (and setting a beautiful dinner table). The cabal-like secrecy, lurking in the shadows of legitimacy and legality, with which procontraception activists were forced to operate could only be distasteful to the Kenwood family, still settling into their newly acquired status as respectable bourgeois citizens.

One year after his interview with Hilda, Dickinson appears to have made it into the Kenwood inner sanctum. Among his papers is the typescript of a document titled "Interview of RLD and Mr. and Mrs. George W. Noyes," dated September 14, 1927, recording his conversation with the Oneida Community archivist who, along with his wife, had traveled down to New York to meet with Dickinson. During this meeting, Dickinson noted that G. W. "placed . . . at his disposal . . . the medical data in the archive of the Oneida Community" and that G. W. was "entirely willing for the archives to be over-hauled to get what data might be of service to the CMH [Committee on Maternal Health] and invites RLD . . . to go and stay at his house as long as necessary." G. W. indicated to Dickinson that the data in the archives on the subject of *coitus reservatus* was very complete, as the Oneidans had maintained a weekly bulletin devoted to the subject that was circulated be-tween the main organization and its branches. G. W. confessed to Dickinson that he thought he was probably one of a very few male descendants who was still practicing *coitus reservatus*.[28]

Perhaps most tellingly, in the interview G. W. confided to Dickinson the extreme resistance he had encountered from his family in his efforts to pub-lish the sequel to *The Religious Experience of John Humphrey Noyes*, which he had finished a year and a half before and had distributed to the wider fam-ily for perusal. The new book examined in detail the theological basis of the Oneida Community's peculiar sexual organization and went so far as to suggest that John Humphrey Noyes's uncontrollable passion for Mary Cragin (as, before her, Abigail Merwin) was at the root of the sexual element in his teachings. G. W. admitted that the present generation of Oneida descendants—the children of the stirpicults, now in their teens and twenties—were largely "apologetic or grieved at the radical beliefs of their forefathers." Among the forty family members whom he had shown the manuscript, there was a "small but active group so vigorously opposed to its publication that they might get out an injunction and even attempt to remove the archives from his care," Dickinson reported. G. W., for his part, was consulting a lawyer at the request of his publisher, Macmillan, to see what rights he might have in the matter. Mrs. Noyes lamented the shortsightedness of the family in objecting to her husband's research; given the inevitability of the material appearing in public someday, it would be best if it were to "be issued in this authoritative form from the original sources."[29]

A letter from Dickinson to G. W. dated September 14, 1927, apparently penned immediately after G. W. and his wife had departed from New York, asked if at some time over the winter he and his secretary, who was "editing the birth control material," could visit Kenwood. "I have no doubt that evidence of much value can be found," he wrote warmly. In the meantime, he extended to G. W. his heartiest wishes that the latter might be allowed "to issue [his manuscript] without further opposition."[30]

But the projected publication of G. W.'s manuscript never took place; nor did Robert Latou Dickinson ever publish Oneida statistics on *coitus reservatus*. Spooked by this potential traitor in their midst, and no doubt horrified by the discovery that G. W. had agreed to turn over the family secrets to a sex researcher from New York, the Kenwood family, joining forces with Oneida management, sought the advice of the Syracuse law firm Mackenzie, Smith, Lewis and Michell in dealing with their wayward relation. In the twenty-eight-page brief drawn up by the firm, OCL claimed legal rights to G. W.'s documents and argued that if he attempted to publish his work, which "places undue emphasis upon certain social practices of the Community," the company could move to block him on the grounds that publication would "destroy or impair the good will connected with its business."[31]

The Kenwood authorities had spoken. Whatever else it was going to be in this brave new world, Oneida Community, Limited, and the family that owned it was definitely not going to serve as a soapbox for a bunch of New York radicals bent on the feminist cause of sexual liberation. While they were willing to play with images of liberated modern women, bobbed hair and all, in their advertising, Oneida was a company whose bottom line depended on reinforcing middle-class gender expectations: women were best when they stuck to domestic pursuits, curating their silver service and protecting their reputations as hostesses with exquisite taste. G. W. and Dickinson's narrative certainly jarred with this image. With the law behind them, Pierrepont and Dunc Robertson appeared to have steered Oneida's ship clear of scandal. Oneida had reaffirmed its status as a "virile institution," as Dunc once described the company, and the "sissy" specter of feminine equality sank back into the past where it belonged—at least for the moment.

14

"Back Home for Keeps"

ONEIDA COMMUNITY, LIMITED, CONTINUED ON ITS UPWARD RISE throughout the 1920s and 1930s. Even the Depression didn't seem to set sales back by much. With the aid of austere wage cuts—for management as well as workers—Oneida squeaked through 1933 with a profit margin, something no other silver company in America managed to do. Ironically, the crash of 1929 didn't alter the company's advertising psychology. The 1930s saw the introduction of elegant new lines of art deco silver, with such aristocratic patterns as "The Lady Hamilton" (named for designer Grosvenor Allen's wife, Christine Hamilton, with a faux aristocratic title appended to it) and "Noblesse," a testament to Oneida's exerting its hypnotic force on prospective brides and homemakers. "In the beauty of their Silverware, as in the style of their apparel, smart women admit no compromise," a 1931 advertisement for the Noblesse pattern declared. "They are content only with design of an authority that cannot be questioned." New York–based celebrity clothing designer Sally Milgrim—best known for the light blue gown Eleanor Roosevelt wore to her husband's inaugural ball in 1933—even concocted a bridal gown based on the Lady Hamilton motif of geometrically overlapping flower petals. Few brides in the 1930s, no doubt, were able to afford designer-commissioned wedding dresses to match their silver service. Nevertheless, Oneida's dream images of princesses and society balls, rather than being an affront to the grim, penny-pinching reality of the Depression for average Americans, seemed to furnish a kind of collective escape from it.[1]

In 1935, the company changed its name from Oneida Community, Limited, to Oneida Limited. When they first started manufacturing silverware in 1880, Oneida stamped its products with the label "Community Plate," a brand name that soon became synonymous with fashionable silver of the highest quality. By 1929, Oneida had acquired three subsidiary companies from a former silverware powerhouse that was down on its luck, the William A. Rogers Company. Under the Rogers name, Oneida began to sell a range of lesser-quality flatware to corner the bottom end of the silverware market. Soon, however, retailers learned to capitalize on the fact that the low-quality Rogers product was manufactured by the same parent company as Community Plate; eager salesmen were pushing inferior, less costly spoons by bathing them in the glow of their high-class cousin. By eliding the "Community" in the parent company's name, Oneida sought to safeguard Community Plate's reputation from the taint of inferior silver. The hired girl's silver—in this case, the Rogers line—needed to learn its place.[2]

But the run of luck by which Oneida had managed to capitalize on the social ambitions of middle-class American women for more than three decades, turning class anxiety into tidy profits, was about to come to an end. With the outbreak of World War II in 1942, silverware production ceased at Oneida Limited, and they shifted to manufacturing matériel for the war effort, everything from surgical instruments and parachute hardware to bayonets and casings for the M74 chemical bomb. Oneida's most important contribution to the war was manufacturing a bearing essential to the engines of Allied planes and tanks. This silver-plated part kept bombers, fighters, and Sherman tanks running. Dunc Robertson was awarded a special "gold bearing" for Oneida's contribution to the war effort, and the company was given four army-navy Es—the highest industrial accolade of the era.

When the United States entered the war on the eve of 1942, Oneida was the most branded name in flatware in the country, and they weren't about to let the reputation they had so painstakingly built up for themselves in the consumer imagination lie fallow. "While we are taking our crack at the Axis by turning out many different instruments of war, Mr. Hitler has only temporarily interrupted our scheme of things! The day will soon come when bayonets and surgical instruments will once again be teaspoons. And when that day comes we want to make sure that the bride's favorite teaspoons are once again Community Plate," recorded an internal news sheet for company employees, artfully titled *The Community Commando*. But the images of dreamy, bobbed beauties and society starlets staring into silver chests were no longer going to work in an America at war. Women could no longer be represented as insouciant domestic creatures of fashion, not least of all because, with the outbreak of war and the departure of their men, many American women went to work, abandoning the cosseted realm of the home for the world of the factory and office.

Women had always been welcome as factory hands in the stereotypically feminine garment and textile industries. But line jobs in the more hard-core industrial sectors—automobile manufacturing and, with the advent of the war, munitions and aircraft plants—had traditionally been reserved for men. The manpower shortage soon changed all this: women were drafted into "masculine" factory jobs and, to the surprise of many, proved themselves excellent workers. As one (female) personnel officer at an aircraft plant noted, "When we first hired women for the factory we thought that what we needed were big strong girls." But she soon learned she was mistaken. "A lot of these little 90 pounders can outwork the big girls," she observed. With the mass mobilization of women, long-accepted sexist stereotypes about size and strength were put to the test.[3]

The biggest gains for women employees during the war, however, were made in the white-collar sector. Clerical, typing, and secretarial positions had, since the nineteenth century, been largely the domain of men: a vast army of mild-mannered bureaucrats, immortalized in Herman Melville's 1851 short story "Bartleby, the Scrivener," that prescient symbol of gray-flannel middle-class anomie. The number of women employed in clerical positions nearly doubled during the war, and women soon outnumbered men. The war itself, and the enormous amount of paperwork it generated, only accelerated the growth of the white-collar sector. As one observer noted in 1942, "There is a bottomless pit in Washington, D.C., which swallows little girls who can hit typewriters."[4]

As women filled traditionally male slots along assembly lines and behind desks, they achieved a new sense of competence and independence outside the home sphere. Not everyone was comfortable with the newly empowered woman unleashed by the shifting social and economic realities of wartime, however. The specter of the emancipated woman was countered by a series of cultural strategies aiming to defang her and return her to the home, if not in fact, then at least symbolically. Wartime propaganda campaigns designed to boost the female labor force focused on women not as equal replacements for men, but as man's helpmates in a new capacity: standing in for him until he could return and resume his rightful place as breadwinner.

The Office of War Information, which set up liaisons with American magazine publishers to ensure that the public was being fed a steady diet of patriotic-themed stories, welcomed fictional stories that sexualized patriotic duty, and feminine dedication to the war effort was rewarded with romance. Take, for example, the story "Lady Bountiful," by Robert Carson, published in *The Saturday Evening Post* in the spring of 1943. The wealthy heroine, who complains bitterly about the material sacrifices she must make to the war, is roundly condemned by her peers and only earns her romantic reward once she has renounced selfishness and taken a job as a clerical worker at an army base. "Real" women took wartime work, the Office of War Information suggested, not to increase their personal power or comfort, but to support their country and fulfill their duties toward their rightful protectors.[5]

Psychoanalysis, too, was happy to step in and aid the effort to repatriate potentially wayward females who might be lulled into thinking themselves liberated once they had crossed the threshold of the workplace. If Freud had been commandeered in the early decades of the twentieth century as a voice for sexual liberation, his work could also be mobilized in the opposite direction. Despite his conviction that neurosis and illness, both mental and physical, was the result of sexual repression, Freud ultimately offered no real alternative to repression if the species hoped to survive. Infants were messy bundles of untutored instincts, pressing for the attainment of bodily

pleasure with no regard for the needs of others. In delving into the unconscious, Freud discovered an infant who, far from being the innocent, gender-
neutral blank slate of Victorian childhood, was a seething mass of aggression
and desire. The smallest and most innocent-looking of its interactions with
the outside world—suckling at the maternal breast, sitting on a potty—
were rooted in a primal drive for pleasure and power that brooked no interference. The laughing little boy dandling on his father's knee was, in reality,
harboring murderous oedipal wishes against this rival for the mother's
love. Repression was not the enemy of civilization; it was its bedrock.

If Freud discovered that the whole body was one big "erogenous zone"
and that sexual "polymorphous perversity" was the basic human condition,
he nonetheless subjected this chaotic jumble of drives and instincts to a
strict developmental hierarchy: the orally obsessed suckling infant gave way
to the anal eroticism of the potty-training toddler, finally culminating in the
discovery of "genital primacy"—in other words, heterosexual vaginal intercourse—as the proper terminus of this arduous process. Only those who had
successfully completed the series could be expected to become productive,
well-adjusted members of civilized society. Those who got stuck along the
way, or otherwise took a wrong turn, would live lives hampered by neurosis
and sexual and social dysfunction.[6]

By the 1940s, psychoanalysis, with its emphasis on the proper regulation of the sex drive as the key to both civilization and individual character,
had seeped into the popular American vocabulary. Everywhere from movies
to magazines to marriage manuals and child-rearing guides, the question
of sexuality was obsessively regulated and monitored, endlessly dissected to
separate the normal from the abnormal, the socially useful from the aber-
rant. In a 1947 sociological study called *Modern Woman: The Lost Sex*,
journalist Ferdinand Lundberg and psychiatrist Marynia F. Farnham traced
the breakdown of the American family and social structures to women's
displacement from the home by the social and economic forces of moder-
nity. Ever since the Industrial Revolution, when the sphere of home and
child raising lost its sex-specific value, women's primal "injured and outraged ego" had been on a rampage, consumed with self-destructive "penis-
envy" and, as a result of their ambivalent child rearing, populating the earth
with "a steadily increasing quota of neurotics, a painful problem to them-

selves, their associates, and society at large." Awash in a modern sea of "imperfectly genitalized" women, only a concerted effort to revalorize the home and repatriate the "lost sex" could save civilization from ruin.[7]

Amidst this battle for the hearts and minds of American women, and in what can only be called one of the canniest advertising coups of all time, at the outset of World War II Oneida Limited swept in and exploited this reigning atmosphere of sexual panic and gender insecurity to spectacular effect. Seeking the advice of the New York advertising firm of Batten, Barton, Durstine and Osborn (BBDO), Oneida's account landed on the desk of Jean Wade Rindlaub, a wife and mother–cum-adwoman, and one of the first women to make it on male-dominated Madison Avenue. "What does woman want?" Freud once queried of fellow psychoanalyst Marie Bonaparte, a puzzle that truly confounded the great theoretician of desire. In the case of the average American woman in 1942, Jean Rindlaub thought, at least, she had found an answer—and Oneida was all ears.

Rindlaub placed her bets on the fact that, notwithstanding the taste for economic independence American women may have gained in the wartime workplace, they could ultimately be convinced to embrace the patriotic domesticity narrative being woven by the Office of War Information. In Rindlaub's able hands, Community Silver would come to symbolize the American home as it *should* be, or rather the American home as Oneida promised it *would* be once the Allied forces had triumphed in Europe and the Pacific.

Rindlaub's "Back Home for Keeps" campaign started appearing in *Life* and *Ladies' Home Journal* in September 1943 and continued well through the end of the war, until December 1945. The ads featured an apple-cheeked and lipsticked all-American beauty engaged in a passionate kiss with a uniformed sweetheart, presumably just returned from the war, under the simple banner, "Back Home for Keeps." "Today he has a war on his hands," one ad narrates with stern masculine seriousness. "But the day will come, please God, when your Tom or Dick or Jack comes home for keeps . . . when kisses will be real, not paper; when you may know the good feel of a tweedy shoulder, the dear sound of a longed-for voice, a strong hand on yours in a dim-lit room. . . ." Then—wait a beat—Oneida adds its plug: "Then crystal will gleam and silver will sparkle on a table set for two."[8]

Another ad that ran in 1944 in issues of *Life, Cosmopolitan, Charm,* and *Ladies' Home Journal* figured a man in uniform embracing his blond sweetheart while reclining his head on a pillow, as his wife's ringed hand twists a lock of his hair. "In the space of a heartbeat . . . some glad day . . . the lump in your throat will melt away—and the man in your life will be home!" the caption promises breathlessly. "It's the day you dream of . . . and Community is dreaming too. Dreaming of silverware as radiant as that joyous morning, as sparkling as the twinkle in the eyes that feast on you. Dreaming . . . with you . . . for you . . . that we may trade the tools of war for the pleasant crafts of peace."[9]

The artist Rindlaub hired to execute the illustrations was Jon Whitcomb, an innovator in the field of commercial art who pioneered a shift in magazine advertising away from detailed, oil-painted long shots to zoomed-in facial close-ups, executed in the more labile, nervy medium of gouache paint. The heavy, dark oils of Norman Rockwell studding the covers of *The Saturday Evening Post* were suddenly forced to compete with light-filled, Whitcomb-inspired portraits of idealized American beauties. Oneida had cashed in on pretty girls once, with the Coles Phillips advertisements. Jon Whitcomb had spent his career, as he himself once remarked, "devoted principally to pretty girls," so he was a perfect fit for the Oneida profile.[10]

Whitcomb didn't consider himself an artist at all but, rather, a manufacturer—someone who crafted a product people were willing to buy. "I have no ambition to paint for future generations," he commented once in an interview. "All I want is to be good right now." Capturing the present moment, the elusive "now" of fashion, always evolving toward its next form, was his driving passion. Being up-to-date was not good enough; the successful cover artist needed to be able to foresee the future. "My crystal ball must aim for four to six months ahead, when the ad will appear," Whitcomb commented.[11]

Whether it was a question of style in lipstick colors or cultural mores, Jon Whitcomb's job was that of a forecaster. And his work on the Oneida campaign demonstrated his careful attention to capturing, and predicting, American ideas about love and sex. Both Whitcomb and Rindlaub were careful in how they bodied forth American ideals of domestic—and, implicitly, sexual—bliss. Rindlaub designed a questionnaire that she distributed to mixed panels of men and women asking what they liked to see in visual representations of kissing couples: Eyes closed? Eyes shut? Arms around each other? "In the culture of the United States . . . love, as shown in our publications, is never pictured as going very far beyond courtship," Whitcomb observed. "It is necessary to learn where this invisible line of taste is located and to stay on the conservative side of it."

In the case of Oneida, Whitcomb did one mock-up on the "Back Home for Keeps" campaign in which a bedroom was glimpsed in the background behind the embracing couple; it never went through to be published. "So, for the duration of the series, returning warriors were pictured entering the gate, on the front steps, in the hall and all over the living room—but not in the boudoir." In one version of the advertisement, the domestic interior hints toward sexual fulfillment through a background snippet of staircase— leading, one imagines, tantalizingly up to a bedroom. In the Rindlaub campaign, as in the previous Coles Phillips one, Oneida would playfully toe—but never cross—the invisible line of American prudery.[12]

Perhaps most important, Rindlaub and Whitcomb gave audience members the image of themselves they wanted to see, even before they knew that they wanted to see it. American women recognized themselves in Whitcomb's ads; they saw reflected there an image that fit their ideas about themselves and about who—after the turbulence and confusion of war—they wanted to be. Letters from admiring readers, requesting pinup copies of the images, began to stream in to the offices of BBDO and Oneida almost immediately. "Your advertisements are the most human and the most heartwarming that I have ever seen," writes a young woman from Boston. "They give girls like me something to look forward to when this war is over. I hope to have a set of Community Silver in my home." "Your pictures are so lovely," confesses another lonesome stateside girl. "They touch a spot so dear for 'those of us who wait.'"[13]

Nor were women the advertisements' only fans. Sergeant William E. Miller, writing on behalf of the Seventeenth Airborne Division stationed on a lonely moor in England in 1944, wrote to Oneida requesting copies of the illustrations to boost troop morale. "The girls remind us of our own, the ones we've left on the campuses of Vanderbilt, Northwestern, and Ohio State," he confides. "We're letting them dream of Community; we're just looking for a way to fulfill their dream and ours." The May 14, 1945, issue of *Life* magazine, celebrating victory in Europe, reported on the "Back Home for Keeps" pinup craze, confirming that it had spread even to the barracks "of those servicemen who have wearied of the anatomical pinup." While Oneida anticipated the popularity of the ad campaign and had printed fifty thousand copies of the images to send to impatient girlfriends and homesick servicemen, in the end they were overwhelmed by written requests for their sentimental posters, sending out hundreds of thousands of prints.[14]

Even the Office of War Information wrote Oneida with their whole-hearted approval of the ad campaign. "The Office of War Information wishes to comment on the splendid contribution which you are making in your current Community campaign," the letter commends. "Americans generally recognize that this is a war of survival but there is, nevertheless, a great need among individual citizens for clarification of their personal relations to winning the war and the peace that will follow. Your campaign effectively describes what we fight for." Oneida had successfully personalized the war by promising a return to sexual and gender stability in a time of disrupted homes, absent men, and newly independent women.[15]

WHEN THE WAR WAS OVER, ONEIDA HAD PROVED ITSELF PRESCIENT. DE-spite the very real possibility that the change in women's work patterns during the war could have shifted gender relations and opened up a path toward equality, the opposite was in fact the case. Women were unceremoniously requested to vacate their jobs to make way for the returning servicemen and go "back home for keeps," where they belonged. Far from being loosened, rigid gender identities now tightened their grip. With the help of Whitcomb and Rindlaub, Oneida could slide seamlessly into postwar advertising: "This Is for Keeps," the advertisements now read, with reassuring images of ecstatic brides and starry-eyed, girl-and-boy-next-door couples exchanging rings.

Rindlaub—whom some advertising historians credit with inventing the "focus group"—conducted detailed surveys of marriage-aged American women after the war in order to develop a profile of what she called, in a speech delivered to Oneida executives, "YOUR CUSTOMER, 1946." After revealing the hair and eye color preferences of most young ladies ("they like 'em tall, dark and handsome," Rindlaub quipped; Gregory Peck was their favorite movie star), she went on to deliver the genuine goods: "Which do [today's women] want most," she teased her panel of male clients, "a happy marriage, a successful career, or both?" And then she answered her own question: "They want what their mothers wanted—84 [out of 100] want a happy marriage." "Age-old dreams, most of them," she glossed. "A man of my own, a home of our own, children. That's looking inside your customer, 1946."[16]

And so again, in Oneida's postwar advertisements, the home figured front and center as the woman's proper domain. One ad shows the bottom halves of a boy and girl—he, loafered with plaid socks; she, in a yellow hoop skirt and bangles around her wrist—sitting on a floor poring over photo albums together. "Did you really know it was me?" the girl queries playfully in the copy accompanying the ad. "Next thing you know, young man, you'll be asking her the same question, and that's where Community comes in," the ad knowingly prods the groom to be. "Community—because girls with love in their hearts have homes on their minds. Homes shining with pride. Homes glowing with hospitality . . . with Community," the copy coaxes. Another ad in the same series features a couple side by side on a sofa, the boy's arm discreetly draped over the girl's shoulder. "Any moment now . . . her pretty little head will be spinning with warm *homesome* thoughts," the copy narrates. "Candlelight, firelight, Community! The boy won't quite know how he got there—but he'll be helping her pick *their* patterns, for keeps."[17]

Oneida's bottom line relied on an ever-expanding pool of breathless young brides—girls who wanted pretty, shiny things—and obliging husbands who would pay for them. The post–World War II ideal of the cookie-cutter, white-bread American family was beginning to take shape, and Oneida was only too willing to oblige in the concoction of this national fantasy.

By the end of the war, the lingua franca of psychoanalysis and sexuality had expanded beyond a tool to diagnose individual psyches on the couch to become a popularly accepted vocabulary with which to assess the health and fitness of the national psyche, or national "character." In the period immediately following the war, the relief of victory soon collapsed in the face of a new international bogey: Communist Russia. George Kennan's infamous "Long Telegram," dispatched from Russia to Secretary of State George

Marshall in February 1946, depicted Soviet leaders as a "self-hypnotized" and "neurotic" cadre of despots disconnected from any objective sense of reality, steeped in "an atmosphere of oriental secretiveness and conspiracy . . . [where] possibilities for distorting or poisoning sources and currents of information are infinite." This duplicitous world force would stop at nothing in its attempts to "penetrate" and convert the West to its beliefs, infiltrating "labor unions, youth leagues, women's organizations, racial societies, religious societies, social organizations, cultural groups, liberal magazines, publishing houses, etc." From the very outset, the Red Scare—the epic battle between East and West, between a feminine, oriental, neurotic collectivism and virile, clear-eyed individualism—was framed as a battle over gender.[18]

It was but a step from here to identifying Communists, with their soft, effeminate, oriental ways, with the sexual deviance represented by homosexuals. Americans stood in danger of losing their masculinity and needed to "firm up" to face the Soviet menace both abroad and, more insidiously, at home. John F. Kennedy's future court historian, Arthur Schlesinger, captured the paranoid tone of the era in his 1949 collection of essays, *The Vital Center*, in which he warned that America needed to regain its waning masculinity in its foreign policy toward the Soviets. Communists, Schlesinger warned, were suspiciously like homosexuals: they could "pass" in public but would always be able to recognize one another—and carry out their nefarious clandestine plots—by means of secret signs.[19]

Blending together a vocabulary drawn from popular psychology and the emergent realm of cabal-like secrecy heralded by the passage of the National Security Act in 1947 and the creation of the Central Intelligence Agency, homosexuals and other sexual "perverts" were framed as security risks, weak links through which the enemy could easily penetrate. In an incredible report written up by a Senate committee in 1950 and entitled *Employment of Homosexuals and Other Sex Perverts in Government*, homosexuals were specifically portrayed as a contagion to be contained. "One homosexual can pollute a government office," warned the report; the authors went on to note that, by hiring homosexuals, "it is almost inevitable that he will attempt to place other homosexuals in Government jobs." Panicked fears sparked the "Lavender Scare," where gay men and women were hunted down and hounded out of government jobs. Heteronormative sexuality became more vital to the national interest than ever.[20]

In this atmosphere of heightened suspicion and sexual paranoia, Oneida responded with an advertising campaign that emphasized the security and stability of the traditional American home. But this was more than just business savvy. Away from the bustling, public world of *Life* magazine advertisements and the smiling girls on Jon Whitcomb's sketch pads, away from the canny marketing of silverware to a nation avid for reassuring portraits of "normal" American sexuality, Kenwood was struggling with its own personal version of the Lavender Scare, enmeshed in a web of sexual paranoia little less dramatic than that sweeping the Senate and the country at large.

15

The Burning

Ever since the day in 1877 when Dr. Ely van der Warker swept into the Oneida Community to conduct thirty-four gynecological exams in just twelve hours, Kenwood had been able to count on receiving a visit from a curious gynecologist about once every fifteen to twenty years. Theodore Noyes, as resident Community physician, had called in Dr. van der Warker in order to refute the popular assumption that Oneida's deviant sexual practices of multiple partners and contraception necessarily led to disease. In 1891, Dr. Anita Newcomb McGee, a medical doctor and anthropologist, visited to mine the surviving members for details of their sexual experiences in the Community, delivering her findings to a fascinated gathering of Philadelphia physicians. In 1926, Dr. Robert Latou Dickinson came knocking, looking for valuable data to bolster his research into female sexuality and contraception. By 1946, if history was any guide, Kenwood was due for another visit. And, right on cue, on November 4, 1946, Dr. Dickinson, now in his eighty-fifth year, wrote to ask Hilda Noyes if he might drop by Kenwood on the afternoon of November 13. He would arrive on the 2:30 train from New York.

Dr. Dickinson had been busy in the twenty years since his last visit; in conjunction with the Committee on Maternal Health, he had managed to publish "some twenty books and a very considerable number of laboratory and clinical reports" in the fields of fertility, sex education, and statistics before the arrival of the war, when his research team temporarily disbanded. Now, he wrote Hilda hopefully, "we start afresh."

Nor had Dickinson's commitment to producing aesthetically beautiful and detailed renderings of female genitalia waned in the intervening years; in fact, he had recently branched out into three dimensions and, with the aid of "a very able sculptor," had created "over a hundred medical teaching models" of the female reproductive system ("with over three hundred parts," he added parenthetically) that were to be unveiled at the Cleveland Health Museum in a week. It was on his way to Cleveland for the gala opening, Dickinson said, that he proposed to stop by Kenwood.[1]

In the intervening years, the aging Dr. Dickinson had also been cultivating a protégé and hopeful successor in the field of sex research: a young zoologist from Indiana University named Alfred C. Kinsey. An expert on the North American gall wasp, of which species Kinsey had collected hundreds of thousands of samples and carried out an exhaustive taxonomy, the obsessive zoologist wandered into sex research almost by accident in 1938, when he proposed to teach a controversial "marriage course"—in essence, a primer in sex education—to university undergraduates. In a 1941 letter to Dr. Dickinson, he claimed that it was upon reading this pioneer's 1931 case study/marriage manual, A Thousand Marriages: A Medical Study of Sex Adjustment, that he had first been struck with the thought that he, too, might "research in this field." Dickinson's heart leapt at the promise of a successor. When Dr. Dickinson finally met Kinsey in the flesh in 1943, "tears poured down Dickinson's cheeks and into his neat white beard—'At last! At last! This is what I have been hoping and praying for all these years,'" Dickinson exclaimed, weeping.[2]

Like his mentor, Dickinson, Kinsey resented the psychoanalytic establishment's presumption of "genital primacy" as the apex of normal sexual development. "Normal," he concluded from his vast and far-ranging sex research, could not be prescribed according to some moralistic biological timeline; rather, "normal" was whatever it was that the statistical majority of people did in the bedroom most of the time—and this was often at radical odds with what popular opinion *thought* people were doing in the bedroom. Among his most controversial findings, Kinsey would prove that homosexual sex, far from being a statistical anomaly, was a common practice among adolescent and adult American males. Taking down their subjects' most taboo confessions with utter impartiality, Kinsey and his trained assistants blanched at nothing. One particularly illustrative example was the case of a heavily accented Armenian scientist; when asked at what age he had first ejaculated and how, the interviewer interpreted him as having answered, "At fourteen, with a horse." Not about to pass over so novel a sexual initiation, the interviewer pursued, "How often were you having sex with animals at fourteen?" The interviewer had, in fact, misheard, it turned out; the subject had said "whores," not "horse." Still, the scientist, stunned at the interviewer's apparent perspicacity, went on to admit, "Well, yes . . . it is true I had intercourse with a pony at fourteen."[3]

Starting with undergraduates enrolled in Kinsey's enormously popular "marriage course" in 1938 and then gradually expanding outward—Chicago's underground homosexual community; the Sigma Delta Tau sorority at the University of Pennsylvania; penal farm inmates incarcerated at the state asylum—Kinsey and his staff tirelessly collected sex histories for eight years. They used a primitive computer, an IBM Hollerith Calculating Machine that took punch cards loaded with data and did the requisite correlations, in order to process and analyze thousands of interviews. By late 1946, Kinsey was writing up the results of his investigations in a study entitled *Sexual Behavior in the Human Male*, a 735-page report that, when it was finally released on October 16, 1947, sent shock waves through the American academic and scientific establishments, as well as the population at large. Whether motivated by horror or admiration, people bought Kinsey's book: it topped all the bestseller lists, initially selling 270,000 copies. And what is more, they read it. *Sexual Behavior in the Human Male* would become one of the most-discussed books not just of the decade, but of the century.[4]

Naturally, Dickinson thought Kinsey might be an interesting contact for the Kenwood crowd. In a letter he wrote to G. W. Noyes, a carbon copy of which he included in Hilda's November 4 letter, Dickinson suggested that, "because of the unmatched experience of the former members [of the Oneida Community], I believe you will have much interest in a visit, someday,

from A.C Kinsey, Professor of Zoology." Dickinson went on to describe his
protégé in glowing terms as the most unbiased and scrupulously scientific of
contemporary sex researchers: "his personality, his freedom from bias, his thor-
oughness," the doctor effused, "will, I feel sure, appeal to you strongly." "His
book on the white native male will appear in a few months," Dickinson informed his Kenwood friends. At the end of his letter to Hilda, the hopeful doctor appended a kind of postscript: "Would Mr. Pierrepont Noyes have the same
interest[?]" he artlessly queried, "I have not read his biography."[5]

Here, though, the paper trail ends. For in 1946 G. W. had been dead already five years and so never received the kind offer of making Dr. Kinsey's
acquaintance. If, as it is reasonable to surmise, Dickinson sent G. W.'s letter to
the address he had on file, it would have arrived on the doorstep of Pete Trowbridge ("P. T.") Noyes, Pierrepont's son and heir apparent to Oneida Limited.
There is no indication in the written record whether Dickinson's proposed
visit with Hilda ever took place. Whether P. T. Noyes intercepted the letter or
whether Hilda informed the Kenwood elders of the sex doctor's proposed visit
will never be known. One thing is certain, however: Pierrepont Noyes would
most certainly not have "had the same interest" in a visit from Dr. Alfred C.
Kinsey as his more progressive stirpicultural cousins.

The record preserves no written response from the Kenwood family to
Dickinson's query. But when, just a few months later, G. W.'s entire vault full
of Oneida Community documents was hauled out and burned—without a
word breathed, without so much as a wisp of a rumor handed down to posterity as to who had authorized and carried out the auto-da-fé—it was undoubtedly response enough. This time, the Kenwood family had put the
recurring specter of inquisitive gynecologists to rest for good.

OF ALL THE METHODS HUMANS HAVE DEVISED THROUGH THE AGES FOR
making things disappear—grinding them into dust or shredding them to bits;
burying them in the earth or sinking them to the bottom of the sea—burning
has always engendered a peculiar fascination. There is something final
about fire, definitive: God first destroyed the world by water; the fire next
time, the gospel song warns. Fire is reserved for ritual destruction of the
utterly wicked, that which must be made to vanish without a trace. Sodom

and Gomorrah, those twin cities of iniquity, were blasted by fire and brimstone from heaven. "And Abraham looked toward Sodom and Gomorrah, and toward all the land of the plain, and beheld, and, lo, the smoke of the country went up as the smoke of a furnace" (Genesis 8: 28).

Even as it destroys, fire purifies: hence its alternative identity as an agent of cleansing and rebirth. For this very reason, book burnings are as mesmerizing as they are appalling. Burning books is not just the rational removal of a menace; if it were, humans would be content with blacking out the offending words the way a censor does. A book burning is an exorcism. Only the alchemical reduction of paper to ashes, this primitive, magical vanishing act, expresses the depth of the periodic human need to make words disappear in order to purge a culture of its impurities, to cleanse it of its blemishes.

According to a researcher who interviewed Oneida executives in the mid-1960s, my grandfather Robert Wayland-Smith and Pierrepont's son P. T. Noyes were among the family members "elected" to sift through their cousin's material before the decision was made to burn it. My grandfather was forty when the Burning took place; there is no one left from his generation. My father's generation—those born in the 1930s—knows that the Burning happened, but there reigns a kind of collective amnesia when it comes to names or dates or motives. No one knows (or will go on record as knowing) who authorized the Burning or who attended it.

John Humphrey Noyes's great-grandson Geoffrey Noyes was six years old in 1947 and lived with his family in G. W. Noyes's old house. G. W.'s built-in vault, with its treasure trove of Community archives, served as a playroom for him as a child. "I think it was a Moser safe," Geoff observed in a conversation I had with him in 2012. "And inside of this thing were very musty brown shelves filled with papers. Stacks and stacks and stacks of papers in there." One day, men came to his house to empty the vault. "They took all this stuff . . . and they burned everything and that was the end of it," he confirmed. Not that Geoff was present at the actual burning of the papers. The only eyewitness proof of it is buried in an obscure 1962 sociological study, dedicated to the history of alternative family structures in America. Sociologist William Kephart, after interviewing a number of Community descendants, found one Oneida executive who agreed to go on record anonymously as affirming that the Burning had, in fact, taken place. "So one morning we got a truck—and believe me, there was so much stuff we needed a truck—loaded all the material on and took it out to the dump and burned it."[6]

We might read the Burning as a local outbreak of the general national mood of paranoia in 1947. It was the year the "Hollywood Ten" would be convicted for contempt of Congress for refusing to testify before the House Un-American Activities Committee. Three years later in 1950, Congress released its report entitled *Employment of Homosexuals and Other Sex Perverts in Government*. With his "sissy" intellectual pursuits, G. W. would appear to have been the perfect Cold War scapegoat: the sacrificial victim, in absentia, of Oneida's own version of the Red and Lavender Scares.

"G. W. was the egghead of the world," one family member recalled of his elder cousin with a smile. He didn't play golf and so fell outside the circle of Kenwood's band of brothers. His abstention from sport, as Edith Kinsley keenly observed in her 1917 diary entry, opened him to suspicion of "throwing sand in the machinery," if not worse. An egghead: an intellectual, someone whose passionate—effeminate—devotion to ideas could prevent him from seeing reality for what it was and subvert his manly capacity to act in his family's best interests. "Oh, G. W.—The Last Apostle," recalled another cousin with a chuckle, pulling up a name that had clearly been used behind his kindred's back. This descendant's abiding memory of G. W. was of an old man shuffling around the Mansion House after dinner in his slippers. An apostle: a dotty, feminine follower of John Humphrey Noyes's oddball theology—in slippers, no less, not even properly shod in masculine footwear.

G. W. died in 1941. Both of the descendants I interviewed knew this distant uncle only as young children, once he was already very old. Through the eyes of youth, the elderly inevitably appear sad and weakened shadows of life and thus vulnerable to ridicule. But while there was bemusement and even affection in their recollections of G. W., there was also a touch of something else; suspicion would be too strong a word—wariness, perhaps. Wariness as the stock inheritance of a family who had been trained, for one hundred years, to anticipate attack and to promptly shut it down—even, or perhaps especially, when the attack was an inside job.

Did my grandfather and his peers act out of purely practical motives, seeking to protect the financial interests and reputation of Oneida Limited against public exposure, as the original legal injunction against G. W. suggests? In this

case the Burning would have been a rather ham-fisted response to the perceived threat, but one that at least would have had the advantage of closing
down for good the possibility of future leaks. Alfred C. Kinsey, for one, could
not undertake a scientific study of sexual practices in the Oneida Community
if the records documenting these sexual practices no longer existed.

There can be no doubt that the Burning stemmed at least in part from a
fierce, almost visceral commitment to family privacy, balanced by an ancestral suspicion of—even contempt for—the world outside. For the Oneida
descendants to reduce their history to ashes was to sacrifice a piece of themselves, to be sure. But such a sacrifice might have seemed a small price to
pay if it meant protecting the family against "outsiders"—the nosy academic,
the meddling tabloid reporter—once and for all. To burn their history was, in
a sense, to thumb their noses at the uninitiated, those who would never
have been able to faithfully represent the lives contained in the now vanished
pages, because they would never have been able to understand what it meant
to be a part of this peculiar chosen tribe.

Perhaps, too, there was an element of apology, even expiation, in the
Oneida descendants' decision to set their patrimony on fire. Bound together
by the knowledge that they had violated some of mainstream society's
strongest taboos in deliberately breaking the marriage vow, the original
Oneidans had ritually sealed their separation from the world outside their
doors. Was the Burning a kind of reverse ritual: an offering laid at the altar of
traditional American mores, a belated atonement for the transgressions of
their fathers? "I often wish the old people had had a regular system of marriage," one of the family members interviewed by William Kephart admitted wistfully. "Then we wouldn't have had such bad publicity."[7]

Or was it less an expiation and more a form of magical thinking: if they
burned all trace of their ancestors' sexual irregularities, wouldn't it be almost as if it had never happened?

But this is all speculation. The real reasons my relatives decided, on a
certain day in 1947, to burn their patrimony, in all its confused and no doubt
contradictory complexity, will never be known for certain. In my mind,
though, when I picture the Burning, I see my grandfather as he listens to the
crack and sigh of burning paper; see him as he watches the plumes of smoke
twist up into the night sky and disappear among the cold, white stars.

Epilogue

O NEIDA LIMITED AND THE KENWOOD COMMUNITY OF DESCENDANTS
who ran the company continued to prosper for nearly half a century
after the Burning. When I grew up in the 1970s and 1980s, my family spent
every Christmas and summer in Kenwood, whose neat, tree-lined streets
were populated with aunts and uncles and cousins of varying degrees. Great-
Grandpa Lou was still alive, tucked away in a corner apartment of the Mansion House; we would visit him at cocktail hour and chat as he smoked a
Cuban cigar and sipped his old-fashioned. In the winter, my cousins and I
sledded at the golf course and warmed up in the Mansion House in front of
a fire, blazing beneath a stately oil portrait of Pierrepont Noyes. We took off
our shoes and mock-skated in our socks across the slippery floor of the Big
Hall, where Evening Meeting had always been held, or banged on the
off-key piano up on the stage (most of the residents at this point were deaf
old aunties and uncles, so it didn't much matter).

Across the street from the Mansion House was the sales office, the
stately gray-stone Tudor building that Pierrepont Noyes had commissioned
in 1926 to the tune of half a million dollars—a monument to industrial

respectability—and where management had their offices. As kids, we would sneak into the cafeteria to buy hot tomato soup in a paper cup or fifty-cent tuna fish sandwiches from a Horn and Hardart–style rotating vending machine. We would pass by the "Blue Room," where visitors were ushered ceremoniously through a pair of swinging glass doors to see Oneida's latest silver designs, gleaming smartly in their crushed blue velvet display cases.

Part of Oneida's success from the 1950s through the 1980s can be traced to the company's unerring instinct, developed over time like some evolutionary sixth sense (could there have been an element of truth to John Humphrey Noyes's eugenic fantasies?), for gauging the shifting social aspirations of anxious American brides and hostesses. Oneida had built its reputation on being the arbiter of domestic taste, every housewife's best friend in her efforts to create a tasteful home and impress her guests. With the introduction of stainless steel flatware in the late 1950s, mostly in the form of low-priced imports from Asia, Oneida's silver plate was suddenly under threat. The OL annual report for 1958 announced "very disappointing" domestic sales in sterling and silver plate, attributing the downturn to the sudden surge in popularity of "lower quality, short-profit, stainless steel knives, forks and spoons, with their positives of no tarnish, easy to keep clean, wear forever."[1]

Dunc Robertson lamented this lapse in American taste, hoping it would be short-lived: "The art of gracious living, the desire to dine rather than to eat, has been temporarily, we hope, overlooked by many hostesses." Oneida's task, he said, was to convince women that proper civilization demanded sterling, not cheap stainless knockoffs. "It is our problem to revitalize these desires," Robertson reminded his shareholders. Those committed to Oneida as makers of the highest-quality sterling silver plate felt stainless would cheapen their brand: "Stainless is a metal made for sewer-pipes," grumbled one speaker at a meeting of Community Plate sales agents.[2]

But the trend toward practicality over "gracious living" proved unstoppable. Oneida was forced to adapt, and adapt it did. As it had done once before (in 1900, when it offered its pennywise customers stylish new designs in the cheaper medium of silver plate), Oneida expanded its market share not only by entering the stainless market, but also by upping the ante for stainless aesthetics. "Nature Makes It Carefree; Oneida Makes It Beautiful!" ran the snappy new slogan concocted to sell stainless, challenging the reigning assumption that style was incompatible with practicality. Oneida's "Paul Revere" pattern, mimicking the naive lines of the early American style, brilliantly imbued the modern, no-nonsense advantages of stainless with an aura of pedigreed Yankee good sense: the best of both worlds. Soon, Oneida's unparalleled team of engineers and designers succeeded in producing flowery Victorian motifs in the tricky medium of stainless, a feat none of their competitors had managed to pull off. "Chateau," introduced in 1956, offered consumers an "intricate pattern on heavier weight stock and in bigger pieces" than any other flatware design on the market. By the 1966 annual shareholders' report, Pierrepont's son and the OL president, P. T. Noyes, announced that stainless sales had "surged ahead, maintaining its position as our most important product."[3]

In 1969, the Oneida brand even made interstellar history when Paul Revere stainless spoons were selected by NASA to accompany the astronauts on the *Apollo 12* mission to the moon. Charles "Pete" Conrad and Alan L. Bean were presented with two spoons apiece, each engraved with the NASA seal and their name: one for use aboard the command module *Yankee Clipper* and one for use—should they desire some liquid nutrients while out exploring the moon's surface—aboard the *Intrepid* lunar module. Oneida's domestic competitors were so flummoxed by the silverware maker's surge in stainless sales and popularity that one rival company stooped to desperate measures: in 1972, they sent an industrial spy to Oneida headquarters posing as a federal safety inspector. (The crafty impostor was intercepted by state police at the Utica airport, and the guilty competitor settled out of court to avoid a lawsuit.)[4]

THE DEMISE OF ONEIDA LIMITED, BOTH AS A COMPANY AND AS A FAMILY-run enterprise, is a complicated story, as most tales of unraveling are. Business wisdom in the early to mid–twentieth century held that family companies lacked the capital and talent to compete with public companies. Family patriarchs, a new breed of business gurus warned, were going the way of the horse and buggy, to be replaced by professional "management experts." Under P. T. Noyes's administration, from 1960 to 1981, Oneida Limited witnessed precisely such a shift. The year after he took over the presidency, Noyes brought in an outside "efficiency expert" to evaluate the company's organization, a symbolic step toward establishing more bureaucratic and impersonal methods of employee "control" within the company.[5]

In 1965, Oneida management's proposed slate for the board of directors included for the first time three "outsiders," industry and management professionals neither descended from the Community nor employed previously by Oneida Limited; in 1967, Oneida put its shares up for sale on the New York Stock Exchange. No doubt in order to shore up investor confidence, P. T. Noyes amended the "Oneida Limited Creed" for the occasion to include a clause affirming the company's answerability to shareholders: "We believe that the business of the corporation must be conducted in every respect so that the shareholders' investment will be safe and will earn an adequate return," he assured his public. As commonplace as this might have sounded to the untrained ear, the Kenwood family and Oneida employees alike would have recognized in this formal announcement of the company's commitment to the "bottom line" a clear departure from Pierrepont's initial vision for Oneida.[6]

When P. T. Noyes retired as president in 1981, the first "outsider" in Oneida's 130-year history ascended to the post; all four succeeding presidents, right up until the bankruptcy in 2006, would be outsiders. When Oneida was forced to restructure in 2004, management's official explanation to stockholders attributed the collapse to the competition of cheap labor abroad, as well as the termination of Oneida's contracts to provide tableware to airlines in the wake of 9/11. A *Forbes* magazine article from 2004 hailed Oneida CEO Pete Kallet as having waged a valiant, if losing, battle, not so much against cheap foreign imports as against the "inbred" culture of the OL board of directors and their stubborn adhesion to the communal values of the old Oneida Community. Pierrepont's legacy—a "squeamishness about firing workers," according to *Forbes* journalist Chana Schoenberger— prevented Kallet from being able to close Oneida's U.S. manufacturing plants and ship the jobs overseas in time to save the company from foundering. "The communal spirit is no match for globalization," she concludes sternly.[7]

Such may indeed be the case, although others would argue that Oneida's rushed decision to acquire a number of companies in 2000, boosting its long-term debt to $238 million, or more than twice stockholder equity, was hardly immaterial to Oneida's eventual financial collapse. Be that as it may, even accepting that Oneida's old communist legacy tragically blinded it to the changed economic realities of globalization, Pierrepont's "communal spirit" couldn't have been more conspicuously absent in the desperate shedding of company liabilities required by its debtors once they moved in to take control. The first "disposable" asset to go was the underfunded worker pension plan and retiree health benefits. Executive retirements were safe, however, thanks to an amendment made to the pension plan in 2002 that awarded top managers up to $300,000 a year in retirement benefits that remained untouched by the bankruptcy proceedings. In one of the bitterest ironies of the entire Oneida saga, by the time the 158-year-old company collapsed, Pierrepont's founding ideal of shared ownership—of an equitable distribution of both pain and profit across the whole body of the organization—had not just disappeared; it had been made a mockery.[8]

THE BURNING, THEN, MAY NOT HAVE MARKED THE END OF ONEIDA LIMITED; the company would continue on, albeit in altered and diluted form, for another half century. But in a certain sense, it symbolized a crucial shift in the spirit of the company and the eccentric family dynasty that had built it. The decision by my grandfather's generation to burn their history may, indeed, have been intended as a snub to outsiders who sought to turn their parents' noble experiment into sex statistics or, worse, material for the tabloids. But in the end, it curiously had the opposite effect: it marked a consolidation in the company of a kind of middle-class smallness, a kowtowing to conformity, a loss of the energy and imagination behind the original dream. It marked the ascendance of an ethos of "professionalism," a bureaucratic devotion to impersonal efficiency and the bottom line over the more quirky, humane "amateur spirit" that Pierrepont had always hailed as the distinctive mark of the company's management class.

As the company shot up in popularity through the twentieth century, John Humphrey Noyes, once a family asset, became more and more a feared liability, a noisome skeleton whose periodic emergence from the closet had to be pushed back at all costs. Certainly, there were legitimate reasons for pushing him back. He was weird; he was perverted; there was no question he had abused his power, especially toward the end of the Community. The generation of women who had been young adults at the breakup found the memory of John Humphrey Noyes nothing short of loathsome. When, in 2012, I asked my uncle to speculate on the motives behind the Burning, he responded only half jokingly that he had always suspected it was his stirpicult grandmother, Pierrepont's wife, Corinna Noyes, who had thrown the first match.

Whether or not my uncle's hunch about her part in the Burning is correct, Corinna's abiding ambivalence toward "the Old Community"—a term the younger stirpicults adopted, no doubt, by way of taking their distance from it—was passed on to her daughter Barbara Noyes Hatcher, who, in 1960, played her own part in the now-serial family effort to make John Humphrey Noyes disappear. In that year the tabloid *True: A Man's Magazine* published an article by the titillating title of "Father Noyes and His Fabulous Flock," presumably a freely adapted riff on John Humphrey Noyes's sexual exploits. My great-aunt paid two of her nephews to drive to all the train stations and dime stores around Kenwood to buy up offending copies of the issue. The salacious report on "Father Noyes" was, distressingly, followed up two years later by Anson Hunter's pulp novel, *King of the Free Lovers.* The cover features a rakish-looking figure with slicked-back black hair, wearing a topcoat and, incongruously, a string tie that makes him look as if he has just pushed through the swinging doors of an Old West saloon. On the bed below him, two buxom sex kittens lounge in various states of undress. I can only imagine my great-aunt's horror when, nearly one hundred years after his death, John Humphrey Noyes suddenly resurfaced in the guise of a B-movie lothario in a dime store novel—as if, by a prankish turn of fate (and one by no means appreciated by his descendants), Noyes had somehow in death achieved the prize that had always eluded him in life: immortality.

But in so assiduously beating back its freakish origins, in so thoroughly internalizing, like a Pavlovian dog, the reflexive flinch of the assailed, the Kenwood family ended up mimicking the very same middle-class terror of the unconventional, the very same compulsive middle-class conformity from which they had once so proudly dissented.

THE GROUP OF HEDGE FUNDS THAT ACQUIRED THE BANKRUPT ONEIDA IN 2006 shifted its management to New York City, although they retained a small residual staff in Kenwood who continued to work in the sales office. Then, in 2011, Everyware, "a leading global marketer of tabletop and food preparation products for the consumer and foodservice markets," according to its Web site (http://everywareglobal.com), acquired Oneida for its portfolio.

John Humphrey Noyes's great-great-great-grandson and a distant cousin of mine, Paul Gebhart, who began working for Oneida Limited in 1980, was one employee who managed to weather the company's tempestuous shifts in fortune, and he was perhaps the last of the clan to remain. I visited him in the summer of 2012 in his office. He explained that when he first started working at Oneida, they still had "the shared ownership perspective that was in the Community." "Everyone had a certain amount of skin in the game," he reminisced, from the toolmaker to the factory operative to top management. Bit by bit, though, that culture had disappeared. With the takeover by the hedge funds in 2006, Oneida moved from being in a "control position to not being able to set those values anymore," he observed matter-of-factly. "Oneida became just another brand in a portfolio."

At the end of our chat, he handed me his card, first flipping it over and penciling in "Everyware," the name of his new employer, by way of updating the expired "Oneida" logo on the front. Everyware hadn't had time to make new business cards yet or to set up new e-mail accounts. Did he regret the changes that he'd witnessed at Oneida over the past thirty years, the eclipse of his ancestor's vision? I queried. "Nothing lasts forever," he offered, smiling affably at me across the desk, the very embodiment of what is most cheerful—or chilling, depending on one's temperament—in the typical American attitude toward the past.

He was right, of course. Nothing lasts forever, least of all dreams, and after our interview I felt a bit silly having expected my cousin to join me in my sentimental nostalgia. But if nothing lasts forever, then, by the same token, not everything disappears. One family relic that remains, stubbornly imposing and magisterial in the face of the vanished family, is the Mansion House, the rambling, 93,000-square-foot Victorian chateau that my communist ancestors constructed for themselves between 1861 and 1878.

Today, it houses a museum devoted to the history of the Oneida Community, "among the most radical and radically successful utopias in history," according to the Oneida Community Mansion House literature; it doubles as a bed-and-breakfast for the occasional upstate visitor. My parents occupy a suite of rooms on the second floor—the last genetic link to the original occupants— and, in an unofficial capacity, act as regents for the upkeep of the sprawling property.

When I visit my parents in the Mansion House every summer, I have to do my laundry in the coin-operated machines in the basement. Last summer, while waiting for my clothes to dry, I poked around the cavernous underground realm. Still there—though boarded up now—is the Turkish bath where Victor Hawley once sought to ease his broken heart, as though the steam might somehow absorb or dissipate his sorrow. There are little padlocked doors in crevices whose uses remain mysterious (who holds the key?); storage rooms full of caged, dusty furniture; damp, cryptlike openings in the brick, unlighted, that seem to serve no purpose whatsoever. I stumble across a vault in one wall, its heavy door hanging open, its shelves lined with what look like tarnished silver serving dishes. One room is a graveyard for unused bathroom fixtures, an assortment of dusty claw-foot tubs and stacked toilet bowls.

I pass into another room, where a mountain of white china choked with dust and cobwebs is sprawled on a table under a naked light bulb. Looking more closely, I recognize the service that was used, when I was a child, to serve Thanksgiving and Christmas dinner upstairs in the dining room to the extended family: chunky white jugs that were once filled with hot gravy; sweeping platters once piled high with freshly carved turkey; sundae dishes, with ice cream and chocolate sauce and Spanish peanuts, served up by local girls hired for the occasion as waitresses. When the kitchen closed ten years ago, they must have stashed the lot down here, not knowing what else to do with it. Does anyone remember it is still here?

At the end of one corridor is a thick door with an engraved copper plate embedded in the wall next to it: "The Oneida Room." Entering, you take a step down into a dark vault, wall-to-wall carpeted in burgundy. This was once the management's clubhouse and bar, a men's-only space for after-golf drinks. On the walls hang dozens of black-and-white photograph collages from the 1960s and 1970s, documenting the annual Silver Niblick Golf Tournament, sponsored by the company for its advertising agents. Peering out from behind the glassy frames are smiling groups of men with bushy sideburns and tube socks, brandishing golf clubs and cocktails. Some careful family historian took the time to clip and collate dozens of photographs, arranging them no doubt according to a social typology that would have been instinctively legible once, long ago, to those who gathered here. But the space has been long since deserted, and the pictures have, now, the bland opacity of an inscription written in a language whose code has been lost.

In recent years, the Mansion House has somehow made it on to a list of "haunted places" in America, with a smattering of paranormal bloggers and TripAdvisor commentators testifying to flickering shadows and floating orbs. "It smelled old," one visitor blogged warily, by way of warning, while one college boyfriend I brought home commented—rather churlishly, I thought—that the Mansion House was a dead ringer for the hotel in *The Shining*.

I have never experienced any ectoplasms or auras in the house. But, in a sense, these ghost hunters are not wrong. Anyone who visits and wanders the now-silent, labyrinthine halls and staircases cannot escape a sense that the Mansion House is itself a ghost: an errant soul, forgotten by Charon and trapped on the far side of the river, when all the family who once built its walls and swelled its rooms with life have disappeared across the Styx, and its descendants—scattered, now, to the four corners of the continent—have slipped silently back into the great gray mass of the American middle class.

NOTES

INTRODUCTION

1 Oneida Community Collection, Syracuse University Library, cited hereafter as OCC. Oneida Limited Annual Report, Fiscal Year Ended January 31, 1948.

2 Theodore Pitt, "The Future of Commerce," *Circular* 7, no. 51 (January 13, 1859).

3 Walter Edmonds, *The First Hundred Years*, rev. ed. (Oneida, NY: Oneida Limited, 1958), 6.

4 George Wallingford Noyes, *John Humphrey Noyes: The Putney Community* (Oneida, NY: 1931), 3; Hubbard Eastman, *Noyesism Unveiled* (Putney, VT, 1849), V.

5 Robert Latou Dickinson Collection, Kinsey Institute Library archival collection, hereafter cited as RLD Collection. Folder "Dickinson's Notes on the O.C.," interview of Robert Latou Dickinson with Mr. and Mrs. George W. Noyes, September 14, 1927.

6 Edmund Wilson, *Upstate: Records and Recollections of Northern New York* (1971; Syracuse, NY: Syracuse University Press, 1990), 125.

1. A MINISTER IS BORN

1 George Wallingford Noyes, *Religious Experience of John Humphrey Noyes* (New York: Macmillan, 1923), 8.

2 G. W. Noyes, *Putney Community*, 87–91.

3 ——, *Religious Experience*, 6; John Humphrey Noyes, *Bible Communism: A Compilation from the Annual Reports and Other Publications of the Oneida Association* (Brooklyn, NY: 1853), 45; John Humphrey Noyes, *Home Talks*, ed. Alfred Barron and George Noyes Miller (Oneida, NY, 1875), 1:64.

4 G. W. Noyes, *Religious Experience*, 9–13.

5 Ibid., 20.

6 Ibid., 21.

7 Ibid., 28.

8 Ibid., 28, 30, 22. David Thomas has written a fascinating psycho-biographical portrait of Noyes in *The Man Who Would Be Perfect: John Humphrey Noyes and the Utopian Impulse* (Philadelphia: University of Pennsylvania Press, 1977).

9 Ibid., 34. For a fascinating study of how the 1820s religious revivals in New York State were linked to shifting economic and class structures, see Paul E. Johnson, *A Shopkeeper's Millennium: Society and Revivals in Rochester, New York, 1815–1837* (New York: Hill and Wang, 1978).

10 Ibid., 40.

11 Charles Grandison Finney, *The Autobiography of Charles G. Finney*, condensed and ed. Helen Wessel (Minneapolis, MN: Bethany House Publishers, 1977), 22.

12 Ibid., 33.

13 Quoted in *Christian Spectator*, "Review of *Methodist Error*" (New Haven: Howe and Spalding, 1820): 2:301.

14 Ibid., 303.

15 Ibid.; quoted in Charles A. Johnson, "The Frontier Camp Meeting: Contemporary and Historical Appraisals, 1805–1840," *Mississippi Valley Historical Review* 37, no. 1 (1950): 91.

16 John Humphrey Noyes, "Heaven Coming," *Home Talks*, 314–19.

17 ———, *The Confessions of John Humphrey Noyes Part I: Confession of Religious Experience, Including a History of Modern Perfectionism* (Oneida Reserve, NY: Leonard, 1849), 2, 3.

18 Ibid., 3.

19 G. W. Noyes, *Religious Experience*, 47, 51.

20 The definitive study of millenarianism in medieval Europe remains Norman Cohn, *The Pursuit of the Millennium*, rev. and exp. ed. (New York: Oxford University Press, 1970), 312.

21 Donald D. Hall, *The Antinomian Controversy, 1636–1638: A Documentary History*, ed. David D. Hall, 2nd ed. (Durham, NC: Duke University Press, 1990), 388.

22 J. H. Noyes, "The River of Life," *Home Talks*, 306–08.

23 ———, *Confessions*, 18.

24 Ibid., 26.

25 Ibid., 27.

26 Ibid., 27, 20, 21; *Autobiography of Charles G. Finney*, 22; J. H. Noyes, *Confessions*, 18.

27 J. H. Noyes, *Confessions*, 21; G. W. Noyes, *Religious Experience*, 365.

28 J. H. Noyes, *Confessions*, 29.

29 Ibid., 30.

2. NOYES IN THE UNDERWORLD

1 Tyler Anbinder, *Five Points: The Nineteenth-Century New York City Neighborhood That Invented Tap, Stole Elections, and Became the World's Most Notorious Slum* (New York: Simon and Schuster, 2001), 16.

2 J. H. Noyes, *Confessions*, 34.

3 Teresa of Avila, *The Book of My Life*, trans. Mirabai Starr (Boston: New Seeds Books, 2007), 225; Simon Schama, "When Stone Came to Life," *Guardian*, September 15, 2006.

4 J. H. Noyes, *Confessions*, 93.

5 Ibid., 94.

6 Ibid., 37.

7 Ibid., 37, 42.

8 Ibid., 39, 46.

9 J. H. Noyes, "Waiting and Watching," *Home Talks*, 240, 239.

10 G. W. Noyes, *Religious Experience*, 154.

11 Ibid., 155.

12 John Humphrey Noyes, *The Way of Holiness: A Series of Papers Formerly Published in "The Perfectionist" at New Haven* (Putney, VT, 1838), 7.

13 William Hepworth Dixon, *Spiritual Wives* (London: Hurst and Blackett Publishers, 1868), 2:15.

14 G. W. Noyes, *Religious Experience*, 199.

15 Ibid., 198.

16 Ibid., 352, 354.

17 Ibid., 356.

18 G. W. Noyes, *Putney Community*, 3.

19 Charles Coleman Sellers, *Theophilus, the Battle-Axe: A History of the Lives and Adventures of Theophilus Ransom Gates and the Battle-Axes* (Philadelphia: Press of Patterson and White, 1930).

20 G. W. Noyes, *Putney Community*, 7.

21 Ibid., 17, 20, 21.

3. NEW JERUSALEM (IN VERMONT)

1 G. W. Noyes, *Putney Community*, 27–32.

2 Ibid., 33.

3 Dixon, *Spiritual Wives*, 96, 103.

4 Ibid., 115, 118, 119.

5 Robert Allerton Parker, *A Yankee Saint: John Humphrey Noyes and the Oneida Community* (New York: G. P. Putnam, 1935), 78.

6 G. W. Noyes, *Putney Community*, 48.

7 Ibid., 32.

8 Robert H. Abzug, *Cosmos Crumbling: American Reform and the Religious Imagination* (New York: Oxford University Press, 1994), 31.

9 Lyman Beecher, *A Plea for the West*, 2nd ed. (Cincinnati: Truman and Smith, 1835), 10; Ernest Lee Tuveson, *Redeemer Nation: The Idea of America's Millennial Role* (Chicago: University of Chicago Press, 1968); Ruth Bloch, *Visionary Republic: Millennial Themes in American Thought, 1756–1800* (Cambridge: Cambridge University Press, 1986).

10 William Breitenbach, "Unregenerate Doings: Selflessness and Selfishness in New Divinity Theology," *American Quarterly* 34, no. 5 (1983): 495; Breitenbach also provides an excellent bibliography on America's cultural and economic shift to an industrial market society. For a detailed study of how the early-nineteenth-century transportation revolution, in particular the construction of canal systems, transformed the economic and social landscape of America, see Carol Sheriff, *The Artificial River: The Erie Canal and the Paradox of Progress, 1817–1862* (New York: Hill and Wang, 1996).

11 Charles Sellers critiques what he calls our "historical mythology of capitalist transformation as human

fulfillment," arguing that American democracy developed in tension with capitalism. See Sellers, *The Market Revolution: Jacksonian America, 1815–1846* (New York: Oxford University Press, 1991); Thomas Carlyle, *Past and Present*, Introduction and Notes by Chris R. Vanden Bossche (Berkeley: University of California Press, 2005), 148.

12 Sellers, *Market Revolution*, 207; Catharine Beecher and Harriet Beecher Stowe, *The American Woman's Home* (New York: J. B. Ford, 1869), 19. The classic contemporary study of the development of a "domestic ideology" in America is Nancy Cott, *The Bonds of Womanhood: "Woman's Sphere" in New England, 1780–1835*, 2nd ed. (New Haven: Yale University Press, 1997). See also Mary P. Ryan, *Cradle of the Middle Class: The Family in Oneida County, New York, 1790–1865* (Cambridge: Cambridge University Press, 1981).

13 Jessie Catherine Kinsley, *A Lasting Spring: Jessie Catherine Kinsley, Daughter of the Oneida Community*, ed. Jane Kinsley Rich, with the assistance of Nelson M. Blake (Syracuse, NY: Syracuse University Press, 1983), 34.

14 G. W. Noyes, *Putney Community*, 50.

15 Ibid., 72.

16 Hesiod, *Works and Days, Theogony, and The Shield of Heracles*, trans. Hugh G. Evelyn-White (Mineola, NY: Dover Publications, 2006), 6; Ovid, *The Metamorphoses*, translated by John Dryden and others, edited by Sir Samuel Garth, with an introduction by Garth Tissol (Wordsworth Editions Limited, 1998), 6.

17 Cohn, *Pursuit of the Millennium*, 193.

18 Ibid., 249.

19 *Selections from the Works of Fourier*, trans. Julia Franklin with an Introduction by Charles Gide (London: Swan Sonnenschein and Co., 1901), 55.

20 Albert Brisbane, *The Social Destiny of Man; or, Association and Reorganization of Industry* (Philadelphia: C. F. Stollmeyer, 1840), 5.

21 *Harbinger*, quoted in John Codman Thomas, *Brook Farm: Historic and Personal Memoirs* (Boston: Arena Publishing, 1894), 102. For the decisive account of the Fourierist movement in America, see Carl J. Guarneri, *The Utopian Alternative: Fourierism in Nineteenth-Century America* (Ithaca, NY: Cornell University Press, 1991).

22 G. W. Noyes, *Putney Community*, 168.

4. ELECTRIC SEX; OR, HOW TO LIVE FOREVER

1 Song of Songs, https://archive.org/details/St.BernardOnTheSongOfSongs, 27, 41; J. H. Noyes, *Bible Communism*, 56, 32.

2 Mary Wollstonecraft Shelley, *Frankenstein*, ed. Susan J. Wolfson, 2nd ed. (New York: Pearson Education, 2007), 90. For a good general account of eighteenth-century electrical science, see Martin Willis, *Mesmerists, Monsters, and Machines* (Kent, OH: Kent State University Press, 2006).

3 E. J. Fraser, *Medical Electricity: A Treatise on the Nature of Vital Electricity in Health and Disease* (Chicago: S. Halsey, 1863), 11.

4 John Humphrey Noyes, *The Berean: A Manual for Those Who Seek the Faith of the Primitive Church* (Putney, VT, 1847), 76; ibid.; J. H. Noyes, "Grace Better Than Suffering," *Home Talks*, 258–63.

5 J. H. Noyes, *Bible Communism*, 33; J. H. Noyes, *Berean*, 493.

6 J. H. Noyes, *Bible Communism*, 44; J. H. Noyes, *Berean*, 493.

7 J. H. Noyes, *Bible Communism*, 60.

8 Parker, *Yankee Saint*, 111.

9 Dixon, *Spiritual Wives*, 289.

10 Parker, *Yankee Saint*, 123.

11 G. W. Noyes, *Putney Community*, 205, 206.

12 Ibid., 207.

13 Letter quoted in Robert S. Fogarty, *Desire and Duty: Tirzah Miller's Intimate Memoir* (Bloomington: Indiana University Press, 2000), 21.

14 *Spiritual Magazine* 2, no. 8 (September 1, 1847): 120.

15 *Spiritual Magazine* 3, no. 5 (July 15, 1847): 65, 67.

16 *Spiritual Magazine* 2, no. 10 (October 15, 1847): 153, 154.

17 *Spiritual Magazine* 2, no. 5 (July 15, 1847): 70.

18 Ibid., 73.

19 Ibid., 72.

20 Ibid., 71–73.

21 *Spiritual Magazine* 2, no. 10 (October 15, 1847): 155.

22 Ibid., 156.

23 G. W. Noyes, *Putney Community*, 283.

24 Ibid.

25 Ibid., 289.

26 Letter from David Crawford, of Putney, Vermont, to Rev. Elisha D. Andrews, of Armada, Michigan; Putney Historical Society Archives.

27 G. W. Noyes, *Putney Community*, 302.

28 Ibid., 317, 309.

29 Ibid., 393.

5. MARRIAGE GROWS COMPLEX

1 Constance Noyes Robertson, *The Oneida Community: An Autobiography, 1851–1876* (Syracuse, NY: Syracuse University Press, 1970), 13.

2 J. H. Noyes, *Bible Communism*, 60; Robertson, *Oneida Community: An Autobiography*, 27.

3 "Basis and Prospects of the Circular," *Circular* 1, no. 1 (November 6, 1851).

4 J. H. Noyes, "The Law of Miracles," *Home Talks*, 301; "Conditions of Spiritual Government," *Circular* 1, no. 21 (August 8, 1864).

5 *First Annual Report of the Oneida Association* (Oneida Reserve, NY: Leonard, 1849), 6; Lawrence

Foster, ed., *Free Love in Utopia: John Humphrey Noyes and the Origin of the Oneida Community*, compiled by George Wallingford Noyes (Chicago: University of Illinois Press, 2001), 54.

6 J. H. Noyes, *Bible Communism*, 27, 30.

7 Ibid., 35, 37.

8 Foster, *Free Love in Utopia*, 215, 249, 231.

9 Ibid., 230, 240, 241.

10 Ibid., 236, 229.

11 Ibid., 223, 224, 229.

12 Ibid., 238–39.

13 Amy Dru Stanley, *From Bondage to Contract: Wage Labor, Marriage, and the Market in the Age of Slave Emancipation* (Cambridge: Cambridge University Press, 1998), 177.

14 Stephen Pearl Andrews, ed., *Love, Marriage, and Divorce and the Sovereignty of the Individual: A Discussion by Henry James, Horace Greeley, and Stephen Pearl Andrews* (New York: Stringer and Townsend Publishers, 1853), 36, 67.

15 Stephen Pearl Andrews, *The Science of Society* (Boston: Sarah E. Holmes Publisher, 1888), 15.

16 T. L. Nichols and Mrs. Mary Gove Nichols, *Marriage: Its History, Character, and Results* (New York: T. L. Nichols, 1854), 119. On the free love movement more generally, see John C. Spurlock, *Free Love: Marriage and Middle-Class Radicalism in America, 1825–1860* (New York: New York University Press, 1988). In addition to reproducing key texts from the movement, Taylor Stoehr gives an excellent overview of the topic in *Free Love in America: A Documentary History* (New York: AMS Press, 1979).

17 Anthony Wonderley, ed., *John Humphrey Noyes on Sexual Relations in the Oneida Community* (Clinton, NY: Richard W. Couper Press, 2012), 99.

18 Wonderley, *John Humphrey Noyes*, 102. Scholars have long debated the "feminist" implications of Oneida's radical restructuring of gender roles, with some touting Noyes's visionary liberation of women and others condemning him as a sexist autocrat. For an excellent summary and analysis of these contradictory assessments, see Lawrence Foster, "Free Love and Feminism: John Humphrey Noyes and the Oneida Community," *Journal of the Early Republic* 1, no. 2 (1981): 165–83.

19 J. H. Noyes, *Home Talks*, 346, 119, 118.

20 Andrews, *The Science of Society*, 15.

21 John Humphrey Noyes, "Good and Bad Attractions," *Circular* 11, no. 52 (December 21, 1873).

22 Ibid.

23 J. H. Noyes, *Bible Communism*, 42.

24 Ibid., 53, 43.

25 Ibid., 44, 46; John Humphrey Noyes, *Male Continence* (Oneida, NY, 1872; repr. New York: AMS Press, 1974), 8, 18.

26 J. H. Noyes, *Male Continence*, 9, 21; Foster, *Free Love in Utopia*, 218.

27 *Circular* 5, no. 8 (March 13, 1856).

28 Robertson, *Oneida Community: An Autobiography*, 294.

29 "Industrial Marriage," *Circular* 3, no. 45 (March 18, 1854); "Occupations and Amusements of Women,"
    3, no. 47 (March 23, 1854); "Fashion a Separator," 5, no. 32 (August 26, 1856).

30 *Daily Journal of the Oneida Community, vols. 1–3: The O.C. Daily, vols. 4–5,* with a new introduc-
    tion by Robert S. Fogarty (Philadelphia: Porcupine Press, 1975), August 28, 1866, September 13,
    1866. Hereafter cited as Fogarty, *Daily Journal.*

31 Robert S. Fogarty, ed., *Desire and Duty at Oneida: Tirzah Miller's Intimate Memoir* (Bloomington:
    Indiana University Press, 2000), 59, 60.

32 "Arrival of a New Recruit at the Oneida Community," in John B. Ellis, *Free Love and Its Votaries*
    (San Francisco: A. L. Bancroft and Co., 1870), 360.

33 Henry James, *The Bostonians,* ed. Richard Lansdown (London: Penguin Books, 2000), 18, 25, 33.

34 Ibid., 56, 383, 47.

6. THE MACHINE IN THE GARDEN

1 J. H. Noyes, *Bible Communism,* 60; Robertson, *Oneida Community: An Autobiography,* 57.

2 Robertson, *Oneida Community: An Autobiography,* 59, 60, 64.

3 Ibid., 61.

4 Quoted in Anthony Wonderley, "Oneida Utopia: Bible Communism to Welfare Capitalism" (forth-
   coming from Cornell University Press, Fall 2016), 52.

5 George E. Cragin, "Trap Making on Oneida Creek, Part I," *Quadrangle* 6, no. 4 (April 1913).

6 G. W. Noyes, *Putney Community,* 72.

7 "Financial View of the Second Coming (Adapted to Wall Street)," *Circular* 3, no. 19 (January 17,
   1854); *Circular* 1, no. 1 (November 6, 1851).

8 Quoted in Leo Marx, *The Machine in the Garden: Technology and the Pastoral Ideal in America*
   (1964; Oxford: Oxford University Press, 2000), 144.

9 Quoted in Charles Sellers, *Market Revolution,* 35.

10 "The Future of Commerce," *Circular* 7, no. 51 (January 13, 1859).

11 "A Business Glance," *Circular* 3, no. 127 (September 26, 1854): 506; Fogarty, *Daily Journal,* October
    9, 1867.

12 *Circular* 3, no. 49 (March 28, 1854): 194; "Working Schools," *Circular* 3, no. 47 (March 23, 1854):
    186.

13 "Industrial Equality,"*Circular* 4, no. 38 (October 11, 1855): 150.

14 George E. Cragin, "Trap Making on Oneida Creek, Part II," *Quadrangle* 6, no. 5 (May 1913).

15 ——, "Trap Making on Oneida Creek, Part III," *Quadrangle* 6, nos. 6 & 7 (June/July 1913).

16 Ibid.

17 Robertson, *Oneida Community: An Autobiography,* 245.

18 "Dedication of the New Community Mansion House," *Circular* 11, no. 3 (February 27, 1862): 9.

19 "Communism and Labor," *Circular* 8, no. 45 (December 1, 1859): 178.

20 Eric Foner, *Free Soil, Free Labor, Free Men: The Ideology of the Republican Party Before the Civil War*
    (Oxford: Oxford University Press, 1995), xvi.

21 Ibid., 16, 16, 13. For a history of the shift from an artisanal workforce to wage labor, see Bruce Laurie, *Artisans into Workers: Labor in Nineteenth-Century America* (Urbana: University of Illinois Press, 1997).

22 Ibid., xviii; "Dedication of the New Community Mansion House," *Circular* 11, no. 3 (February 27, 1862).

23 "How We Began Making Machine Twist," *Quadrangle* 6, nos. 10 & 11 (October/November 1913): 4.

24 Robertson, *Oneida Community: An Autobiography*, 60, 73.

25 "Community Journal," *Circular* 5, no. 44 (January 18, 1869): 350; *Circular* 6, no. 46 (January 31, 1870): 364; *Circular* 6, no. 49 (February 21, 1870): 390.

26 Fogarty, *Daily Journal*, August 14–15, 1867; Fogarty, *Daily Journal*, March 11, 1867.

27 Ibid., August 16, 1867.

28 Andrew J. Downing, *The Architecture of Country Houses* (New York: D. Appleton, 1851), foreword.

29 "Researches in Landscape Gardening, No. 1," *Circular* 11, no. 6 (March 20, 1862): 24.

30 Quoted in Wonderley, "Oneida Utopia," 75.

7. STICKY LOVE

1 Harriet Skinner, "Heavenly Electricity," *Circular* 7, no. 36 (September 30, 1858): 143.

2 "Conversion to a Soft Heart," *Circular* 4, no. 30 (October 7, 1867): 233.

3 Rich, *Lasting Spring*, 29.

4 *Mutual Criticism* (Oneida, NY: Office of the American Socialist, 1876), 30; Rich, *Lasting Spring*, 30.

5 OCC, box 16, "James Herrick Criticism."

6 OCC, box 48, Beulah Hendee to Annie Hatch, August 2, 1878.

7 Ibid., August 3, 1878.

8 OCC, box 73, John Sears to Beulah Hendee, May 23, 1877.

9 OCC, box 48, Beulah Hendee to Annie Hatch, August 15, 1878.

10 Ibid., August 10, 1878.

11 Ibid., August 15, 1878; August 21, 1878.

12 Ibid., September 4, 1878; September 15, 1878.

13 Ibid., September 4, 1878.

14 Ibid., November 24, 1878; September 18, 1878.

15 Ibid., September 17, 1878; J. H. Noyes, "First Love and Tried Love," *Circular* 11, no. 50 (December 7, 1874).

16 OCC, box 47, Hatch to Hendee, October 25, 1878; box 48, Hendee to Hatch, November 19, 1878, and January 1, 1879.

17 OCC, box 48, Hendee to Hatch, January 6, 1879; November 19, 1878; Fogarty, *Desire and Duty*, 130.

18 OCC, box 73, John Sears to Beulah Hendee, October 9, 1878; box 48, Hendee to Hatch, November 19, 1878.

19 Ibid., Sears to Hendee, January 12, 1879; February 28, 1879.

20 OCC, box 47, Hatch to Hendee, December 12, 1878.

21 Ibid., Hatch to Hendee, January 17, 1882.

22 Ibid., Hendee to Hatch, January 23, 1879.

23 Rich, *Lasting Spring*, 44.

24 Ibid., 48.

25 Thomas Merton, *The Wisdom of the Desert* (New Haven, KY: Abbey of Gethsemani, 1960), 8.

26 Rich, *Lasting Spring*, 41.

8. BRAVE NEW WORLD

 1 Fogarty, *Desire and Duty*, 174. This chapter is indebted to Fogarty's painstaking archival work both in *Desire and Duty* and in an earlier volume reproducing the diary of the Oneida member Victor Hawley, *Special Love/Special Sex: An Oneida Community Diary* (Syracuse, NY: Syracuse University Press, 1994).

 2 Fogarty, *Desire and Duty*, 126, 58.

 3 Robertson, *Oneida Community: An Autobiography*, 355.

 4 Fogarty, *Desire and Duty*, 124.

 5 Pierrepont B. Noyes, *My Father's House: An Oneida Boyhood* (New York: Rinehart, 1937), 29.

 6 Ibid., 66; Corinna Ackley Noyes, *Days of My Youth* (Utica, NY: Widtman Press, 1960), 17.

 7 Corinna Ackley Noyes, *Days of My Youth*, 16.

 8 John Humphrey Noyes, "Essay on Scientific Propagation," reprinted in *Male Continence* (New York: AMS Press, 1974), 15.

 9 Robertson, *Oneida Community: An Autobiography*, 343; "The Leading Race," *Circular* 2, no. 4 (April 10, 1865).

10 Letter from George Washington Noyes to Harriet Skinner, September 13, 1869, quoted in Fogarty, *Desire and Duty*, 21.

11 Fogarty, *Desire and Duty*, 21.

12 Robertson, *Oneida Community: An Autobiography*, 338.

13 Ibid., 349.

14 Fogarty, *Desire and Duty*, 62.

15 Ibid., 69.

16 Ibid., 66.

17 Ibid., 66–68.

18 Ibid., 67, 70.

19 Ibid., 70, 73.

20 Ibid., 72.

21 Ibid., 111.

22 Ibid., 109–10.

23 Ibid., 117, 151.

24 Ibid., 158, 159.

25 Fogarty, *Special Love/Special Sex*, 55.

26 Ibid., 94.

27 Ibid., 56.

28 Ibid., 56–63.

29 Ibid., 65.

30 Ibid., 67.

31 Ibid.

32 Ibid., 92.

33 Ibid., 95.

34 Entries from Victor Hawley's diary from June through September 1876.

35 Ibid., 120.

36 Ibid., 135–40.

37 Ibid., 149.

38 Ibid., 161.

39 Ibid., 152.

40 Ibid., 164.

9. TWILIGHT OF THE GODS

1 OCC, box 71, Theodore Noyes, notebook, 1864–65.

2 John Humphrey Noyes, "Anastatism," *Circular* 2, no. 10 (May 22, 1865).

3 OCC, box 71, Theodore Noyes, correspondence, Noyes to Tirzah Miller, February 7, 1867.

4 Richard Hofstadter, *Social Darwinism in American Thought* (Boston: Beacon Press, 1983), 16.

5 Ibid., 29.

6 *Vestiges of the Natural History of Creation* (London: John Churchill, 1844), 58.

7 Constance Noyes Robertson, *Oneida Community: The Breakup*, 1876–1881 (Syracuse, NY: Syracuse University Press, 1972), 24.

8 Ibid., 27.

9 Joseph Langdon Skinner's journal, 1873–75 (unpublished manuscript).

10 Robertson, *Breakup*, 29.

11 Ibid., 30.

12 Gardner Murphy and Robert O. Ballou, eds., *William James on Psychical Research* (New York: Viking, 1960): 369.

13 Francis Wayland-Smith, "Controls I," *Circular* (August 24, 1874).

14 ——, "Controls III," *Circular* (September 7, 1874).

15 Roberston, *Breakup*, 32.

16 Fogarty, *Desire and Duty*, 106–07.

17 Robertson, *Breakup*, 40.

18 Ibid., 49.

19 Ibid., 55, 53.

20 Ibid., 57.

21 Ibid., 62, 61.

22 Ibid.

23 Anthony Comstock, quoted in Molly McGarry, *Ghosts of Futures Past: Spiritualism and the Cultural Politics of Nineteenth-Century America* (Berkeley: University of California Press, 2008), 94.

24 Nancy F. Cott, *Public Vows: A History of Marriage and the Nation* (Cambridge: Harvard University Press, 2000), 128.

25 Ibid.

26 Robertson, *Breakup*, 103–04.

27 Ibid., 102.

28 Ibid., 107.

29 Ibid., 110.

30 OCC, box 69, John Humphrey Noyes, "1881–1885 Niagara Journal and Stone Cottage Talks."

10. THINGS FALL APART

1 Robertson, *Breakup*, 116.

2 Ibid., 120.

3 OCC, box 71, Theodore Noyes, interview with Anita Newcomb McGee.

4 Robertson, *Breakup*, 126, 129, 130.

5 Ibid., 136–137.

6 Ibid., 141, 132.

7 Ibid., 92.

8 Ibid., 149.

9 Ibid., 252.

10 See Stanley, *From Bondage to Contract*.

11 Theodore Pitt, "The Failure of Individualism," *American Socialist*, May 8, 1879; OCC, box 73, Theodore Pitt, "Koinonia: The Socialism of Jesus," in folder "Theodore Pitt: Writings."

12 George Washington Noyes, "A Social Need," *Circular* 12, no. 10 (March 8, 1875).

13 William Graham Sumner, *What the Social Classes Owe to Each Other* (New York: Harper, 1884), 25.

14 Robertson, *Breakup*, 145.

15 Ibid., 153, 155.

16 Ibid., 159.

17 Ibid., 161, 165.

18 Ibid., 168, 176.

19 OCC, box 48, Beulah Hendee to Alfred Barron, September 3, 1879; September 1879.

20 Ibid., September 7, 1879; Noyes quoted in Barron to Hendee, November 27, 1879; Barron to Hendee, December 9, 1879; Hendee to Barron, December 10, 1879.

21 Ibid., Hendee to Barron, September 10, 1879.

22 Robertson, *Breakup*, 191, 192, 194, 196.

23 Ibid., 273.

24 Ibid., 287.

25 Ibid., 289, 223.

26 OCC, box 20, "Agreement to Divide and Reorganize."

27 "1877—The Iron Spoon," *Quadrangle* 7, no. 9 (September 1913): 15–17.

28 Ibid.; Robertson, *Breakup*, 282.

29 "Private Property in the O.C.," *Quadrangle* 5, no. 3 (August 1930): 6–9.

30 Quoted in Spencer Klaw, *Without Sin: The Life and Death of the Oneida Community* (New York: Penguin, 1993), 172; quoted in P. B. Noyes, *My Father's House*, 193.

31 Ibid., 189.

32 Robertson, *Breakup*, 312.

33 Cornelia Worden Wayland-Smith, diary (unpublished manuscript).

34 OCC, box 47, Hatch to Hendee, December 28, 1879.

35 Rich, *Lasting Spring*, 62.

36 Cornelia Worden Wayland-Smith, diary (unpublished manuscript).

37 OCC, box 69, John Humphrey Noyes, "1881–1885 Niagara Journal and Stone Cottage Talks."

38 Ibid., letter from Theodore Pitt to Princess Louise, dated July 26, 1880, as recopied in Noyes's "Niagara Journal."

11. SELLING SILVER

1 P. B. Noyes, *My Father's House*, 35–36, 60.

2 Ibid., 25, 85.

3 Ibid., 85.

4 Ibid., 206, 241; Pierrepont B. Noyes, *A Goodly Heritage: Oneida Limited Silversmiths* (New York, Holt, Rinehart and Winston, 1958), 9.

5 Ibid., 41.

6 OCC, box 73, Theodore Pitt, "Interview with J. H. Noyes," April 30, 1886.

7 Ibid., letter to George Miller from Theodore Pitt, February 4, 1888.

8 P. B. Noyes, *Goodly Heritage*, 47.

9 See Karen Halttunen, *Confidence Men and Painted Ladies: A Study of Middle-Class Culture in America, 1830–1870* (New Haven: Yale University Press, 1982).

10 Walter Dill Scott, *Influencing Men in Business: The Psychology of Argument and Suggestion*, 2nd ed. (New York: Ronald Press, 1919), 50, 51; William Jessup Sholar, ed., *Salesmanship: The Standard Course of the Y.M.C.A. Schools* (New York: Association Press, 1920), 2:175.

11 P. B. Noyes, *Goodly Heritage*, 54.

12 William Morey Maxwell, *The Training of a Salesman* (Philadelphia: J. B. Lippincott, 1919), 47.

13 P. B. Noyes, *Goodly Heritage*, 70.

14 Ibid., 82.

15 Ibid., 94–95.

16 Ibid., 145.

17 Ibid., 172, 187.

18 Ibid., 186.

19 Ibid., 205.

20 Ibid., 191; "Dramatizing Community Silver into Prestige and Popularity," reprinted from *Printers Ink* (Fulton, NY: Merrill Press, n.d.), 5.

21 Ibid.

22 Ibid., 8.

23 Ibid., 12.

24 Advertisements and copy reproduced on the back page of the *Quadrangle*, 1928.

25 "Editorial," *Quadrangle* 5, no. 4 (April 1912): 4–5; 4.

26 Stephen Rose Leonard, "Introduction," *Quadrangle* 1, no. 1 (April, 1908).

12. SURVIVAL OF THE FITTEST

1 P. B. Noyes, *Goodly Heritage*, 111.

2 Eugene V. Debs, *The Socialist Party and the Working Class* (Chicago. C. H. Kerr, 1904), 4; Linda Gordon, *The Moral Property of Women: A History of Birth Control Politics in America* (Urbana: University of Illinois Press, 1974), 139.

3 "Labor and Capital," *Circular* 8, no. 44, October 9, 1871; OCC, box 73, Theodore Pitt, "The Socialism of Jesus" (undated typescript).

4 Francis Wayland-Smith, *Shall We Choose Socialism?* (Kenwood, NY: F. Wayland-Smith, 1907).

5 Upton Sinclair, *The Jungle* (Simon and Brown, 2012): 395–96.

6 P. B. Noyes, "Basswood Philosophy III," *Quadrangle* 2, no. 1 (April 1909).

7 G. W. Noyes, *Putney Community*, 283.

8 Esther Lowenthal, "The Labor Policy of the Oneida Community Limited," *Journal of Political Economy* 35, no. 1 (February 1927): 117.

9 Maren Lockwood Carden, *Oneida: Utopian Community to Modern Corporation* (Baltimore: Johns Hopkins University Press, 1969), 143.

10 P. B. Noyes, speech at the 1913 Annual Agents' Banquet, *Quadrangle* 6, no. 1 (January 1913): 9–11; Lowenthal, "Labor Policy," 124, 125.

11 Andrea Tone, *The Business of Benevolence: Industrial Paternalism in Progressive America* (Ithaca, NY: Cornell University Press), 1997; Lowenthal, "Labor Policy," 124.

12 P. B. Noyes, "Basswood Philosophy II," *Quadrangle* 1, no. 12 (March 1909): 10–11; 11.

13 ——, "Basswood Philosophy III," *Quadrangle* 2, no. 2 (April 1909); P. B. Noyes, speech at the 1909 Annual Agents' Banquet, *Quadrangle* 1, no. 2 (February 1909): 9–11; 11.

14 G. W. Noyes, "A Social Need"; P. B. Noyes, speech at the 1910 Annual Agents' Banquet, *Quadrangle* 2, no. 11 (February 1910): 7–9; 8, 9.

15 P. B. Noyes, George Wallingford Noyes, speeches at the 1912 Annual Agents' Banquet, *Quadrangle* 5, no. 1 (January 1912).

16 P. B. Noyes, speech at the 1912 Annual Agents' Banquet, ibid.; P. B. Noyes, quoted in Edith Kinsley, undated diary extracts, OCC, box 62.

17 Sumner, *What the Social Classes Owe to Each Other*, 154.

18 Andrew Carnegie, "Wealth," *North American Review* 148, no. 391 (June 1889).

19 P. B. Noyes, *Goodly Heritage*, 214.

20 George Bernard Shaw, *Man and Superman: A Comedy and a Philosophy* (New York: Brentanos, 1903), 185–86.

21 Julian S. Huxley, "Eugenics and Society," *Eugenics Review* 28, no. 1 (1936): 26, 29.

22 Daniel J. Kevles, *In the Name of Eugenics: Genetics and the Uses of Human Heredity* (Cambridge: Harvard University Press, 1985): 45; Charles Davenport, *Heredity in Relation to Eugenics* (New York: Henry Holt Publishers, 1911): 8.

23 Kevles, *Eugenics*, 55.

24 Davenport, *Heredity*, iv, 67.

25 P. B. Noyes, *Goodly Heritage*, 173.

26 H. G. Wells, *The Future in America: A Search After Realities* (New York: Harper, 1906), 164–66.

27 Hilda Herrick Noyes, "The Woman's Club: Report on Eugenics," *Quadrangle* 5, no. 12 (December 1912).

28 Stephen Rose Leonard, "Strange Reasoning Again," *Quadrangle* 2, no. 4 (July 1909).

29 G. W. Noyes, speech at the 1912 Annual Agents' Banquet, *Quadrangle* 5, no. 1 (January 1912): 19–22; 21.

30 *Eugenics, Genetics and the Family, Second International Congress of Eugenics, 1921, Volumes 1 and 2* (New York and London: Garland Publishing, 1985). First quotes are from Vol. 1, Leonard Darwin, "Aims and Methods of Eugenical Societies," 5–19; 7, 19. Second set of quotes from Vol. 2, Dr. E. A. Hooton, "Observations and Queries as to the Effect of Race Mixtures on Certain Physical Characteristics," 64–74; 66.

31 Ibid., 376.

32 Ibid., 380.

33 Anita Newcomb McGee, "An Experiment in Human Stirpiculture," *American Anthropologist* 4, no. 4 (October 1891): 325.

34 Theodore Skinner, speech at the 1912 Annual Agents' Banquet, *Quadrangle* 5, no. 1 (January 1912): 6–7.

35 P. B. Noyes, speech at the 1910 Annual Agents' Banquet, *Quadrangle* 2, no. 11 (February 1910): 9.

36 "Kenwood Letter," *Quadrangle* 3, no. 4 (August 1928): 23.

37 "The Community Album," ibid.: 13.

13. "THE STRIKE OF A SEX"

1 OCC, box 62, Edith Kinsley (undated typescript).

2 Michael S. Kimmel, *Manhood in America: A Cultural History*, 3rd ed. (Oxford: Oxford University Press, 2011).

3 Theodore Roosevelt, "The American Boy," *Saint Nicholas Magazine*, May 1900; "Citizenship in a

Republic," speech at the Sorbonne, Paris, France, April 23, 1910, excerpts printed in *The American Heritage Book of Great American Speeches for Young People*, ed. Suzanne McIntire (John Wiley and Sons, 2001), 125–26.

4 Edmonds, *First Hundred Years*, 61; Geoffrey P. Noyes Collection, Syracuse University Library, box 7, undated letter from Dunc Robertson to P. T. Noyes.

5 Geoffrey P. Noyes Collection, Syracuse University Library, box 7, undated letter from Dunc Robertson to P. T. Noyes.

6 OCC, box 62, Edith Kinsley, "Kenwood Mores" (undated typescript).

7 Ibid.

8 Ibid.

9 OCC, box 67, folder "George Wallingford Noyes." Letter from G. W. N. to Pierrepont Noyes, December 17, 1884; letter from G. W. N. to Tirzah Miller, February 19, 1885; anecdote recounted in John B. Teeple, *The Oneida Family: Genealogy of a Nineteenth-Century Perfectionist Commune* (Cazenovia, NY: Gleaner Press, 1985), 240.

10 RLD Collection, "Interview by Robert Latou Dickinson of Hilda Herrick Noyes," September 1926, in folder entitled "Dickinson's Notes on the O.C."

11 OCC, box 67, folder "George Wallingford Noyes." Letter from G. W. N. to William Findlay, June 14, 1923; RLD Collection, folder "Dickinson's Notes on the O. C.," "Interview of RLD of Mr. and Mrs. G. W. Noyes (9/14/27)."

12 J. H. Noyes, *Male Continence*, 32.

13 Ely van de Warker, "A Gynecological Study of the Oneida Community," *American Journal of Obstetrics and Diseases of Women and Children* 17, no. 8 (August 1884): 809.

14 Quoted in Gordon, *Moral Property*, 114.

15 See Hal D. Sears, *The Sex Radicals: Free Love in High Victorian America* (Lawrence: Regents Press of Kansas, 1977): on Ezra Heywood, 182; on Ida Craddock, 262.

16 For a general history of the birth control movement in America, see Gordon, *Moral Property*, and Peter C. Engelman, *A History of the Birth Control Movement in America* (Santa Barbara: Praeger ABC-CLIO, 2011).

17 On Dickinson's role in the birth control movement, see Engelman, *History of the Birth Control Movement*, 92, 154–56.

18 RLD collection, folder "Letters Given by Dr. McGee to Dr. Dickinson, 1924," unpublished manuscript by Anita Newcomb McGee, "The Oneida Community."

19 Marsha Silberman, "The Perfect Storm: Nineteenth-Century Chicago Sex Radicals: Moses Harman, Ida Craddock, Alice Stockham and the Comstock Obscenity Laws," *Journal of the Illinois State Historical Society* 2, nos. 3/4 (Fall–Winter 2009): 324–67; 330, 335.

20 George N. Miller, "Author's Preface," *The Strike of a Sex*, 4th ed. (New York: Twentieth Century Publishing, 1891).

21 Ibid., 159–61; Margaret Sanger, "Magnetation Methods of Birth Control," August 1915, https://www.nyu.edu/projects/sanger/webedition/app/documents/show.php?sangerDoc=129014.xml.

22 RLD Collection, folder "Dickinson's Correspondence with Drs. McGee and Noyes Concerning the Oneida Community," letter from Robert Latou Dickinson to Hilda Herrick Noyes, January 1926.

23 RLD Collection, folder "Miscellaneous Materials on the Oneida Community," newspaper clippings, Hilda Herrick Noyes, "The Development of Useful Citizenship," *Journal of Heredity* 11, no. 2 (February 1920); Hilda Herrick Noyes, "Insurance and Eugenics," *Eugenical News* 4, no. 8 (August 1919); RLD Collection, folder "Dickinson's Correspondence," letter from Hilda Herrick Noyes to RLD dated February 7, 1926.

24 RLD Collection, folder "Dickinson's Correspondence with Drs. McGee and Noyes," Robert Latou Dickinson to Hilda Herrick Noyes, September 24, 1926.

25 RLD Collection, folder "Dickinson's Notes on the O.C.," "Interview by Robert Latou Dickinson of Hilda Herrick Noyes," September 1926.

26 The definitive history of Freud's reception in America is Nathan G. Hale's two-volume series, *Freud and the Americans: The Beginnings of Psychoanalysis in the United States, 1876–1917* (New York: Oxford University Press, 1971), and *The Rise and Crisis of Psychoanalysis in the United States: Freud and the Americans, 1917–1985* (New York: Oxford University Press, 1995). On the origins of the science of "sexology," see Jonathan Gathorne-Hardy, *Kinsey: Sex the Measure of All Things* (Bloomington: Indiana University Press, 1998), particularly ch. 8, "A Brief History of Sex Research."

27 Quoted in Engelman, *History of the Birth Control Movement*, 93.

28 RLD Collection, folder "Dickinson's Notes on the Oneida Community," "Interview by Robert Latou Dickinson of George Wallingford Noyes," September 14, 1927.

29 Ibid.

30 RLD Collection, folder "Dickinson's Correspondence," letter from by Robert Latou Dickinson to George Wallingford Noyes, September 14, 1927.

31 Quoted in Foster, *Free Love in Utopia*, xi. The original legal document held in the Syracuse University Library carries no date; some historians have hypothesized that it was issued in 1938. While the question may never be settled definitively, the letters between Dickinson and G. W. Noyes at the Kinsey Institute suggest the injunction may have been issued as early as 1927, in the aftermath of G. W.'s circulation of his manuscript to his Kenwood relatives, and in response to his apparent offer to open up the family archives to outsiders.

14. "BACK HOME FOR KEEPS"

1 Nancy Gluck, *The Community Table* (Norwalk, CT: Silver Season, 2006), 56, 57.

2 Walter D. Edmonds, *The First Hundred Years*, 62.

3 Quoted in D'Ann Campbell, *Women at War with America: Private Lives in a Patriotic Era* (Cambridge: Harvard University Press, 1984), 115. There are a number of excellent studies devoted to American women and shifting gender roles both during and after World War II. See, e.g., Susan M. Hartmann, *The Home Front and Beyond: American Women in the 1940s* (Boston: Twayne Publishers, 1982); Karen Anderson, *Wartime Women: Sex Roles, Family Relations, and the Status of Women During World War*

II (Westport, CT: Greenwood Press, 1981); and Elaine Tyler May, *Homeward Bound: American Families in the Cold War Era* (New York: Basic Books, 1988).

4 Campbell, *Women at War*, 106.

5 Maureen Honey, "New Roles for Women and the Feminine Mystique: Popular Fiction of the 1940s," *American Studies* 24, no. 1 (1983): 43.

6 See Nathan Hale, *Rise and Crisis of Psychoanalysis*, particularly ch. 16, "The 'Golden Age' of Popularization, 1945–1965."

7 Ferdinand Lundberg and Marynia F. Farnham, *Modern Woman: The Lost Sex* (New York: Harper, 1947), 156, 353, 317.

8 Oneida Community Mansion House archives, "Back Home for Keeps" advertisement, 1943.

9 Ibid., "Back Home for Keeps" advertisement, 1944.

10 Jon Whitcomb, *All About Girls* (Englewood Cliffs, NJ: Prentice-Hall, 1962), viii.

11 ———, "How I Paint a Picture," in *Famous Artists Course Lessons 1–24*, by Albert Dorne et al. (Famous Artists Schools, n.d.): 6–24.

12 Ibid., 2.

13 Jean Wade Rindlaub Papers, Schlesinger Library, Radcliffe Institute, Cambridge, MA, letters quoted in a speech given to Oneida Limited, December 15, 1944, Series 5, Subseries C, folder 16.11.

14 Ibid., letter from Sergeant William E. Miller to Oneida, December 3, 1944, folder 16.11; "Speaking of Pictures: Sentimental Advertisements Start a New Kind of Pin-Up Craze," *Life*, May 14, 1945.

15 OCMH archive, undated letter to OL from the Office of War Information, presented in "Wartime at Oneida Ltd., An Exhibit in the Oneida Community Mansion House," November 2012, curated by Anthony Wonderley.

16 Jean Wade Rindlaub Papers, Schlesinger Library, Radcliffe Institute, Cambridge, MA, speech dated August 28, 1946, Series 5, Subseries C, folder 16.12.

17 OCMH archives, Oneida advertisements from the 1950s.

18 Telegram ["Long Telegram"], George Kennan to George Marshall, February 22, 1946, Harry S. Truman Administration File, Elsey Papers, 7, 12; https://www.trumanlibrary.org/whistlestop/study_collections/coldwar/documents/pdf/6-6.pdf. For an interesting discussion of how sexuality and national "character" became intertwined in the Cold War era, see Miriam G. Reumann, *American Sexual Character: Sex, Gender, and National Identity in the Kinsey Reports* (Berkeley: University of California Press, 2005).

19 Quoted in Robert D. Dean, *Imperial Brotherhood: Gender and the Making of Cold War Foreign Policy* (Amherst: University of Massachusetts Press, 2001), 68.

20 Ibid. See also David K. Johnson, *The Lavender Scare: The Cold War Persecution of Gays and Lesbians in the Federal Government*, rpt. ed. (Chicago: University of Chicago Press, 2005).

15. THE BURNING

1 RLD Collection, folder "Miscellaneous Materials on the Oneida Community," letter from Robert Latou Dickinson to Hilda Herrick Noyes, November 4, 1946.

2 Gathorne-Hardy, *Kinsey*, 87, 202.

3 Ibid., 176.

4 Ibid., 270.

5 RLD Collection, folder "Miscellaneous," draft of a handwritten letter from Robert Latou Dickinson to George Wallingford Noyes, November 4, 1946.

6 William M. Kephart, "Experimental Family Organization: An Historic-Cultural Report on the Oneida Community," *Marriage and Family Living* 25, no. 3 (1963): 261–71, 266.

7 Ibid., 266.

EPILOGUE

1 Oneida Limited Annual Report, January 31, 1958.

2 Quoted in J. P. L. Hatcher, A *"Goodly Heritage" Gone Wrong* (unpublished manuscript), 32. I am deeply indebted to Lang Hatcher, Pierrepont Noyes's grandson, for giving me access to this learned account of Oneida Limited's history.

3 Ibid., 56.

4 *Chittenango Times*, November 27, 1969, 6; ibid., 42.

5 "To Have and to Hold," An *Economist* Special Report: Family Companies, *Economist*, April 18, 2015, 3–16; Maren Lockwood Carden, *Oneida: Utopian Community to Modern Corporation* (Baltimore: Johns Hopkins University Press, 1969), 184.

6 Carden, *Oneida*, 185; quoted in Wonderley, "Oneida Utopia," 127.

7 Wonderley gives an account of the 2004 stockholder meeting in "Oneida Utopia," 129; Chana Schoenberger, "Tarnished," *Forbes*, March 15, 2004.

8 Ellen E. Schulz, *The Retirement Heist: How Companies Plunder and Profit from the Nest Eggs of American Workers* (New York: Portfolio/Penguin, 2011).

BIBLIOGRAPHY

MANUSCRIPT COLLECTIONS

Oneida Community Collection, Syracuse University Library. (Cited as OCC)

P. Geoffrey Noyes Papers, Syracuse University Library.

Robert Latou Dickinson Collection, Kinsey Institute for Research in Sex, Gender, and Reproduction, University of Indiana, Bloomington. (Cited as RLD Collection)

Jean Wade Rindlaub Papers, Arthur and Elizabeth Schlesinger Library on the History of Women in America, Radcliffe Institute, Cambridge, MA.

Robert Allerton Parker Papers, Bancroft Library, University of California, Berkeley.

FREQUENTLY CITED PERIODICALS

The American Socialist

The Circular

Daily Journal of the Oneida Community

The O.C. Daily

The Quadrangle

The Spiritual Magazine

PRIMARY AND SECONDARY SOURCES

Abzug, Robert H. *Cosmos Crumbling: American Reform and the Religious Imagination.* New York: Oxford University Press, 1994.

Anbinder, Tyler. *Five Points: The Nineteenth Century New York City Neighborhood That Invented Tap, Stole Elections, and Became the World's Most Notorious Slum.* New York: Simon and Schuster, 2001.

Anderson, Karen. *Wartime Women: Sex Roles, Family Relations, and the Status of Women During World War II.* Westport, CT: Greenwood Press, 1981.

Andrews, Stephen Pearl, ed. *Love, Marriage, and Divorce and the Sovereignty of the Individual: A Discussion by Henry James, Horace Greeley, and Stephen Pearl Andrews.* New York: Stronger and Townsend Publishers, 1853.

———. *The Science of Society.* Boston: Sarah E. Holmes Publisher, 1888.

"The Battle Axes of Free Love Valley." *Mercury,* January 4, 2009.

Beecher, Catharine, and Harriet Beecher Stowe. *The American Woman's Home.* New York: J. B. Ford, 1869.

Beecher, Lyman. *A Plea for the West.* 2nd ed. Cincinnati: Truman and Smith, 1835.

Bloch, Ruth. *Visionary Republic: Millennial Themes in American Thought, 1756–1800.* Cambridge: Cambridge University Press, 1986.

Breitenbach, William. "Unregenerate Doings: Selflessness and Selfishness in New Divinity Theology." *American Quarterly* 34, no. 5 (1983): 479–502.

Brisbane, Albert. *The Social Destiny of Man; or, Association and the Reorganization of Industry.* Philadelphia: C. F. Stollmeyer, 1840.

Campbell, D'Ann. *Women at War with America: Private Lives in a Patriotic Era.* Cambridge: Harvard University Press, 1984.

Carden, Maren Lockwood. *Oneida: Utopian Community to Modern Corporation.* Baltimore: Johns Hopkins University Press, 1969.

Carlyle, Thomas. *Past and Present.* Introduction and Notes by Chris R. Vanden Bossche. Berkeley: University of California Press, 2005.

Carnegie, Andrew. "Wealth." *North American Review* 148, no. 391 (1889): 653–65.

Cohn, Norman. *The Pursuit of the Millennium.* Rev. and exp. ed. New York: Oxford University Press, 1970.

Cott, Nancy. *The Bonds of Womanhood: "Woman's Sphere" in New England, 1780–1835.* 2nd ed. New Haven: Yale University Press, 1997.

———. *Public Vows: A History of Marriage and the Nation.* Cambridge: Harvard University Press, 2000.

Davenport, Charles. *Heredity in Relation to Eugenics.* New York: Henry Holt Publishers, 1911.

Dean, Robert D. *Imperial Brotherhood: Gender and the Making of Cold War Foreign Policy.* Amherst: University of Massachusetts Press, 2001.

Debs, Eugene V. *The Socialist Party and the Working Class.* Chicago: C. H. Kerr, 1904.

Dixon, William Hepworth. *Spiritual Wives.* 2 vols. London: Hurst and Blackett Publishers, 1868.

Downing, Andrew J. *The Architecture of Country Houses.* New York: D. Appleton, 1851.

Eastman, Hubbard. *Noyesism Unveiled.* Putney, VT, 1849.

Edmonds, Walter. *The First Hundred Years.* Rev. ed. Oneida, NY: Oneida Limited, 1958.

Ellis, John B. *Free Love and Its Votaries; or, American Socialism Unmasked.* New York: A. L. Bancroft, 1870.

Engelman, Peter C. *A History of the Birth Control Movement in America.* Santa Barbara, CA: Praeger ABL-CLIO, 2011.

Eugenics, Genetics and the Family. 2 vols. Scientific Papers of the Second International Congress of Eugenics. Baltimore: Williams and Wilkins, 1923.

Finney, Charles Grandison. *The Autobiography of Charles G. Finney.* Edited by Helen Wessel. Minneapolis, MN: Bethany House Publishers, 1977.

Fogarty, Robert, ed. *Desire and Duty at Oneida: Tirzah Miller's Intimate Memoir.* Bloomington: Indiana University Press, 2000.

———. *Special Love/Special Sex: An Oneida Community Diary.* Syracuse, NY: Syracuse University Press, 1994.

Foner, Eric. *Free Soil, Free Labor, Free Men: The Ideology of the Republican Party Before the Civil War.* Oxford: Oxford University Press, 1995.

Foster, Lawrence. "Free Love and Feminism: John Humphrey Noyes and the Oneida Community." *Journal of the Early Republic* 1, no. 2 (1981): 165–83.

———, ed. *Free Love in Utopia: John Humphrey Noyes and the Origin of the Oneida Community*. Compiled by George Wallingford Noyes. Chicago: University of Illinois Press, 2001.

Fourier, Charles. *Selections from the Works of Fourier*. Translated by Julia Franklin with an Introduction by Charles Gide. London: Swan Sonnenschein and Co., 1901.

Fraser, E. J. *Medical Electricity: A Treatise on the Nature of Vital Electricity in Health and Disease*. Chicago: S. Halsey, 1863.

Gathorne-Hardy, Jonathan. *Kinsey: Sex the Measure of All Things*. Bloomington: Indiana University Press, 1998.

Gluck, Nancy. *The Community Table*. Norwalk, CT: Silver Season, 2006.

Gordon, Linda. *The Moral Property of Women: A History of Birth Control Politics in America*. Urbana: University of Illinois Press, 1974.

Guarneri, Carl J. *The Utopian Alternative: Fourierism in Nineteenth-Century America*. Ithaca, NY: Cornell University Press, 1991.

Hale, Nathan G. *Freud and the Americans: The Beginnings of Psychoanalysis in the United States, 1876–1917*. 2 vols. New York: Oxford University Press, 1971.

———. *The Rise and Crisis of Psychoanalysis in the United States: Freud and the Americans, 1917–1985*. New York: Oxford University Press, 1995.

Hall, David D. *The Antinomian Controversy, 1636–1638: A Documentary History*. 2nd ed. Durham, NC: Duke University Press, 1990.

Halttunen, Karen. *Confidence Men and Painted Ladies: A Study of Middle-Class Culture in America, 1830–1870*. New Haven: Yale University Press, 1982.

Hartmann, Susan M. *The Home Front and Beyond: American Women in the 1940s*. Boston: Twayne Publishers, 1982.

Hesiod. *Works and Days, Theogony, and The Shield of Heracles*. Translated by Hugh G. Evelyn-White. Mineola, NY: Dover Publications, 2006.

Hofstadter, Richard. *Social Darwinism in American Thought*. Boston: Beacon Press, 1983.

Honey, Maureen. "New Roles for Women and the Feminine Mystique: Popular Fiction of the 1940s." *American Studies* 24, no. 1 (1983): 37–51.

Huxley, Julian. "Eugenics and Society." *Eugenics Review* 28, no. 1 (1936).

James, Henry. *The Bostonians*. Edited by Richard Lansdown. London: Penguin Books, 2000.

Johnson, Charles A. "The Frontier Camp Meeting: Contemporary and Historical Appraisals, 1805–1840." *Mississippi Valley Historical Review* 37, no. 1 (1950): 91–110.

Johnson, David K. *The Lavender Scare: The Cold War Persecution of Gays and Lesbians in the Federal Government*. Rpt. ed. Chicago: University of Chicago Press, 2005.

Johnson, Paul E. *A Shopkeeper's Millennium: Society and Revivals in Rochester, New York, 1815–1837*. New York: Hill and Wang, 1978.

Kephart, William M. "Experimental Family Organization: An Historic-Cultural Report on the Oneida Community." *Marriage and Family Living* 25, no. 3 (1963): 261–71.

Kevles, Daniel K. *In the Name of Eugenics: Genetics and the Uses of Human Heredity.* Cambridge: Harvard University Press, 1985.

Kimmel, Michael S. *Manhood in America: A Cultural History.* 3rd ed. Oxford: Oxford University Press, 2011.

Kinsley, Jessie Catherine. *A Lasting Spring: Jessie Catherine Kinsley, Daughter of the Oneida Community.* Edited by Jane Kinsley Rich, with the assistance of Nelson M. Blake. Syracuse, NY: Syracuse University Press, 1983.

Klaw, Spencer. *Without Sin: The Life and Death of the Oneida Community.* New York: Penguin, 1993.

Laurie, Bruce. *Artisans into Workers: Labor in Nineteenth-Century America.* Urbana: University of Illinois Press, 1997.

Lowenthal, Esther. "The Labor Policy of the Oneida Community Limited." *Journal of Political Economy* 35, no. 1 (1927): 114–26.

Lundberg, Ferdinand, and Marynia F. Farnham. *Modern Woman: The Lost Sex.* New York: Harper, 1947.

Marx, Leo. *The Machine in the Garden: Technology and the Pastoral Ideal in America.* Oxford: Oxford University Press, 2000.

Maxwell, William. *The Training of a Salesman.* Philadelphia: J. B. Lippincott, 1919.

May, Elaine Tyler. *Homeward Bound: American Families in the Cold War Era.* New York: Basic Books, 1988.

McGarry, Molly. *Ghosts of Futures Past: Spiritualism and the Cultural Politics of Nineteenth-Century America.* Berkeley: University of California Press, 2008.

McGee, Anita Newcomb. "An Experiment in Human Stirpiculture." *American Anthropologist* 4, no. 4 (October 1891): 319–26.

Merton, Thomas. *The Wisdom of the Desert.* New Haven, KY: Abbey of Gethsemani, 1960.

Review of *Methodist Error.* In *Christian Spectator* 2: 300–06. New Haven: Howe and Spalding, 1820.

Miller, George N. *The Strike of a Sex.* 4th ed. New York: Twentieth Century Publishing, 1891.

Murphy, Gardner, and Robert O. Ballou, eds. *William James on Psychical Research.* New York: Viking, 1960.

Nichols, T. L., and Mrs. Mary Gove Nichols. *Marriage: Its History, Character, and Results.* New York: T. L. Nichols, 1854.

Noyes, Corinna Ackley. *Days of My Youth.* Utica, NY: Widtman Press, 1960.

Noyes, George Wallingford. *John Humphrey Noyes: The Putney Community.* Oneida, NY, 1931.

——. *Religious Experience of John Humphrey Noyes.* New York: Macmillan, 1923.

Noyes, John Humphrey. *The Berean: A Manual for Those Who Seek the Faith of the Primitive Church.* Putney, VT, 1847.

——. *Bible Communism: A Compilation from the Annual Reports and Other Publications of the Oneida Association.* Brooklyn, NY, 1853.

——. *The Confessions of John Humphrey Noyes Part 1: Confession of Religious Experience, Including a History of Modern Perfectionism*. Oneida Reserve, NY: Leonard, 1849.

——. *Home Talks*. Edited by Alfred Barron and George Noyes Miller. Oneida, NY, 1875.

——. *Male Continence*. Oneida, NY: 1872; repr. New York: AMS Press, 1974.

——. *The Way of Holiness: A Series of Papers Formerly Published in "The Perfectionist" at New Haven*. Putney, VT, 1838.

Noyes, Pierrepont B. *A Goodly Heritage: Oneida Limited Silversmiths*. New York: Holt, Rinehart and Winston, 1958.

——. *My Father's House: An Oneida Boyhood*. New York: Rinehart, 1937.

Ovid. *The Metamorphoses*. Translated by John Dryden and others, edited by Sir Samuel Garth, with an introduction by Garth Tissol. Wordsworth Editions Limited, 1998.

Parker, Robert Allerton. *A Yankee Saint: John Humphrey Noyes and the Oneida Community*. New York: G. P. Putnam, 1935.

Reumann, Miriam G. *American Sexual Character: Sex, Gender, and National Identity in the Kinsey Reports*. Berkeley: University of California Press, 2005.

Robertson, Constance Noyes. *The Oneida Community: An Autobiography, 1851–1876*. Syracuse, NY: Syracuse University Press, 1970.

——. *Oneida Community: The Breakup, 1876–1881*. Syracuse, NY: Syracuse University Press, 1972.

Ryan, Mary P. *Cradle of the Middle Class: The Family in Oneida County, New York, 1790–1865*. Cambridge: Cambridge University Press, 1981.

Schama, Simon. "When Stones Came to Life." *Guardian*, September 15, 2006.

Schoenberger, Chana. "Tarnished." *Forbes*, March 15, 2004.

Schulz, Ellen E. *The Retirement Heist: How Companies Plunder and Profit from the Nest Eggs of American Workers*. New York: Portfolio/Penguin, 2011.

Scott, Walter Dill. *Influencing Men in Business: The Psychology of Argument and Suggestion*. 2nd ed. New York: Ronald Press, 1919.

Sears, Hal D. *The Sex Radicals: Free Love in High Victorian America*. Lawrence: Regents Press of Kansas, 1977.

Sellers, Charles. *The Market Revolution: Jacksonian America, 1815–1846*. New York: Oxford University Press, 1991.

Sellers, Charles Coleman. *Theophilus, the Battle-Age: A History of the Lives and Adventures of Theophilus Ransom Gates and the Battle-Axes*. Philadelphia: Press of Patterson and White, 1930.

Shaw, George Bernard. *Man and Superman: A Comedy and a Philosophy*. New York: Brentanos, 1903.

Shelley, Mary Wollstonecraft. *Frankenstein*. Edited by Susan J. Wolfson. 2nd ed. New York: Pearson Education, 2007.

Sheriff, Carol. *The Artificial River: The Erie Canal and the Paradox of Progress, 1817–1862*. New York: Hill and Wang, 1996.

Sholar, William Jessup, ed. *Salesmanship: The Standard Course of the Y.M.C.A. Schools*. Vol. 2. New York: Association Press, 1920.

Silberman, Marsha. "The Perfect Storm: Nineteenth-Century Chicago Sex Radicals: Moses Harman, Ida Craddock, Alice Stockham and the Comstock Obscenity Laws." *Journal of the Illinois State Historical Society* 2, no. 3/4 (Fall–Winter 2009): 324–67.

Spurlock, John C. *Free Love: Marriage and Middle-Class Radicalism in America, 1825–1860.* New York: New York University Press, 1988.

Stanley, Amy Dru. *From Bondage to Contract: Wage Labor, Marriage, and the Market in the Age of Slave Emancipation.* Cambridge: Cambridge University Press, 1998.

Stoehr, Talyor. *Free Love in America: A Documentary History.* New York: AMS Press, 1979.

Sumner, William Graham. *What the Social Classes Owe to Each Other.* New York: Harper, 1884.

Teeple, John B. *The Oneida Family: Genealogy of a Nineteenth-Century Perfectionist Commune.* Cazenovia, NY: Gleaner Press, 1985.

Teresa of Avila. *The Book of My Life.* Translated by Mirabai Starr. Boston: New Seeds Books, 2007.

Thomas, David. *The Man Who Would Be Perfect: John Humphrey Noyes and the Utopian Impulse.* Philadelphia: University of Pennsylvania Press, 1977.

Thomas, John Codman. *Brook Farm: Historic and Personal Memoirs.* Boston: Arena Publishing, 1894.

"To Have and to Hold." An *Economist* Special Report: Family Companies. *Economist*, April 18, 2015.

Tone, Andrea. *The Business of Benevolence: Industrial Paternalism in Progressive America.* Ithaca, NY: Cornell University Press, 1997.

Tuveson, Ernest Lee. *Redeemer Nation: The Idea of America's Millennial Role.* Chicago: University of Chicago Press, 1968.

Vestiges of the Natural History of Creation. London: John Churchill, 1844.

Warker, Ely van de. "A Gynecological Study of the Oneida Community." *American Journal of Obstetrics and Diseases of Women and Children* 17, no. 8 (August 1884): 785–810.

Wayland-Smith, Francis. *Shall We Choose Socialism?* Kenwood, NY: F. Wayland-Smith, 1907.

Wells, H. G. *The Future in America: A Search After Realities.* New York: Harper, 1906.

Whitcomb, Jon. *All About Girls.* Englewood Cliffs, NJ: Prentice-Hall, 1962.

——. "How I Paint a Picture." In *Famous Artists Course Lessons 1–24,* by Albert Dorne et al. Famous Artists Schools, Inc., 1954.

Willis, Martin. *Mesmerists, Monsters, and Machines.* Kent, OH: Kent State University Press, 2006.

Wilson, Edmund. *Upstate: Records and Recollections of Northern New York.* 1971. Syracuse, NY: Syracuse University Press, 1990.

Wonderley, Anthony. *John Humphrey Noyes on Sexual Relations in the Oneida Community.* Clinton, NY: Richard W. Couper Press, 2012.

——. "Oneida Utopia: Bible Communism to Welfare Capitalism." Unpublished manuscript.

ACKNOWLEDGMENTS

THE IDEA FOR THIS BOOK ORIGINATED WITH MY LITERARY AGENT, ROB McQuilkin, who, when he discovered I was an Oneida descendant, encouraged me to "write a book about my family." I am deeply indebted to Rob not only for convincing me that this was a topic worth writing about but also for providing me with critical feedback, both painstaking and brilliant, at every step along the way. Without Rob, this book never would have seen the light of day.

A number of friends and colleagues provided much-appreciated advice on the manuscript as it developed. A special thanks to Colin Hamilton, who read all the early chapters and whose responses helped me shape the voice and narrative pace of the story. I received expert historical advice from Lynn Hunt, Margaret Jacobs, Teo Ruiz, and Scarlett Freund, who all encouraged me to situate John Humphrey Noyes's millenarianism within the larger context of European Christian mysticism and millennial thought. Karen Halttunen helped me deepen my treatment of the nineteenth-century American social and economic context within which Perfectionism flowered.

I would like to thank Anthony Wonderley, curator of the Oneida

Community Mansion House museum, for his encouragement and for facilitating my access to archival materials as I researched my project. He was particularly generous in sharing his own research, including his yet-to-be-published manuscript exploring Oneida's industrial development and labor policies between 1848 and 1948. Langford Hatcher was kind enough to share with me his research regarding the demise and eventual 2006 bankruptcy of Oneida Limited, a precious and illuminating look at the final decades of the company. Thank you to Geoffrey Noyes for his candid interviews, access to private Oneida Limited archival material from the 1970s and 1980s, and his general spirit of genial encouragement.

Librarians and archivists at Syracuse University Bird Library Special Collections provided tireless and trusted help in wading through the Oneida Community Collection. Thank you, as well, to the librarians who facilitated my access to the Robert Latou Dickinson Collection at the Kinsey Institute at the University of Indiana, Bloomington; the Jean Wade Rindlaub Papers at the Arthur and Elizabeth Schlesinger Library on the History of Women in America at the Radcliffe Institute in Cambridge, Massachusetts; and the Robert Allerton Parker Papers at UC Berkeley's Bancroft Library.

I would like to thank the University of Southern California, Dornsife, College of Letters, Arts and Sciences, and the Writing Program in particular, for their unstinting support and for providing a lively and engaged intellectual community. Thank you to Lisa Bitel, Vanessa Schwartz, and Peter Mancall for supporting my research and for encouraging me to apply for research funds from USC's Center for Religion and Civic Culture. The CRCC's generous Interdisciplinary Research Grant helped fund my bicoastal travel and research in 2013–14.

Thank you, finally, to my editor at Picador, Anna deVries, whose patience and unwavering belief in the value of this project helped me navigate the rough patches. Her gentle guidance and implicit trust in my voice carried the book through.

Thank you to Jacob Soll, who taught me how to love history and who (most important) was patient with my predawn writing schedule during the two years I worked on the book.

To my parents, Giles and Kate Wayland-Smith, who taught me by example the Oneidan value of selflessness, my gratitude knows no bounds.

INDEX